LITERARY
CULTURES
of the
CIVIL WAR

LITERARY CULTURES *of the* CIVIL WAR

Edited by
TIMOTHY SWEET

THE UNIVERSITY OF
GEORGIA PRESS
Athens

Paperback edition, 2020
© 2016 by the University of Georgia Press
Athens, Georgia 30602
www.ugapress.org
All rights reserved
Designed by Kaelin Chappell Broaddus
Set in 10/13 Adobe Caslon Pro by Kaelin Chappell Broaddus

Most University of Georgia Press titles are
available from popular e-book vendors.

Printed digitally

Library of Congress Cataloging-in-Publication Data

Names: Sweet, Timothy, 1960– editor.
Title: Literary cultures of the civil war / edited by Timothy Sweet.
Description: Athens : The University of Georgia Press, 2016. |
Includes bibliographical references and index.
Identifiers: LCCN 2015043959 | ISBN 9780820349602 (hardcover : alk. paper) |
ISBN 9780820349596 (ebook)
Subjects: LCSH: United States—History—Civil War, 1861–1865—
Literature and the war. | War and literature—United States—History. |
American literature—History and criticism. | War in literature.
Classification: LCC PS217.C58 L58 2016 | DDC 810.9/358—dc23
LC record available at http://lccn.loc.gov/2015043959

ISBN 9780820357843 (paperback : alk. paper)

CONTENTS

LIST OF FIGURES vii

ACKNOWLEDGMENTS ix

Introduction
Shaping the Civil War Canon
TIMOTHY SWEET 1

I. African American Literary Cultures

"if we Ever Expect to be a Pepple"
The Epistolary Culture of African American Soldiers
CHRISTOPHER HAGER 23

The Color of Quaintness
*Thomas Wentworth Higginson,
Black Song, and American Union*
JEREMY WELLS 39

The Negro in the American Rebellion
*William Wells Brown and the
Design of African American History*
JOHN ERNEST 57

"Naked Genius"
The Civil War Poems of George Moses Horton
FAITH BARRETT 77

II. Poetics of War

Melville's *Battle-Pieces* and Vernacular Poetics
TIMOTHY SWEET 99

"Help'd, Braced, Concentrated"
Transatlantic Tensions and Whitman's National War Poetry
SAMUEL GRABER 119

Surplus Patriotism
William Gilmore Simms's War Poetry of the South and the Afterlife of Confederate Literary Nationalism
COLEMAN HUTCHISON 141

III. Mediations of Nation and Region

Traces of the Confederacy
Soldier Newspapers and Wartime Printing in the Occupied South
JAMES BERKEY 167

The Turn against Sentiment
Kate Cumming and Confederate Realism
JANE E. SCHULTZ 189

Mourning and Substitution in *The Gates Ajar*
SHIRLEY SAMUELS 207

"Near Andersonville"
Place and Race in Early American Regionalism
JILLIAN SPIVEY CADDELL 225

Emancipation and Grizzly Reckoning
The Advent of Photography, California's Overland Monthly, and the Model of Parallax
KATHLEEN DIFFLEY 245

CONTRIBUTORS 265

INDEX 267

LIST OF FIGURES

1. Higginson's surreptitious recording of the words of a spiritual, likely "I hear de bell done ringing." — 51
2. "The Union Army Entered Savannah," *Harper's Weekly*, January 21, 1865. — 168
3. Two runaway slave ads, *First Minnesota*, March 11, 1862. — 178
4. Advertising pages of the *Newbern Progress*, March 22 and April 5, 1862. — 182
5. "To the Patriotic Citizens of St. Landry," *Opelousas Courier*, April 25, 1863. — 184
6. Winslow Homer, *Near Andersonville*, 1865–66. — 226
7. "Taking Stereoscopic Picture of Near Objects." *Harper's Monthly*, September 1869. — 246
8. Alexander Gardner, "The 'Sunken Road' at Antietam." — 249
9. Edwin Forbes, "Brilliant and Decisive Bayonet Charge of Hawkins's Zouaves." *Frank Leslie's Illustrated Weekly*, October 11, 1862. — 250
10. Edwin Forbes, "The battle of Antietam—Charge of Burnside's 9th Corps." — 250
11. Alexander Gardner, "Antietam, Maryland. Bodies of dead, Louisiana Regiment." — 252
12. First issue title page, *Overland Monthly*, July 1868. — 255
13. Wartime title page image, *Atlantic Monthly*, January 1865. — 256

ACKNOWLEDGMENTS

Some of the essays in this collection emerged from the Civil War Caucus, which for the past several years has met annually at the Midwest Modern Language Association conference for two days of panels on Civil War literary studies. Kathleen Diffley, tireless organizer of the caucus, deserves our special thanks. I am grateful to all members of the caucus with whom I have discussed the project, and especially to Kathleen for consultation throughout the process and for reading the introduction with a careful eye and a ready pen. The flaws and omissions, of course, remain mine.

Martha Schoolman, who read the manuscript for the University of Georgia Press, offered numerous constructive suggestions that improved the introduction, many of the individual essays, and the overall shape of the collection. The comments of another anonymous reader were helpful as well. Walter Biggins at the press has been a pleasure to work with. The Department of English at West Virginia University supported the project by providing research assistants. Thus, I am grateful to James Holsinger and especially to Beth Staley for their careful attention to the manuscript.

"Melville's *Battle-Pieces* and Vernacular Poetics" is a somewhat expanded version of an essay that was first published in *Leviathan* 17, no. 3 (October 2015) and appears here by permission.

Some of the material in "Surplus Patriotism: William Gilmore Simms's *War Poetry of the South* and the Afterlife of Confederate Literary Nationalism" is taken from the critical introduction to the Simms Initiatives' digital and print-on-demand edition of *War Poetry of the South*, and appears here by permission.

LITERARY
CULTURES
of the
CIVIL WAR

Introduction
Shaping the Civil War Canon

TIMOTHY SWEET

On the fiftieth anniversary of the Civil War, the venerable literary historian Fred Lewis Pattee proclaimed a new definition of American literature. No longer should the antebellum flowering of New England's literary culture be regarded as our "National Period," Pattee argued, "for national it certainly was not." Rather, "our first really national period" originated "shortly after the close of the Civil War with those new forces and new ideals and broadened views that grew out of that mighty struggle." American writers finally ceased to imitate European predecessors, declared "literary independence," and "looked to their own land for materials and inspiration," especially to the West, to produce "autochthonic" works.[1] Deploying the central trope of Lincoln's Gettysburg Address, *autochthones*, to characterize a new birth of American literature, Pattee seems to have taken Lincoln's nationalizing political program as forecasting an analogous literary program.[2]

Beyond a mention of the Gettysburg Address and a quick dismissal of Stephen Crane's *Red Badge of Courage* as "manufactured realism," Pattee said little about the literature of the war itself (397). However, one book did claim his attention: Walt Whitman's *Drum-Taps*. Pattee argued that the war changed the nationalist project of America's most important poet, who transmitted its influence to subsequent writers: "Henceforth the poet will sing of Men—men not as magnificent bodies, but as triumphant souls. *Drum-Taps* fairly quivers and sobs and shouts with new life. America has risen at last—one feels it in every line. The book gives more of the actual soul of the great conflict and the new spirit that arose from it than any other book ever written" (175). Unsurprisingly, Pattee's literary history omitted any mention of African American writers while relegating the question of race to the postwar development of the "darky" character type in southern regionalist literature (83). Thus, Pattee enacted by means of exclusion David Blight's familiar thesis that by the fiftieth anniversary, reconciliationism—here taking the form of a nationally unifying, westward-looking declaration of American literary independence—had eclipsed the war's emancipationist promise.[3]

Even so, Pattee's partial account suggests in retrospect that the war's literary canon would emerge, albeit gradually, from a central preoccupation with national identity ("soul" or "spirit," as both Pattee and Whitman would have put it) and a claim that literature has privileged access to that identity. The repressed emancipationist promise would return, and subsequent critics would focus on body as well as "spirit" in relation to the newly reconfigured nation-state. These critics would elaborate related analytical categories such as violence, affect, and citizenship, as well as the central category of nationhood, while claiming a larger role for literature as not merely representing but actively shaping these categories.

Literary Cultures of the Civil War makes the most of that larger role. This collection of essays delivers on Pattee's promise by returning to the unsettled moment when the memory of the war was not yet overwritten by topoi that would later come to dominate, such as the Lost Cause, the romance of reunion, and the reconciliation of veterans. These essays address texts produced by writers who lived through the war and wrote about it before the end of Reconstruction, well before second-generation works such as *The Red Badge of Courage* (1895). To explore the ground of alternative memories, the essays in this book engage with the diversity of literary cultures—ensembles of discourses, conventions, and practices shaping and shaped by verbal production—that existed in the postwar United States. Such ensembles, often regionally or locally differentiated, include Euroamerican and African American vernacular oral cultures, manuscript journals and letters, and print cultures structured by newspapers, magazines, or books; overlapping discourses of politics, protest, domesticity, and sentiment; unsettled literary nationalism and emergent literary regionalism; and vernacular and elite aesthetic traditions. While most of the essays address a given text as participating in more than one of these ensembles, they fall into three groups that would have surprised Pattee and the critics who followed him: African American literary cultures, poetics of war, and mediations of nation and region. Tracing the emergence of these concerns from the crucial centennial moment of canon formation through the sesquicentennial will be the project of this introduction.

The Centennial Moment

As Blight and others have observed, centennial reflections of the Civil War were informed by two contexts: the civil rights movement and the Cold War.[4] Civil rights activism had resurrected the war's emancipationist promise, while Cold War politics had reconfigured the terms of reunion.[5] In a 1961 review-essay on the Civil War's literary canon for the *Reporter*, Alfred Kazin addressed civil rights by asserting, against a prominent line of popular historiography exemplified by Bruce Catton's work, that slavery was central and that the war had been inevitable. Kazin characterized the body of writing on slavery, North and South, as exhibiting a unified literary style grounded in reference to Revolutionary era patriotism and gaining affect through "the extraordinary hold of the images and rhythms of the King James Bible."[6] The assurance of divine mandate in both pro- and antislavery discourse brought about an ideological hardening, in which Kazin also found a modern (Cold War) analog in Marx's theory of class conflict, as contrasted with the values of "classical" politics and "loyalty to the commonwealth" (37). As a Cold War liberal, Kazin valued those few writers whom he saw as standing outside of ideological polarization and asserting humanism against totalitarianism: Lincoln for his capacity to deploy biblical rhetoric without being blinded by it; Mary Chesnut for her ability to articulate "the complex human relationships of slavery" with "humor, detachment, and patience"; Walt Whitman for the experiential truth of *Specimen Days* and some of his "impressionistic" *Drum-Taps* poems; Herman Melville for the "stoic and classical distrust of human nature" evident in *Battle-Pieces* (37, 38, 42).

That same year, Robert Penn Warren opened a book-length reflection on the war by citing two "clear and objective facts": the cause of slavery, "which looms up mountainously and cannot be talked away," and the Unionist result.[7] Warren observed the ways in which cause and result remained intertwined in the present, remarking on the North's abandonment of the war's emancipationist potential and discussing African American writers' critiques of the North's redemptivist history of the war, from W. E. B. Du Bois through civil rights activist and journalist Carl Rowan. Yet in the Cold War context, Warren was equally interested in the legacy of Unionism.[8] Warren argued that the Civil War had created a climate favorable to the development of pragmatism, which was modeled by Lincoln and later elaborated on in the jurisprudence of Oliver Wendell Holmes Jr. and the philosophy of William James. Warren offered pragmatist philosophy as an antidote to the Cold War's ideological hardening by pointing the question of the Civil War's inevitability toward the present moment: "does the naked geo-political confrontation with Russia doom us to the struggle? ... Or can we learn that we can make, or at least have a hand in the making of, our future?"

(101–2). Warren's concluding meditation on the war as a "tragedy" in the classical sense returned him to the question of inevitability and thus, by way of the cathartic potential of the Gettysburg Address, to Melville's tragic reading of the war in *Battle-Pieces*.[9] Warren argued that the nation had not been instructed by the war's "catharsis of pity and terror," as Melville had hoped: "We have not yet created a union which is, in the deepest sense, a community" (107). Differentiating Melville's pragmatic Unionism from Whitman's unattainable "mystic" Unionism, Warren argued that Melville's "tragic insight" consisted in "the necessity for action in the face of the difficulty of knowing truth."[10]

Where Kazin's and Warren's assessments of the war's literary legacy were selective, Edmund Wilson's *Patriotic Gore* attempted to be exhaustive. A staunch critic of Cold War militarism, Wilson compared Lincoln's historical role to Lenin's, positing that both leaders suffered untimely removal from office with negative consequences for the state. Beyond this analogy, whose limits Wilson fully realized, the Cold War frame motivated a critique of the state as a mechanism for organizing instinctual aggression. Wilson granted Warren's characterization of the two structures of feeling—or as Wilson put it, "two fraudulent traditions"—that resulted from the war: the "Great Alibi" that enabled southerners to blame every ill on the war and the northern exceptionalist "Treasury of Virtue" that had been adopted as a unifying rhetoric to "carry along into all our subsequent wars."[11] As Wilson framed the Civil War, its literature demonstrated "how automatically, on both sides of the contest, ... a divided and arguing public may be converted into a national near-unanimity, a flood of energy which will carry the young to destruction" (xxxii).

In practice, Wilson's literary canon was not so narrow as his opening critique suggested. If he denigrated most war poetry, including Melville's, as mere "patriotic journalism," he valued instances of psychological realism (for example, some of Whitman's poems), as did his Cold War ideological antagonist Kazin (470). Wilson praised *Uncle Tom's Cabin* as a complex and sectionally balanced critique plausibly demonstrating that "the national ideal is in danger," before he criticized it as an example of the "Northern myth" that organized so much writing, according to which the Union cause was God's cause and Lincoln a "martyred Messiah" (8, 98). He concluded with a survey of postwar southern regionalism (Albion Tourgée, George W. Cable, Kate Chopin, Thomas Nelson Page) followed by an account of the war's literary and philosophical legacy in realism and pragmatism. In contrast to the "verbose untidy" style of Cooper or the static style of Hawthorne, Melville, and Poe, Wilson traced two opposing tendencies in American prose formed from opposing responses to the war (636). On one hand, "a lack of confidence, a diffidence and a mechanism of self-defense" became manifest in a literature of "ambiguity, prolixity, [and] irony," especially by noncombatants such as Henry Adams and Henry James (654). On the other hand, the war's lesson of "efficiency" gave rise to the "lucidity, precision, [and] terseness" of Lincoln's speeches and the memoirs of Ulysses S. Grant and Thomas Wentworth Higginson (649). Ambrose Bierce developed this new "firmer and quicker" style in short stories that "make us feel the indignity and absurdity of war" (638, 619). Yet the most important "precursor of realism" to emerge from the war, Wilson argued, was John W. De Forest's novel *Miss Ravenel's Conversion from Secession to Loyalty*, which he recognized as influencing Stephen Crane's *Red Badge of Courage*, among others (670, 684). Despite De Forest's accomplishments as a realist, however, Wilson criticized his contempt for the South and his unquestioning promotion of the Union cause.

Wilson found literary realism's philosophical analogue in pragmatism, a product of the war that Kazin noted implicitly and Warren discussed explicitly. Thus, Wilson closed *Patriotic Gore* with a nod toward William James, followed by an extensive account of the career of Oliver Wendell Holmes Jr. If the ideological conclusion of the eight-hundred-page survey could be brought down to one point, it might be Wilson's skeptical account of Holmes's pragmatic belief in "the general validity of any corpus of law as the expression of the dominant will of any considerable social group"; or, to put it bluntly, "what is left, without God's direction, is simply a conflict of forces, in which the party that wins rules" (766, 762).[12]

Daniel Aaron's *The Unwritten War*, which was invited for the Civil War Centennial Commission series called the Impact of the War though not completed until 1973, followed Warren and Wilson in defining grand fictions that northerners and southerners used to organize their understandings of the conflict. Where Warren referred to "tragedy" and Wilson to "myth" (in the sense of false consciousness), Aaron used the term "epic" to evoke a missing "literary masterpiece" that critics as early as 1862 had hoped the war would inspire.[13] Aaron suggested that a federal epic might have begun with Daniel Webster's apostasy in defending the Fugitive Slave Act in 1850 and might have continued through a providentially directed chastisement of North and South for the crimes of materialism and slavery, a progress that would depict Lincoln as both an Abraham who guided the nation to safety and a messiah who died to redeem its suffering. But for Aaron, writers north and south were unable to produce a work on this moral scale. They failed "to say something revealing about the meaning ... of the War," Aaron argued, because of their "emotional resistance" to the sociopolitical fact of race; thus, while "the Negro" was central to the war, "yet he figured only peripherally in the War literature" (xxii).

Aspiring to the breadth of Wilson's survey, Aaron began by charting the polarization of the 1850s, which he argued nevertheless left writers conceptually unprepared for war. The few who refused partisan rhetoric included Hawthorne, a "lonely dissent[er]" from the Unionist program; Whitman, a healer who translated soldiers' suffering into poetry and conceived of Lincoln as "the blessed offering" in a "national fertility rite"; and Melville, a poet of "paradoxes, ironies, and conflicts" who "tells of a dearly bought national 'enlightenment' acquired in the glare of bursting bombs—and not retained" (39, 53, 88, 90). Of the generation of northerners young enough to enlist, Aaron observed that "the four most talented"—Henry Adams, William Dean Howells, Henry James, and Mark Twain—refused combat and looked back with "nostalgia for what the War destroyed or made obsolete" (92). Combatants such as De Forest and Bierce showed the "hard reality" of war based on personal experience but without engaging the larger ideological frame (92). Although no southerner accomplished an epic account of the war, Aaron argued, a few wrote "unrhetorically and with some detachment." These included Henry Timrod, a noncombatant who nevertheless was "'educated' by events in the Melvillean sense"; David Hunter Strother ("Porte Crayon"), a Union veteran whose unpublished diaries contained scenes "that out-horror Bierce" and whose views on race underwent a conversion after hearing Frederick Douglass speak in 1864; George Washington Cable, a Confederate veteran who came to criticize Lost Cause ideology and the postwar disenfranchisement of African Americans; and especially Mary Chesnut, whom social conventions likely prevented from "turn[ing] to novel-writing" (228, 234, 250, 251).

Describing the literary response to the war as largely unified, North versus South, the centennial critics structured their interpretations in terms of the dynamic of reunion, though not in the form of Pattee's forgetful reconciliationism. Kazin mapped the legacy of the slavery debates onto civil rights activism while valuing writers such as Whitman, Melville, and Chesnut, who seem to have stood outside of such polarization, and Lincoln, who attempted to resolve it while maintaining a moral compass. The southerner Warren felt more deeply than the New Yorker Kazin the legacy of slavery and imagined that critical reflection on Cold War politics might prompt the kind of self-aware pragmatism he found in Melville. Wilson, on the other hand, saw too much national unity in Cold War America, a kind of groupthink that so many Civil War writers had represented for their respective sides. If Wilson, like Warren, embraced pragmatism, it was in ironic rather than tragic form—and with Holmes rather than Melville as its paradigmatic figure. Even more than Kazin, however, Wilson imagined that writers could stand outside of ideology. Aaron too imagined such a dispassionate standpoint from which writers could have developed a critical perspective on the postwar question of race. Valuing many of the same figures as did his precursors (Whitman, Melville, Chesnut) and for similar reasons (objectivity, irony, detachment), Aaron brought his assessment of Civil War literature up through the centennial era, pausing to explore Crane's late nineteenth-century depoliticization of the war in *The Red Badge of Courage* before turning to William Faulkner, an author who was finally able "to read the War's meaning ... in the consciousness of a people" (311).

Postcentennial Interventions

The Unwritten War marked a turn from public-sphere criticism to academic criticism.[14] Yet key themes persisted. As the Cold War waned, politically motivated criticism came to focus on the national security state, with its investment in the management of bodies.[15] Where the Cold War context encouraged centennial critics to embrace or ironically acknowledge pragmatism as the war's largest cultural result, postcentennial critics showed relatively little interest in the political genesis of pragmatism. The centennial critics' other motivating context, the civil rights movement, continued to march under the more inclusive banner of social justice. In these new contexts, critics intervened either skeptically, by interrogating the relation of bodies to the state, or optimistically, by resurrecting the war's emancipationist legacy and, in some cases, extending that legacy to read gender into the discussions surrounding the Fourteenth and Fifteenth Amendments. Tempered by a poststructuralist suspicion of foundational narratives, this new work deepened the investigations of violence, citizenship, and nationhood begun by the centennial critics while expanding the survey of literary cultures begun especially by Wilson and Aaron.

The first significant postcentennial studies focused on violence. Shira Wolosky brought Emily Dickinson into the war's canon, revising the received image of Dickinson as a self-enclosed eccentric to argue that she responded profoundly to the war's violence as a theodicean problem.[16] The meaning of death in war was similarly the central focus of my comparative study of Whitman's and Melville's poetry and battlefield photography, *Traces of War*, which took as its point of departure Elaine Scarry's account of the relation between violence and language.[17] According to Scarry, the wounds and deaths of war are "broken away from the body and relocated elsewhere" by means of language in the process of instantiating the victor's "ideas" and "beliefs."[18] This process of instantiation is often complex and, especially in the case of the Civil War, the specification of the victor's beliefs was controversial: Was the war really about slavery or the federal union or both? Was it consistently so over time, and for whom? In this context, the Whitman of realistic observation, valued by Kazin and Wilson, receded in favor of the Whitman who questions the possibility of representation—"the real war will never get in the books," as he famously wrote in *Specimen Days*—while nevertheless attempting to transact national reunion through mourning.[19] Melville was seen as struggling critically with this process, especially with the demands that the state made on the bodies of the soldiers who were, at the same time, supposed to be citizens. Subsequent studies (discussed below) picked up the connection between literature and photography, including Elizabeth Young's "Verbal Battlefields," an analysis of Alexander Gardner's captions for his 1866 *Photographic Sketch Book* of the war.[20] James Dawes extended the investigation of the split between object and representational medium in *The Language of War*, juxtaposing the "emancipatory" model favored by Scarry, in which language and violence are mutually exclusive, with a poststructuralist model in which language and violence are mutually constitutive. After reading Sherman's and Grant's memoirs to exemplify his claim that "counting is the epistemology of war," Dawes presented Louisa May Alcott's *Hospital Sketches*, which develops a sentimental discourse of individual sympathy, as a counterpoint to the nationalizing tendencies of Whitman's poetics of naming, counting, and cataloging.[21]

Subsequent studies along this line of inquiry focused increasingly on the body as a site of meaning production. Franny Nudelman's *John Brown's Body* extended the analysis from the bodies of soldiers (battlefield photography, Whitman's *Drum-Taps* and *Specimen Days*) to the bodies of slaves (*The Confessions of Nat Turner*, "Benito Cereno") and the body of John Brown (the eponymous soldiers' marching song, Thoreau's "A Plea for Captain John Brown," Melville's "The Portent").[22] Interrogating the means by which nationalist culture abstracts the effects of violence, Nudelman connected the literature of the war per se to antebellum cultural contexts via three discursive regimes: sentiment, science, and punishment. Science, particularly medical discourse, also provided the context for Lisa Long's *Rehabilitating Bodies*, which argued that the understanding of "invisible wounds" associated with the Civil War—phantom limb pain, neurasthenia, hysteria, and similar maladies—was shaped by the sexism and racism of nineteenth-century medical discourse.[23] Readings of Alcott's *Hospital Sketches* and Elizabeth Stuart Phelps's best-selling novel *The Gates Ajar* helped consolidate these texts' new canonical status. Notable also was Long's attention to "The Case of George Dedlow," a bizarre story of a quadruple amputee written by Silas Weir Mitchell.[24] Medical imagery composed just one part of the archive of Shirley Samuels's wide-ranging study of American iconography, *Facing America*.[25] Samuels argued that photography, which came of age during the war, marked a significant divide in iconographic form. Close attention to faces particularly revealed the anxieties over race, gender, and sexuality structuring familiar icons (Washington embracing Lincoln in heaven, Jefferson Davis wearing a dress) as well as less familiar but no less iconic images (medical photographs of soldier amputees, or a portrait of Mary Todd Lincoln's modiste, Elizabeth

Keckley). This context enabled productive new readings of *Uncle Tom's Cabin*, Whitman's writings on Lincoln, and Keckley's 1868 memoir, *Behind the Scenes, or, Thirty Years a Slave and Four Years in the White House*. Drew Gilpin Faust's comprehensive history of death in the Civil War, *This Republic of Suffering*, returned the focus to the soldier's body. Arguing that massive wartime losses exacerbated an antebellum crisis of belief, Faust used literary texts to index two kinds of personal response: those who found consolation in the Christian concepts of immortality and heaven, as exemplified in popular ballads and newspaper verse, and those who refused consolation and focused on death as loss, such as Melville and Bierce. Especially consoling, argued Faust, was a Swedenborgian image of heaven as a perfected earth where family relations persisted, as presented for example in Phelps's *Gates Ajar*.[26]

Another postcentennial line of inquiry took as its organizing categories the configurations of citizenship and nationhood, beyond (as Warren put it) Whitman's mystic Unionism or Melville's pragmatic Unionism. The first such was Kathleen Diffley's *Where My Heart Is Turning Ever*, which investigated the ways in which popular fiction engaged with the issues surrounding the war's great legal result, constitutional reform.[27] Working with an archive of more than three hundred magazine stories about the war published from 1861 through 1876, Diffley identified three genres, each paired with a constitutional amendment: the Thirteenth with "Old Homestead" stories such as Mark Twain's "A True Story, Repeated Word for Word and I Heard It," which strains to incorporate freedpeople into a national domestic narrative; the Fourteenth with romances such as John W. De Forest's "Parole D'Honneur" or anti-romances such as Constance Fenimore Woolson's "Rodman the Keeper," in which gender provides the ground for negotiating race and class; and the Fifteenth with adventure stories such as Rebecca Harding Davis's "How the Widow Crossed the Lines," often with female protagonists whose exploits questioned the formal exclusion of women from citizenship. After Diffley's canon-expanding project, Deak Nabers returned to old-canon authors in *Victory of Law*, which took as its organizing context the due process and equal protection clauses of the Fourteenth Amendment. Starting from the premise that literature and law can both enact ideas of freedom, Nabers argued that Thoreau's antislavery writings, Melville's *Battle-Pieces*, and Whitman's *Drum-Taps* paralleled constitutional debate and that the Fourteenth Amendment itself was in some sense a "poetic achievement."[28]

Other studies explored questions of nationhood and citizenship through the cultural work of particular literary forms such as romance fiction, lyric poetry, or epic. Nina Silber's *The Romance of Reunion* charted the postwar emergence of the subgenre of reconciliation fiction, which targeted a northern readership in allegorizing the power relations of national reunion as marital union between a northern veteran and a southern belle while creating an idyllic image of the South.[29] Silber argued that while the romance plot of De Forest's *Miss Ravenel's Conversion* (a novel that Wilson and Aaron had valued for its realistic attention to combat) anticipated the paradigm, only in the 1880s did it emerge full blown, when reconciliation novels by the likes of Thomas Nelson Page painted an idealized image of the South as a refuge from social and economic upheaval. Henry James's *The Bostonians*, however, went against this popular current in turning a Confederate veteran and a New England women's rights reformer against each other.

Faith Barrett's more recent *To Fight Aloud Is Very Brave* approached the question of nationalism through poetic rather than fictional form, particularly "voice-effects" conveyed in modes of address, pronoun usages, songlike structures, and similar formal features that specify an audience's relation to a text.[30] Chapters addressed popular song, soldiers' poetry, and old-canon stalwarts (Dickinson, Melville, Whitman) while making a case for sustained critical attention to new-canon poets such as Frances Harper, who frequently recited her own poems during antislavery lectures and whose postbellum poetry criticized the ongoing disenfranchisement of African Americans; George Moses Horton, a former slave and freelance poet who attached himself to the Ninth Michigan Cavalry; and Sarah Piatt, whose critical play with romantic landscapes and gender conventions earned her substantial popularity in northern magazines. Whereas Barrett examined varieties of pre-Modernist lyric, Julia Stern answered Aaron's complaint by arguing that Mary Chesnut's wartime diary, as revised in the 1880s, constituted a prose epic of the Confederacy, featuring Chesnut herself in the persona of Cassandra. Stern argued that while Chesnut's narrative is inevitably "beset by race prejudice," nevertheless it "inadvertently gives voice" to the "reality and power of slave consciousness."[31]

Thematically focused studies also investigated mediating categories of national identity, such as memory, loyalty, or moral ideals. Martin Griffin's *Ashes of the Mind* engaged with the northern response to the white South's apparent success in controlling the collective memory of the war.[32] Whereas in southern literature, a realistic history of the war was gradually replaced by the nostalgic romance of nobility and lost organic social relations, according to Silber's paradigm, Griffin traced the dissipation of a specifically northern cultural memory of victory as the century drew on, through studies of James Russell Lowell's writings (especially the "Ode Recited at the Harvard Commemoration"), Melville's *Battle-Pieces*, James's *Bostonians*, Bierce's short fiction, and Paul Laurence Dunbar's poetry (especially his sonnet on Robert Gould Shaw). Elizabeth Duquette's *Loyal Subjects* traced the wartime discourse of loyalty that posed an alternative to the antebellum discourse of sympathy as a model for understanding social bonds.³³ Duquette charted loyalty's affective appeal in various literary domains, notably in the structure of romance narratives (De Forest's *Miss Ravenel*, James's *Bostonians*), in Charles Chesnutt's engagement with the loyal slave trope, and in the shape of nineteenth-century philosophy. In the latter case, Duquette focused not on the pragmatism that Wilson and Warren saw emerging from the war, but rather on idealism, as exemplified by Josiah Royce's emphasis on ethical culture. Whereas Griffin's and Duquette's studies were weighted toward the later nineteenth century, Randall Fuller's *From Battlefields Rising* returned to the war years to argue that the Civil War tested the commitments of antebellum and especially New England literature that was oriented toward moral transformation and social reform.³⁴ Organized chronologically, Fuller's study traced the war's impact on numerous literary careers, weighting old-canon writers such as Emerson, Dickinson, Hawthorne, Melville, and Whitman more heavily than new-canon figures such as Alcott, Phelps, and Thomas Wentworth Higginson.

With the exception of Stern's recent reading of Mary Chesnut, studies of the literary dimensions of nationhood and citizenship discussed so far all took an implicitly (or sometimes explicitly) Unionist point of view. Only recently has the literary dimension of Confederate nationhood received significant, sustained attention. Given its rapid emergence, brief life, and troubled afterlife, Confederate nationalism presents an interesting test case for Benedict Anderson's account of nationalism as a modern phenomenon, according to which a nation exists in the minds of its members, as imagined and disseminated through print culture.³⁵ Thus, beginning with Drew Gilpin Faust's brief but suggestive *The Creation of Confederate Nationalism*, Anderson's thesis has been important in shaping research.³⁶ The first sustained account was Michael Bernath's *Confederate Minds*, which extended the study of southern intellectual history from the antebellum era, where it had already received significant attention, to the Confederate era.³⁷ Focusing less on particular authors and texts and more on the periodicals that were their vehicles, Bernath argued that since the originality required to articulate a distinct national literature was at odds with the Confederacy's ideological conservatism, Confederate literary nationalism was doomed to fail. Ian Binnington's *Confederate Visions* focused on a particular constellating symbol of nationalism, the Confederate military.³⁸ Binnington followed Alice Fahs (discussed below) in drawing examples of popular poetry and fiction from newspapers and periodicals. Both Bernath and Binnington mentioned Henry Timrod's and William Gilmore Simms's poetry and the handful of novels that were published in the Confederacy, many of which were first serialized in periodicals. Of the novels, only Augusta Jane Evans's *Macaria; or, the Altars of Sacrifice* has received critical attention to date. Whereas Faust, Bernath, and Binnington used literature as an index to nationalist symbolism and ideology, Coleman Hutchison's *Apples and Ashes* asked "literary questions of the literary texts of the Confederacy."[39] Focusing on the formal and rhetorical structures that invite readers to invest texts with meaning, Hutchison organized his study by genre: literary criticism (the London-based *Index* as well as the *Southern Literary Messenger*); the novel (Evans's *Macaria*); popular song (the parallel northern and southern lives of the antebellum minstrel song "Dixie"); and memoir (Loreta Janeta Velazquez's geographically restless *The Woman in Battle*). The chapter on poetry ranged widely from ephemera to newspaper poetry to Timrod to postwar anthologies such as Simms's *War Poetry of the South*.

A third line of postcentennial criticism incorporated the work of the two lines discussed above—on violence and the body, on nationhood and citizenship—into the project of canon expansion. One kind of canon-expanding project was explicitly motivated by the feminist and African American recovery work of the 1970s and 1980s that resulted, for example, in the Heath anthology of American literature.[40] An important instance was Elizabeth Young's *Disarming the Nation*. Young observed that while studies of Civil War literature had traditionally emphasized the "generative power of [white] masculinity," nevertheless Wilson's eclectic approach, which included Stowe, Howe, Chesnut, and Forten, hinted at alternative genealogies of women's and African Americans' experience. Arguing that women writers especially exploited the symbolic possibilities of the word "civil," Young focused on six sets of women's texts dating from the war years through the centennial: the wartime and postwar reception of *Uncle Tom's Cabin*; Alcott's writings from *Hospital Sketches* through *Little Women* and its sequels; Keckley's *Behind the Scenes*; Velazquez's *The Woman in Battle* (emphasizing gender where Hutchison would emphasize geography); Frances Harper's novels *Minnie's Sacrifice* and *Iola Leroy* (as compared with Barrett's study of Harper, which would focus on poetry); and Margaret Mitchell's *Gone with the Wind*.

As Young remarked, one reason the Civil War canon was slow to include women's writing was that earlier feminist criticism tended to focus on the domestic sphere.[41] Lyde Cullen Sizer's *The Political Work of Northern Women Writers and the Civil War* demonstrated, however, that numerous northern women writers actively engaged with national issues through various public genres, including novels, short stories, poetry, periodical essays, and letters to the editor.[42] Sizer argued that these writers developed an implicitly white, middle-class rhetoric of unity among women that was exclusionary as well as motivating and community building. Jennifer James took up other rhetorics of exclusion in *A Freedom Bought with Blood*: the imagination of the citizen's body as male and the classification of the black body as naturally inferior and institutionally disabled by slavery.[43] In this context, James argued, many African American men went to war to prove their rehabilitation and claim citizenship. One of two chapters on Civil

War literature examined how the war affected William Wells Brown's revisions for the 1867 edition of his novel *Clotel; or, The Colored Heroine* (first published in 1853). Another focused on Harper's *Minnie's Sacrifice* and *Iola Leroy* as well as Dunbar's reconciliation fiction, with some mention of the poetry that was Griffin's primary object of analysis.

Another kind of canon-expanding project turned to popular literature, which was largely neglected by the centennial critics, as an index of ideologies and a shaping force of wartime culture. Informed, like many of the studies discussed thus far, by Anderson's print-culture theory of nationalism, Alice Fahs's *The Imagined Civil War* examined how northern and southern popular literature produced affective bonds of national consciousness.[44] Reminding us that the modernist dichotomy of "high" and "low" culture oversimplifies the nineteenth-century literary field, Fahs took popular literature to encompass everything from song sheets to newspaper verse, the latter including the work of such contemporarily well-known but since neglected poets as Paul Hamilton Hayne. Fahs found that issues of race and women's experience featured prominently in a range of genres and modes, such as romance fiction, adventure fiction, sensational literature, and humor. Like those who examined more-canonical literature, Fahs argued that primary themes of popular Civil War literature included the devastating impact of violence, the tension between the needs of the individual and the needs of the nation, and the exploration of the war's liberationist potential.

Recent anthologies have consolidated these canon-expanding projects. Reprinting short stories with wartime settings published in monthly magazines during the war and Reconstruction, Kathleen Diffley's anthology *To Live and Die* mixes stories by well-known authors such as Rebecca Harding Davis and Mark Twain with less familiar stories such as Mitchell's "The Case of George Dedlow" (discussed above).[45] Edward Everett Hale is represented here not by his much reprinted "The Man without a Country" but by a humorous story of improvisation amid wartime shortages in Richmond. Faith Barrett and Cristanne Miller's anthology of poetry that was published during and immediately following the war, "*Words for the Hour*," similarly mixes familiar and unfamiliar authors.[46] Along with selections from newspaper and popular anthology verse, several authors are given more-substantial representation, thus solidifying their canonical status: Whitman, Melville, Dickinson, Whittier, Timrod, Harper, Horton, and Piatt. Ian Finseth's multigeneric anthology, *The American Civil War*, construes the bounds of Civil War literature more expansively, stretching to the early twentieth century to include retrospective accounts and commentaries on the issue of race by African American writers such as Dunbar and W. E. B. Du Bois as well as wartime writings by Horton and Frederick Douglass.[47]

The Sesquicentennial Context and the Shape of the Collection

While the centennial critics moved beyond the reconciliationist memory that shaped fiftieth-anniversary reflections, they nevertheless looked for unanimity in the literary response to the war. By contrast, the postcentennial critics largely refused to organize the literature of the war in terms of a unifying narrative frame such as Warren's "tragedy," Wilson's "myth," or Aaron's phantom "epic." Rather, influenced by both the theoretical ferment of the 1970s and 1980s and the historicizing responses of the 1980s and 1990s, they returned to the categories that wartime writers themselves had used to make sense of the war: violence, the body, nationhood, law, freedom, citizenship. On the occasion of the Civil War's sesquicentennial, the essays in the present collection continue these investigations as shaped by current priorities of nineteenth-century American literary study. These priorities include recovery work and canon formation, especially in African American literature; a recognition of the importance of poetry in nineteenth-century American culture; continued interest in the print mediation of nation and region; and a renewed interest in aesthetics.[48] Thus while many of the essays in this collection share an interest in aesthetics, they otherwise fall into three groups.

The "African American Literary Cultures" group continues postcentennial recovery work and with it the explicit recognition of the war's emancipationist promise. Christopher Hager documents the formation of a culture of literacy in black regiments during the war, showing how protest letters by newly literate soldiers became vehicles for identity formation. Adapting interests and expectations to contemporary political realities, these soldiers nevertheless used epistolary conventions to assert their rights as citizens. Their letters thus provide a counterpoint to the disciplinary narrative that locates the origin of African American literature in the slave narrative. Another verbal culture of black regiments is the context for Jeremy Wells's essay on transcriptions of songs made by Thomas Wentworth Higginson, the commander of the First South Carolina Volunteers. Wells argues that Higginson, who is best known to literary history as Emily Dickinson's correspondent and editor, had no doubts regarding black soldiers' rights of citizenship, but he was puzzled by the challenge that their songs posed for the sound of American culture as he attempted to understand them according to the conventions of poetry and song that he knew. African American military experience and its potential implications for citizenship and social being were central to William Wells Brown's *The Negro in the American Rebellion*. John Ernest argues that Brown responded to the memorialization of the war in white popular culture by producing a transformative text in African American historiography, using a hyperdocumentary form to show that the war was larger and more complex than any claims made by whites concerning its purpose or significance. Although African American poet George Moses Horton did not serve as a soldier, a military environment also proved fertile ground for his artistic development, as Faith Barrett demonstrates. Attached as a freedman to the Ninth Michigan Cavalry, Horton wrote in a variety of forms, addressing a broad range of readers with divergent views on race, emancipation, and citizenship. By adapting poetic conventions to claim a black poetic voice, Horton positioned himself as both exceptional and representative.

The "Poetics of War" group elaborates on the understanding established by Barrett's essay regarding the importance of poetry in nineteenth-century American cultural life. My essay situates the unusual forms of Melville's *Battle-Pieces* poems in the context of vernacular poetic forms such as ballad, hymn, and epitaph. I argue that where such somatically familiar forms conventionally produce the emotional satisfactions of community belonging or national identification, Melville intervened to propose a critical experience of citizenship. Offering a new account of Whitman's nationalist literary project, Samuel Graber argues that Whitman found in wartime British anti-Unionism a means to wean American literary culture from foreign influence. In place of a transatlantic lineage, in *Drum-Taps* and its sequel Whitman imagined an autochthonous origin for American poetics in the blood-soaked ground. Within any such configuration, the postbellum fate of Confederate literary nationalism remained problematic. Thus, Coleman Hutchison argues that the South's most prominent man of letters, William Gilmore Simms, in contrast to Whitman, looked to England for a model that made sectionalism integral to postbellum literary nationalism. Documenting the extraordinary productivity of Confederate literary culture, Simms's *War Poetry of the South* demonstrated by way of anthology the American assimilation of English poetic forms. Like Barrett's essay, Hutchison's develops significant insights into nineteenth-century American poetic culture by using methods beyond the kind of close reading that developed as a technique for reading modernist works.

The essays in the "Mediations of Nation and Region" group investigate the production of identification in various sites and forms, including the development of two of the war's most significant and lasting literary legacies, regionalism and realism. During the war, as James Berkey demonstrates, literary cultures of North and South often met on a single page in the soldier newspapers printed in the occupied South. Here Union soldiers adapted materials at hand in southern printing offices, using familiar practices of the mid-nineteenth-century American culture of reprinting to attempt to control prior journalistic traces of Confederate ideology. Another means of engagement with larger literary cultures was private writing that later became public. For example, Confederate Army nurse Kate Cumming's wartime diary, published in 1866 as *A Journal of Hospital Life*, responded to the norms of southern femininity encoded in antebellum sentimental discourse, as Jane Schultz demonstrates. Developing what Schultz terms a "Confederate realism" opposed to sentimentalism during the war, Cumming reverted to a sentimental mode more suitable for the production of reconciliationist memory in a revised version of the journal published three decades later. Elizabeth Stuart Phelps also responded to antebellum sentimental discourse in her best-selling novel *The Gates Ajar*, as Shirley Samuels demonstrates in her geographically attentive reading, by representing a postwar culture of mourning in which the loss of future reproductive possibility enables women to bond with other women in a new form of national family. As Phelps brings domestic discourse into the public arena, she questions the ideological boundaries of "separate spheres" by bringing the violent legacy of the Kansas-Nebraska Act into the heart of New England domesticity. Sometimes taken as sentimentalism's pragmatic other, literary realism emerged from the war bound up with a regionalist consciousness and questions of race, as essays by both Jillian Spivey Caddell and Kathleen Diffley indicate. Caddell traces the relationship between regionalization and the marginalization of the black subject in multiple media, comparing the perspectives of war fiction published in the *Atlantic Monthly*—Rebecca Harding Davis's "John Lamar" and Constance Fenimore Woolson's "Rodman the Keeper"—with that of Winslow Homer's painting *Near Andersonville*. Diffley investigates the ways in which the memory and purpose of the war were retrospectively shaped by fiction published in the San Francisco–based *Overland Monthly*, edited during the late 1860s by Bret Harte. Elaborating on the common analogy of realistic fiction and photography, Diffley extends the analogy to a form that came to prominence during the war, the stereograph. She argues that the *Overland*, a western challenger to the Boston-based *Atlantic*'s claim to cultural dominance, implicitly revised northeastern orthodoxies regarding emancipation, even while its fiction was structured by the new stereoscopic logic of parallax.

Both wide-ranging and effectively focused, this collection thus begins to explore the diversity of literary cultures that emerged during the 1860s and 1870s. The Civil War reshaped or enabled new ensembles of discourses, conventions, and practices, with the result that new questions arose regarding fundamental categories such as nation, violence, liberty, citizenship, community, and identity. As the postcentennial expansion of the war's literary canon has already indicated, more voices spoke to these questions, and in more registers, than were recognized either by fiftieth-anniversary assessments given to reconciliationism or

Introduction

centennial assessments framed by the Cold War and the civil rights movement. The Civil War's sesquicentennial, then, provides an occasion to listen again to de-familiarized voices from the war and to hear others for the first time.

NOTES

1. Fred Lewis Pattee, *History of American Literature since 1870* (New York: Century, 1915), vii, viii, hereafter documented parenthetically.
2. See Pattee's discussion of the Gettysburg Address (14). On the trope of *autochthones*, see Gary Wills, *Lincoln at Gettysburg: The Words That Remade America* (New York: Simon and Schuster, 1992), 41–62.
3. David Blight, *Race and Reunion: The Civil War in American Memory* (Cambridge, Mass.: Harvard University Press, 2001).
4. David Blight, *American Oracle: The Civil War in the Civil Rights Era* (Cambridge, Mass.: Belknap–Harvard University Press), 2011. See also Jon Wiener, "Civil War, Cold War, Civil Rights: The Civil War Centennial Context, 1960–1965," in *The Memory of the Civil War in American Culture*, ed. Alice Fahs and Joan Waugh (Chapel Hill: University of North Carolina Press, 2004), 237–57.
5. Viewing post–World War II U.S. race relations in global context, Mary Dudziak argues that through civil rights reform, the federal government wanted to tell a progressive story about American democracy and demonstrate American moral superiority. *Cold War Civil Rights: Race and the Image of American Democracy* (Princeton: Princeton University Press, 2000).
6. Alfred Kazin, "And the War Came," *The Reporter*, May 11, 1961, 42, hereafter documented parenthetically.
7. Robert Penn Warren, *The Legacy of the Civil War: Meditations on the Centennial* (New York: Random House, 1961), 7, hereafter documented parenthetically.
8. Warren would return to the civil rights agenda with his 1965 oral history compilation, *Who Speaks for the Negro?* (New York: Random House, 1965).
9. On Warren's interpretation of the war as tragedy, see Blight, *American Oracle*, 31–79.
10. Robert Penn Warren, "Melville's Poems," *Southern Review* 3 (1967): 820, 822.
11. Edmund Wilson, *Patriotic Gore: Studies in the Literature of the American Civil War* (New York: Oxford University Press, 1962), xxxi–xxxii, hereafter documented parenthetically. See Warren, *Legacy*, 53–76.
12. While George Frederickson's important study does not refer explicitly to the centennial moment, his concluding remarks on Henry James's anti-imperialism resonate with the Cold War context. See *The Inner Civil War: Northern Intellectuals and the Crisis of the Union* (New York: Harper and Row, 1965), 229–36.
13. Daniel Aaron, *The Unwritten War: American Writers and the Civil War*, 2nd ed. (1973; repr., Madison: University of Wisconsin Press, 1987), xx, hereafter documented parenthetically.
14. This turn is signaled, for example, by the 1987 republication of Aaron's book, not by

a commercial press (Knopf had published the first edition), but by an academic press. On the decline of public-sphere criticism, see Russell Jacoby, *The Last Intellectuals: American Culture in the Age of Academe* (New York: Basic, 1987).

15. For a critique of the national security state predating the governmental reaction to the events of September 11, 2001, see Gore Vidal, "The National Security State" (1988), and "Monotheism and Its Discontents" (1992), *Selected Essays of Gore Vidal*, ed. Jay Parini (New York: Vintage, 2009), 399–407, 408–16.

16. Shira Wolosky, *Emily Dickinson: A Voice of War* (New Haven: Yale University Press, 1984). See also Aaron's suggestive but undeveloped comments, *Unwritten War*, 355–56.

17. Timothy Sweet, *Traces of War: Poetry, Photography, and the Crisis of the Union* (Baltimore: Johns Hopkins University Press, 1990).

18. Elaine Scarry, *The Body in Pain: The Making and Unmaking of the World* (New York: Oxford University Press, 1985), 124, 125.

19. Walt Whitman, *Prose Works 1892*, 2 vols., ed. Floyd Stovall (New York: New York University Press, 1963), 1:115.

20. Elizabeth Young, "Verbal Battlefields," in Anthony W. Lee and Elizabeth Young, *On Alexander Gardner's "Photographic Sketch Book" of the Civil War* (Berkeley: University of California Press, 2007), 52–94.

21. James Dawes, *The Language of War: The Literature and Culture of the U.S. from the Civil War through World War II* (Cambridge: Harvard University Press, 2005), 3, 29; on Alcott and Whitman, see 43–55.

22. Franny Nudelman, *John Brown's Body: Slavery, Violence, and the Culture of War* (Chapel Hill: University of North Carolina Press, 2004).

23. Lisa Long, *Rehabilitating Bodies: Health, History, and the American Civil War* (Philadelphia: University of Pennsylvania Press, 2004), 4.

24. Mitchell, an army surgeon, is best known today as the inventor of the "rest cure" for neurasthenia that is critically depicted in Charlotte Perkins Gilman's short story "The Yellow Wallpaper."

25. Shirley Samuels, *Facing America: Iconography and the American Civil War* (Oxford: Oxford University Press, 2004).

26. Drew Gilpin Faust, *This Republic of Suffering: Death and the American Civil War* (New York: Knopf, 2008), 171–210.

27. Kathleen Diffley, *Where My Heart Is Turning Ever: Civil War Stories and Constitutional Reform, 1861–76* (Athens: University of Georgia Press, 1992).

28. Deak Nabers, *Victory of Law: The Fourteenth Amendment, the Civil War, and American Literature, 1852–1867* (Baltimore: Johns Hopkins University Press, 2006), 198.

29. Nina Silber, *The Romance of Reunion: Northerners and the South* (Chapel Hill: University of North Carolina Press, 1993), 105–23.

30. Faith Barrett, *To Fight Aloud Is Very Brave: American Poetry and the Civil War* (Amherst: University of Massachusetts Press, 2012).

31. Julia Stern, *Mary Chesnut's Civil War Epic* (Chicago: University of Chicago Press, 2010), 15.

32. Martin Griffin, *Ashes of the Mind: War and Memory in Northern Literature, 1865–1900* (Amherst: University of Massachusetts Press, 2009).

33. Elizabeth Duquette, *Loyal Subjects: Bonds of Nation, Race, and Allegiance in Nineteenth-Century America* (New Brunswick: Rutgers University Press, 2010).

34. Randall Fuller, *From Battlefields Rising: How the Civil War Transformed American Literature* (Oxford: Oxford University Press, 2011).

35. Benedict Anderson, *Imagined Communities: Reflections on the Origin and Spread of Nationalism* (London: Verso, 1983).

36. Drew Gilpin Faust, *The Creation of Confederate Nationalism: Ideology and Identity in the Civil War South* (Baton Rouge: Louisiana State University Press, 1988). On Anderson, see 16, 18.

37. Michael Bernath, *Confederate Minds: The Struggle for Intellectual Independence in the Civil War South* (Chapel Hill: University of North Carolina Press, 2010). On antebellum southern intellectual history, see especially Michael O'Brien, *Conjectures of Order: Intellectual Life in the American South, 1810–1860*, 2 vols. (Chapel Hill: University of North Carolina Press, 2004).

38. Ian Binnington, *Confederate Visions: Nationalism, Symbolism, and the Imagined South in the Civil War* (Charlottesville: University of Virginia Press, 2013).

39. Coleman Hutchison, *Apples and Ashes: Literature, Nationalism, and the Confederate States of America* (Athens: University of Georgia Press, 2012), 14.

40. Ironically, Civil War literature itself has remained a marginalized category in the Heath and similar anthologies that break at 1865. On the shape of American literary history without this split, see Christopher Hager and Cody Marrs, "Against 1865: Reperiodizing the Nineteenth Century," *J19* 1, no. 2 (2013): 259–84.

41. Elizabeth Young, *Disarming the Nation: Women's Writing and the American Civil War* (Chicago: University of Chicago Press, 1999), 6.

42. Lyde Cullen Sizer, *The Political Work of Northern Women Writers and the Civil War, 1850–1872* (Chapel Hill: University of North Carolina Press, 2000).

43. Jennifer C. James, *A Freedom Bought with Blood: African American War Literature from the Civil War to World War II* (Chapel Hill: University of North Carolina Press, 2007).

44. Alice Fahs, *The Imagined Civil War: Popular Literature of the North and South, 1861–1865* (Chapel Hill: University of North Carolina Press, 2001). See also Fahs, "Northern and Southern Worlds of Print," in *Perspectives on American Book History: Artifacts and Commentary*, ed. Scott E. Casper, Joanne D. Chaison, and Jeffrey D. Groves (Amherst: University of Massachusetts Press, 2002), 195–222.

45. Kathleen Diffley, ed., *To Live and Die: Collected Stories of the Civil War, 1861–1876* (Durham: Duke University Press, 2002).

46. Faith Barrett and Cristanne Miller, eds., *"Words for the Hour": A New Anthology of Civil War Poetry* (Amherst: University of Massachusetts Press, 2005).

47. Ian Frederick Finseth, ed., *The American Civil War: An Anthology of Essential Writings* (New York: Routledge, 2006).

48. On African American literature as an archival concern, see John Ernest, *Chaotic*

Justice: Rethinking African American Literary History (Chapel Hill: University of North Carolina Press, 2009); Eric Gardner, *Unexpected Places: Relocating Nineteenth-Century American Literature* (Jackson: University of Mississippi Press, 2009); and Lara Langer Cohen and Jordan Alexander Stein, eds., *Early African American Print Culture* (Philadelphia: University of Pennsylvania Press, 2012). On the cultural importance of poetry, see Paula Bennett, *Poets in the Public Sphere: The Emancipatory Project of Women's Poetry, 1800–1900* (Princeton: Princeton University Press, 2003); Mary Loeffelholz, *From School to Salon: Reading Nineteenth-Century American Women's Poetry* (Princeton: Princeton University Press, 2004); Eliza Richards, *Gender and the Poetics of Reception in Poe's Circle* (Cambridge: Cambridge University Press, 2004); and Max Cavitch, *American Elegy: The Poetry of Mourning from the Puritans to Whitman* (Minneapolis: University of Minnesota Press, 2006). On the print mediation of nation and region beyond Benedict Anderson, see Meredith McGill, *American Literature and the Culture of Reprinting, 1834–1853* (Philadelphia: University of Pennsylvania Press, 2003); Trish Loughran, *The Republic in Print: Print Culture in the Age of U.S. Nation Building* (New York: Columbia University Press, 2007); and Phillip Round, *Removable Type: Histories of the Book in Indian Country* (Chapel Hill: University of North Carolina Press, 2010). On the aesthetic turn, see Christopher Castiglia and Russ Castronovo, eds., "Aesthetics and the End(s) of Cultural Studies," special issue of *American Literature* 76, no. 3 (2004); Russ Castronovo, *Beautiful Democracy: Aesthetics and Anarchy in a Global Era* (Chicago: University of Chicago Press, 2007); Christopher Castiglia, *Interior States: Institutional Consciousness and the Inner Life of Democracy in the Antebellum United States* (Durham: Duke University Press, 2008); Samuel Otter and Geoffrey Sanborn, eds., *Melville and Aesthetics* (New York: Palgrave Macmillan, 2011); and Cindy Weinstein and Christopher Looby, eds., *American Literature's Aesthetic Dimensions* (New York: Columbia University Press, 2012).

PART I

AFRICAN AMERICAN LITERARY CULTURES

"if we Ever Expect to be a Pepple"

The Epistolary Culture of African American Soldiers

CHRISTOPHER HAGER

A few weeks after disembarking in South Carolina and taking command of a black regiment, Thomas Wentworth Higginson strolled through camp one evening and observed a bazaar of expressive culture. Gathered around fires, soldiers were

> telling stories and shouting with laughter over the broadest mimicry, in which they excel, and in which the officers come in for a full share. The ever-lasting "shout" is always within hearing, with its mixture of piety and polka, and its castanet-like clapping of the hands. Then there are quieter prayer-meetings, with pious invocations and slow psalms, "deaconed out" from memory by the leader, two lines at a time, in a sort of wailing chant. Elsewhere, there are *conversazioni* around fires, with a woman for queen of the circle,—her Nubian face, gay head-dress, gilt necklace, and white teeth, all resplendent in the glowing light. Sometimes the woman is spelling slow monosyllables out of a primer, a feat which always commands all ears,—they rightly recognizing a mighty spell, equal to the overthrowing of monarchs, in the magic assonance of *cat, hat, pat, bat,* and the rest of it. Elsewhere, it is some solitary old cook, some aged Uncle Tiff, with enormous spectacles, who is perusing a hymn-book by the light of a pine splinter, in his deserted cooking booth of palmetto leaves. By another fire there is an actual dance, red-legged soldiers doing right-and-left, and "now-lead-de-lady-ober," to the music of a violin which is rather artistically played, and which may have guided the steps, in other days, of Barnwells and Hugers. And yonder is a

stump-orator perched on his barrel, pouring out his exhortations to fidelity in war and in religion.[1]

Like a living Venn diagram, the circles around campfires chart the rich and variegated terrain of African American culture in the Civil War South. Higginson's stroll takes him from old forms to new: the ring shout of African origins to the prayer meeting inspired by North American Christianity. It juxtaposes the radical transformations occasioned by emancipation—the "magic" emergence of literacy from a spelling book—with the continuities of oral traditions. Even if marred by Higginson's tendency to patronize and exoticize African Americans, the passage highlights the distinctive overlaps of black cultural life's many origins and resonances.

It also raises many of the same questions that have shaped our understanding of African American culture from then until now. What had survived the middle passage, and what emerged during slavery? What was borrowed from whites? Are black cultural practices distinguished by their aesthetics (like the violin music) or their ideology (like the stump speeches)? And what might Higginson have misperceived or mislabeled? (Surely none of the participants in the "*conversazioni*" conceived it as such.) The ambiguities in what Higginson saw, amid the darkness of an army camp by night, are essential to understanding the Civil War as a crucial moment in African American literary history. Kenneth Warren has recently argued that African American literature "gained its coherence as an undertaking in the social world defined by the system of Jim Crow segregation." Higginson catalogued the ingredients that would go into the subsequent, more organized "undertaking."[2]

It took an army camp for many of those ingredients to surface—not only for them to become visible to Higginson (who, like most New England abolitionists, would never have had much first-hand knowledge of African Americans in the South had the war not brought them down there) and thus to become part of a published record of the war, but also for them to emerge from slavery's hiding places. Evening gatherings of black men around campfires did not abound in the Confederacy. Neither did spelling books. Wartime emancipation made it possible for black southerners to assemble, and at essentially the same time it freed them to become literate. For the formerly enslaved, these two effects of the Civil War—these vital ingredients of a literary culture—converged nowhere more suddenly and intensely than in those military regiments, like Higginson's, made up of southern black men.

The writings of black soldiers during the war thus form a counterweight (not exactly the same as Kenneth Warren's) to a narrative of African American literature that originates with fugitive slave narratives and their tropes of stolen literacy as a tool of liberation. Frederick Douglass learned to write in slavery, escaped alone to the North, and penned a masterful autobiography, but very few people experienced anything similar. Far more numerous, and equally important, were ordinary southern blacks who embarked on a less dramatic but unmistakably literary project. Colonel Higginson did not notice, or was less interested by, those soldiers who drew upon the campfires' cultural mélange when they wrote letters. The act of writing was more private than dances, ring shouts, and orations, yet the letters African American soldiers wrote were in another way their most public cultural products—engaged with worlds beyond the glow of the campfire and better preserved today. These men's Civil War letters constitute a collective work of expressive and political innovation.

Throughout the nation and for everyone, the mobilization for war sparked literary activity—not the kinds of literary activity scholars like Edmund Wilson and Daniel Aaron have famously looked for and not found, but a rich outpouring of written expression by ordinary Americans. Letter writing became an even bigger part of everyday life than it had been before. White soldiers and their families back home could communicate only in writing, and the volume of letters flowing into and out of Union camps alone has been estimated at 180,000 per day.[3] Even barely literate young men took up pen and paper to remain connected with their home places. Better-educated servicemen, keenly aware that they were participating in historic events, kept diaries and mailed pages home to parents, wives, and sisters. Moreover, the many idle hours in camp turned countless soldiers into readers, poring over their caches of letters from home, even forming a crucial market for dime novels.[4]

Southern black soldiers had these same occasions for reading and writing, and with particular urgency. The circumstances of their parting from family members usually were not the same as for white soldiers. These men did not march off to war in a parade. They might have fled a plantation under cover of night in the hopes of getting behind Union lines, then enlisted and wanted to tell a wife or parent that they were free and safe. They might have been separated from loved ones long ago by the domestic slave trade and only now have found the opportunity to ask someone to write a letter for them, or learned enough to write a letter on their own, to some vaguely remembered address.[5]

Black soldiers also had reasons for writing that most white soldiers did not, and they faced special pressures on their entry to and behavior in the world of letters. For them, joining the army was a pathway to citizenship—the leading edge of a new era after slavery. As Frederick Douglass famously said, "Once let the black man get upon his person the brass letters US, let him get an eagle on his button, and a musket on his shoulder, and bullets in his pocket, and there is no power on earth or under the earth which can deny that he has earned the right of citizenship in the United States."⁶ With that at stake, black soldiers' acts of writing did more than the personal and practical work of epistolary communication; they also did the conceptual and political work of shaping African American civic identity. As birthplaces of both citizenship and literacy, black regiments witnessed the convergence of linked projects, political and literary: to secure a place in the legal and the discursive United States. One black soldier, in a letter he obviously labored to write, deplored the conditions of his unit's service—"we Expected to be Treeated as men but we have bin Treeated more Like Dogs"—and articulated the stakes of his protest: "if we Ever Expect to be a Pepple & if we Dont Reply to some one of a thourety we Shall for Ever be Troden Down under foot of man."⁷

As this anonymous writer understood, the citizenship to which black men aspired—their hopes of being, in the eyes of the nation, *a people*—depended on more than military service alone. It required nipping second-class status in its every bud, protesting each injustice, laying claim to the rights without which African Americans would "be trodden down under foot of man." In the Union-occupied South, holding this line required recourse to "someone of authority" (he sent his letter to the secretary of war). And *that*, in a literate society and an increasingly bureaucratic military, meant writing—even if one's ability to write fell short of the audience's expectations, as this writer knew his did. "Pleass to Excuse bad writing & also mistakes," he wrote at the end (*BM* 655).

If the cultural life of the army camp comes to us filtered through a white observer, Thomas Wentworth Higginson, this letter is mediated, too, by the observer whom the writer expects to judge his writing "bad." What makes such letters interesting is not that they are somehow unmediated and authentic. They are not. The epistolary writing of aggrieved black soldiers constitutes a literary project precisely because it is highly constructed, characterized by rhetorical balancing acts and experiments, and mediated in manifold ways. They emerged from the crucible of their writers' political will and verbal expressiveness; their limitations as well as their abilities as writers and penmen; and, not least, their calculations—with the prospects for African American citizenship in mind—about what they should and should not say to white authority figures, and how they should and should not say it. It was a recipe for anxiety about one's legitimacy—as a political actor, as a writer of standard English. As we will see, manuscripts often reflect a nerve-wracking process of composition. Yet freedmen's uncertainties and struggles also inspired shrewd political and rhetorical maneuvering, from which sprang a notable identification of freedom with nationalism. The archive of enlisted freedmen's letters to white authorities is incomplete in many respects—it excludes writings by northern black soldiers (most of whom were just as literate before the war as during) and, of course, women—but it shows in incomparable detail how African American soldiers, in the churn of the war's progress and meaning, developed expressive modes of civic integration and political protest.[8]

For all these reasons, the epistolary culture of black soldiers reproduces in microcosm some of the Civil War's central interpretive problems. As the historian Yael Sternhell has recently suggested, "We must approach the Civil War with all the uncertainty, skepticism, and realism with which we treat other wars and other historical events. Yet we may do so while simultaneously appreciating that the liberation of 4 million Americans was a tremendously positive outcome of the war."[9] What Sternhell here articulates is the literary quality of a historiographical dilemma: how can a single thing—the American Civil War—harbor such very different meanings as *bloody tragedy* and *triumph of justice*? In the written record of the war they produced, southern black soldiers were contending with precisely this conundrum: how to hold in balance the glory and the horror of the events swirling around them? A former slave, now donning the uniform of the U.S. Army and exercising his burgeoning skills as a writer, might at once wish to celebrate freedom, literacy, and emergent citizenship, and also to condemn the racism, lament the sufferings, and protest the injustices that afflicted most black soldiers and their families. By negotiating that tension in their letters, these writers created a literary record of a complex process of identity formation—one characterized by the careful adaptation of freedpeople's interests to prevailing political realities, as well as the adamant assertion that, in the wake of emancipation, American political reality ought to adapt itself to freed people's claims.

Like most aspects of wartime emancipation, the black military experience was a study in contrasts. It did become, as advocates and recruiters like Frederick Douglass foresaw, a proving ground for black manhood. Engagements such as the assault on Fort Wagner captured the nation's attention and banished doubts about African Americans' courage. When *Harper's Weekly* depicted "A Typical Negro" in 1863, it framed military service as a process whereby, as Douglass had put it in his 1845 *Narrative*, "a slave was made a man." In these famous images, the scarred back of an escaped slave named Gordon—seated and stripped to the waist—is displayed next to a (smaller) picture of Gordon standing and facing the viewer "in his uniform as a U.S. soldier."[10] At the same time, African American soldiers were paid less than whites (a controversy Higginson wrote about in an appendix to *Army Life in a Black Regiment*); could not become officers; faced execution or re-enslavement if captured by Confederate forces; suffered greatly from disease, for which they often received inadequate treatment; and worried that their wives and families would starve if free or, if still enslaved, face violent retaliation by white southerners.[11] African American military service entailed less tangible sacrifices, too. As Carole Emberton has recently argued, the equation of citizenship with military service and "manhood" depended on whites' disavowal of "black men's capacity for violence" and in turn "complicated their understanding of black men's capacity for freedom."[12]

Access to literacy was perhaps the one unadulterated good. African American regiments unquestionably were venues for cultural and intellectual development. Reading lessons like the one Higginson saw around a campfire were widespread enough that later historians could refer to the Union Army as a "School" or "an Educational Institution for Negroes."[13] Teachers of various stripes abounded. An illiterate serviceman could seek lessons from a modestly more learned comrade or a missionary teacher, among others. Susie King Taylor, an escaped slave not yet twenty years old, worked as a laundress for Higginson's regiment and led an informal school for the men.[14] But if the acquisition of literacy traced a simple upward arc, the practice of literacy—particularly written literacy—reflected the deep complexities of black military service, emancipation, and the war. If knowing how to write was undeniably a good thing, it was nevertheless unclear to most freedmen exactly how to use their new knowledge.

While the military made literacy accessible and allowable, it also, of course, subjected enlisted men to considerable discipline and compulsion. For the recently freed, it represented a wholly unfamiliar epistemic regime, characterized by byzantine-seeming systems of communicating and transacting affairs: hidebound bureaucracies, entrenched social and linguistic protocols, unfamiliar assumptions and sensitivities. When a black soldier wrote a letter to "Mr Abebrem Lenken" in 1865 to complain about his treatment in the army, he had to figure out, all at once, what he was entitled to and how he should express that conviction: "i have ben sick Evy since i Come her and i think it is hard to make A man go and fite and Wont let him vote and wont let him go home when he is sick." Venturing new alphabetic combinations, he was unsure what rules he might be violating: "i Dont wont you to get mad with what i say for i Dont mene any harm rite soon if you pleze and let me no how you feel." After signing his name to the letter, he took his pen and made dozens of small dots in a cloud around his signature, to what end—amusement? artfulness? a little pomp for a missive to the president?—it is impossible to know.[15]

Despite their many idiosyncrasies, the manuscripts that survive from southern blacks' wartime military service do share some generic features. As the remainder of this essay will detail, these letters with some consistency display certain habits of writing, including an anxious will to adhere to norms; they document certain compositional events, especially a tendency to experiment and retry ideas in postscripts; and they advance certain kinds of claims, primarily appeals to ideas of justice and contractual agreement. From each of these angles, enlisted freedmen's writings constitute an effort to negotiate a place in the nation. In their relationships to epistolary and linguistic customs, to audiences, and to American political culture, these writings suggest that the way to emerge from slavery into citizenship—to become "a Pepple"—is to integrate, partially, to the polity as it exists; and then, with a wedge entered, to assert an unyielding identity.

Soldiers showed a keen awareness of conventions and a willingness, even eagerness, to conform to them. Even the most untutored writers generally knew they ought to begin their letters by saying something like, "i Seat myself to Rite you a few lines," "I am nesseriley compelled to write you a few Lines," or "please indulg me the liberty of writing you afew lines" (*BM* 424, 646, 82). Yet originality came easily to these beginning writers, if you count as original something like a cloud of dots, a peculiar twist of syntax, or a brutal frankness that proper Victorian education would have stifled. A black soldier in Louisiana wrote General Sherman to complain about his commander's "excesive cruelty," which included forcing the soldier to march "untill I have deposited the excrement of my body in my pants" (*BM* 456).

Still, the imperatives of standard spelling and usage, the considerations of a reading audience's expectations—to which a well-educated writer might not give a second thought—could be a matter of great anxiety, especially when the stakes were as high as proving a race's fitness for citizenship. A man from the Thirty-fifth U.S. Colored Troops tried four times to form the numeral 3 before he felt he had got it right and could spell out the rest of his regiment's name. Men doubled back with their pens and overwrote words with other, still incorrect spellings; scratched out signatures that apparently didn't look very good; and apologized constantly: "i am Sory that I am not able to write good." "my writing is none of the best for Slaves are poorly learned." "Sir I cant mot write very well an I lives so agreat wais of from eny one that can wrigh So I have to try an do it my self" (*BM* 156, 641, 655, 798–99).

One common result of neoliterate anxiety is what linguists call hypercorrection—overusing rules not fully understood, or trying too hard to sound proper. For adult men who had enjoyed the use of spoken English for years, to leap into the realm of written expression was to encounter bewildering new rules and dilemmas: silent letters, homonyms, and all manner of dissonance between how they talked and how they were supposed to write. Why is "right" not spelled the same as "write"? (One black soldier penned the sentence, "I have bin ronged out of my Writes.") Why can the letter C sometimes sound like a K and sometimes like an S (as the man who called himself a "colored colder" evidently had learned)? What's the point of extra letters that aren't pronounced? A former slave and preacher named Abram Mercherson didn't quite know but figured he ought to use them, writing "abought" for "about" and "wrape" for "rape" (*BM* III, 646).[16]

The hypercorrections and eccentricities of freedmen's words offer glimpses of their scattershot educations. Some soldiers wrote mostly phonetically, inadvertently creating a fascinating record of the sound of local speech (one South Carolinian signed off a letter, "No Mor to asatain your attanchins at present").[17] In other instances, writers showed some facility with English orthography, but a lexicon apparently acquired for one purpose helped express something else: a construction foreman consistently wrote "wood" for "would," an infantryman "reguard" for "regard." A group of soldiers composed a petition in 1865 amid pitched debates about voting rights—suffrage—in which they described their wives' hardships as "thir suferage." Overheard words, bits of conversations, and fragments of writing lessons reveal themselves in minutiae of trial and error. Rufus Wright probably asked the men in his unit how to spell the name of a dead comrade, and their answer opened his eyes to yet another quirk of English spelling. In a letter to his wife remembering the fallen "Sergent Stephensen," Wright decided to sign his name differently than he had before: now he was "Ruphus" (*BM* 820, 754, 725, 663).

In the new realms of literacy and freedom, one encountered strange and enigmatic customs and hesitated to question them. George Johnson, a black sailor aboard a Union ship in the Gulf of Mexico, apparently got a few writing lessons from someone who taught him about silent terminal *E*s. Johnson used them liberally: "Cane" for can, "Gite" for get, "Eate" for eat. He evidently was told that when it came to participles—the kinds of words he pronounced like *somethin* and *nothin*—he was supposed to spell them with an -ing. And so he did: "somthingin," "nothingin," "payingin," "douingin."[18] This extra syllable must have struck him as mysterious—it took a written word that resembled a spoken one and turned it into a cryptic symbol—but he heeded the rule he was given. That shouldn't lead us to think Johnson was a meek or submissive person. How many writers, after all, acquaint themselves with the phonological history of Middle English before employing the silent *gh* in "night" or "taught"? Writing in English entails a certain acceptance of the arbitrary.

Someone like George Johnson thus would have had no illusions that literacy was a tool entirely at his disposal. It no doubt was frustrating, but it could not have been surprising—and perhaps, therefore, not especially demoralizing—when he found it hard to write down what he wanted to say. His readiness to accept some arbitrary constraints, his willingness to adhere to inhospitable norms, did not diminish his capacity to assert claims of his own, as we will see.

For most soldiers recently escaped from slavery, the blank page was as new an environment as the army camps in which they now lived. It took some getting used to, and writers had many ways of exploring it. One former slave used part of a sheet of paper for penmanship practice—rows of lowercase Ys and Gs run across the bottom—and the rest of it for a letter to Abraham Lincoln. William B. Gould, an escaped slave serving in the U.S. Navy, kept a diary in a cheaply bound composition book, and in addition to logging his daily activities, he drew a picture of his ship and experimented with writing left-handed. John Boston, who fled slavery in Maryland near the beginning of the war, sent a letter to his wife, who remained behind. He had received enough tutelage in epistolary practices to know he should set off his signature from the body of the letter. But after signing his letter, he decided it was more worthwhile to make use of the blank spaces around his name. Below his signature he added, "Give my love to Father and Mother," and above the signature, below the letter proper, he barely squeezed in the words "Kiss Daniel for me."

Alongside their physical experimentation with pen and ink, they experimented with language and the stuff of their political and cultural surroundings. A petition submitted to the Freedmen's Bureau in 1865 concluded its litany of grievances by declaring: "This is not the persuit of happa ness."[19] An anonymous former slave in New Orleans composed a four-page treatise in which he juxtaposed passages copied verbatim from the U.S. Constitution with irregularly spelled declamations against the Union army's treatment of blacks. He argued for racial equality with sentimental inflection—"the black men has wives and Sweet harts Jest like the white men"—and called out hypocrisy and licentiousness as sharply as a New England abolitionist: "Some white men has Collored wives and Sweet hearts . . . it is not a City rule for Collored people to ride in the white peoples cars but the bed togeather."[20]

Such experimentation, hemmed in by rules and apprehensions, could take awhile to unfold. Like letters by relatively uneducated writers of all races, these letters tend to show heavier ink and more frequent blotting near the ends of pages than near the beginnings. But to a surprising extent, the letters black soldiers sent to military and government officials include postscripts—often very long ones, even longer than the letters themselves. Sometimes it seems these writers were pleasantly surprised to discover, after they had filled a sheet with writing and painstakingly inscribed their signature at the bottom, that the back of the page also was there for them to use. Garland H. White, who would become chaplain of the Twenty-eighth U.S. Colored Troops, wrote to Secretary of War Edwin Stanton offering to help recruit black soldiers (before the federal government had begun doing so). He filled the front of a sheet of letter paper with a decorous explanation of himself and his proposal. At the bottom he signed himself "your most humble servant, Garland H. White." When he turned the sheet over, his first thought apparently was a worry about how his letter would be received: "please excuse my bad writing as I never went to School a day in my left."

But the act of having composed the letter on the front, however imperfect, may have emboldened him as much as it made him anxious. As he let his pen run on through the blank expanse of the verso, he left the apologetic mode behind and throttled up his persuasive tactics. In a second-page plea fully as long as the first, he almost dares Stanton to let him undertake the revolutionary work of enlisting African American soldiers: "it might prove one of the greatest acts of your life. an act which might redown to your honor to the remotest generation." *Redound* was probably a word White had heard but not commonly seen in print. His approximation of it, "redown," is the only phonetically spelled word in the letter (as opposed to simple solecisms, like "accomplishs" for accomplishes or "faverorabl" for favorable)—a sign he had perhaps abandoned his scruples about such things. With a page of "bad writing" already committed to paper, why let the inability to spell a good word he once heard stand in the way of more impassioned expression? White closes his postscript, almost two hundred words after starting it and more than four hundred after commencing the letter—far removed from the deferential tone with which he began: "I shall not be happy till I hear from you on this very important subject & not then if I am denied."[21]

As the war progressed and the reach of emancipation spread, black soldiers found themselves part of an ever-larger community, in part solidified by expanding literacy and the circulation of text. Leading black newspapers, such as the *Weekly Anglo-African* and *Christian Recorder*, achieved large readerships in the ranks, and dispatches from soldiers became a mainstay of their reporting. The sailor William Gould was not only an avid newspaper reader himself; he also plainly cared about the broader community of black servicemen he imagined reading along with him. As he wrote in his diary in 1864, "I took up A subscription to assist in sending A News Paper (The Anglo Affrican) to the colard soldiers of the Army of the United States."[22]

Perhaps fired with confidence by their expanding numbers, perhaps prone to imitate the arguments to which they now were exposed, black soldiers' letters made increasingly vigorous demands for justice. Put down on paper, these demands are often suggestive of the voluble political discussions that preceded most acts of writing—like the stump orations and campfire discussions that Thomas Wentworth Higginson observed. The word *justice* itself, no doubt loud in the ears of men who wrote letters of grievance or petition to military officials, carries in its phonetically written form the sounds of men's voices: "I hav ben always ben faithfull and don My Duty as a Souldier should and concequencely I want Justice don me in return"; "I ask for them,—I ask for myself,—Jestice"; "I ought not to be in prson if I had Jested done me;" "the unjesteness that is dun to us as Black Men..." (*BM* 453; *LL* 724; *BM* 455, 647).

These men keenly grasped the logic of justice, too. A soldier whose unit had been transferred to Texas after Appomattox wrote to an unnamed official demanding aid for their families back east: "Wee onley wish the pertecttion of our wifes and as we has been all ways been so acomodated with the Law for any thing that wee do young wee now wish to be comodated for what wee have done right and if I have said any thing young I pray to be exc" (*BM* 725–27). Though sensitive to the risks of having *said anything wrong*, this writer is unafraid to make a sweeping but reasonable demand upon his government: to the same extent African Americans have been held to legal account for *anything that we do wrong*, so must they now, in the wake of Union victory, receive the full protection and benefits of their service to the nation.

In the letter that gives this essay its title, a soldier serving in North Carolina likewise made sure to remind his reader, Edwin Stanton, that African Americans deserved equal protection under the law. "We have men that bin on Duty now for Near Two months havent bin Releve from guard," he complained, "& when we Put men on guard in Town we hafto Leve them there for a Weeke at a Time & i Know that it tis not milertary to Keepe men on guard Longer 48 Hours at the Longes.... i have Read the Reagulations Enough to Know that it is Rong but i Supose that because we are colored that they think that we dont no any Better." This writer may sense that he will be judged by the quality of his writing, as his compatriots are presumed ignorant of military regulations, but he presses the point that, even if he cannot spell perfectly, he does in fact know what is allowable and what is not: "if thare is any Reagulation in this; Kind of Buisness then i will Sey that i arnt United States Soldier nor Dont Know any thing army Reagulations" (*BM* 654–55). In short, it goes both ways: if he is subject to the rules of being a "United States Soldier," then so must be his officers, and he must enjoy the protections afforded a soldier.

Some claims, less apt to be practiced in spoken language, proved harder to put into writing. Still, a writer could, as Garland White did in a postscript, work his way around to a novel formulation, very often predicated on the idea of the nation's political obligations to black soldiers. George Johnson (of the misplaced -*ing*s) began his 1863 petition to a white general with bluntness and confidence: "Genarl Butler Promest Me if i Went in the Sivest that My Fambely Should be taken Car of by the Govenment but i dou not think that it is so For My Sister has been in Jail now vere nere a Month Suffern and i Would Wish to Gite her out if there is any Possibely Chance of douingin so." General Benjamin Butler's recruiting advertisements in Union-occupied New Orleans had promised that black soldiers would receive the same wages and benefits as white soldiers, including support for wives and children. Newly enlisted black men probably talked with one another a great deal about whether military service was living up to promises. Johnson's interpretation of Butler's promise to include his sister's freedom from wrongful imprisonment may be a bit of a stretch (and he was in the navy, not the army), but he clearly grasped that the postslavery era had a new political logic. White people had contractual obligations to black people, not only the other way around.

When Johnson tried to explain his sister's predicament in greater detail, he left behind the logic of contracts, the stuff of commiseration with fellow recruits. Trying to give voice to something more private, probably unrehearsed, his writing falters: "so i Will ask of you intesede of Giten her out if you so pleas For i think that she has been in there Most Longe or nouff Suffern She has not Got very Good health For hes has not been Longe Sence been out of her Clild bad way taken and put in Jail." He signs off: "her Brother George W. F. Johnson border of the U.S Ship Pampero Gulf Squrd off Pilot town." Then—something about this declaration of his identity and his official position perhaps having restored his verbal buoyancy—he rallies. A postscript at last makes clear the meaning of the sentence that faltered: "also you Will Pleas to answer this Letter and if I Can Gite her out you Will beso Kinde as Give Me a permit to Go in and See her For I Lern that the ponish them slily in Jail and i Woulden For to be ille treted What Sowever because She has Misscarred a Childe." Having pushed to the other side of his signature, Johnson did find the words for what he wanted to say, or realized that he wanted to say it. Not only as a matter of keeping promises, but also out of compassion for his sister's recent suffering, should the government be concerned with her plight.

Johnson's plea did not ring in the halls of power, in part because his signature got lost along the way. Instead of being set off at the bottom of the page, it runs together with the text of the letter and postscript. The clerk at military headquarters who received this letter didn't spot a signature of the ordinary sort and apparently did not read closely enough to locate the one there was. He labeled the letter "No Name" and filed it away. Johnson's civic identity not having been fully credited, his letter sits today, bundled by faded ribbon with several dozen other "miscellaneous letters," in an uncatalogued box at the National Archives in Washington.

His letter may have been ignored, but nine months later, he sent another letter up the chain of command and made another audacious assertion. Requesting a transfer from the navy into the army, he wrote: "[I] think that i am Capabel of Commading a Squard i Would haft to be in stuckted alittle. after that i Would beabel to Lede a Company i Would wish to try it any Way." It may have been Johnson's tenacious acts of writing that convinced him of just how much he could accomplish if only "in stuckted alittle."[23]

What black soldiers' letters show is what Colonel Higginson could not see: the private cogitations that followed from the expressions of intellect and culture he could overhear. From those campfires, men retired to their tents turning over phrases in their heads, applying ideas to their own experience, preparing to craft representations of their world and their minds, building the resolve to send those representations before the eyes of powerful men. Imagining those nighttime denouements to evening conversations, seeing in soldiers' letters a thousand ricocheting fragments of the explosion of wartime emancipation, we can see a part of the Civil War otherwise barely recoverable from history: the inspiring, frightening, vertiginous experience of being newly free and extremely vulnerable.

We also can see from a different angle the roots of postbellum culture. For Kenneth Warren, Jim Crow–era African American literature "had been produced within constraints."[24] Arguably, that literature was initiated by the men who became writers in a military world that both promised freedom and teemed with constraints. Navigating that world, they scouted the terrain African American literature would yet explore. Like Paul Laurence Dunbar writing verse for William Dean Howells's America, these writers' words were encircled by expectations (though, for them, moving between standard English and something like dialect was no aesthetic choice, however circumscribed). Trying to figure out how they should sound, southern black soldiers developed a canny awareness that white American nationalism was constituted by words—that seizing the language of freedom, justice, and civil rights must precede the seizing of those things themselves.

The anonymous soldier with whom I began wrote to Edwin Stanton: "We came out in 1[8]63 as Valent hearted men for the Sacke of our Surffring Courntury & Since that Time things has chings a Round."[25] In his formulation, a type of reform-minded sentimentalism—"valiant-hearted men," "for the sake of our suffering country"—pivots toward a form of postwar disillusionment: "things has changed around." Nonetheless, valiant hearts and concern for suffering were not suddenly bygone values; the war did not so abruptly terminate what we associate with antebellum culture.[26] Rather, what had changed is that black soldiers like this one, in their efforts to participate in what they perceived to be white American culture, had often found themselves frustrated. The nation to which they were rhetorically adhering was not entirely willing to admit them. Yet these remained the premises of protest. In addition to the event of the war, it was the conjunction of literacy with incorporation into the national army—it was these letters and their experiments—that nurtured a tradition of black expression steeped in nationalist culture. The imperative to appeal, in this anonymous writer's words, "to some one of a thourety" remained in force "five score years" later, during the Civil War centennial, when Martin Luther King would commence his most famous speech, adapting the words of a white leader "in whose symbolic shadow we stand."[27]

NOTES

1. Thomas Wentworth Higginson, *Army Life in a Black Regiment and Other Writings* (1870; repr., New York: Penguin, 1997), 18–19.

2. Kenneth W. Warren, *What Was African American Literature?* (Cambridge: Harvard University Press, 2011), 1.

3. David M. Henkin, *The Postal Age: The Emergence of Modern Communications in Nineteenth-Century America* (Chicago: University of Chicago Press, 2006), 137.

4. Chandra Manning draws on extensive research in letters by rank-and-file soldiers in *What This Cruel War Was Over: Soldiers, Slavery, and the Civil War* (New York: Alfred A. Knopf, 2007). On soldiers' reading and the proliferation of dime novels, see Alice Fahs, *The Imagined Civil War: Popular Literature of the North and South, 1861–1865* (Chapel Hill: University of North Carolina Press, 2001).

5. For an overview of black soldiers' letter writing, see Keith P. Wilson, *Campfires of Freedom: The Camp Life of Black Soldiers during the Civil War* (Kent: Kent State University Press, 2002), 71–72. On former slaves' efforts to locate family members, see Heather Andrea Williams, *Help Me to Find My People: The African American Search for Family Lost in Slavery* (Chapel Hill: University of North Carolina Press, 2012).

6. *Douglass' Monthly* 5, no. 10 (1863), 852 (from speech delivered July 6, 1863).

7. Unsigned letter to Edwin M. Stanton, October 2, 1865, A-396 1865, Letters Received, ser. 360, Colored Troops Division, Record Group 94, National Archives, in Ira Berlin, Joseph P. Reidy, and Leslie S. Rowland, eds., *The Black Military Experience*, ser. 2, vol. 1 of *Freedom: A Documentary History of Emancipation, 1861–1867* (Cambridge: Cambridge University Press, 1982), 654, hereafter documented parenthetically as *BM*. In this essay, I have chosen to discuss primarily letters that appear in the *Freedom* series so that interested readers may easily consult them. Letters I have examined in the archives are cited both by their location at the National Archives in Washington and their publication in *Freedom*, if applicable; others are cited only as published.

8. Black women could participate meaningfully, if indirectly, in epistolary negotiations with white authorities. For an example, see my discussion of a letter by Martha Glover in chapter 5 of *Word by Word: Emancipation and the Act of Writing* (Cambridge: Harvard University Press, 2013). The archive to which I refer consists of holograph letters written by formerly enslaved men enlisted in the Union Army and directed to superior officers and government officials. Because they were so directed, a significant number of such letters has been preserved—far more than any other type of writing by African American southerners during the Civil War. Wilson numbers "protest letters about the behavior of

[white] line officers" in the thousands (*Campfires of Freedom*, 72). Many such letters are available in the multivolume series *Freedom: A Documentary History of Emancipation*.

9. Yael A. Sternhell, "Revisionism Reinvented?: The Antiwar Turn in Civil War Scholarship," *Journal of the Civil War Era* 3, no. 2 (2013): 252.

10. *Harper's Weekly*, July 4, 1863, 429. Douglass, *Narrative of the Life of Frederick Douglass, An American Slave*, ed. David W. Blight (Boston: Bedford, 2003), 84.

11. Most of these issues are discussed in all the major works on African American soldiers in the Civil War, which include Berlin et al., *The Black Military*; Dudley Taylor Cornish, *The Sable Arm: Black Troops in the Union Army, 1861–1865* (1956; repr., Lawrence: University Press of Kansas, 1987); Joseph T. Glatthaar, *Forged in Battle: The Civil War Alliance of Black Soldiers and White Officers* (New York: Free Press, 1990); John David Smith, ed., *Black Soldiers in Blue: African American Troops in the Civil War Era* (Chapel Hill: University of North Carolina Press, 2002); and Wilson, *Campfires of Freedom*. On issues of health and medical treatment, see in particular Margaret Humphreys, *Intensely Human: The Health of the Black Soldier in the American Civil War* (Baltimore: Johns Hopkins University Press, 2008), as well as Jim Downs, *Sick from Freedom: African-American Illness and Suffering during the Civil War and Reconstruction* (New York: Oxford University Press, 2012). For a distinctive angle on black soldiers' concern for their families' welfare, see Andrew L. Slap, "The Loyal Deserters: African American Soldiers and Community in Civil War Memphis," in *Weirding the War: Stories from the Civil War's Ragged Edges*, ed. Stephen Berry (Athens: University of Georgia Press, 2011), 234–48.

12. Carole Emberton, "'Only Murder Makes Men': Reconsidering the Black Military Experience," *Journal of the Civil War Era* 2, no. 3 (2012): 372.

13. Dudley Taylor Cornish, "The Union Army as a School for Negroes," *Journal of Negro History* 37, no. 4 (1952): 368–82; John W. Blassingame, "The Union Army as an Educational Institution for Negroes, 1862–1865," *Journal of Negro Education* 34, no. 2 (1965): 152–59.

14. Susie King Taylor, *Reminiscences of My Life in Camp: An African American Woman's Civil War Memoir*, ed. Catherine Clinton (1902; repr. Athens: University of Georgia Press, 2006).

15. Zack Burden to Mr Abebrem Lenken, February 2, 1865, B-110 1865, Letters Received, ser. 360, Colored Troops Division, Record Group 94, National Archives, Washington, D.C., in *BM* 647–48.

16. Ira Berlin, Thavolia Glymph, Steven F. Miller, Joseph P. Reidy, Leslie S. Rowland, and Julie Saville, eds., *The Wartime Genesis of Free Labor: The Lower South*, ser. 1, vol. 3 of *Freedom: A Documentary History of Emancipation, 1861–1867* (Cambridge: Cambridge University Press, 1990), 314.

17. Steven Hahn, Steven F. Miller, Susan E. O'Donovan, John C. Rodrigue, and Leslie S. Rowland, eds. *Land and Labor, 1865*, ser. 3, vol. 1 of *Freedom: A Documentary History of Emancipation, 1861–1867* (Chapel Hill: University of North Carolina Press, 2008), 970, hereafter documented parenthetically as *LL*.

18. George Johnson to Genarl Franch, 7 January 1863, Miscellaneous Records, ser. 1796,

Department of the Gulf, Record Group 393 Part I, National Archives, Washington, D.C., in Berlin et al., *The Wartime Genesis*, 407–8.

19. Prince Murrell to Gen. Swain, 17 December 1865, Alabama Assistant Commissioner, Freedmen's Bureau, ser. 9, Record Group 105, National Archives, Washington, D.C.

20. Statement of a Colored Man, enclosed in Lt. Col. Jas. A. Hopkins to Brig. Gen. James Bowen, 2 September 1863, H-99 1863, Letters Received, ser. 1920, Civil Affairs, Department of the Gulf, Record Group 393 Part I, National Archives, Washington, D.C., in *BM* 153–57.

21. Garland H. White to E. M. Stanton, 7 May 1862, W-561 1862, Letters Received, ser. 23, Record Group 107; M221, Letters Received by the Secretary of War, Roll 208. National Archives, Washington, D.C., in *BM* 82–83.

22. William B. Gould IV, ed., *Diary of a Contraband: The Civil War Passage of a Black Sailor* (Stanford: Stanford University Press, 2002), 179. The term "imagined community," of course, and the idea that newspapers create such communities, both derive from Benedict Anderson, *Imagined Communities: Reflections on the Origin and Spread of Nationalism*, rev. ed. (New York: Verso, 1991).

23. George Willford Johnson to Genarl, 9 September 1813 [1863], J-41 1863, Letters Received, ser. 360, Colored Troops Division, Record Group 94, National Archives, Washington, D.C.

24. Warren, *What Was African*, 42.

25. Unsigned letter to Edwin M. Stanton, 2 October 1865, in *BM* 654.

26. On continuities between antebellum and postbellum U.S. culture, see Christopher Hager and Cody Marrs, "Against 1865: Reperiodizing the Nineteenth Century," *J19: The Journal of Nineteenth-Century Americanists* 1, no. 2 (2013): 259–84.

27. Martin Luther King Jr., "I Have a Dream. . .": Speech by the Rev. Martin Luther King at the "March on Washington," National Archives, http://www.archives.gov/press/exhibits/dream-speech.pdf.

The Color of Quaintness
Thomas Wentworth Higginson, Black Song, and American Union

JEREMY WELLS

"Quaint" is a curious word. In fact among the definitions the *Oxford English Dictionary* provides for "quaint" is "curious, unusual ... strange," a sense of the word that, were it its only meaning, would make rather redundant Edgar Allan Poe's use of it in the first stanza of "The Raven": "while I pondered, weak and weary, / Over many a quaint and curious volume of forgotten lore." Poe perhaps had in mind a sense of the word closer to what it meant in the original Anglo-Norman: "quaint" as "cunning, ingenious ... elegant" or "carefully or ingeniously elaborated," meanings now obsolete but still very much in circulation during the mid-nineteenth century. It is unlikely, however, that what Poe meant by "quaint" was what we mean by it, namely "attractively or agreeably unusual in character or appearance; *esp.* pleasingly old-fashioned. Now the usual sense." This "quaint"—a "quaint" we might attach to a courtship ritual or canopy bed, a saying still spoken by your grandmother or how one might describe the scene of a Thomas Kinkcade painting—began to emerge during the late eighteenth and early nineteenth centuries, no doubt as a result of the fact that, with industrialization and other forms of technological development, something could become "unusual," perhaps "attractively" so, simply by remaining (or by trying to seem) not new, not modern.

What Thomas Wentworth Higginson meant by "quaint" is the subject of the present essay. More precisely, I explore here what he means when he uses the word to describe black song throughout *Army Life in a Black Regiment*, Higginson's 1869 narrative detailing his experiences as colonel of the first regiment of former slaves formed during the Civil War. I wonder what he means when he uses the term, and I wonder why he uses it so often. The word appears eleven times in *Army Life*, five in the chapter most relevant to my discussion, "Negro Spirituals."[1] Of the other six instances, three occur in discussions of black singing. Only three do not: one involves the "quaint complaints" Higginson receives from a soldier eager to cease training and begin combat, another the "quaint challenge" he is issued at one point by a soldier on guard duty, and a third the "quaint ... handwriting" he perceives in the letters sent to him by former soldiers after the war.[2] The other instances of "quaint"—eight of the eleven—all pertain to black song.

I began this essay by discussing the range of potential meanings of "quaint" because I think Higginson's late 1860s observations about spirituals and other forms of African American vernacular song reflect more than one. There is in them surely the sense of quaintness as signifying strangeness and curiosity, quaint as unfamiliar. There may also be that older sense of quaintness as indicating ingenuity, a meaning dying out but not yet quite dead by the time Higginson was writing. More interesting, there may be in Higginson's descriptions of black song as "quaint" something of the newer meaning that had emerged by the 1860s: quaint as old-fashioned, as oddly familiar, perhaps as uncanny. This matters, first, because of the place *Army Life in a Black Regiment* occupies in an American ethnomusicological record. W. E. B. Du Bois alludes to it in the "Sorrow Songs" chapter of *The Souls of Black Folk* (1903) when he cites Higginson as among the first figures to try to preserve the music of the black South, "the singular spiritual heritage of the nation and the greatest gift of the Negro people."[3] More recent commentators also point to nationalism in order to explain Higginson's and his readers' sudden and surprisingly deep fascination with spirituals during the war years. "They represent a psychological stronghold against ... national disintegration" to which "white Americans were attracted ... during a time of national crisis," according to literary scholar John M. Picker; or they afforded "white Americans ... the means by which to construct a racially transcendent, national selfhood" because, once they had been written down, they separated black bodies from "the sounds themselves," "a primordial natural voice," according to musicologist Ronald Radano.[4] Such readings call attention to Higginson's Transcendentalism and see his encounter with spirituals as affirming, in one way or another, his understanding of "negroes" and what they might mean to a reconstructed "America." Yet I will argue here that *Army Life in a Black Regiment* is considerably less settled on this point, that indeed the prose in which it tries to record black song tends in a different direction than the prose in which it seeks to represent black soldiery.

A second reason a fixation on "quaint" proves illustrative, then, is that Higginson published *Army Life in a Black Regiment* in order to change how Americans used words to engage matters of race and nationality. Sermonist, essayist, editor, and poet, Higginson was a man of letters in a notably full sense of the term. A man of action, too—he had fought in "Bleeding Kansas" and conspired with John Brown, among his other prewar abolitionist activities—he had assumed command of the First South Carolina volunteers with pencil and notebook in hand, assured that, if he survived, he would have a fateful story to relate. As Don Dingledine has observed, *Army Life* "dramatizes the power of words, the importance of what stories we tell and how we tell them."[5] A narrative that quite literally from its first sentence to its last invites its reader to reimagine "the soldier" as something other than "white," it positions its subjects—"eight hundred men suddenly transformed from slaves into soldiers"—as avatars of a newly egalitarian nationhood (4). It becomes confused, however, when those same soldiers start singing. It does not know whether what it then tries to record in words is strangely "African" or perhaps uncannily "American." It cannot say, in short, whether the sounds produced by the mouths and especially the bodies of former slaves lost in song represent a form of culture belonging essentially to *them* or one perhaps also somehow indicative of *us*. Positioning it instead as "quaint," Higginson's narrative suggests that black folk culture may have posed an even more interesting challenge to a U.S. national imaginary during the pivotal 1860s than black bodily assertiveness and sacrifice.

"These pages record some of the adventures of the First South Carolina Volunteers,—the first slave regiment mustered into the service of the United States during the late civil war" (1). So begins Higginson's memoir, with a sentence in which the former colonel absents himself, places the emphasis instead on his soldiers, and imparts a sense of agency to the text rather than its author by giving it the action of the opening verb: "These pages record . . ." An act of rhetorical self-sacrifice—the word "I" does not appear in either of *Army Life*'s first two paragraphs—Higginson's initial verbal gesture extends in a way what he had been doing (or at least risking) since he had become a radical abolitionist years earlier, one willing to court danger and risk death for the cause. The sentence is noteworthy also in that it makes no direct mention of race—no reference to soldiers as "black," "negro," "dusky," "Ethiopian," or any of the other adjectives that appear later to demarcate racial difference. It does call attention to the soldiers' former condition of servitude and, in so doing, distinguishes the First South Carolina from the regiments of free black soldiers formed soon afterward, most famously the Fifty-Fourth Massachusetts. Yet the language of Higginson's opening sentence may be described as otherwise egalitarian, for what "army life" had provided him—what it had furnished in terms of both experiences and terminology, signifieds and signifiers—were ways of eliding racial difference, ways at times even of denying it. "Mustered into the service of the United States during the late civil war," after all, described equally well the recent careers of more than two and a half million men, the vast majority of them white.

From its very first words, then, *Army Life* asks its reader to see similitude as much as difference and to recognize service to the nation as a transcendent activity. It devotes plenty of words to delineating between "black" and "white" in the pages that follow. Having subordinated race to nationality so early on, however, it can do so while still insisting, as it later makes explicit, that the soldiers of the First South Carolina "were very much like other men" (255). The book's final paragraph makes something of a performance of these linguistic tendencies:

> We who served with the black troops have this peculiar satisfaction, that, whatever dignity or sacredness the memories of the war may have to others, they have more to us.... [T]he peculiar privilege of associating with an outcast race, of training it to defend its rights and to perform its duties, this was our especial meed. The vacillating policy of the Government sometimes filled other officers with doubt and shame; until the negro had justice, they were but defending liberty with one hand and crushing it with the other. From this inconsistency we were free.... If this was not recognized on our side of the lines, we knew that it was admitted on the other. Fighting with ropes round our necks, denied the ordinary courtesies of war till we ourselves compelled their concession, we could at least turn this outlawry into a compliment. We had touched the pivot of the war.... Till the blacks were armed, there was no guaranty of their freedom. It was their demeanor under arms that shamed the nation into recognizing them as men. (266–67)

John Mead has identified *Army Life* as a "documen[t] in which the barrier between black and white Americans was, if not erased, tested and blurred," while Christopher Looby has noted Higginson's tendency to represent himself "as having felt ... a disoriented feeling of identification with his black soldiers, a physical oneness with them, a feeling of alienation from his own given identity."[6] A similar merging can be seen here. In a passage that draws numerous distinctions—between black and white, those who trained black soldiers and those who did not, a "vacillating ... Government" and principled subcitizenry, and "our side of the lines" and "the other"—there is nevertheless a sense of unification, an implication that what the Civil War had created above all else were the circumstances in which black and white males could fight together as "men." Just as in *Army Life*'s first sentence, there is an emphasis from the outset on the idea of service as a shared enterprise. There is a parallel also between the "freedom" for which black soldiers are fighting and the rectitude of the First South Carolina's officer corps: "From this inconsistency we were free." The "we" that is distinct from "the black troops" at the beginning of the passage, once it has traversed a rhetorical field marked by patriotism, shared memories, and common enemies North and South, seems larger by its end; it is hard not to read the concluding "we" who "had touched the pivot of the war" as biracial. This link is made strongest by the image of the noose, especially since, only a few pages earlier, Higginson had addressed "why this particular war was an especially favorable test of the colored soldiers. They had more to fight for than the whites.... They fought with ropes round their necks" (251). By *Army Life*'s final paragraph, the "ropes" encircle "*our* necks," and an image of soldierly union replaces those that, earlier in the text, had emphasized differences of race, region, and rank.

Higginson's method in *Army Life* may thus be described, appropriately enough, as regimented. In terms of demonstrating black soldiers' battlefield capabilities, the text knows where it is going from its outset, and it gets there. In terms of its own implications, it makes clear that soldiers' conduct in combat signifies their readiness for citizenship, that "army life" refers metonymically to life itself. Their "manly" comportment during the war stands "both for the credit and for the discipline of the regiment,—as well as for the men's subsequent lives" (86). Higginson hardly could have been more deliberate, then, in terms of how he imbued his memoir with meaning. He was not like Russell Conwell, a fellow Union officer who revisited the South during 1869, the year *Army Life* was published, only to find himself ambivalent about the war and surprisingly sympathetic toward his former foes. For Conwell, writing was a means of making sense of contradiction: "God bless the man who invented diaries! They are the only preventatives now in use to keep wandering correspondents from insanity ... so strangely and inconsistently are the evils and virtues, pleasures and pains of life jumbled together in the experience of a Northern man who visits and observes the people of the South."[7] For Higginson, by contrast, the meaning of the war had remained the same from beginning to end to the postwar. The purpose of a "diary" was to make a point, to realize a plan. It was to render into narrative something like what Frederick Douglass had said to an audience of potential black recruits in Philadelphia in July 1863, not quite six months after the First South Carolina had seen its first combat: "Once let the black man get upon his person the brass letters US, let him get an eagle on his button, and a musket on his shoulder, and bullets in his pocket, and there is no power on earth or under the earth which can deny that he has earned the right of citizenship in the United States."[8] Higginson had seen his men "suddenly transformed from slaves into soldiers." From soldiers into citizens was to be the next step, and like Douglass's speech, Higginson's memoir models a rhetorical economy and efficiency meant to make so radical a change seem tenable. Both could write purposefully, for these were changes to a national imaginary each had been contemplating for more than a decade by the time emancipation and the enlistment of black troops made them appear at long last immanent.

Given how preplanned *Army Life in a Black Regiment* therefore seems, it is noteworthy that the first unscripted moment it allows itself to relate involves African Americans breaking into song. On New Year's Day 1863, just over one month into the soldiers' training, Camp Saxton hosted a ceremony honoring the issuance that day of the Emancipation Proclamation. A "multitude of people" attended, including a brigadier general, officers from other regiments, white "ladies on horseback and in carriages," and a number of now-former slaves, women as well as men, from the nearby plantations of coastal South Carolina. In a long section detailing the "festival," Higginson recounts how a prayer was spoken, the colors presented, and "the President's Proclamation" read by a sequence of white guests. "All this was according to the programme." But then took place an event "so simple, so touching, so utterly unexpected and startling, that . . . it gave the key-note to whole day." Once the proclamation had been read, three African Americans—one old man and two women whose ages he does not identify—began singing "My Country 'Tis of Thee." "Firmly and irrepressibly the quavering voices sang on, verse after verse; others of the colored people joined in." Their thorough knowledge of the song impressed Higginson, their sense of occasion, even more. So taken was he by the improvised performance that, when white members of the congregation tried to join in the singing, Higginson "motioned them to silence," apparently believing that the moment belonged to the newly free women and men (40–41). Appropriating "white" song and U.S. nationality after years of repression and alienation, they were performing a sense of belonging to a national "we," and Higginson, displaying something of an improvisational genius of his own, recognized that they did not require the sort of validation that might be implied by white accompaniment.

Yet here is the language Higginson later found to interpret the event:

> I never saw anything so electric; it made all other words cheap; it seemed the choked voice of a race at last unloosed. . . . If you could have heard how quaint and innocent it was! Old Tiff and his children might have sung it; and close before me was a little slave-boy, almost white, who seemed to belong to the party, and even he must join in. Just think of it!—the first day they had ever had a country, the first flag they had ever seen which promised anything to their people, and here, while mere spectators stood in silence . . . these simple souls burst out in their lay, as if they were by their own hearths at home! (41)

While it may be true, as Robert James Branham has argued, that this "act of singing ... marked" the performers' "first symbolic step toward citizenship," the temporality of Higginson's interpretation of the event is complicated and ambiguous.[9] He seems carried away, and in more than one sense of the phrase. On the one hand, he thinks of the future—of a changing "country" that must now accommodate "their people," even of historians who may one day deem the day's proceedings unbelievable. Yet on the other, he is carried away from Camp Saxton, site of what he terms elsewhere in *Army Life* "a vast experiment," and into the imagined, much more familiar "home[s]"—the Uncle Tom's cabins, almost—of the former slaves in attendance (4). Indeed, he is carried into an actual Harriet Beecher Stowe novel, *Dred* (1856), and reminded of scenes in which a slave named Old Tiff sings to console the white children to whom he is devoted. Higginson is transported, in short, into a curious recent past in which slavery still exists and lends itself moreover to sentimental representation. This may explain why he refers to the "almost white" youngster standing near him as "a little slave-boy"; Higginson forgets momentarily why such *former* slaves as the boy have gathered at Camp Saxton, let alone why they are singing what they are singing.

The entire episode he sums up meanwhile as "quaint and innocent." The words jump out, since the passage seeks initially to celebrate African Americans as, at the very least, great interpreters of U.S. culture. They end up "innocent[s]," however, as if the irony of the scene is evident only to such "mere spectators" as Higginson. And their performance ends up seeming "quaint." The ambiguity of the word captures just how impressed Higginson seems to have been by the impromptu and yet how disoriented he was by the singers' incursion into the day's highly ritualized, regularized "programme." In fact, Higginson was scheduled to speak next when the three singers broke into "My Country 'Tis of Thee." He recovered as best he could: with the audience "waiting for my stupid words ... I went on." Yet while this confession of humility creates a sense of equipoise, the colonel descending into "stupid" prose after the ex-slaves had lifted their voices into soaring, "electric" song, Higginson ends up affirming difference. He may feel stupefied, but they seem "simple." Summing up what the event had meant, he makes this sense of difference seem even greater: "the life of the whole day was in those unknown people's song" (41). The three who began the singing may have been unknown to Higginson in a strict sense of the word, for they were not his soldiers. Yet there is the implication also that they and those they represent are unknowable, their souls remaining shrouded in mystery. Even as they are claiming "my country" as their own, they seem to Higginson to occupy a terra incognita he cannot imagine penetrating.

Higginson's characterization of the New Year's Day "key-note" as "quaint" links it with his accounts of black musical performance throughout *Army Life*, including a description late in the text of "their prayer-meetings," which were marked by "a mingling, often quaint enough, of the warlike and the pious" (255). Quaintness links the Jubilee celebration more directly to the "Negro Spirituals" chapter, in which Higginson reproduces the words of thirty-six of the religious songs he overheard during his time commanding the First South Carolina. With most of these he endeavors, to the best of his linguistic abilities, to give a sense of what they sounded like. Neither a trained musician nor a would-be musicologist, Higginson instead called upon what he knew best, language and literature, in order to "record" the songs, to offer "the fantasy of sound in print," as Michael Cohen has explained the synesthetic experience "Negro Spirituals" tries to achieve. "Higginson's dialect transcriptions ... stood at the limit to which the eye could be confused into creating 'the peculiarity of sounds.'"[10] Yet since dialect alone could not reproduce the sounds of the new music he was hearing, Higginson used adjectives: more than sixty appear in the chapter, and they range from "simple" and "monotonous" to "graceful" and "operatic," from "mystical" and "Oriental" to "touching" and "sweet." Most adjectives appear only once in the chapter. A few are used twice. "Strange" appears four times. Only two words, "quaint" and "plaintive," appear five, and of the two, "plaintive" seems comparatively unremarkable, denoting as it does grief and lamentation, and in any event describing the quality of a song itself.

"Quaint," by contrast, expresses a relationship. Like "strange," it implies the writer's subjectivity: what seems "quaint" or "strange" to one might seem ordinary and unremarkable to someone else, especially to someone excluded from the writer's principal frames of reference. Much more so than "strange," however, "quaint" had come by the mid-1860s to suggest also a relationship to modernity. If "quaint" now can be applied to something made to seem past-like—quaintness as simulacrum—"quaint" then denoted something more like the surprising persistence of the past into the present, something that may have genuinely troubled the distance between the two.[11] It is therefore noteworthy that Higginson keeps coming back to it in "Negro Spirituals," sometimes in brief, relatively off-handed comments ("Here is an infinitely quaint description of the length of the heavenly road" or "the chorus alone was identical; the words ... given are quaint enough"), yet sometimes in more substantial passages, like the one that begins the chapter:

> The war brought to some of us ... many a strange fulfilment of dreams of other days. For instance, the present writer had been a faithful student of the Scottish ballads, and had always envied Sir Walter the delight of tracing them out amid their own heather, and of writing them down piecemeal from the lips of aged

crones. It was a strange enjoyment, therefore, to be suddenly brought into the midst of a kindred world of unwritten songs, as simple and indigenous as the Border Minstrelsy, more uniformly plaintive, almost always more quaint, and often as essentially poetic. (207, 212, 197)

Higginson's likening his musical discoveries to Scott's *Minstrelsy of the Scottish Border* (1802–1803) has drawn frequent notice from critics. Picker focuses on Higginson's use of the word "unwritten": "For Higginson, writing a work *down* appears to be the most crucial part of the musical composition process" (237). Jon Cruz understands this impulse as evidence of Higginson's "romantic naturalism," a preservationist tendency "less concerned with actual black lives than with a more inchoate feel for finding authenticity on the edges of modernity."[12] Radano finds similarly that the inscription of spirituals "erase[d] blackness in the name of its preservation," though he concedes that Higginson's comparing them to Scottish ballads "subtly challenged the absolutes of black and white" (523–24, 514). Such mixed appraisals are not surprising, given the ambivalences that pervade the passage. Imagining similitude and familiarity, Higginson also emphasizes oddity and excess: the spirituals are "*more* . . . plaintive," "*more* quaint." They embody something "essentially poetic," seem "indigenous," and evoke a "kindred world," a space he thinks he knows how to navigate. Yet the "fulfilment" and "enjoyment" he experiences are both labeled "strange," two of the four instances of the word in the "Negro Spirituals" chapter coming in its first three sentences.

This simultaneous sense of novelty and return, of venturing toward outlandishness while experiencing the homely, might be better described as "uncanny," and Higginson does use the word once in *Army Life*. It occurs in a scene suffused with tactile rather than audible imagery, however, for Higginson has taken a swim at night and felt something brush against his skin: "It appeared impossible that anything uncanny should hide beneath that lovely mirror; and yet when some floating wisp of reeds suddenly coiled itself around my neck, or some unknown thing, drifting deeper, coldly touched my foot, it caused that undefinable shudder which every swimmer knows, and which especially comes over one by night" (157). Looby has noted the frequency with which "scenes of watery suspension" occur in the text, and he explains them in terms of Higginson's desire to identify with his black soldiers, even to immerse his denuded body in a blackness both literal and metaphorical (129). Something similar—or to be more exact, something similarly simultaneously pleasure-filled and frightening—takes place when Higginson first encounters black song and dance. The extended description comes early in the "Camp Diary" chapter, Higginson having been in camp just over one week when he writes it. It begins, uncannily enough, with a mention of water:

> What a life is this I lead! It is a dark, mild, drizzling evening, and as the foggy air breeds sand-flies, so it calls out melodies and strange antics from this mysterious race of grown-up children with whom my lot is cast. All over the camp the lights glimmer in the tents, and as I sit at my desk in the open doorway, there come mingled sounds of stir and glee. Boys laugh and shout,—a feeble flute stirs somewhere in some tent, not an officer's,—a drum throbs far away in another,—wild kildeer-plover flit and wail above us, like the haunting souls of dead slave-masters,—and from a neighboring cook-fire comes the monotonous sound of that strange festival, half pow-wow, half prayer-meeting, which they know only as a "shout." These fires are usually enclosed in a little booth, made neatly of palm-leaves and covered in at top, a regular native African hut, in short, such as is pictured in books, and such as I once got up from dried palm-leaves for a fair at home. This hut is now crammed with men, singing at the top of their voices, in one of their quaint, monotonous, endless, negro-Methodist chants, with obscure syllables recurring constantly, and slight variations interwoven, all accompanied with a regular drumming of the feet and clapping of the hands, like castanets. Then the excitement spreads: inside and outside the enclosure men begin to quiver and dance, others join, a circle forms, winding monotonously round some one in the centre; some 'heel and toe' tumultuously, others merely tremble and stagger on, others stoop and rise, others whirl, others caper sideways, all keep steadily circling like dervishes; spectators applaud special strokes of skill; my approach only enlivens the scene; the circle enlarges, louder grows the singing, rousing shouts of encouragement come in, half bacchanalian, half devout, "Wake 'em, brudder!" "Stan' up to 'em, brudder!"—and still the ceaseless drumming and clapping, in perfect cadence, goes steadily on. Suddenly there comes a sort of snap, and the spell breaks, amid general sighing and laughter. And this not rarely and occasionally, but night after night, while in other parts of the camp the soberest prayers and exhortations are proceeding sedately. (16–18)

The longest paragraph in the early entries of the "Camp Diary" and one containing some of the longest single sentences in all of *Army Life*, Higginson's initial presentation of black music offers much to consider. One might begin by noting that, in this single passage, a "shout" is described as both "half pow-wow, half prayer-meeting" and "half bacchanalian, half devout." Were one to want to quantify the racial uncanny, one might add together Higginson's fractions and discover in a "shout" a ritual performance that seemed 100 percent strange and 100 percent familiar. The physical structure that houses it propels Higginson's imagination toward "Africa" yet also, in the same sentence, toward something he had once built "for a fair at home." The sense of geography expands in other directions, too: toward Spain, perhaps, given the "castanets" he hears when his soldiers beat rhythms with their bodies; toward Turkey, when he likens their dancing to the whirling of dervishes; toward ancient Rome, when he perceives a "bacchanalia"; toward a Native American settlement, when he senses a "pow-wow"; and toward some mysterious realm haunted by the "souls of dead slave-masters," some spectral South that almost anticipates the writings of William Faulkner.

There is "skill" alongside "stagger[ing]," "excitement" in the presence of "monoton[y]," and "perfect cadence" adjacent to "tumul[t]." Surrounding all of this is a sense of sobriety and sedation, and the calm to which the passage returns at its end parallels the composure of its beginning, when Higginson was still safely ensconced at his desk in his tent. What comes between, however, is some of the most vortical prose written by a nineteenth-century U.S. writer: sentences that grow longer and longer; parallel clauses that nevertheless grow shorter and shorter within them; a sudden switch to the historical present; a dizzying sequence of images, perhaps meant to simulate the whizzing-by of the world as it would have been experienced by the twirling men within the revolving circle of dancers; and a centrifugal energy that pulls in Higginson ("my approach only enlivens the scene") as well as his reader. There may be no body of water, but that sense of "immersion" in blackness that Looby describes—"a trancelike release from the social inscriptions that are all too coercively present in the stringently hierarchized and regulated military context"—is perhaps nowhere more evident in the text than here, in the veritable whirlpool of men that becomes a vortex of words, introduces the subject of black music into *Army Life*, and represents perhaps the most undisciplined prose the staid Higginson ever allowed himself to publish (129).

The regimentation of *Army Life* has been restored by the end of the passage, to be sure. The "spell" broken, the narrative returns in its next paragraph to a much more distanced, observational prose ("A simple and lovable people, whose graces seem to come by nature, and whose vices by training"). It returns also to the past tense ("Dr. Zachos told me last night ... 'they had absolutely no vices'") (18). For a considerable while prior to this, however, it had courted, via its descriptions of black musical performance, connection and confusion. It had touched something unfamiliar, something certainly compelling, something perhaps even dangerous—not unlike the "uncanny" that Higginson says might "hide beneath [the] lovely mirror" of a surface of water, threatening to "coi[l] itself around my neck." The circular image of a shared noose that comes close to concluding *Army Life* thus appears, albeit in strange ways, in passages from much earlier in the text. A sense that he and his soldiers would have proudly hanged together if they had been captured by Confederate troops—an image of political union that transcends race—provides Higginson an ending to his memoir consistent with long-held views. The widening gyre of cultural attachment that begins to form earlier sends it spiraling off in unforeseen, unpredictable directions, however. The writing that results expresses initially an even stronger sense of union than the ties of politics, yet it also leads Higginson to recoil from a vision of himself thus textualized. He withdraws from the circle of associations that had begun to encompass him and seeks out instead a prose that reestablishes detachment, discipline, and linearity.

Higginson returns to the scene of a "shout" at the outset of the "Negro Spirituals," which he completed several years after his earliest encounters with black musical performance. The later prose does not exude the same energy of the moment captured in "Camp Diary," for while some images and descriptive phrases survive from the initial account to the later one—"plover" still "haunt" him at the outset of "Negro Spirituals," for example—Higginson manages to keep his distance the second time around. He does this, in part, by calling attention to the writing processes whereby he reconstructed the spirituals:

> Writing down in the darkness, as I best could,—perhaps with my hand in the safe covert of my pocket,—the words of the song, I have afterwards carried it to my tent, like some captured bird or insect, and then, after examination, put it by. Or, summoning one of the men at some period of leisure,—Corporal Robert Sutton, for instance, whose iron memory held all the details of a song as if it were a ford or a forest,—I have completed the new specimen by supplying the absent parts. The music I could only retain by ear. (197–98)

Every bit the "romantic naturalist" here that Cruz has named him, Higginson mobilizes metaphors representing multiple sciences—ornithology, entomology, even the military science of topography—and in so doing detaches himself from a music that, curiously enough, is in some ways more a "part" of him now than it was when he first overheard it. Elsewhere in the chapter he deploys what Picker terms his "favorite metaphor," "turning spirituals into plants," for he calls the songs "strange plants, which I had before seen as in museums alone" but "could now gather on their own soil" (197). He also calls them "flowers of poetry," and another way in which *Army Life* recontextualizes the spirituals is to present them as lyric poems—textual objects in which indentation, alignment of parallel lines, punctuation, and enumeration give rise to what might be thought of as a poetic gestalt.

In some ways like the soldiers themselves, then, the spirituals have been regimented by the end of *Army Life*. Higginson's troops enter the war as volunteers; by the end they seem candidates for the regular army. Similarly, the spirituals first appear in *Army Life* as an unruly force. Indeed, they had resisted Higgin-

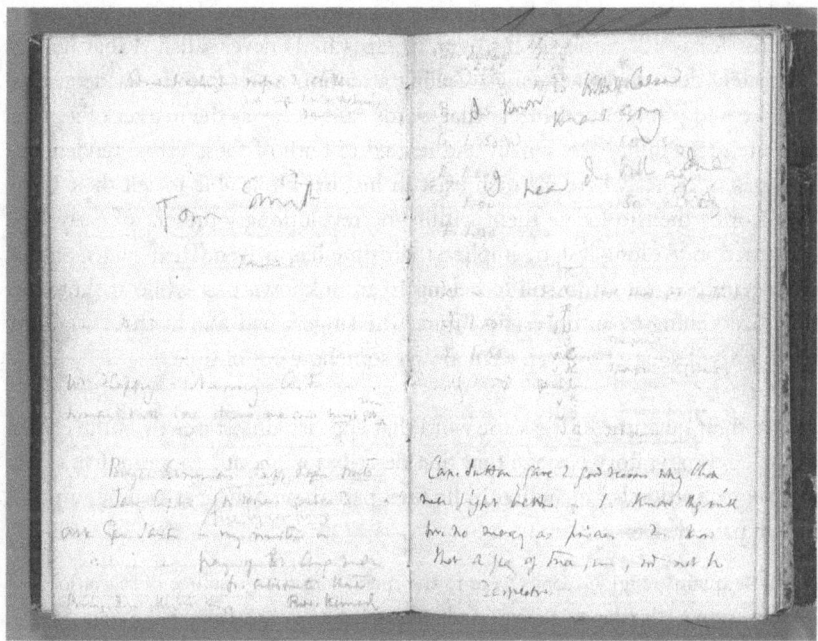

FIGURE 1. Higginson's surreptitious recording of the words of a spiritual, likely "I hear de bell done ringing" (upper right, diagonally across the rules of one of the notebooks he kept during the Civil War). MS Am 1162.2 (2), Houghton Library, Harvard University.

son's initial efforts to write them down. Writing in the dark—perhaps with his pencil and notebook in his pocket, as he claims above—Higginson scrawled in an almost illegible hand the words he thought he was hearing. His notebooks are otherwise full of carefully constructed tables: records of military orders received, loans made to individual soldiers, and so forth. The handwriting is typically easy to decipher. When it came time to record the songs, however, his writing became undisciplined. Words are frequently crossed out. Some appear on top of an already written table, superimposing disorder upon order. Some even appear at odd angles, quite literally defying the rules on the paper. (See figure 1.) By the time they reappear as "Negro Spirituals," the words have been "captured," corrected, studied, straightened out, and made to conform more or less to the standards of printed poetry. Like soldiers, they have in a sense been trained.

Yet the representational fate of the spirituals within *Army Life* is fundamentally different from that of the men who sing them. For one thing, the men end up "men," having demonstrated during the war essential similarities to their white counterparts. The spirituals conversely remain exotic, even as they have been domesticated into poems worthy of such adjectives as "kindred" and "convivial." For another, the soldiers never resist representation. Higginson is never at a loss for words to depict his men, whereas he is never satisfied that he has adequately described their songs. Calling attention instead to the inadequacies of prose and print, he fetishizes what words cannot say as the marker of a more absolute racial difference. Finally and related to both of these verbal tendencies, Higginson knows where his men exist in history. He is able to tell their Civil War stories then to locate them within the revolutionary present of early Reconstruction. At long last, he implies, their time has arrived. Their songs, on the other hand, seem to him still to belong to an unknown past while at the same time hearkening to an uncertain future. The singers had fought their way into history. Their songs, however, seem always somehow out of time.

Hence their quaintness. The same word that appears almost exactly at the center of the circumgyratory passage that first describes a "shout" reappears five times in "Negro Spirituals," including in its final paragraph, where it assumes a position of precedence:

> These quaint religious songs were to the men more than a source of relaxation; they were a stimulus to courage and a tie to heaven.... A few youths from Savannah, who were comparatively men of the world, had learned some of the 'Ethiopian Minstrel' ditties, imported from the North. These took no hold upon the mass; and, on the other hand, they sang reluctantly, even on Sunday, the long and short metres of the hymn-books, always gladly yielding to the more potent excitement of their own "spirituals." By these they could sing themselves, as had their fathers before them, out of the contemplation of their own low estate, into the sublime scenery of the Apocalypse.... [H]istory cannot afford to lose this portion of its record. There is no parallel instance of an oppressed race thus sustained by the religious sentiment alone. These songs are but the vocal expression of the simplicity of their faith and the sublimity of their long resignation. (221–22)

The final reference to quaintness in "Negro Spirituals" comes closest perhaps to indicating the word's manifold meanings. There is an explicit sense of otherworldliness, the "tie to heaven" appearing at the outset. There is a sense also of ingenuity, the spiritual being praised at the end as an unsurpassed cultural coping mechanism. There is throughout a sense of the persistence of the past, really of multiple pasts. Contrasted with an inauthentic, "imported" modern music, the "ditties" of the minstrel stage, spirituals evoke "generations" of slave singing. Contrasted with the predictable hymns of the white church, meanwhile, they reflect a sense of time—of tempo, time signature, and rhythm—that can convey both "more potent excitement" and "the sublimity of their long resignation."

It is the passage's other reference to the sublime, namely "the sublime scenery of the Apocalypse," that stands out as its most significant image. What is remarkable about the sentence that contains it is that it bypasses the present. It gestures backward toward the soldiers' "fathers before them" and forward toward an awe-inspiring end time, yet it suggests that the present, namely the activity of "contemplat[ing] ... their own low estate," is what the spirituals get them "out of." The notion that his soldiers might have been singing about the present, namely the war and the possibilities it already entailed, seems suddenly lost to Higginson. Instead, he consigns the spirituals to "history." Rather than depicting them as still capable of leaving him spellbound, as they had during the war, he sees them as already sealed-off, vestiges of a time now past. They betoken "the simplicity of their faith" rather than a more complicated cultural syncretism still taking place.

In short, here and elsewhere in *Army Life*, Higginson seems inclined to imagine the singing ex-slave a singing *still*-slave. He views the spiritual, whose relevance his soldiers had been revealing to him continually since the day he had assumed his command, nevertheless as a relic. Reluctant to conceive it as a still-living form, he rather insists upon its deadness: its having become an uprooted plant, a specimen ready for dissection, an object now for historical study only. One wonders whether Higginson had not kept singing the songs to himself as he worked to reconstruct them for publication. One pictures him at least humming a few measures in order to jog his memory as he sought out a word—even if he did think that, in so doing, he was "complet[ing] the new specimen." One suspects he began to internalize the rhythms, to acquire an ear for the melodies, to be able to reconstruct the polyphonies, at least in his mind if never quite on paper. One supposes that, over time, he simply grew to like them.

This is not how the spirituals register over the course of *Army Life*, however. Instead, they go from seeming to possess a gravitational pull Higginson can barely resist to being relatively inert objects on the page. They go from being performance pieces marked by variability and amplified by bodily movement—dancing, clapping, and so forth—to becoming standardized, disembodied texts in which, as Radano phrases it, "writing ... overwhelm[s] the originary presence of vernacular orality" (506). More straightforwardly, they go "from ambiguity towards refinement and clarity," as Picker has argued (236). And they go from occasioning a momentary "us" in the description of the "shout" in "Camp Diary" to becoming signs of a very different "them" at the end of "Negro Spirituals," an unparalleled "oppressed race ... sustained by the religious sentiment alone." Respectful, perhaps, of the spirituals as a kind of cultural property that does not belong to him, Higginson is nevertheless conspicuous in his efforts to hold black culture at arm's length. He insists on seeing former slaves as fellow soldiers. He defers, however, when presented a parallel opportunity to see them as "co-worker[s] in the kingdom of culture," as Du Bois would envision them less than forty years later (4).

Writing closer to one hundred years after the publication of *Army Life in a Black Regiment*, Sterling Brown mentions Higginson at the very outset of his essay "Negro Folk Expression" (1953): "Thomas Wentworth Higginson, one of the very first to pay respectful attention to the Negro spiritual, called it a startling flower growing in dark soil. Using his figure, we might think of this flower as a hybrid, as the American Negro is a hybrid. And though flowers of its family grew in Africa, Europe, and other parts of America, this hybrid bloom is uniquely beautiful."[13] It is noteworthy that Higginson occupies so eminent a position in Brown's cultural history. Yet it is equally significant that the later writer needed to revise his predecessor, to make expanded "us[e] of his figure," in order to construct a genealogy and place Higginson at its head. In *Army Life*'s discussions of the spirituals, after all, there is scant notice of their hybridity and perhaps even scanter acknowledgment of the possibility of interpreting them as "American"; they are instead explicitly linked with "Africa," the "Orient," and other distant spaces. Higginson seeks to preserve them for the historical record, specimen-like, transforming cultural history into something more like natural history. Even thus domesticated, the spirituals never threaten to enter the domains of "American art," "expression," "civilization," or some similar imaginary. They come nowhere close to being designated what Du Bois dubs them in *The Souls of Black Folk* when, just before he thanks Higginson for having noticed them, much like Brown does, he calls the spirituals "the sole American music ... the most beautiful expression of human experience born this side the seas" (251).

Higginson's choice of words would not be worth highlighting were not *Army Life* so otherwise intent on representing black soldiery as portending American citizenship. He could reimagine the body politic; he had in fact risked life and limb to help bring about the change. Yet he could not, or would not—or in any event did not—recalibrate his sense of culture. Perhaps the man of letters from Cambridge was unable to see in the songs of the black South an opportunity for reassessing what counted as national music. Perhaps Higginson understood American art as something eventually to be bestowed upon former slaves, not something that could be redefined in order to incorporate the art they were already producing. Perhaps he had simply not yet had enough time to arrive at so new a way of thinking, as he had joined the Civil War effort for military, not musicological reasons.

Or perhaps the recalibration was taking place, only he lacked the words to express it. This might explain *Army Life in a Black Regiment* and why it possesses the peculiar relationship with language it does: why it is marked by distinctive crosscurrents of discourse and depends on particular words to do more than customary work. I will end this essay by underscoring that, for Higginson, quaintness may not have possessed a color, a nationality, nor even fundamentally a sense of space, a geographic dimension that makes possible the differentiation between the "exotic" and the "domestic." Rather it seems to have possessed a temporality, and a rather personalized one at that: it may have implied that what initially seems strange may someday be regarded as familiar and even celebrated as emblematic. For in April of 1862, seven months before he would accept the commission to become colonel of the First South Carolina Volunteer Regiment, Higginson received out of the blue a letter from an aspiring poet from Massachusetts asking his opinion of her efforts. In an essay that appeared thirty years later in the *Atlantic*, Higginson describes his initial reaction to the letter and the poems it contained: "The letter was postmarked 'Amherst,' and it was in a handwriting so peculiar that it seemed as if the writer might have taken her first lessons by studying the famous fossil bird tracks in the museum of that college town. Yet it was not in the slightest degree illiterate, but cultivated, *quaint*, and wholly unique. Of punctuation there was little; she used chiefly dashes."[14] The poet was of course Emily Dickinson, and the occasion of Higginson's 1891 essay was the posthumous publication of her first book of poetry one year earlier. Writing in 1891 about their 1860s correspondence, Higginson could celebrate that American literature had finally become "modern" enough to accord Dickinson a place. Writing from 1862 to 1869 about the strange music he encountered during his military sojourn in the black South, Higginson was perhaps searching for the words to indicate that "Negro Spirituals" would one day be accorded their place in American culture, too, and that thus what had once seemed quaint in multiple senses of the word might seem, as Du Bois would later call them, "the singular spiritual heritage of the nation."

NOTES

1. "Negro Spirituals" was one of nine chapters of *Army Life in a Black Regiment*, published earlier as an article in the *Atlantic Monthly*. "Negro Spirituals" was published in 1867; others had appeared as early as 1864.

2. Thomas Wentworth Higginson, *Army Life in a Black Regiment* (Boston: Fields, Osgood, and Company, 1870), 63, 164, 266, hereafter documented parenthetically.

3. W. E. B. Du Bois, *The Souls of Black Folk* (Chicago: A. C. McClurg, 1903), 251.

4. John M. Picker, "The Union of Music and Text in Whitman's *Drum-Taps* and Higginson's *Army Life in a Black Regiment*," *Walt Whitman Quarterly Review* 12, no. 4 (1995):

240, hereafter documented parenthetically; Ronald Radano, "Denoting Difference: The Writing of the Slave Spirituals," *Critical Inquiry* 22, no. 3 (1996): 523, hereafter documented parenthetically.

5. Don Dingledine, "'The Whole Drama of the War': The African American Soldier in Civil War Literature," *PMLA* 115, no. 5 (2000): 1113.

6. John Mead, "Declarations of Liberty: Representations of Black/White Alliances against Slavery by John Brown, James Redpath, and Thomas Wentworth Higginson," *Journal for the Study of Radicalism* 3, no. 1 (2008): 112; Christopher, Looby, "Flowers of Manhood: Race, Sex, and Floriculture from Thomas Wentworth Higginson to Robert Mapplethorpe," *Criticism* 37, no. 1 (1995): 129, hereafter documented parenthetically.

7. Russell Conwell, *Magnolia Journey: A Union Veteran Revisits the Former Confederate States*, ed. Joseph Carter (1869; repr., Tuscaloosa: University of Alabama Press, 1974), 101.

8. Frederick Douglass, "Address for the Promotion of Colored Enlistments," in *Frederick Douglass: Selected Speeches and Writings*, ed. Philip S. Foner (1863; repr., Chicago: Lawrence Hill, 1999), 536.

9. Robert James Branham, "'Of Thee I Sing': Contesting 'America,'" *American Quarterly* 48, no. 4 (1996): 636.

10. Michael Cohen, "Paul Laurence Dunbar and the Genres of Dialect," *African American Review* 41, no. 2 (2007): 250.

11. On quaintness as a quality that depends not on the actual passage of time but rather its commodified illusion, see Daniel Harris, *Cute, Quaint, Hungry and Romantic: The Aesthetics of Consumerism* (New York: Basic Books, 2000).

12. Jon Cruz, *Culture on the Margins: The Black Spiritual and the Rise of American Cultural Interpretation* (Princeton: Princeton University Press, 1999), 150.

13. Sterling A. Brown, "Negro Folk Expression: Spirituals, Seculars, Ballads, and Work Songs," in *A Son's Return: Selected Essays of Sterling A. Brown*, ed. Mark A. Sanders (1953; repr., Boston: Northeastern University Press, 1996), 243.

14. Thomas Wentworth Higginson, "Emily Dickinson's Letters," *Atlantic Monthly* 68, no. 408 (1891): 444, emphasis added.

The Negro in the American Rebellion
William Wells Brown and the
Design of African American History

JOHN ERNEST

———◆———

Although William Wells Brown's 1867 publication, *The Negro in the American Rebellion: His Heroism and His Fidelity*, has been hailed as "the first military history of African Americans by a member of any race," the great irony of Brown's career as historian is that his contribution to history is largely limited to the fact of the book's publication.¹ Like many of Brown's publications—and he was prolific—*The Negro in the American Rebellion* is celebrated, in effect, as a historical artifact, an African American first, a significant statement, but not one that anyone need either read or take seriously. Even the great African American writer Charles W. Chesnutt, then only twenty-three and looking ahead to his own writing career, noted in his journal that his skimming of Brown's history only confirmed his opinion "that the Negro is yet to become known who can write a good book." Noting that he reads such books "merely for facts," Chesnutt adds, "I could appreciate the facts better if they were well presented. The book [*The Negro in the American Rebellion*] reminds me of a gentleman in a dirty shirt. You are rather apt to doubt his gentility under such circumstances. I am sometimes doubtful of the facts for the same reason—they make but a shabby appearance."² Most other readers have been more or less kind, but have come to similar conclusions, presenting *The Negro in the American Rebellion* as, at best, a sourcebook of information, but one to be approached with care if approached at all for historical understanding.

Certainly, Chesnutt would have found many facts in Brown's history, but if he was deeply familiar with Brown's writing career, he would have found ample reason to distrust the facts. In another of Brown's historical works, *The Black Man; His Antecedents, His Genius, and His Achievements*, Brown includes a sketch of a man who might not have existed, a sketch that Brown's biographer, William Edward Farrison, locates "in the shadowland between the real and the imaginary."[3] This is, indeed, where Brown typically worked throughout his career, though his contributions to the antislavery movement, the temperance movement, Civil War recruitment, and other causes were substantial and quite real. But in all of his work, Brown plays (sometimes openly, sometimes not) with facts, even in his autobiographical work, and certainly in his histories. Stories that were once presented as fact become part of a larger fictional narrative, and stories once presented as fiction turn up as history, and sometimes for no observable reason. *The Negro in the American Rebellion*, for example, includes in a chapter titled "Wit and Humor of the War" a two-sentence example of such humor that Brown had first presented, more extensively, in his 1853 fictional narrative *Clotel*. The 1867 history also includes a chapter titled "A Thrilling Incident of the War" that borrows directly from a story Brown had told of himself in his autobiography, now ascribed to a different man in a different time.

Can a history be taken seriously when its devotion to facts is so demonstrably questionable? Although the answer to this question might seem clear, we should pause to consider how many white-authored histories of the United States, or white commentaries on that history, have been taken seriously, even in their presentation of African American life and culture. As Thomas J. Ward has noted, "Whatever its weaknesses, *The Negro in the American Rebellion* was certainly no more flawed (or romanticized) than many of the 'Lost Cause' accounts of the war, which either grossly misrepresented black attitudes towards the war or left African Americans out completely."[4] Deeply aware of what might be called the cultural politics of objectivity, Brown was a transitional historian, working to bring African American identity and experience into the theater of authoritative history but still very much distrustful of the possibility of a fair hearing on the historical stage. Like William C. Nell before him and George Washington Williams after him, Brown worked to gather the materials that would demonstrate African American achievement, promote African American collective self-definition, and establish those of African origins as historical agents throughout history and in the United States. But like Nell and others before him and somewhat unlike Williams after, Brown adopted a narrative method that both responds to and challenges the epistemological assumptions of the white supremacist culture that both contained and defined African American identity and experience. In *The Negro in the American Rebellion*, Brown addresses the history he knows best, the history not directed or even informed by historical accuracy, but rather the history one encountered in the press, in popular culture, and in the various commemorative memorials that shaped the American cultural landscape after the Civil War. Brown's purpose was not only to record but to shape history, and to direct the American historical consciousness toward a different perspective than those provided by other forums for historical remembrance.

Brown's formal experimentation in earlier works led him to develop the particular documentary form of *The Negro in the American Rebellion*. In *Clotel*, for example, Brown had deliberately mixed documentary and nondocumentary sources. Blurring the lines between fact and fiction in *Clotel* by representing some fictional elements as truth while framing historical fact as fiction, Brown troubled the category of authenticity that was both the burden of the slave narrative's address to a white readership and the warrant by which the Fugitive Slave Law could (re)enslave African Americans.[5] Shaping *The Negro in the American Rebellion* to address white supremacist culture's persistent misrepresentation of African American experience, Brown amplified the documentary practice of antebellum abolitionist newspapers, which had frequently reprinted articles from other papers, sometimes without comment, so as to allow readers to sift truth from reportorial framing. This practice complicates any reading of Brown's work, historical or otherwise, for any given paragraph might or might not represent Brown's views. Even that most intimate marker of a writer's work, the voice, is elusive—for we cannot be sure that the sentence or paragraph or even the chapter we are reading is wholly Brown's own. A close reading of Brown's work, then, as I will demonstrate, comes down to a reading of his method, to the interplay of voices and perspectives Brown artfully and purposefully choreographs in his work. In the case of the hyperdocumentary form of *The Negro in the American Rebellion*, Brown's method is designed to reveal that the war was larger and more complex than any white claims concerning its purpose, thus allowing Brown's canny readers to discern from the war's complexities and contradictions a hopeful trajectory for the African American future.

History without Authority

Although all of Brown's critics acknowledge that it can be problematic to hold Brown to current historical standards, few have considered the extent to which Brown himself might have expected and anticipated a critical or even hostile response to his work. The great nineteenth-century American historians were white gentlemen of means who owned great libraries and were well connected to those in power. It is not surprising that anyone interested in studying William H. Prescott, George Bancroft, John Lothrop Motley, Francis Parkman, or Henry Adams will be assisted by published letters and journals, and will find in those letters and journals names of some of the most influential national and international figures of the day. Some were gentlemen of independent means; Motley was a diplomat; Bancroft was secretary of the navy; and Adams was the grandson and great-grandson of U.S. presidents. Such men lived in worlds fundamentally different from Brown's. But I say this not to offer the conventional move of accounting for Brown's lack of a formal education or lack of access to positions of power and authority, but rather to suggest that Brown's world, and the history and education that had shaped his life, was itself inaccessible to such men as Prescott, Bancroft, Motley, Parkman, and Adams. As their work reveals hauntingly well, the leading white American historians were men of great but limited vision, particularly when it came to issues of slavery and race. But while Brown was positioned to tell a story they could not, a story arguably central to any understanding of U.S. history, the cultural politics of historical authority made it unlikely that his contributions would be either recognized or acknowledged.

Consider, for example, one of the most imposing of the many works of African American history published in the last decades of the nineteenth century, and one often referenced as the beginning of African American historiography, George Washington Williams's *History of the Negro Race in America from 1619 to 1880: Negroes as Slaves, as Soldiers, and as Citizens; Together with a Preliminary Consideration of the Unity of the Human Family, a Historical Sketch of Africa, and an Account of the Negro Governments of Sierra Leone and Liberia* (1883). Williams explores everything from the vagaries of race science to the challenge of recovering and even naming the history of various regions of Africa, but most of this history is devoted to people of African descent in the United States. Williams's research for this two-volume history was extensive, and he involves the reader in that research regularly, both by way of commentary and by way of reprinted documents—and he is quite clear at the beginning of the *History* about the reasoning behind his methods. "Where I have used documents," he states, "it was with a desire to escape the charge of superficiality. If, however, I may be charged with seeking to escape the labor incident to thorough digestion, I answer, that, while men with the reputation of Bancroft and Hildreth could pass unchallenged when disregarding largely the use of documents and the citation of authorities, I would find myself challenged by a large number of critics."[6] In many ways, Williams offers readers a grand narrative of U.S. history, one that has become almost standard in accounts of American racial history. Addressing the constitutional convention at the end of the Revolutionary War, Williams states, "It was then and there that the hydra of slavery struck its fangs into the Constitution; and, once inoculated with the poison of the monster, the government was only able to purify itself in the flames of a great civil war" (1:vii). Williams states that he has been motivated "not as the blind panegyrist of my race, nor as the partisan apologist, but from a love for '*the truth of history*,'" and he presents the book in the hope for an ideal world that would today be labeled racially blind, in hopes that "the day will hasten when there shall be no North, no South, no Black, no White,—but all be American citizens, with equal duties and equal rights" (1:x).

Williams's *History*, though, is representative of African American experience less in the story it tells than in the historical perspective it embodies, in its confrontation and negotiation with a world of experience that resists not simply resolution but clear narrative lines. Indeed, Williams's subject is frequently and ultimately overwhelmed by the documents that support it. Tracing the origins of the great majority of African Americans to an inherently inferior type, "the lowest strata of the African race," Williams retroactively endorses those who argued that slavery had a civilizing effect on the enslaved, who having gained their freedom were again in danger of degradation (1:109). Williams, then, constructs a double narrative: the story of an ancient degradation and the story of a providential rise to a "higher," more "civilized" type of humanity. By these and other means, Williams effectively rewrites the untold stories of enslavement into an exclusionary narrative of citizenship. At the same time, Williams's own involvement in that history, his failure to be as removed or as objective as he promises in the introductory pages, comes through in the various fissures of his narrative and in the commentary he can't keep himself from presenting. In his opening pages, he states, "I have avoided comment so far as it was consistent with a clear exposition of the truth" (1:x). The comments he presents, though, are extensive, and they speak volumes about what Mark M. Smith calls the "emotional, visceral, and febrile understanding of racial identity," which became especially prominent markers of race toward the end of the century.[7] At the beginning of his second volume, Williams comments on his position as a historian of slavery, noting, "I have tracked my bleeding countrymen through the widely scattered documents of American history; I have listened to their groans, their clanking chains, and melting prayers, until the woes of a race and the agonies of centuries seem to crowd upon my soul as a bitter reality" (2:iii). Approaching that scattered community though the evidence collected from scattered archives, Williams notes that he brings more to this text than a hopeful ideal. "Many pages of this history," he states, "have been blistered with my tears; and, although having lived but a little more than a generation, my mind feels as if it were cycles old" (2:iii). Williams's *History* is, in effect, bursting at the seams, unable to contain the many narrative trajectories involved in the "history of the race."

Although Brown shares Williams's desire to present a record of African American achievement, he does so without anxiety about his use of documents. Indeed, the great bulk of *The Negro in the American Rebellion* is made up entirely of documents that Brown draws from various sources. As Ward observes, "Much of Brown's account of the war is simply the reprinting of often page-long primary documents—mainly newspaper accounts, letters, government documents, even songs—interspersed with his commentary" (review of *The Negro*). Indeed, Brown presents these documents with relatively little commentary and virtually no narrative bridges. We simply proceed from one episode of the Civil War to the next, and often we find ourselves immediately immersed in a document—or, at times, something that we might suspect is a reprinted document. Predictably, this is not a method that earns Brown praise for his historical method. Ward's judgment is characteristic: "Brown provided no footnotes, and only a smattering of the accounts give the source; too often Brown relies on unnamed observers. This style, as one might expect, also does not lead to cohesive narrative, which is one of the great weaknesses of the book" (review of *The Negro*). To be sure, one can follow Brown's developing commentary toward a kind of narrative arc, one dealing with the struggle against racial oppression before, during, and after the Civil War. John David Smith, the primary champion of *The Negro in the American Rebellion*, observes that "in his book Brown condemned slavery, documented anti-Negro sentiment among Southerners and white Northerners, championed the role of the U.S. Colored Troups (USCT), interpreted the war as a struggle for blacks to attain social equality, and assailed those who oppressed blacks after Appomattox" (xvi). These concerns lead Smith to an identifiable purpose in Brown's approach: "*The Negro in the American Rebellion* was less a traditional 'history' than a loosely literary and polemical work that interpreted the causes and consequences of the Civil War from the perspective of African Americans. Brown constructed a thematically arranged historical narrative, weaving in and out of imaginary scenes to illustrate his points" (xxxiii).

Even with such a map, though, it can be difficult to follow Brown's documentary approach. For example, the ninth chapter of *The Negro in the American Rebellion*, "Intelligent Contrabands," begins with the dramatic promise of an embedded reporter: "I spent three weeks at Liverpool Point, the outpost of Hooker's Division, almost directly opposite Aquia Creek, waiting patiently for the advance of our left wing to follow up the army, becoming, if not a participator against the dying struggles of rebellion, at least a chronicler of the triumphs in the march of the Union army."[8] This is presented without introduction and without quotation marks, and one might accordingly expect that Brown himself is narrating this account—until we reach the end of the account, that is, and find that the piece is attributed to a "War Correspondent of the New York Times" (35). It can, in fact, be difficult to know how to read this book—to know at any given moment who is talking, on what authority, and to what purpose. Even Smith, though otherwise an appreciative reader capable of finding in this book "a thematically arranged historical narrative," ultimately concedes that "Brown's *The Negro in the American Rebellion* has serious limitations as 'history' (xxxiv).

And if the book is deeply flawed in the purpose for which it was intended, what claims can be made for it?

Contending Histories

And yet, it might be that Brown is a more savvy and accomplished historian than the evidence against him might suggest. Brown knew well that he was unlikely to encounter any comprehensive, studied, judicious, and accurate history of African Americans authored by the white historians whose authority over historical judgment was relatively unquestioned. But he knew equally well that the historical world he lived in was hardly one that submitted to the authority of historians. He knew that he lived in a world of opinions, prejudices, and judgments that both carried and conveyed history; he lived in a world in which historical views expressed themselves through racial oppression, in which historical actors had been shaped by the absurdities of racial ideology. *The Negro in the American Rebellion* is a history that accounts for the dynamics of racial history and not simply a history that focuses on different historical actors than those encountered in mainstream histories.

In the decades that followed Brown's pioneering work, and into the twentieth century, African American writers produced a great number of historical publications. By and large, these many histories can be grouped into four primary subsets: autobiographies and memoirs, institutional histories, works devoted to recovering individual biographies (and their affiliated histories), and race histories (including but often extending beyond national histories). All of these histories were devoted to the peculiarly difficult task of presenting a coherent history of African Americans. And the challenges were imposing. On the one hand, African Americans were not concentrated into a single geographical area; they did not profess united ideological, religious, or political views; and their lives were not governed by the same economic, political, or legal conditions or practices. Rather, they were subject to a range of state and local governments (not to mention extralegal forces), under which they were variously both recognized and invisible, included and excluded. On the other hand, the force of racial ideology and control bound African Americans to a common sense of affiliation and destiny, and encouraged institutional and cultural formations specific to black life in the United States. Gathering the fragmented history of this collective usually involved a focus on individual stories organized (often only loosely) by regional affiliations. Published before the Civil War, William C. Nell's *The Colored Patriots of the American Revolution* (1855) is made up of chapters devoted to individual states, from Massachusetts to Florida, and even then the chapters often jump without transition from one event, group, or individual to another. After the war, George Washington Williams's *History of the Negro Race in America* begins with chapters devoted to Africa and theories of race, and then it turns to thirteen chapters devoted to the thirteen American colonies. After a long section on slavery, the Civil War, and Emancipation, Williams turns to individual stories and institutional (mainly religious) histories. Through such means, African American historians tried to account for a scattered history connected first by the forces of oppression beyond the control of black Americans and second by the growing networks of African American organizational efforts that gradually spread from local to regional influence. Unsurprisingly, then, a great many of the histories published from 1860 to 1920 were hybrid works, involving two or more of the subsets of historical focus I've summarized, and all feature tenuous connections and often sudden narrative turns from one set of concerns to another.

Brown's *The Negro in the American Rebellion* looks rather different when placed in the context of these histories than when considered against an ideal of either objective or narrative history. Indeed, it is instructive to consider Brown's own claims for his book, presented in the preface. "I waited patiently," he notes, "before beginning this work, with the hope that some one more competent would take the subject in hand; but, up to the present, it has not been done, although many books have been written upon the Rebellion" (xliii). African American historical research and writing had begun, many years before, not only because African Americans were regularly excluded from histories written by others but also because they were occasionally and, one might say, strategically *included*—that is, represented in such a way as to support white historians' presentation of the national story (of which George Bancroft's *History of the United States* is an instructive example). Knowing that "many books have been written upon the Rebellion," Brown attempts to gather the fragments of the stories that were likely to be either omitted or misrepresented in such histories. But significant, too, for our reading of *The Negro in the American Rebellion* is Brown's commentary, at the beginning and end of the book, on its organization. In his preface, Brown accounts for the first six chapters of the book rather incidentally, noting, "It occurred to me [while writing the book] that a sketch of the condition of the race previous to the commencement of the war would not be uninteresting to the reader" (xliii). At the end of the book, after a chapter titled "Caste" that, one might argue, was designed to be the book's culminating argument, Brown includes a final chapter, titled "Sixth Regiment United-States Volunteers," and prefaces it with a brief remark: "The following sketch of the Sixth Regiment United-States colored troops was kindly furnished by a gentleman of Philadelphia, but came too late to appear in its proper place" (214). The chapter ends without commentary, and so does the book. Of course, one could argue that Brown's decision to include early chapters on "the condition of the race previous to the commencement of the war" was not at all incidental, and one could note that, in referring to the closing chapter's "proper" place, Brown is suggesting that the book does indeed have a governing design. In both cases, in my view, one would be right—but more to the point is the tension between a principle of order and a fragmented history that drives the book in virtually every chapter. This is a book that suggests a governing principle that it never quite fulfills, and the resulting tension between principle and practice, or between ideological designs and historical experience, is very much the point in African American historical writing throughout the nineteenth century.

After the Civil War, African Americans, confronted with a newly threatening system of repression that included the competition with immigrant groups that so preoccupied such leaders as Booker T. Washington, found themselves facing the challenge of entering and countering many histories, many narratives, in a racial palimpsest that complicated even the terms by which their collective identity or political unity could be defined.[9] As has often been noted, the tenuous alliance of the white North and South was a political union managed by way of racial unity. "American reunion," David Blight observes, was "achievable in the end only through new regimes of racial subjugation, a fated and tragic struggle still only in its formative years. The sections needed one another, almost as polar opposites that made the center hold and kept both an industrial economy humming and a New South on the course of revival. Some of the war's greatest results, the civil and political liberties of African Americans, were slowly becoming sacrificial offerings on the altar of reunion."[10] The terms of this reunion would become the guiding terms of U.S. politics from that time to the present day, with any alleviation to the ongoing sacrificial offerings, any partial granting of African American rights, marked as progress, regardless of whether the historical effects of the original sacrifice were in any way addressed or compensated. At various stages of U.S. history, African Americans would find themselves in a new configuration of racial identity, approaching with a Du Boisian double consciousness what Alice Fahs has termed white America's "doubled consciousness of blacks" after the Civil War that "enabled whites to maintain older stereotypes while looking ahead to the possibility of new social realities for African Americans."[11] Progress for African Americans was itself folded into a historical narrative that looked back as insistently as it looked forward.

With so many stories to tell, so many overlapping and competing narratives, it is hardly surprising that the Civil War is still the most popular subject among publishers and readers alike. But while many of those publications include mention of African Americans, and many more discuss slavery, relatively few have been examined for what they can tell us about race in the late nineteenth century and beyond. To be sure, in *Black Reconstruction* (1935) Du Bois famously presented excerpts demonstrating the centrality of the racist assumptions informing many white historians' accounts of the failures of Reconstruction, but more difficult to counter was, to draw again from Mark M. Smith, the "emotional, visceral, and febrile understanding of racial identity" behind such narratives that had already qualified Du Bois's faith in the efficacy of historical evidence and scholarly reason in a white supremacist culture.[12] And behind such official narratives were various and influential unofficial histories (the "imagined Civil War," as Fahs has it) in the form of "war poetry, sentimental war stories, sensational war novels, war humor, war juveniles, war songs, collections of war-related anecdotes, and war histories—literature that has often been designated, then dismissed, as popular" (1). "In both the North and the South," Fahs observes, "popular war literature was vitally important in shaping a cultural politics of war. Not only did it mark the gender of men and women as well as boys and girls, but it also explored and articulated attitudes toward race and, ultimately, portrayed and helped to shape new modes of imagining individuals' relationships to the nation" (1–2). The Civil War offered not one but many narratives, various competing and overlapping histories. "This variegated literature," as Fahs puts it, "created not just one but a multitude of different imagined wars, complicating notions of what kind of national community was created through the auspices of print culture" (10).

One might well wonder whether a stable history is even possible under such conditions, especially for those whose lives were governed by the increasing absurdities of racial ideology. Certainly, one doesn't need to look far for reminders of these central concerns in nineteenth-century African American print culture—including the recognition by African Americans that they would need to assert authority over print culture itself if they were to have any hope of controlling, or at least influencing, the dynamics of racial definition. This was quite clear in the 1827 editorial that defined the mission of the first African American newspaper, *Freedom's Journal*. "We wish to plead our own cause," the editorial announced, for "too long have others spoken for us. Too long has the public been deceived by misrepresentations, in things which concern us dearly, though in the estimation of some mere trifles; for though there are many in society who exercise towards us benevolent feelings; still (with sorrow we confess it) there are others who make it their business to enlarge upon the least trifle, which tends to the discredit of any person of color; and pronounce anathemas and denounce our whole body for the misconduct of this guilty one."[13] Similarly, the members of the "Colored National Convention" held in Rochester in 1853 asked in their published proceedings, "What stone has been left unturned to degrade us? What hand has refused to fan the flame of prejudice against us? What American artist has not caricatured us? What wit has not laughed at us in our wretchedness? What songster has not made merry over our depressed spirits? What press has not ridiculed and contemned us? What pulpit has withheld from our devoted heads its angry lightning, or its sanctimonious hate?"[14] Toward the end of the century, in 1892, a time when many white writers were invested in representing caricatures of African Americans in their works, Anna Julia Cooper would echo these comments in her essay "The Negro as Presented in American Literature." Noting the tendency of white writers to base their black characters on the writers' perceptions of whatever black people they happened to encounter, Cooper complains that "a few with really kind intentions and a sincere desire for information have approached the subject as a clumsy microscopist, not quite at home with his instrument, might study a new order of beetle or bug. Not having focused closely enough to obtain a clear-cut view, they begin by telling you that all colored people look exactly alike and end by noting down every chance contortion or idiosyncrasy as a race characteristic."[15] From Joel Chandler Harris's "Uncle Remus" tales to Thomas Dixon Jr.'s threatening celebrations of the Ku Klux Klan, African Americans knew that they were being misrepresented with great force.

In such an environment, the possibilities for objective history were stretched to their limit, and the challenge of representing the ideological fictions that supported the delicate national order, fictions central to African American experience, were formidable. Representing African American experience meant much more than identifying black historical agents, for one needed to account for the multiple ideological, institutional, and social factors that made blackness or whiteness so definitively significant. One needed to account for facts shaped by social fictions, and histories immediately appropriated by historical authorities who either omitted or included pointed misrepresentations of African Americans. One needed to tell a story relegated to the margins of national history that had everything to do with the nation's ideological center, and one needed to work from official historical records that were biased from the start. One needed to transform blackness and whiteness from blandly superficial facts to context-rich signifiers, and relate the realms of experience and understanding that official history both relied upon and held beneath the surface. One needed to record history in such a way as to expose the multiple and competing historical perspectives that constituted the hidden chambers of official history's grand facades.

Reading History's Character

Brown's liberal use of other sources in *The Negro in the American Rebellion* is hardly surprising, for this was his primary method in all of his writing. In everything he published, Brown drew from other sources, often presented in jarring juxtapositions with one another, and frequently presented so as to confound the reader's sense of a stable perspective or definitive narrative thread. As with his presentation of the piece by the *New York Times* correspondent, Brown often leads the reader into a chapter with a clear mode of address only to reveal later that the narrator is other than we might have thought. And he regularly places fragments of newspaper stories, bits from books, and other pieces with and against one another in ways that do not seem, at first, to add up to a coherent whole. I have elsewhere suggested that Brown is most usefully understood as a cultural editor, drawing from various cultural materials, often with little commentary and no source acknowledgment, and then rearranging those materials in a revealing demonstration of cultural contradictoriness and tension. His purpose, I then suggested, was to "establish and then reconstitute a correspondence between realms that are public and private, communal and individual—or, more to the point, between culture and individual character."[16] "The claim of authorship" in Brown's work, I have argued, "extends beyond any given narrative line or any specific episode" (34). Rather, authorship "functions as a response to the text that the community is in the act of writing. Brown does not so much represent a world as capture a world in the act of unconscious self-representation. In his role as cultural editor, Brown gathers the documents that reveal the national disunity—not the meaninglessness of the national text but rather its meaningful incoherence" (34). This understanding of Brown's method, I suggest now, is particularly relevant for *The Negro in the American Rebellion*, for in no other area of concern have U.S. authors been so actively engaged in the process of anxious self-representation than in their ongoing writings on the Civil War, and in no other area of historical writing have the results of that self-representation been so contested or so meaningfully contradictory and, at times, incoherent, even as basic facts of the Civil War have been scrutinized and memorized, from academic halls to Civil War circles, to the last detail.

The Negro in the American Rebellion is a work that emphasizes the extent to which history is mediated through the perspectives of those involved and of those who report on events. Reading this work, the reader jumps from newspaper to magazine to primary document, from the *New York Times* (reporting on a heroic black soldier) to the *Atlantic Monthly* (reporting on "the scenes which Gen. Butler had to pass through in connection with slavery") to the *Louisville Journal* (voicing objections to Lincoln's approval of a bill abolishing slavery in the District of Columbia) to a proclamation issued by the mayor's office of Cincinnati (suggestive of a threatening racial climate in his city) (33–35, 49–50, 52–53, 56–57). Frequently, the narrative pauses for a poem—for example, an "imitation of Leigh Hunt's celebrated poem" taken from the *Boston Transcript*, a poem that celebrates General Butler's evolved views on slavery; or a poem by the prominent African American poet Frances E. W. Harper, celebrating the Emancipation Proclamation; or a version of a poem from *The Liberator* by Edward H. G. Clark, originally titled "To James Gordon Bennett, *High Priest of Northern Treason*," but now adapted (perhaps by Brown himself) to address President Andrew Johnson as the "great Judas of the nineteenth century" and "foul political traitor of the age" (51, 71, 191–92). In short, the reader encounters a great number of perspectives and voices in *The Negro in the American Rebellion*, sometimes rising to a chorus and sometimes dissolving into cacophonous confusion. Each source speaks for history, some insisting on a prominent place in the historical record and others clearly representing the anonymous masses directly involved in history's messy progression—but the real history presented in this book might be said to be that represented in the tensions and unions between and among the various voices and views.

Of course, the primary conflict represented by *The Negro in the American Rebellion* is that of its central focus in relation to typical accounts of the war, North or South. The fact that Brown needs to assert—or, rather, insert—a history of black soldiers is itself significant. This might seem a very basic point in an age when we habitually judge racism by omissions and language, but Brown was hardly struggling against simple racism alone. His task was to get African Americans on the historical map, and thereby to shift the map to different purposes than those to which it was commonly devoted. Douglas L. Mitchell—to date, the best reader of the internal logic and narrative order of *The Negro in the American Rebellion*—offers not only a chapter-by-chapter explanation of Brown's method but also a sound statement on Brown's thesis:

> His Civil War is a fundamentally different war from the accounts focusing on the eastern battlefields and the titanic presence of Grant and Sherman on the one hand, Lee, Jackson, and Longstreet on the other. His war is a heroic struggle for black freedom through arms, conducted on the periphery of the other accounts, in the western theater and on the southern coast, at places like Milliken's Bend, Port Hudson, Fort Wagner, Olustee, and Honey Hill. It is a war that accomplished much, most important the final demonstration of the courage and competence of the black man, but it is one that does not end at Appomattox. Final Union victory will come only with enforced universal suffrage for African Americans, else all is squandered.[17]

Brown looks to the periphery for the center, to find not only in the actions but in the perspectives exposed at the margins of history the driving ideological forces of the nation's center. In this way, Brown anticipates the situation David Blight has illuminated as the war's aftermath, a political and economic re-alliance of white northerners and southerners achieved by transforming African Americans into "sacrificial offerings on the altar of reunion."[18]

In the relatively sparse but forceful commentary Brown brings to this collection of anecdotes and documents, he brings home the point that African Americans are the key to the war, and the key to determining the national character—indeed, the key to measuring the success of the American experiment. Brown sets the stage for this argument from the book's opening page, asserting of African Americans that "the history of this people, full of sorrow, blood, and tears, is full also of instruction for mankind" (1). "Never were the institutions of a people, or the principles of liberty, put to such a severe test as those of the American Republic," he adds, noting that the degradations of slavery extended to enslavers as well as the enslaved (1). The early chapters of *The Negro in the American Rebellion* address both the hope of those institutions and the tensions created by their degradation. He highlights African American military service in the American Revolution, and highlights the praise of General Andrew Jackson, by no means a friend to the antislavery cause, for black fighters in the War of 1812. But Brown also highlights slave rebellions, asserting that "the efforts of Denmark Vesey, Nat Turner, and Madison Washington to strike the chains of slavery from the limbs of their enslaved race will live in history, and will warn all tyrants to beware of the wrath of God and the strong arm of man" (20). In effect, Brown draws from the providential logic behind a great deal of national mythology (and behind such influential histories as George Bancroft's *History of the United States*) to argue that the nation's security was tied to its success in fulfilling its principles. "Every iniquity that society allows to subsist for the benefit of the oppressor," he states, commenting on the slave rebellions, "is a sword with which she herself arms the oppressed. Right is the most dangerous of weapons: woe to him who leaves it to his enemies" (20).

And that point is Brown's entrance to the Civil War. In many ways echoing the argument presented by white southerner Hinton Helper in *The Impending Crisis* (1857), Brown argues that "the vast wealth realized by the slave-holder had made him feel that the South was independent of the rest of the world" (29). Wealth brought laxity as well, for "prosperity had made him giddy. Cotton was not merely king; it was God. Moral considerations were nothing" (29). But in a nation driven by concepts of providential history—a nation ruled by law, guided by an idea, devoted to guiding principles—the inevitable intellectual and moral separation from the larger union was serious: "But, alas! the supreme error of this anticipation lay in omitting from the calculation all power of principle. The right still has authority over the minds of men and in the counsels of nations. Factories may cease their din; men and women may be thrown out of employment; the marts of commerce may be silent and deserted; but truth and justice still command some respect among men; and God yet remains the object of their adoration" (29). Of course, the decades preceding the Civil War were hardly years in which southerners abandoned all claims to "moral considerations," but for Brown, as for others who considered the United States to be the child of providence, history would provide the ultimate test of moral perspective, and Brown's primary charge against the South was that it had long been engaged in a war against history itself. "They dreamed of perpetuating slavery," he observes, "though all history shows the decline of the system as industry, commerce, and knowledge advance. The slave-holders proposed nothing less than to reverse the currents of humanity, and to make barbarism flourish in the bosom of civilization" (29).

This argument contextualizes both the courage and the mistreatment of African Americans throughout Brown's account, but Brown recognized that his vision of progress required more than an argument against the South. Indeed, for many African Americans, the Civil War was significant not only because it led to the abolition of slavery but also because it addressed the oppression of African Americans in the North as well. The Civil War allowed African Americans an argument to enter upon a historical stage recognized by white Americans, north and south, domestic and international. The fact that they had to struggle even for the entrance, to be allowed to serve as soldiers, was itself significant, as was the unequal treatment they received as soon as the honor of service was allowed. Brown emphasizes this point not only in his attention to the views of individual leaders and the poor treatment of black soldiers by fellow soldiers and enemies alike; he emphasizes it as well in highlighting the dubious hopes for African Americans engaged in the national cause:

> The negro has little to hope from Northern sympathy or legislation. Any attempt to engraft upon the organic law of the States provisions extending to the colored man political privileges is overwhelmingly defeated by the people. It makes no difference that here is a pen, and there a voice, raised in his behalf: the general verdict is against him; and its repetition in any case where it is demanded shows that it is inexorable. We talk a great deal about the vice of slavery, and the cruelty of denying to our fellow-men their personal freedom and a due reward of labor; but we are very careful not to concede the corollary, that the sin of withholding that freedom is not vastly greater than withholding the rights to which he who enjoys it is entitled. (82)

Here and elsewhere Brown turns the story to a larger purpose. As Thomas J. Ward observes, "In *The Negro in the American Rebellion*, Brown was ... not simply writing a history of blacks in the Civil War, he was making a case for full citizenship for African Americans in the new Union" (review of *The Negro*). But he knew that this would be a difficult case to make. Accounting for the limited force of advocacy—"here is a pen, and there a voice"—Brown implicitly accounts as well for his own method, in which the voice of advocacy is deeply embedded in the dynamic play of perspectives and prejudices involved in the Civil War. Moreover, he quietly turns his comments about the historically regressive and morally blind South to the North as well.

One could say that the real significance of the Civil War for Brown was its lush messiness, the fact that it encompassed and exposed so many tensions, so many contradictions, so many ideological and moral undercurrents suddenly erupting onto the national landscape. In this way, the Civil War was larger than any claims concerning its purpose, more significant in its causes than in any simple understanding of its resolution. It was, for Brown, the inevitable result of the nation's struggle against principle and progress, and it was as well the necessary intervention if the nation was to proceed beyond the limited vision of white America both north and south:

> All legitimate revolutions are occasioned by the growth of society beyond the growth of government; and they will be peaceful or violent just in proportion as the people and the government shall be wise and virtuous or vicious and ignorant. Such revolutions or reforms are generally of a peaceful nature in communities in which the government has made provision for the gradual expansion of its institutions to suit the onward march of society. No government is wise in overlooking, whatever may be the strength of its own traditions, or however glorious its history, that human institutions which have been adapted for a barbarous age or state of society will cease to be adapted for more civilized and intelligent times; and, unless government makes a provision for the gradual expansion, nothing can prevent a storm, either of an intellectual or a physical nature. Slavery was always the barbarous institution of America; and the Rebellion was the result of this incongruity between it and freedom. (30)

Brown's argument here is ingenious and compelling: the result of a historically regressive mode of social organization, the Civil War made progress possible—progress beyond what even most white Americans were prepared to envision. As Brown presents his case for black enfranchisement and civil rights, he works both with and against the contending forces of the many other speakers in this book. He uses the often limited, usually engaged, sometimes progressive, and occasionally offensive perspectives of those who populate the pages of this history to create the stage upon which he can present a meditation on the historical development of American character. In a manner as reasoned as that of John C. Calhoun in his *Disquisition on Government*, Brown suggests that the Civil War was, in effect, larger than the history Americans understood, but every bit as large as the history they had both created and repressed. And now this maturing history was pressing on the nation, and the various perspectives Brown includes in his documentary study indicate how variously prepared or unprepared most white Americans were to rise to the character demanded by the world emerging from the conflicts involved in and highlighted by the war.

The Negro in the American Rebellion is an important work of history not in spite of its method but because of it. Certainly, it is important to give the book its due for the argument it presents and the history it documents. As John David Smith observes, "Brown's *The Negro in the American Rebellion* nevertheless has real value as 'history'—as history with a purpose. It provided a window into the coming of the war, identified blacks as historical actors in the Civil War, honored their manhood, analyzed the meaning of emancipation, and signaled a call to arms against the neo-slavery of Presidential Reconstruction and the North's ongoing racial proscription" (xxxvii). It is arguably true as well, as Wilson Jeremiah Moses has observed, that Brown is more successful at capturing the experience of African Americans "than anything attempted by a trained historian for another ninety years."[19] Certainly, one cannot miss the force of these achievements when reading this work, but one should not undervalue Brown's method when evaluating this book. This is not to say that Brown's method is a radical departure for his time, however, since the abolitionist press regularly published pieces from other newspapers and other sources, frequently without comment, that represented a broad range of views. Locating oneself with and against such a variety of views was part of the regular discipline of any newspaper reader of the time, and Brown was a devoted student of and contributor to the abolitionist press. Brown simply adopts that method for the purposes of history, and presents a history much as an abolitionist editor might present the news and views of the day—with an array of voices and perspectives, but with a clear editorial focus to guide the way.

The Negro in the American Rebellion captures the immediacy of the war, its complex representation in the press, while also pressing for a vision of history capable of accounting for all of the views represented along the way, an ideal of character against which all of the historical actors in the book might be measured. In his 1861 address to the New Jersey Senate, on his inaugural journey to the White House, Abraham Lincoln exemplified the force of this understanding of American history. "I am exceedingly anxious that this Union, the Constitution, and the liberties of the people shall be perpetuated," he stated, "in accordance with the original idea for which that struggle was made, and I shall be most happy indeed if I shall be an humble instrument in the hands of the Almighty, and of this, his almost chosen people, for perpetuating the object of that great struggle."[20] Brown tells the story of this "almost chosen people," linking their fortune to the idea that remains beyond them, but one that might be fulfilled if the Civil War could lead to a different role for African Americans in the national historical story. In his remarks, Lincoln located the inspiration for his national faith in "Weem's Life of Washington," a good reminder that objective history isn't always the history that captures and guides the national imagination. I am not suggesting that Brown was trying to cast himself as a black Parson Weems, but neither was he preparing for the day when he might apply for membership in the American Historical Association (formed in 1884). Rather, he was trying to both represent and guide history, a task that he, like George Bancroft, Henry Adams, and many lesser lights, understood to be the historian's fundamental role. And he did so by way of a method that was as conflicted, complex, and finally as promising as African Americans of the time understood the United States to be. He didn't just represent history; he reenacted it, and there is still much to learn from his method as well as his matter.

NOTES

1. John David Smith, introduction to *The Negro in the American Rebellion: His Heroism and His Fidelity*, by William Wells Brown (1867; repr., Athens: Ohio University Press, 2003), xv, hereafter documented parenthetically.

2. Charles W. Chesnutt, *The Journals of Charles W. Chesnutt*, ed. Richard Brodhead (Durham: Duke University Press, 1993), 164.

3. William Edward Farrison, *William Wells Brown: Author and Reformer* (Chicago: University of Chicago Press, 1969), 372.

4. Thomas J. Ward, review of *The Negro in the American Rebellion: His Heroism and His Fidelity*, by William Wells Brown (1867; repr., Athens: Ohio University Press, 2003), *H-Civil War*, June 2005, H-Net Reviews, http://www.h-net.org/reviews/showrev.php?id=10618, hereafter documented parenthetically.

5. Trish Loughran, *The Republic in Print: Print Culture in the Age of U.S. Nation Building, 1770–1870* (New York: Columbia University Press, 2009), 404–25.

6. George W. Williams, *History of the Negro Race in America from 1619 to 1880. Negroes as Slaves, as Soldiers, and as Citizens; Together with a Preliminary Consideration of Unity of the Human Family, an Historical Sketch of Africa, and an Account of the Negro Governments of Sierra Leone and Liberia*, 2 vols. (1883; repr., Salem, N.H.: Ayer, 1989), 1:vii, hereafter documented parenthetically.

7. Mark M. Smith, *How Race Is Made: Slavery, Segregation, and the Senses* (Chapel Hill: University of North Carolina Press, 2006), 47. I am drawing here from my broader discussion of Williams, race, and African American writing in *Chaotic Justice: Rethinking African American Literary History* (Chapel Hill: University of North Carolina Press, 2009); see especially 196–215.

8. William Wells Brown, *The Negro in the American Rebellion: His Heroism and His Fidelity* (1867; reprint., Athens: Ohio University Press, 2003), 33, hereafter documented parenthetically.

9. On race as a racial palimpsest, see Matthew Frye Jacobson, *Whiteness of a Different Color: European Immigrants and the Alchemy of Race* (Cambridge: Harvard University Press, 1998), 142. See also my discussion of Jacobson's approach in *Chaotic Justice*, 201–2.

10. David W. Blight, *Race and Reunion: The Civil War in American Memory* (Cambridge, Mass.: Belknap, 2001), 139.

11. Alice Fahs, *The Imagined Civil War: Popular Literature of the North and South, 1861–1865* (Chapel Hill: University of North Carolina Press, 2001), 162, hereafter documented parenthetically.

12. Smith, *How Race Is Made*, 47.

13. "To Our Patrons," *Freedom's Journal*, March 16, 1827.

14. Howard Homan Bell, ed., *Proceedings of the Colored National Convention, Held in Rochester, July 6th, 7th and 8th, 1853*, in *Minutes and Proceedings of the National Negro Conventions, 1830–1864* (New York: Arno Press and The New York Times, 1969), 16–17.

15. Anna Julia Cooper, *A Voice from the South by a Black Woman of the South* (New York: Oxford University Press, 1988), 186–87.

16. John Ernest, *Resistance and Reformation in Nineteenth-Century African-American Literature: Brown, Wilson, Jacobs, Delany, Douglass, and Harper* (Jackson: University Press of Mississippi, 1995), 23, hereafter documented parenthetically.

17. Douglas L. Mitchell, *A Disturbing and Alien Memory: Southern Novelists Writing History* (Baton Rouge: Louisiana State University Press, 2008), 110.

18. Blight, *Race and Reunion*, 139.

19. Quoted in Smith, introduction, xxxvii.

20. Abraham Lincoln, *Collected Works*, ed. Marion Delores Pratt and Lloyd A. Dunlap (Springfield, Ill.: The Abraham Lincoln Association, 1953), 4:236.

"Naked Genius"
The Civil War Poems of George Moses Horton

FAITH BARRETT

In the summer of 1865, a previously enslaved African American named George Moses Horton traveled for three months with the Ninth Michigan Cavalry as the Union army secured North Carolina. It was probably during this time that Horton wrote a poem entitled "The Obstructions of Genius," reflecting on the obstacles that had limited his career as a poet. Reminding readers of Horton's regional fame as the "black bard of North Carolina," the opening stanza suggests that the poet has been treated with mistrust by both blacks and whites:

> I am surveyed by envy's eye.
> By white and colored all the same,
> Which oft draws out a secret sigh,
> To feel the ills that bother fame.[1]

Having reminded readers of Horton's success, however, the second stanza goes on to lament the many difficulties that have thwarted his career:

> Throughout my life I've tried the path,
> Which seemed as leading out of gloom,
> Beneath my feet still kindled wrath,
> Genius seemed leading to a tomb. (157)

Laden with mixed metaphors, this stanza surely evokes the mixture of frustration, anger, and pride that Horton must have felt as he looked back on a writing career that had spanned more than three decades but had never enabled him to purchase his freedom.

Placed as the final poem in Horton's 1865 collection, "The Obstructions of Genius" strikes not a celebratory or conciliatory tone but rather a tone of brooding lament. In its final stanza, the poem calls on readers to forget—for all eternity—the violence of slavery:

> Let us the evil now forget,
>   Which darkened the Columbian shore,
> Till sun shall fail to rise and set,
>   And slavery's cries are heard no more. (158)

In an Isaac Watts hymn that was widely sung in the nineteenth century, "From all that dwell below the skies," the speaker calls on humanity to sing God's praises, until that "praise shall sound from shore to shore," a state of collective exultation marked by the end of earth-bound temporality: "till suns shall rise and set no more."[2] Though it faintly echoes Watts's utopian imagery of a future union with God, Horton's final stanza calls not for a celebration but rather for a collective state of forgetting, one that will surely be easier for whites than for blacks to achieve. Implicitly underlining the gulf that divides white and black memories of slavery, this final stanza seems also to express the speaker's personal despair and longing for death. Like other poems in Horton's 1865 collection, "The Obstructions of Genius" shows evidence of having been written in haste, relying on a simple alternating rhyme scheme and shifting in different metaphoric and argumentative directions from one stanza to the next. The poem foregrounds Horton's use of a patchwork of imitative techniques, echoing the rhetorics of romanticism and abolition, as well as Protestant hymns and popular songs. Yet "The Obstructions of Genius" is also a representative example of what makes Horton's Civil War collection so rich for further study.

As I will go on to suggest, Horton's commitment to imitation is a strategic choice, one that enables him to address a range of different audiences, including both southerners and northerners. Like many nineteenth-century Americans, both white and black, for whom education was a hard-won privilege, Horton used his skill at imitating poetic conventions to write his way toward literary recognition, hoping to demonstrate not only that he was *literate*, but also that he was a *man of letters*. As Emerson notes, the man of letters displays his skill both as a writer and as a reader of others' works. In "Quotation and Originality," Emerson argues that "we are as much informed of a writer's genius by what he selects as by what he originates."[3] Echoing this conflicted account of the relationship between imitation and originality, Horton's Civil War collection proposes an alternative model for "genius," one that echoes the conventions of the English poetic tradition all the while making a space for an African American voice within southern literature.[4]

After situating Horton in the context of Chapel Hill and the cultures of nineteenth-century poetry, this essay will go on to consider the larger project of Horton's Civil War collection, before turning to a group of poems in which Horton speaks to and for soldiers. Through these readings, I will argue that Horton constructs his own authority to speak by ventriloquizing the voices of Civil War soldiers and grieving Americans. In his poems Horton defuses the threat of his literary mastery by reiterating poetic conventions; yet because these conventions allow him to foreground literary style, he can also slip double meanings into the content, thereby retaining traces of the black speaker's voice. Because of their seeming transparency, Horton's poems are not well suited to New Critical methods of close reading; when combined with analysis of the discursive contexts in which Horton lived and wrote, however, careful attention to the poems' rhetorical and formal strategies underlines both their multiple layers of meaning and the skill with which Horton addressed different constituencies of white readers. In their accessibility and their eclectic aesthetic commitments, Horton's poems raise important questions about the cultural functions of poetry, the particular appeal of this genre for newly literate and black writers, and the pathways to recognition and publication for regionally known poets in the nineteenth century.

George Moses Horton in Chapel Hill

A brief account of Horton's remarkable life will help to contextualize my analysis. Born into slavery near the end of the eighteenth century, he began walking to Chapel Hill from his master's farm on the weekends while still a young man. Initially, he sold fruit, ran errands, and gave speeches for the young white male students. When he met with particular success composing love poems for his clients, he began working mainly as a poet-for-hire, eventually persuading his master to let him buy his own time. So skillful was Horton at this work that he would remain in Chapel Hill from the 1830s until the Civil War. During the intervening decades, he had attempted unsuccessfully to raise funds to buy his freedom; he had also published two collections of poetry and established a regional reputation as a poet, having seen his poems appear in the *Chapel Hill Gazette* and the *Raleigh Register*, as well as the *Southern Literary Messenger*. Though Horton never succeeded in buying his own freedom, he was clearly very skillful at winning the support of white sponsors.[5]

In April of 1865, when the Ninth Michigan Cavalry arrived in North Carolina, Horton became friendly with the men of the unit, traveling with them until late July, when the soldiers were released from duty.[6] During this time, he supported himself in part by writing love poems for the wives and sweethearts of these soldiers. He also wrote a third collection of poems, *Naked Genius*, which was published late in the summer of 1865 under the sponsorship of Colonel William Banks of the Ninth Michigan.

Cultures of Poetry in
Nineteenth-Century America

In order to understand Horton's turn toward verse, it is essential that we situate his work in the rich and varied cultures of nineteenth-century American poetry. The rise of sectional tensions between North and South in the mid-nineteenth century coincided, for many whites, with increasing class mobility and rising rates of literacy, particularly in the North. This rise in literacy rates shaped poetry's cultural status in several ways, ensuring its centrality to political discourses throughout the Civil War era. First, poetry became ubiquitous, appearing not only in books, but also in the more affordable and more portable media of newspapers, magazines, pamphlets, and broadsides. Second, the dramatic increase in the number of newspapers and magazines being published brought poetry to new and expanding audiences. In the absence of copyright law, poetry was a frequent choice for reprinting. Enhancing its speed of circulation still further, poetry had particularly close ties with popular song. Finally, poetry was central to the classroom, routinely performed at school exhibitions, and featured prominently in reading primers and spellers. Poetry was also read and recited at church, civic, and political gatherings, as well as around the family hearth. While Horton could not have attended school, he may well have found a means of access to the kinds of primers and readers that white schoolchildren used. On the many trips he made to Chapel Hill as a young man, he would certainly have heard poetry read and recited. During the years that he worked as a poet-for-hire in Chapel Hill, Horton's paying customers provided him with many books of poetry, including works by Homer, Virgil, Milton, Shakespeare, and Byron, among others.[7] From the late 1820s onward, his deft use of the conventions of love poetry suggests that he was well read in the poetry of the eighteenth and nineteenth centuries.

As Horton's life story suggests, many self-educated writers, both black and white, were drawn to poetry because learning to read had brought them into regular contact with rhymed, metrical language. Moreover, poetry would have been particularly accessible to writers who were not born into literate circles because of the ways that it circulated in both oral and written forms. During this same era, the work of the Ploughman Poet Robert Burns met with wide acclaim across the English-speaking world, suggesting that farmer-poets might be well placed to speak for the experience of rural working people. Men whose economic backgrounds or geographic locations kept them from formal schooling—the young Abraham Lincoln, for example—taught themselves to read and write poetry in order to demonstrate their membership in the cohort of educated men.[8] As a result of this confluence of developments, the genre of poetry became extraordinarily capacious in terms of the content and the stylistic commitments it could embrace. Poetry was at once the province of philosophers and learned men and the genre that tripped from the tongue of every schoolchild. Rhymed metrical verse was in effect an alternative language, one that many nineteenth-century readers and writers learned to speak and write. During the Civil War, the centrality of poetry to the political conversation led to an extraordinary outpouring of poetic writing by men and women from all walks of life.[9]

For an African American writer, poetry might have had particular appeal because of its close relationship to song. Ivy Wilson and Mary Louise Kete both emphasize the strong ties between song and poetry in black culture.[10] Moreover, Max Cavitch notes that "poetry—sung, chanted, or spoken—was ... often the only resource slaves had for the palliation of monotony—the monotony of physical work."[11] As Christopher Hager points out in his study of newly literate blacks, Horton composed his first poems in his head while pushing a plough for his master.[12] Horton's strong reliance on meter and rhyme throughout his career was likely shaped by this early practice of oral composition. Moreover, for African American writers, the turn toward poetry was a particularly ambitious choice, a means of refuting claims made by Jefferson, among others, that the genre was beyond the reach of blacks: "Among the blacks is misery enough, God knows, but no poetry."[13]

While mid-twentieth-century critics generally dismissed Horton's work as imitative, the current reassessment of nineteenth-century poetry reminds us that nineteenth-century readers valued a poet's fidelity to literary conventions as much or even more than they valued originality. Self-educated writers had a particular investment in demonstrating their mastery of poetic conventions, and in a culture where readers encountered poetry on a daily basis, competence with those conventions had considerable value. Several recent analyses offer nuanced frameworks for reading the rhetoric of imitation in the poetry of this period. Eliza Richards's groundbreaking study of the women poets in Poe's circle considers how women writers negotiate their relationship to the work of male models, calibrating a careful balance between mimicry and originality; still other studies have considered how both male and women poets use facility at following poetic conventions as a means of achieving the professional status of authorship.[14] Enslaved black writers would find imitation to be a particularly productive means of balancing deference to whites with indirect forms of protest and self-expression. In a foundational text of African American studies, Henry Louis Gates argues that black writers draw on a range of imitative and double-voicing techniques, using intertextual response to create a "hidden polemic" within their writings.[15] Because Horton's cultural position makes explicit parody risky, he typically situates his poems between the poles of critique and homage, threading moments of polemic into poems that display deference, either through conventional thematic content or through conventional poetic forms.

The Project of Naked Genius

The critical dismissal of Horton's work in the twentieth century was likely also shaped by the eclectic range of conventions he worked with across his three collections. And no collection is more eclectic than his Civil War book, *Naked Genius*. In this collection, Horton's imitative strategies embrace a range of poetic traditions, as he responds to popular songs and hymns as well as love poetry, classical war poetry, and the elegy. Befriended by a group of Union soldiers, Horton writes many poems that are well suited for a military audience, and a Union audience in particular: he includes victory marches for the Union, elegies for Union generals, elegies for Lincoln, first-person song-poems in which the soldier laments his separation from home, sentimental pieces in which a soldier addresses his absent family, high-literary responses to the terrors of war, and occasional poems about specific incidents from the summer he spent with the Michigan cavalry. Horton describes with horror the devastation wrought by the war, and he also frequently holds white southerners accountable for their fate. Yet while his immediate audience of Union soldiers is evident in many aspects of this collection, Horton also includes love poems, romantic lyrics about nature, temperance poems, laments about the trials of an unhappy marriage, elegies for female relatives, abolitionist poems, and animal ballads, a list that makes clear he wanted to write a book that would do more than just respond to the war. Indeed the eclectic range of the volume suggests that Horton also hoped to reach white southerners who knew of his work. This seemingly contradictory embrace of both northern and southern white audiences underlines the complex layering of voices that Horton achieves in this collection. Moreover, throughout *Naked Genius*, Horton orders poems in the volume in such a way as to set up implicit echoes among the different thematic groups. For example, poems that protest the frustrations of marriage or romantic love gone sour are interspersed among poems that lament the dividing of the nation; the broken marriage thus becomes for Horton a metaphor for the broken nation.

In *Naked Genius*, Horton includes a staggering ninety new poems, as well as an additional forty poems reprinted from his 1845 collection *Poetical Works*. Many of the new poems were clearly written around the war's end, though some may predate the war. In his late sixties at the time, Horton must have had to work diligently to assemble a third collection while traveling.[16] As a formerly enslaved African American man writing in his late sixties about the mixture of joy, relief, and sorrow he feels at the war's end, Horton's emotional perspective on the conflict is both powerful and distinctive. No longer a slave, not a soldier, not a northerner, and yet also not a Confederate southerner, Horton nonetheless speaks to and for these different constituencies. Known as a performer of speeches and perhaps also his poems in Chapel Hill, Horton likely performed his poems while traveling with the Ninth Michigan. Horton's poems thus trade on their own speakerliness, reminding readers of the voice of the writer, even as that writer also uses poetic conventions as a partial mask for his own identity as a once-enslaved black man.

Evidence suggests that Horton left North Carolina for Philadelphia sometime in 1866, and many of the poems in *Naked Genius* already register sorrow at parting from one's homeland. As Sherman notes, the powerful mix of emotions Horton must have felt during his travels with the Ninth Michigan is reflected in the collection's many poems about home and homesickness.[17] These evocations of home would surely have resonated with many white readers, including both northern soldiers and the many southerners who were displaced by the war. More powerfully still, Horton also gives dignified voice to the experience of the many southern blacks—himself included—who struggled with poverty and displacement after emancipation.

Horton calls his third collection *Naked Genius*, underlining that the black writer too can be inspired by the muses. In the second poem in the collection, "George Moses Horton Myself," Horton's speaker declares: "My genius from a boy, / Has fluttered like a bird within my heart" (11). Yet by using the epithet white southerners used for all black males regardless of their age, "boy," these lines point toward the ways that the exercise of that genius has been severely curtailed in the slave-holding South. By titling this collection *Naked Genius*, Horton shows an acute awareness of the complexity of his relationship to white audiences. "Naked" implies that the poet bares his soul, but Horton relies on a careful layering of speakers' voices to elide—for the most part—the specificity of his own experience as a once-enslaved black man. Horton uses the figure of "genius" to emphasize his exceptional gifts, but he also works within recognized poetic conventions—the soldier-elegy, the marching song, the poem about a specific battle or wartime event—displaying his mastery of these antecedents. With inspiration as a foundation and poetic convention as a guide, the "genius" can claim the authority to write about war, mortality, and the long view of human history. Such "genius" can also claim the authority to speak to and for soldiers, as I will suggest in reading a group of Horton's poems.

Reconciling Soldiers

In "Like Brothers We Meet," dedicated to "the Federal and late Confederate soldiers," Horton seeks to bridge the gap between North and South by imagining reconciliation between the two armies (47). The poem underlines two of Horton's goals for this collection: he writes to contribute to national reunification, and he writes with the hope that he might expand his reading audience. Having worked for most of his life in Chapel Hill, Horton would have known many men who fought for the Confederacy. In "Like Brothers We Meet," Horton uses a paternal and didactic tone, one that is softened both by his age—Horton was in his late sixties at the war's end—and by his judicious choice of a first-person plural speaker:

> Like heart-loving brothers we meet,
> And still the loud thunders of strife,
> The blaze of fraternity kindles most sweet,
> There's nothing more pleasing in life. (47)

While this poem explicitly addresses soldiers, many poems in the volume offer advice to young men in general and college students in particular, a rhetorical stance that Horton had fine-tuned over the course of his many years of work at the university. In "Like Brothers We Meet," Horton layers a call for soldierly reconciliation onto his many exhortations to young men to live upright and virtuous lives.

The poem offers a varied array of images in support of its argument for reconciliation, with nature and familial metaphors dominating. While no explicit mention is made of slavery, the second stanza suggests that greater harmony between northern and southern "brothers" will lead to better living conditions for the poor. These lines also imply that national reconciliation will lead to better treatment for freed slaves:

> The black cloud of faction retreats,
> The poor is no longer depressed,
> See those once discarded resuming their seats,
> The lost strangers soon will find rest. (47)

In these lines, Horton sidesteps explicit mention of slavery, though the "black cloud of faction" surely suggests the slavery debate; moreover, the phrase "lost strangers" evokes freed slaves as much as it does soldiers who have been freed from their military obligations. The image of "those once discarded resuming their seats" suggests the possibility of a familial table where all will be welcome. Indeed, one of the most powerful features of this volume is its implicit linking of the position of the freed slave with that of the soldier released from duty: both will need to establish a new identity and new ways of living in the aftermath of the war and emancipation. Here and elsewhere in the volume, Horton's careful layering of the collective "we" of soldiers' voices onto subtle traces of the solitary "I" of the black-poet speaker strongly suggests this possibility. Read in relation to the poem's second stanza, when the first stanza declares "Like heart-loving brothers we meet," this declaration seems to call not only for national harmony but also for interracial harmony. The boldness of this implicit call for interracial harmony is contained in part by the poem's formal regularity.

As this second stanza already suggests, however, even as the poem calls for reconciliation, the speaker admits that what he is envisioning is a utopia:

> Hang closely together like friends,
> By peace-killing foes never driven,
> The storm of commotion eternally ends,
> And earth will soon turn into Heaven. (47)

Observing that "the storm of commotion eternally ends," the speaker implies a weary awareness of the cycles of war and peace throughout history. And while this final stanza imitates the millennial rhetoric so common during the Civil War, in this case, that millennial imagery underlines the vast distance that separates the reunited nation from the kingdom of Heaven. Ultimately, what is at stake in this poem is Horton's utopian "we," a pronoun that both does and does not include the voices of emancipated slaves. While Horton's "we" seems mainly to include the collective of Union and Confederate soldiers, the poet's life story suggests the possibility of including emancipated slaves as well. The suggestion of the speaker as a newly freed slave remains muted, however, broadening the poem's potential appeal among white readers not sympathetic to abolition.

Horton's formal choices in this poem are conventional ones: the poem follows a regular metrical pattern of alternating iambs and anapests—a lively and upbeat galloping meter—and alternating rhyme, which he frequently chooses. Because of the poem's meter, it is easy to imagine it being sung or performed. Both the regularity of the form and the galloping meter imitate countless popular songs of the era, though the anapestic pattern is less frequently seen in songs than two-syllable patterns. Yet if Horton's formal choices are conventional, his approach to the content is not: few poets or lyricists writing popular songs chose to call for reconciliation in pieces written immediately after the war's end. While poets like Whitman and Melville might grapple with the moral complexities of reconciliation between North and South in the more literary poems they published in book form, Horton here uses a popular form to contain political content not usually encountered in this medium. While the defeat of the South necessarily limited the printing of sheet music in southern cities, northern presses churned out popular songs for a pro-Union public eager to celebrate the war's end. In songs like "Sherman's March to the Sea," with lyrics by Lieutenant S. H. M. Byers, Union victories were celebrated in wholly partisan fashion:

> Then sang we a song for our chieftain
> That echoed o'er river and lea
> And the stars in our banner shone brighter
> When Sherman marched down to the sea.[18]

Even in northern songs where the central theme was celebration of the peace, Lincoln's assassination made partisan pro-Union sentiments all but unavoidable. In "Peace: National Hymn in the Form of a March," the original celebratory lyrics by "Miss Fay" were published with an added set of new lyrics by W. J. Hoppin to acknowledge the tragedy of Lincoln's assassination. Though Miss Fay's lyrics make reference to the Union victory, their larger emphasis is on peace and national reconciliation: "Throughout the land, let all rejoice Once more shall peace and plenty reign / Sing with a Nation's heart and voice Glory in the Highest Good will toward all men!" In Hoppin's added lyrics, however, cannons mark what is emphatically presented as a Union triumph: "Let the bells ring out the tidings, / Let the joyful cannon roar; / Truth and Right shall win the battle, / Peace and Union reign once more!"[19] Lacking a victory to celebrate, published southern songs tended to lament the devastation of southern landscapes and the deaths of Confederate soldiers, often using sentimental stances as a placeholder for the kind of angry partisan rhetoric that would have been too politically risky in 1865 or 1866. In "Like Brothers We Meet," Horton controls the political risks of his message of reconciliation by couching that message in a regular poetic form. It is Horton's position as a previously enslaved black southerner that allows him to articulate this plainspoken call for reconciliation between North and South. He likely also relied on the strength of his personal ties with the men of the Ninth Michigan and with young Confederate soldiers from Chapel Hill in presenting this argument for peace and reunion between the two regions.

The Execution of Private Henry Anderson

While "Like Brothers We Meet" offers a utopian vision of peace and reunion, in many other poems in *Naked Genius*, Horton seems far more skeptical about the future of the nation. In a group of three interconnected pieces, Horton meditates on a specific incident that took place during his travels with the Ninth Michigan, namely the execution of a Union soldier, Private Henry Anderson, who was convicted of murder. While the group of three opens with an occasional poem that offers details about Anderson's conviction and execution, the two poems that follow implicitly take the occasion of the execution as an impetus for reflection on the moral complexities of guilt and innocence. In the first poem, "Execution of Private Henry Anderson," Horton uses iambic pentameter in six-line stanzas to add a rhythmic heft to his description of the scene:

> This verse is plain, that all may understand,
> The scene is solemn and expressly grand;
> The must'ring concourse formed in grand array,
> Betrayed the fate of the expiring day;
> Gazing spectators seemed completely dumb,
> Beneath the sound of bugle and the drum. (51)

The stanza makes clear how the formal ceremony preceding the execution moves all onlookers to a tense silence. The regularity of Horton's meter and rhyme scheme reinforces the drum's steady beating.

In stanzas 4 through 6, the second half of the poem, Horton explains Anderson's crime and meditates on the punishment and suffering that must follow such an action:

> This seems to bear the mark, tho' justly done,
> A case that every sober man may shun;
> 'Twas for the deed of open homicide,
> This guilty malefactor fell and died.
> See well arrayed the attentive squadrons stand,
> Thus to discharge their guns at one command;
> Till pointing at one mark the shaft of death,
> He breaths at last his one decisive breath.
>
> It is, indeed, a sad infernal crime
> To one's own self, thus hurried out of time;
> He introduces first the murderous strife,
> By his own hand he spurns away his life!
> How many creatures thus have fell,
> Imbibing nectar from the bowls of hell!
>
> Inspiring depredations all the night,
> And thus betrayed the death at morning light;
> Thus flies the deadly shaft without control—
> He fell upon his coffin, O, my soul!
> Let all that live the scene appall—
> He dies! no more to live at all, at all! (52)

Stanza 4 uses the present tense to recreate the scene of the execution—"See well arrayed the attentive squadrons stand"—before culminating in a present-tense description of Anderson's death: "He breaths [*sic*] at last his one decisive breath." Stanza 5 meditates on the consequences of such a crime in the afterlife, and stanza 6 builds to a climax whose drama is only heightened by the plainspoken language Horton here uses. Returning one more time to the present-tense moment of Anderson's death, the poem concludes: "He dies! no more to live at all, at all!" While Horton probably had only limited opportunities to observe wartime fighting, in witnessing this execution, his speaker observes firsthand the deadly force both of military justice and of military firepower. While his poems responding to the war typically evoke combat in more general or literary gestures (as in "The Spectator of the Battle of Belmont," for example), the plainspoken specificity of this piece underlines the contrast between what he could and could not witness of the war as a slave.

What begins as a meditation on crime and punishment in this first poem develops into a meditation on mortality and isolation in the second poem Horton writes in response to the same events, "A Dirge on the Same." While the first poem makes clear Horton's moral condemnation of the crime, the second poem imagines the inner anguish of the condemned man in the first person, representing him as a solitary figure wracked by fear and pain. The poem begins:

> Look! my soul, O, look and wonder!
> Tears distil from every eye;
> Soul and body torn asunder—
> What a dreadful death I die!
>
> Hark! the knell of death is tolling!
> Just before me lies the grave!
> For the pain there's no controlling—
> Shoot! I fall! no longer brave! (53)

In a particularly dramatic moment, the second stanza of "Dirge" closes by reminding readers of Anderson's former occupation as a soldier, as he declares he is "no longer brave." The poem thus begins to reflect on the moral ambiguity of executing a soldier for murder when other forms of killing in contexts sanctioned by the military would have instead led to his being celebrated for bravery.

The poem's fifth stanza notes that Anderson's crime has deprived him of the right to be defended—or even mourned—by family members:

> Void of father or of mother
> In this land, to take my part;
> Void of sister or a brother
> To appease my broken heart. (53)

By emphasizing Anderson's separation from his family, this quatrain of "Dirge on the Same" also offers a subtle but insistent reminder of the ways that slavery breaks apart families. Indeed Horton's speaker's empathy for Anderson seems in part to be empathy with his isolated condition: his crime has deprived him of the right to any comfort or attempt at defense by his family. The poem concludes with a partisan image that suggests that Anderson will find himself surrounded by a host of his former enemies when he descends to hell:

> Hark! I hear the imperial rebels
>   Rattling in accursed chains;
> Crowded by a group of devils
>   Wailing in eternal pain!

Thus while the poem's second stanza reminds us of the moral complexity of the military executing one of its own soldiers for murder, the poem's remaining stanzas faintly evoke slavery and then remind readers of the partisan divide that led to the war in the first place, a divide that the poem suggests will persist in the afterlife. Beneath its smooth formal surface, the poem taps into a range of distinct—even conflicting—moral issues, underlining the complexity of this tangle. And in reminding readers of the speed with which justice can be dealt out by the military, the poem perhaps begins to question the moral authority that underpins such power over life.

The third poem in this sequence amplifies still further this ambivalent perspective on Anderson's execution, this time suggesting that those who are quick to condemn are often stained by guilt themselves. While the poem makes no explicit reference to Anderson's conviction or execution, its placement immediately after the two preceding pieces strongly suggests the possibility of reading the three together. The central message of "The Guilty Judge" is that anyone who assumes the authority to judge others would do well to examine his own conscience, for moral rectitude may well be a sign of hidden guilt. The somewhat tangled phrasing suggests that Horton may have written the poem in haste, yet more importantly, shifts and contradictions in the phrasing also register the many layers of Horton's thinking about the powers of the judiciary in particular and the state in general. The first stanza reminds readers that there are sinners who go unpunished, suggesting that some might even accuse others of crimes they themselves committed:

> That thoughtless soul is hard to find,
>   Not guilty of some dirty plan,
> Utters the charge, yet breaks behind—
>   Thou art the man!

Stanza 5 explains how one accuser can fan the flames of suspicion, bringing out a whole multitude of accusers:

> Some coward may lend the deed a wing
> That cruel blaze of guilt to fan;
> To them the sounding wheel distinct—
> Thou art the man!

The "wheel" suggests the speed with which a rumor can turn from suspicion into accusation, as well as the turning of the Wheel of Fortune. Throughout the poem, Horton uses hypnotic repetition of "Thou art the man!" to suggest how fine the line is that separates the guilty from the innocent. The refrain also underlines how quickly a man's life might be derailed by a false accusation. Moreover, reiteration of the refrain perhaps also underlines the contrast between the condition of being "a man," even an accused or guilty man, and the condition of being a slave. As an emancipated slave, Horton would have been a particularly keen observer of the ways that punishment might be arbitrarily dealt out to blacks by whites. In this group of three poems, Horton offers Anderson as an object for his readers' moral contemplation; moving beyond merely condemning Anderson's crime, Horton takes the private's execution as an occasion for an ambitious meditation on the dynamic relationship between military and judicial power, and between accusation and guilt. Read as a group, the three poems suggest that both the state and the judiciary dispossess men of their rights and that those who hold judicial power often use such powers to protect themselves. The relationships among the three poems suggest both the strength of Horton's empathy with the executed man and his deeply felt skepticism about the power structures of the military and the state.

Closing Gestures

Given how varied *Naked Genius* is, it is not surprising that Horton elects to offer multiple gestures of argumentative closure in the final poems in the sequence. From the several closing gestures Horton includes, I want to focus on just two, considering the ways that Horton says farewell both to the men of the Ninth Michigan and to his broader readership. In "At Leaving Camp," he uses plain-spoken language and a simple meter to imagine the disorientation and melancholy of soldiers now released from their military obligations. In "The Obstructions of Genius," he uses the first person to lament bitterly the ways that slavery has limited his work as a poet. Echoes between the two pieces reiterate the parallels between the situation of the released soldier and that of the emancipated slave.

"At Leaving Camp" is just one of Horton's many responses to the disbanding of the Union and Confederate armies. Both "The Soldier on His Way Home" and "The Soldier at Home" use short lines and regular meter to strike a celebratory, if measured tone in response to the soldiers' dismissal, and both of these poems close with positive images of harmony. In "At Leaving Camp," however, Horton's speaker expresses a more mixed set of emotions, suggesting that dismissed soldiers—and emancipated slaves—may share a sense of melancholy and identity confusion in the war's aftermath. The poem opens with a quatrain that suggests that the natural world will be left in peace with the departure of the noisy camp and its crew:

> The ramping of the noisy camp,
>   Beneath the sky serene;
> Like evening with a starlight lamp,
>   It soon will close the scene. (137)

As further stanzas unfold, however, the speaker suggests that the natural surroundings will be left both blighted and deprived of their purpose once the soldiers depart:

> These fields all fenceless void of flowers,
>   Will soon be left in shame;
> To fade with all the falling showers,
>   Whence none its loss reclaimed.

Moving away from these romantic images, stanzas 7 through 9 evoke a life of hard wandering, the life Horton himself has been living for the past three months, and the life he sees in his future as well:

> We've wandered thus from place to place,
>   On life's precarious way;
> Until you run life's transient race,
>   And camp beyond the grave.
>
> Where'er we lodged, we there must stay,
>   Forever hence to dwell;
> Hence never to be called away,
>   From heaven or from hell.
>
> Still slow, we move from place to place,
>   Like bees from flower to flower;
> Or faithful saints from grace to grace,
>   Move by superior power.

In this group of quatrains, Horton's imagery oscillates uncomfortably between wandering and settling, as the many changes of metaphor and shifts in grammatical structure make clear. The final stanza suggests that some provisional closure may be possible:

> But soon we trust to move our last,
>   No more the States to roam;
> When the decision will be past,
>   And all arrive at home. (138)

But in view of the several stanzas' worth of oscillation that precedes this claim, it is difficult to imagine the speaker settling into a "home." Though Horton likely suffered from fatigue and homesickness during his travels with the Ninth Michigan, his interlude of travel with them had allowed him to resume his work as a poet-for-hire, and it also brought him Colonel William Banks's invaluable sponsorship for his third collection. Thus, his time with the Ninth Michigan offered him both a new audience and a new sense of purpose as a writer. The disbanding of the Union army leaves Horton without an immediate means of supporting himself, however; "At Leaving Camp" suggests that the disbanding of the army shook Horton's confidence that he would continue to find audiences for his poetry.

Horton reiterates these concerns in the more personal and more explicit poem with which he ends the collection, "The Obstructions of Genius." In this piece, the speaker laments the many obstacles that have thwarted both his path to freedom and his creative ambitions. While the first stanza suggests that Horton's reputation as a poet has been extensive enough to provoke jealousy, the second stanza makes clear that Horton's poetic "genius" never allowed him to escape the bonds of slavery:

> I am surveyed by envy's eye.
>   By white and colored all the same,
> Which oft draws out a secret sigh,
>   To feel the ills that bother fame.
>
> Throughout my life I've tried the path
>   Which seemed as leading out of gloom,
> Beneath my feet still kindled wrath,
>   Genius seemed leading to a tomb. (157)

In these two stanzas, Horton obliquely evokes the paradox of his position: that his work as a poet always depended on his status as an exception, a poetic "genius" who rose above the ranks of enslaved black men around him. Far from setting him free, "genius" thus led him only to the "tomb" of continuing enslavement. In stanza 4, he laments the failure of white supporters and sponsors to intervene in any way in his condition:

> Has philanthropic vigor slept,
> So long in cells of disregard,
> While genius in his fetters wept,
> Devoid of favors or reward. (157)

Though the poem closes with the speaker enjoining his readers "Let us the evil now forget" until "slavery's cries are heard no more," this one-stanza gesture of closure is undermined by the six stanzas of lament, protest, and frustration that precede it. This is a dark and despairing finish to the collection, its despair only heightened by the strong contrast with the exclamatory energy of the advertising page that immediately follows it in *Naked Genius*.[20] Hoping to recruit agents to sell the collection, the advertisement calls on "energetic young men"—particularly disabled veterans—who want to "build up a fortune for themselves" to contact William Banks (159). It insists that "THE BLACK POET will be read with admiration and wonder by all" (159). The final poem in the collection belies this advertising confidence, however. Horton closes the volume by figuring himself as "genius in fetters," a "genius" headed toward the tomb (157). The nakedness that Horton shows us in "The Obstructions of Genius" is the embittered weariness of a seventy-year-old man who had spent his life trying to end his enslavement and trying against all odds to pursue his vocation as a poet.

As "The Obstructions of Genius" makes clear, Horton uses imitation of poetic conventions as a way to address his own liminal status: he is not a soldier and is no longer a slave, yet in the context of the white southern literary tradition, he cannot really be a poet either. Keenly aware of the power imbalance in the patronage relationships that had sustained his work in Chapel Hill, he would certainly have understood that it was in part his status as a contradiction in terms that had enabled him to work as a poet. The advertising page that follows the text argues that white readers sympathetic to the cause of abolition will want to read this important work by a talented black writer; more importantly still, the ad copy argues that those white readers who have doubted the abilities of blacks will be persuaded by the volume to recognize that the newly emancipated are "possessed of genius" (159). The copy thus reveals Horton's awareness that where he once presented himself as *exceptional*, he must now begin to present himself as *representative*. With the decline of the university on which his livelihood depended, the collapse of the Confederacy, and the disbanding of the Ninth Michigan, he must begin again to carve out a position for himself, to cultivate relationships with new readers and sponsors, and to develop new approaches to the careful balance of masking and self-disclosure he had worked with as a poet for more than fifty years. His weariness in response to these formidable challenges is palpable throughout *Naked Genius*, but particularly in the collection's final poem. With the deeply personal lament "Obstructions of Genius," Horton closes the volume, vanishing from the pages of his own book and ending—so far as we know—his print career. Yet if Horton's personal despair is readily apparent in this final poem, the meditation on genius that runs throughout this collection nonetheless underlines his extraordinary achievement: Horton is the paradigm of Emersonian genius insofar as he is both exceptional and representative, standing "among partial men for the complete man."[21] And Emerson's model of genius explicitly includes the possibilities of imitation and quotation: "Genius borrows nobly."[22] Like Emerson's Poet then, Horton stands "balked and dumb, stuttering and stammering," using rage to draw out his "*dream*-power."[23] Only by attending to Horton's strategic use of imitation can we begin to understand both the rage and the power of the poems in *Naked Genius*.

NOTES

I am grateful to Theresa Strouth Gaul, Kathy Glass, Timothy Sweet, and Megan Ward for their helpful responses to earlier versions of this essay.

1. George Moses Horton, *Naked Genius* (Raleigh, N.C.: William B. Smith, 1865), 157, hereafter documented parenthetically.

2. First published in 1719, Watts's hymn was included in many American hymnals and songbooks across the nineteenth century. I cite it here from *Hymns for the Camp*, 2nd ed. (Raleigh, N.C.: General Tract Agency, 1862), 27.

3. Ralph Waldo Emerson, "Quotation and Originality," *Letters and Social Aims* (Boston: Houghton Mifflin, 1884), 185.

4. For analysis of the discourses of genius that attends to the intersection of racial difference and aesthetic culture in emergent models of American identity across the second half of the nineteenth century, see Gustavus Stadler, *Troubling Minds: The Cultural Politics of Genius in the United States, 1840–1890* (Minneapolis: University of Minnesota Press, 2006).

5. I draw my account of Horton's life from Joan Sherman's introduction to *The Black Bard of North Carolina: George Moses Horton and His Poetry* (Chapel Hill: University of North Carolina, 1997), 1–46, and from Leon Jackson's "The Black Bard and the Black Market" in his *The Business of Letters: Authorial Economies in Antebellum America* (Stanford: Stanford University Press, 2008), 53–88. Sherman's introduction provides a helpful overview of Horton's life and work, assesses the history of his reception, and also proposes key questions for analysis of the poems. Jackson reads Horton as an important figure for retheorizing the profession of authorship in antebellum America. See also my analysis of Horton's antebellum and Civil War–era work in *To Fight Aloud Is Very Brave: American Poetry and the Civil War* (Amherst: University of Massachusetts Press, 2012), 225–50.

In this chapter, I argue that Horton reclaims the stances of southern romanticism for a black voice.

6. As Sherman notes, we do not know for certain whether Horton escaped slavery by traveling to Raleigh and crossing the Union lines or whether he waited for the Union army to reach his master's farm in Chatham. See *Black Bard*, 29.

7. Ibid., 8.

8. For analysis of Abraham Lincoln's use of imitative strategies in his poetry, see my "Abraham Lincoln and Poetry," in *The Cambridge Companion to Abraham Lincoln*, ed. Shirley Samuels (Cambridge: Cambridge University Press, 2012), 22–39.

9. For a discussion of Civil War poetry that attends to its rhetoric of nation building, see my *To Fight Aloud Is Very Brave*.

10. For analysis of how African American poets use musical forms to imagine alternative models of community, see Ivy Wilson, *Specters of Democracy: Blackness and the Aesthetics of Politics in the Antebellum U.S.* (Oxford: Oxford University Press, 2011), 59–79. For discussion of the relationship between music and poetry in African American communities across the nineteenth century, see Mary Louise Kete, "The Reception of Nineteenth Century American Poetry," in *The Cambridge Companion to Nineteenth-Century American Poetry*, ed. Kerry Larson (Cambridge: Cambridge University Press, 2011), 18–19. For an overview of the thematic concerns of African American poets across the nineteenth century, see Joan Sherman's introduction to *African American Poetry of the Nineteenth Century* (Urbana: University of Illinois Press, 1992), 1–14. For a critical reassessment of the place of poetry in African American writing of the nineteenth century, see Ivy Wilson's "The Color Line: James Monroe Whitfield and Albery Allson Whitman," in *The Cambridge Companion to Nineteenth-Century American Poetry*, ed. Kerry Larson (Cambridge: Cambridge University Press, 2011), 208–24. For a detailed analysis of African American responses to the conventions of the elegy, see Max Cavitch, *American Elegy: The Poetry of Mourning from the Puritans to Whitman* (Minneapolis: University of Minnesota Press, 2007), 180–232.

11. Max Cavitch, "Slavery and Its Metrics," *The Cambridge Companion to Nineteenth-Century American Poetry*, ed. Kerry Larson (Cambridge: Cambridge University Press, 2011), 100.

12. Christopher Hager situates Horton's writing practices in relation to the writing of newly literate blacks in his *Word by Word: Emancipation and the Act of Writing* (Cambridge: Harvard University Press, 2013), 69, 72–73. For analysis of how African Americans in the South provided an education for themselves during and after slavery, see Heather Andrea Williams's *Self-Taught: African American Education in Slavery and Freedom* (Chapel Hill: University of North Carolina Press, 2005).

13. Thomas Jefferson, *Notes on the State of Virginia*, ed. Frank Shuffelton (New York: Penguin, 1999), 147.

14. For analysis of the tensions between originality and imitation in the work of women poets in Poe's circle, see Eliza Richards, *Gender and the Poetics of Reception in Poe's Circle* (Cambridge: Cambridge University Press, 2004). Richards's nuanced and insightful account of the relationship between genius and mimicry in nineteenth-century poetry

has shaped my thinking here. See in particular 18–25. For an analysis of how reiteration of poetic conventions could lead to publishing success and recognition, see Jennifer Putzi, "'Some Queer Freak of Taste': Gender, Authorship, and the 'Rock Me to Sleep' Controversy," *American Literature* 84, no. 4 (2012): 769–95. For analysis of the cultural position of a nineteenth-century ballad-peddler, see Michael C. Cohen, "Peddlers, Poems, and Local Culture: The Case of Jonathan Plummer, a 'Balladmonger' in Nineteenth-Century New England," *ESQ: A Journal of the American Renaissance* 54, no. 1–4 (2008): 9–32. See also my analysis of Abraham Lincoln's use of imitative strategies in "Abraham Lincoln and Poetry." For a discussion of the relationship between imitation and Horton's career as a poet, see also Jackson, *Business of Letters*.

15. See Henry Louis Gates, *The Signifying Monkey: A Theory of African American Literary Criticism* (New York: Oxford University Press, 1988), esp. 44–124. For Gates's rereading of Bakhtin's account of parody and "hidden polemic," see 110–11.

16. Sherman notes that Horton walked nearly three hundred miles with the Ninth Michigan that summer. See *Black Bard*, 30.

17. Ibid.

18. "Sherman's March to the Sea," music by Lieutenant J. L. Rockwell, lyrics by Lieutenant S. H. M. Byers (Chicago: H. M. Higgins, 1865).

19. "Peace: National Hymn in the Form of a March," music by Charles Moulton, lyrics by Miss Fay, alternate lyrics by W. J. Hoppin (New York: Scharfenberg and Luis, 1865).

20. I am grateful to Will Powell for drawing my attention to this juxtaposition.

21. Ralph Waldo Emerson, "The Poet," in *Selections from Ralph Waldo Emerson*, ed. Stephen Whicher (Boston: Houghton Mifflin, Riverside Press, 1957), 223.

22. Ralph Waldo Emerson, "Quotation and Originality," 182.

23. Emerson, "The Poet," 240.

PART II

POETICS OF WAR

Melville's *Battle-Pieces* and Vernacular Poetics

TIMOTHY SWEET

The growing interest in Melville's poetry over the past two decades has drawn on a larger recognition of the importance of poetry in mid-nineteenth-century America.[1] Where we used to see Melville's turn to poetry as a turn away from an unappreciative audience, we can now see it as a turn toward a different, culturally prominent literary mode. Undeterred by his failure to find a publisher for the volume of poetry he completed in 1860, Melville seemed to have found in the Civil War an occasion to reconstitute the public he had lost with *Pierre* and *The Confidence-Man*. The commercial failure of *Battle-Pieces* only sharpens the resulting question: how did Melville understand poetry to hail a constituency?

Melville's dedication of the volume "TO THE MEMORY OF THE THREE HUNDRED THOUSAND WHO IN THE WAR FOR THE MAINTENANCE OF THE UNION FELL DEVOTEDLY UNDER THE FLAG OF THEIR FATHERS" suggests that he counted on the power of elegiac commemoration to constitute an audience through the production of common memory.[2] But what form would this commemoration take? Melville addresses the problem of form in the preface: "I seem, in most of these verses, to have but placed a harp in a window, and noted the contrasted airs which wayward winds have played upon the strings" (3). The figure of the Aeolian harp signals Melville's critique of representation; it is a way of explaining why, as Whitman put it, "the real war will never get in the books."[3] It also signals his address to his audience in terms of poetics and suggests an engagement with the question of the forms of national identification and citizenship. If the "strings" of the harp evoke a lyre, the poetics that Melville developed in *Battle-Pieces* was not lyric in the sense that modernist criticism has prepared us to understand: the fiction of "feeling confessing itself to itself" in the "utter unconsciousness of a listener," in John Stuart Mill's well-known formulation.[4] Rather, Melville's poetics was lyric in the sense of bardic song, in which a poet deliberately addresses and thereby constitutes an audience.[5]

For Melville, the project of reconstituting a fragmented nation meant engaging not with the private subjectivity of emergent modernist lyric but rather with the possibilities for public address offered by the vernacular forms of hymn, ballad, song, and epitaph, while subordinating the elite omniscience of epic.[6] Vernacular forms, somatically satisfying in their quatrains of four-stress or alternating four- and three-stress lines rhyming *abcb* or sometimes *abab*, produced communities of experience in churches, work sites, and leisured gatherings or, in the case of epitaphs, through reminders of our common fate. These satisfactions are suggested, for example, by the popularity of a Currier and Ives lithograph depicting an inscribed gravestone on which grieving loved ones could write the soldier's name, military unit, place of death, and date: "in memory of [blank] of the [blank] who died at [blank] 186_ a brave and gallant soldier, and a true patriot." Framed by images of a grieving woman, flowers, and a weeping willow, the stone includes a generic epitaph in vernacular verse form, 4/3/4/3 *abab*:

> His toils are past, his work is done,
>   And he is fully blest
> He fought the fight, the victory won,
>   And enters into rest.[7]

Melville often engages critically with such forms, disrupting the ways in which vernacular poetics have been vehicles for discourses that legitimate violence, such as glory, patriotism, or religion. Thus, while *Battle-Pieces* includes some nostalgic poems in undeviating vernacular stanza, as well as pentameter poems deriving from an elite tradition, the volume's baseline form is that of the hymn, ballad, or epitaph in the process of becoming something else. Often, Melville inscribes traces of this process in the openings of poems, some portion of a quatrain remaining as a reminder of the poem's formal and ideological ground.

In recognizing the vernacular poetic context of *Battle-Pieces*, we return Melville to his military experience aboard the frigate *United States* and to his work on merchant and whaling ships, all ventures that took place against a background of song.[8] In *White-Jacket*, Jack Chase, the captain of the maintop, sings traditional ballads while the sailor-poet Lemsford pens new ones.[9] In *Moby-Dick*, the *Pequod*'s crew receive copies of Isaac Watts's *Hymns*; they heave on the windlass to a hymn or a "wild chorus"; off duty, they sing naval ballads and whaling songs.[10] Melville also had a career-long interest in the naval and martial songs of

Charles Dibdin, which were printed in broadside, circulated orally, and then collected and published posthumously in 1841.[11] A line from Dibdin's "Poor Jack"—"as for my life, 'tis the king's"—provides a deadly bit of foreshadowing in *Billy Budd*.[12] Such patriotic ventriloquism is the norm in Dibdin's songs, many of which take the first-person voice of a common sailor or soldier. Products of the late eighteenth-century ballad revival, these songs capitalize on the core value of authenticity by means of which the literati helped the middle class invent "the folk."[13] Thus, a standard collection of English songs that Melville owned claimed of Dibdin's songs, "the pictures are true, ... the feelings are real"; readers would recognize their truth even if they had never been to sea and had "received only the old traditionary or stage notions of [sailors'] character."[14] White-Jacket had affirmed this closed circuit of authentication, with its familiar distinction between elite and vernacular forms: "I do not unite with high critical authority in considering Dibdin's ditties 'slang songs,' for most of them breathe the very poetry of the ocean." Even so, he recognizes that they are contrived to produce a particular image of the authentic sailor: "It is remarkable that those songs—which would lead one to think that man-of-war's men are the most care-free, contented, virtuous, and patriotic of mankind—were composed at a time when the English Navy was principally manned by felons and paupers .... Dibdin was a man of genius; but no wonder, Dibdin was a government pensioner at £200 per annum" (383). Which is to say, the government rewarded Dibdin's success in hailing "the people," as a ship's crew were called, such that they would recognize themselves as subjected to authority.

The vernacular poetic context of Melville's work thus opens the question of the constitution of "the people" and their relation to authority, a microcosm of the Civil War's central problem. Developing a poetics of supplement to the vernacular tradition, Melville hoped that enough would remain of familiar forms to transact the people's self-recognition, while enabling deeper, critical reflection and national reconstitution on an enlightened foundation, much as White-Jacket, one of the people of the *Neversink* (Melville's fictional name for the frigate *United States*), was an appreciative but critical reader of Dibdin. Using the device of ventriloquism sparingly in *Battle-Pieces*, Melville usually takes the depersonalized stance of hymn, ballad, or epitaph. In the few poems that do take a first-person voice, it is usually plural, "the people" speaking in ballad or song from differing positions: representative southerners in "Stonewall Jackson (Ascribed to a Virginian)" and "The Frenzy in the Wake," for example, and representative northerners in "Stonewall Jackson. Mortally Wounded at Chancellorsville." By contrast, elites North and South speak in pentameter monologue. "The House-top" uses a blank verse soliloquy to characterize a New Yorker who approves the violent suppression of the 1863 draft riots fomented by the city's immigrant "rats" (64). In "Lee in the Capitol," Robert E. Lee's testimony before Congress in 1866 takes the form of heroic couplets, thus locating Lee within the elite antebellum southern culture in which Dryden's Virgil and Pope's Homer were the literary standard. This marking off of elite from vernacular forms suggests Melville's awareness that the postwar reconstitution of the nation was not limited to the question of North and South, but rather raised broad questions of political authority. In thus shaping the vernacular voice, Melville avoids the easy cooptation of patriotic verse while attempting to constitute "the people" in a critical, self-aware relation to traditional political and poetic forms.[15]

The question of political authority emerges in the volume's opening poem, "The Portent," formally in its address to the reader's expectation of ballad stanza as well as thematically in the naming of John Brown:

> *Hanging from the beam,*
>   *Slowly swaying (such the law),*
> *Gaunt the shadow on your green,*
>   *Shenandoah!*
> *The cut is on the crown*
>   *(Lo, John Brown),*
> *And the stabs shall heal no more.*
>
> *Hidden in the cap*
>   *Is the anguish none can draw;*
> *So your future veils its face,*
>   *Shenandoah!*
> *But the streaming beard is shown*
>   *(Weird John Brown)*
> *The meteor of the war.* (5, italics in original)

Lines 1 and 2 invert the ballad's expected 4/3 stress pattern. The apparent restoration of the 4/3 pattern with the next two lines adds a stressed final syllable to "Shenandoah," rhyming it with "law" and "war."[16] Thus bringing key sites of contested meaning, law and war, into emphatic alignment, the form draws together culturally prestigious regions of the Union and the Confederacy: native speakers in New England, in Tidewater and Piedmont Virginia, and in low-country South Carolina would all have pronounced "more" and "war" without a postvocalic /r/ thus naturally rhyming these words with "law" and "draw."[17] Yet to stretch "Shenandoah" into a four-syllable word is to pull the name of the river where Brown was executed away from local speakers who, to this day, pronounce it with three syllables (Shanan-doe). In the folksong that emerged from such local speakers—"Oh Shenandoah, I long to see you"—any attempt to add an extra syllable ("-ah") is naturally elided into the stressed vowel, "I."[18] "Oh Shenandoah" voices the melancholia of continental expansion, orienting national division along an east–west axis, as figured in the pull of two rivers, the Shenandoah and the "wide Missouri." Melville maps this axis onto the war's north–south axis. In the context of the execution at Harper's Ferry, the allusion to the Missouri River and westward expansion evokes the Missouri Compromise and John Brown's abolitionist activities in northeastern Kansas during the mid-1850s.

Such regional and class differentiations might be bridged by a bardic poet who hopes to speak for all through vernacular forms. As critics have observed, the image of John Brown's "streaming beard" alludes to an actual meteor that flashed between the time of Brown's trial and his execution, as well as to Thomas Gray's poem "The Bard."[19] Gray depicts a thirteenth-century Welsh bard who addresses the English conqueror Edward I. After foretelling Edward's doom and subsequent civil wars that will end only when Elizabeth accedes to the throne, the bard commits suicide, plunging into the Conway River gorge. This allusion suggests that as Wars of the Roses laid waste to the Conway valley, so the Shenandoah Valley was devastated by fighting throughout the war, beginning with Brown's suicidal raid. Pursuing the analogy at various points, for example in "Battle of Stone River," Melville entertains the idea that, as in the English civil wars, ideological legitimacy in the U.S. Civil War may be a product of mere force. However, where Gray's bard invokes other "ancestral bards" to "join" in "dreadful harmony" and shape the future—"Weave the warp and weave the woof"—Melville refuses Gray's fantasy of shaping fate, even while claiming from the mute Brown the role of prophet: "So your future veils its face, / Shenandoah!"[20] From the retrospect of 1866, Brown's execution predicts and even in some sense causes (as do Gray's "ancestral bards") the violence of civil war. The future that remained veiled to the would-be bard Melville was the question of national reconstitution.

Two explicit statements of poetic theory early in the volume, in "Dupont's Round Fight" and "A Utilitarian View of the Monitor's Fight," clarify Melville's formal engagement with the common meter tradition in "The Portent" while pressing its political questions. Although these poems offer apparently conflicting accounts of the relation of poetic form to content, both argue that form ought to have a mimetic function. A historicized reading suggests, however, that Melville was more concerned with form's rhetorical power to constitute and affect an audience. "Dupont's Round Fight" proposes that poetic forms find contents that match their representational capacities, thereby sorting events to identify correspondences between world and words.

> In time and measure perfect moves
>   All art whose aim is sure;
> Evolving rhyme and stars divine
>   Have rules, and they endure.
>
> Nor less the Fleet that warred for Right,
>   And, warring so, prevailed,
> In geometric beauty curved,
>   And in an orbit sailed.
>
> The Rebel at Port Royal felt
>   The unity overawe,
> And rued the spell. A type was here,
>   And victory of Law. (20)

As if to comment on Emerson's dictum that "the thought and the form are equal in the order of time, but in the order of genesis the thought is prior to the form," here "rhyme" is said to have "evolv[ed]" so as to realize its fated end, an invariantly iambic regularization of 4/3/4/3 hymn stanza.[21] The first stanza provides a natural-law analog to poetic "rule" against which the second stanza measures the astral "orbit" of Dupont's fleet during the Battle of Port Royal. Melville saw from a map in the *Rebellion Record* that the fleet sailed in a neatly elliptical path, first upstream to fire on Fort Beauregard and then downstream to fire on Fort Walker.[22] The "unity" of these analogous regularities stands as a "type" of the ultimate Union victory, which would reconstitute the nation on the basis of "Law," much as a congregation constitutes itself through the singing of a hymn professing God's law.

Yet the final line, invoking a juridical sense of "Law" for the confirmation of the "type" made visible in the orders of battle and meter, introduces a metaphysical disjunction. The question of "victory" is inapplicable to the sense of natural law that governs the stars: gravity, momentum, and so on. The question of poetic form is similarly poised between natural and constructed standards: if sonic phenomena such as rhyme and meter are, on the one hand, natural features of all oral language, they are on the other hand conventionally organized patterns that come to feel familiar (that is to say, natural) as verse. As Deak Nabers has argued, this is one of many instances in which Melville demonstrates his awareness of the dual valence of law, natural and positive, that was at stake in the war and remained at stake in Reconstruction.[23]

Against this already troubled poetic theory, the first stanza of "A Utilitarian View of the Monitor's Fight" registers a contrasting claim that traditional forms ought to be malleable in taking on new content:

> Plain be the phrase, yet apt the verse,
>   More ponderous than nimble;
> For since grimed War here laid aside
>   His Orient pomp, 'twould ill befit
> Overmuch to ply
>   The rhyme's barbaric cymbal. (44)

As critics have observed, lines 4 and 5 disrupt the anticipated rhythm and rhyme of 4/3/4/3 ballad or hymn stanza, as thematically the poem claims that the new mechanized warfare exemplified by the clash of the ironclads disrupts certain discourses that legitimate warfare: heroism, glory, and so on.[24] These discourses are staples of patriotic hymns and ballads, whose formal and representational capacities, Melville suggests, have been exceeded by a new kind of event. The contrast is the more emphatic since this poem immediately follows "The Temeraire," a nostalgic paean to sailing ships set in a 3/3/3/3 *abcb* song stanza framed by three stanzas in the 4/3/4/3 *abcb* form that is the base for "A Utilitarian View" (41). Even so, in "A Utilitarian View," the repetition of the first stanza's novel pattern through four subsequent stanzas establishes a new formal regularity. The expected rhyme does return in each stanza rather than remaining unresolved. The battle is celebrated, albeit in a new fashion: "Hail to victory without the gaud / Of glory" (44). Analogously, if "warriors / Are now but operatives" and "a singe runs through lace and feather," still the traditional discourses are not obliterated but rather blemished and battle scarred, bearing traces of violence into peacetime commemorations (45). The hymn or ballad form and its patriotic or heroic associations persist as the ground against which these new judgments and accommodations make sense. This point is the more evident if we recognize that the historical content of "Dupont's Round Fight" is similar in one key respect to that of "A Utilitarian View." The ships of the South Atlantic Blockading Squadron were steam powered and propeller or wheel driven.[25] Melville's readers would have known that sailing ships would not have been capable of the neatly elliptical maneuver executed by Captain Dupont's squadron in the mouth of Port Royal Sound. Here, no less than in the *Monitor*'s fight, the maneuvers were conducted by means of "crank, / Pivot, and screw, / And calculations of caloric" (44). However, although the sailors who manned Dupont's ships were mere "operatives," like those of the *Monitor*, in the new mechanized mode of naval warfare, they are only revealed to be such as the hymn or ballad becomes another form.

Melville's engagement with vernacular poetics takes three general forms in *Battle-Pieces*: repetition, internal modification, and larger transformation. In the first case, Melville sometimes constitutes his audience by simply retaining the familiar forms of hymn, ballad, or refrain-driven song. Even here, as we have seen in "Dupont's Round Fight," material details may complicate straightforward affirmation, especially when the poem is read in the context of other poems such as "A Utilitarian View." Melville counts on vernacular forms' affirmative rhetorics to produce affective bonding, as in the case of "The Temeraire," in which Englishmen, Unionists, and Confederates alike can recognize in one another a shared nostalgia for the time before steamships. Yet Melville also dramatizes nationally divisive consequences that cut against mutual recognition, as for example in a pair of songs commemorating Sherman's March. "The March to the Sea (December 1864)" begins as a Union soldiers' marching song—"It was glorious and glad marching, / A marching glad and free"—but turns in the last stanza to anticipate the southern civilian response:

> For behind they left a wailing
> A terror and a ban,
> And blazing cinders sailing,
> And houseless households wan,
> ....
> They will long remember Sherman
> Marching to the sea. (94, 96)

This response is taken up in the first-person plural voice of the paired poem "The Frenzy in the Wake," which ends with a vehement iteration of Lost Cause ideology: "Have we gamed and lost? But even despair / Shall never our hate rescind" (98).

Whereas in poems about the war's destruction Melville develops a critical perspective on the ballad's transmission of the legitimating discourses of patriotism, in poems bearing on the incorporation of emancipated slaves into the national body politic he counts on the vernacular poetic tradition's power to summon assent, as for example in "'Formerly a Slave.'" This poem is a response in modified hymn form to a painting by Elihu Vedder of an aged New York street vendor, which Melville had seen on exhibition at the National Academy of Design in 1865. Had Melville chosen to ventriloquize the vendor's voice, literary convention would have dictated a dialect poem. Instead, he proposes reading the street vendor's character through her physiognomy, projecting a meliorist view of race relations through a small formal modification introduced in the first stanza and followed uniformly thereafter:

> The sufferance of her race is shown,
> And retrospect of life,

> Which now too late deliverance dawns upon;
>   Yet is she not at strife.
>
> Her children's children they shall know
>   The good withheld from her;
> And so her reverie takes prophetic cheer—
>   In spirit she sees the stir
>
> Far down the depth of thousand years,
>   And marks the revel shine;
> Her dusky face is lit with sober light,
>   Sibylline, yet benign. (115)

The unrhymed third lines of each quatrain, bearing five stresses rather than the expected four, each imagine the vendor's "dawn[ing]" sense of hope, evident not through the luminist technique that Melville had seen at the exhibition, but rather through the "sober light" of character study.[26] As the ballad stanza accommodates the elevating five-stress third line with only a slight strain, so might the American body politic strain just slightly to incorporate the emancipated slaves' descendants.

The slight strain of the base meter in "'Formerly a Slave'" contrasts with greater formal strain in "A Utilitarian View." Melville's approach in the latter is comparable to that in "The Apparition (A Retrospect)," a first-person-plural voice account of an incident from the 1864 siege of Petersburg, Virginia, in which Union troops dug a tunnel to undermine the Confederate line and exploded dynamite, blowing a hole in the defenses.[27] As in many other poems, violence disrupts the pastoral scene:

> Convulsions came; and, where the field
>   Long slept in pastoral green,
> A goblin-mountain was upheaved
> (Sure the sense was all deceived),
>   Marl-glen and slag-ravine.
>
> The unreserved of Ill was there,
>   The clinkers in her last retreat;
> But, ere the eye could take it in,
> Or mind could comprehension win,
>   It sunk!—and at our feet.
>
> So, then, Solidity's a crust—
>   The core of fire below;

> All may go well for many a year,
> But who can think without a fear
> Of horrors that happen so? (116)

The third line of each stanza, which would remain unrhymed in traditional ballad stanza, here is rhymed by a fourth, before the fifth line recovers the form. In each case the doubling line—which momentarily explodes the ballad scheme as dynamite "upheaved" the ground—focuses on the mechanism of perception. By the third stanza, the doubling line anticipates future perceptions as the event persists in a post-traumatic trace.[28] The poem's plural subjectivity could represent the nearby Confederate soldiers as well as the Union soldiers who were at first too stunned to charge the gap and later became trapped in the hole at the mercy of the surrounding Confederates. The final three lines shift the response from the eternal metaphysics of the stanza's first two lines to a specific postbellum national allegory, in which the plural voice could speak for all Americans. The return of a similar image in the supplement ponders further sectional crisis: "Wherefore in a clear sky do we still turn our eyes toward the South, as the Neapolitan, months after the eruption, turns his toward Vesuvius?" (185).

In his most complex kind of engagement with vernacular forms, Melville transforms these forms into something else over the course of the poem, developing more profuse and complexly interwoven rhymes, while leaving a trace of the original. Moments that delegitimate war, such as the interjection "what like a bullet can undeceive!" from "Shiloh," thus claim the ballad's broad cultural authority rather than the subjective authority of the lyric voice that would develop in later antiwar poems such as Wilfred Owen's *"Dulce et Decorum Est."*[29] "Shiloh" takes as its poetic baseline the familiar 4/3 form of songs such as Will S. Hays's "The Drummer Boy of Shiloh: A Beautiful Ballad," which was published as sheet music. The five-verse song opens,

> On Shiloh's dark and bloody ground,
> The dead and wounded lay;
> Amongst them was a drummer boy,
> Who beat the drum that day.
> A wounded soldier held him up –
> His drum was by his side;
> He clasp'd his hands, then rais'd his eyes,
> And prayed before he died.[30]

In addition to the question of religious consolation, as we will see, Melville engages with two other popular topoi in "Shiloh," pastoral recuperation and reconciliation in death. An example combining the latter two topoi is "On the

Heights of Mission Ridge" by J. Augustine Signaigo, from William Gilmore Simms's postwar anthology, *War Poetry of the South*. Signaigo tells of the deaths of "two opposing colonels" who had been schoolmates "and had loved each other well." Simultaneously seeing each other wounded in battle, that "old time, full of feeling, / Came upon them once again." Thus, in the final quatrains,

> When that night the moon came creeping,
>   With its gold streaks o'er the slain,
> She beheld two soldiers sleeping,
>   Free from every earthly pain.
> Close beside the mountain heather,
>   Where the rocks obscure the sand,
> They had died, it seems, together,
>   As they clasped each other's hand.[31]

As "Heights of Mission Ridge" closes, so "Shiloh" opens with the promise of pastoral recuperation, associating this promise with ballad stanza. Melville then marks the trace of violence by a shift to couplets:

> Skimming lightly, wheeling still,
>   The swallows fly low
> Over the field in clouded days,
>   The forest-field of Shiloh—
> Over the field where April rain
> Solaced the parched ones stretched in pain (46)

Couplets in turn give way to an embedded ballad quatrain as the violence becomes the object of political interpretation, which is counterpoised to "natural prayer," a phrase that evokes Enlightenment categories of natural religion, natural rights, and natural law. With death comes enlightenment, as Melville had suggested in an earlier poem, "The March into Virginia":

> The church so lone, the log-built one
>   That echoed many a parting groan,
>   And natural prayer
>   Of dying foemen mingled there—
> Foemen at morn, but friends at eve—
>   Fame or country least their care:
> (What like a bullet can undeceive!) (46)

Shifting from terms of universal agreement in the first line of the embedded quatrain (the soldiers were "foemen") to delegitimation in the third by means of the temporal caesura in the second ("morn" / "eve"), Melville turns the soldiers' knowledge into another claim, also apparently universal, clinched by rhyme. Not only have the soldiers agreed to put aside the discourses of "fame" and "country" that positioned them as "foemen"; they have also come to recognize that these discourses are deceptions that make war possible. Locating this recognition with respect to the opening pastoral frame, the poem's final three lines pick up the rhyme of the opening ballad quatrain:

> But now they lie low,
> While over them the swallows skim,
> And all is hushed at Shiloh. (46)

The unrhymed line's internal rhyme ("them" / "skim") marks the natural environment's indifference to human suffering. Melville thus identifies claims of legitimation and delegitimation alike as products of politics and therefore tenuous, requiring human agreement and capable of modification.

Disrupting the audience's formal expectations without obliterating them, such poems invite complex or critical interpretations of events without grounding such interpretations in a lyric speaker's subjectivity. Thus, for example, "On the Slain Collegians," which opens with two 4/3/4/3 ballad quatrains rhymed *abcb*, introduces a new stanza form midway through the poem:

> Woe for the homes of the North,
> And woe for the seats of the South:
> All who felt life's spring in prime,
> And were swept by the wind of their place and time— (118–19)

The fourth line here, which maintains the four-stress baseline rhythm despite added syllables, ought to rhyme with "South." Thus, the unexpected couplet "prime" / "time" asks us retrospectively to reconcile "North" and "South" as a couplet, emphasizing an equal distribution of fault and pathos while proposing an uneasy postbellum unification. Yet this is an off-rhyme at best.

This structure of common meter giving way to a more complex form is prominent in the "Verses Inscriptive and Memorial" section. For example, "An uninscribed Monument on one of the Battle-fields of the Wilderness," which comments like "Shiloh" on the popular theme of pastoral recuperation, begins with an evocation of traditional ballad or epitaph form:

> Silence and solitude may hint
>   (Whose home is in yon piny wood)
> What I, though tableted, could never tell—
> The din which here befell,
>   And striving of the multitude. (130)

As the fourth line rhymes with the third, which would have remained unrhymed in the form set up by the first two lines, the poem shifts genres. Following are two more quatrains rhymed *abba*, the pattern set by lines 2 through 5 ("wood" / "tell" / "-fell" / "-tude"), and a closing couplet that commands the living witness's response through the conventional gravestone trope of *sta viator*:

> Thou who beholdest, if thy thought,
> Not narrowed down to personal cheer,
> Take in the import of the quiet here—
> The after-quiet—the calm full-fraught;
> Thou too wilt silent stand—
> Silent as I, and lonesome as the land. (130)

In the latter part of this fifteen-line poem, several lines take the pentameter form of line 3, thus reinforcing the sense that we are hearing a ballad turn into a new form something akin to a sonnet. Yet the topic is outside the sonnet form's conventional purview. The personified monument's bid for the observer's identification forces a confrontation with mortality.[32] "Personal cheer" would be a natural response, even if tinged with survivor's guilt. However, the stone redirects any such "narrow," "personal" evasion of violence, urging attention to the cannon balls lying on the ground, "spheres of death / Set round me in their rust," asking for an impossible recognition that transcends human emotion, to become "lonesome as the land."

The concluding poem of the "Verses Inscriptive and Memorial" section, by contrast, directly presents first-person subjectivity. Ventriloquizing the voice of a common soldier in the manner of Charles Dibdin, "The Returned Volunteer to his Rifle" sets up the expectation of four-stress quatrains rhymed *abcb*. Marked by indentations, the opening quatrain is songlike and sentimental as it venerates patriarchy and patriotism. However, the pentameter third line soon strains the meter:

> Over this hearth—my father's seat—
>   Repose, to patriot-memory dear,
> Thou tried companion, whom at last I greet
>   By steepy banks of Hudson here.
> How oft I told thee of this scene—
> The Highlands blue—the river's narrowing sheen.
> Little at Gettysburg we thought
> To find such haven; but God kept it green.
> Long rest! with belt, and bayonet, and canteen. (138)

The sixth line stretches to pentameter again, aestheticizing the Hudson River valley landscape familiar to Melville from his boyhood and gesturing toward blank verse landscape meditation in the vein of Bryant's "The Prairie" or Lowell's "The Cathedral." The poem's base line remains poised uneasily between four and five stresses, between vernacular and elite associations. The next line, however, pulls back to the four-stress base as the scene shifts to a radically different landscape in a flashback recollection of the Gettysburg battlefield. Then a deliberate effort to return to the present moment cuts short this post-traumatic recollection. Sentimental icons in the final couplet ("haven ... God kept it green") begin to recover the tenor of the opening but cannot cover the trace of trauma registered by the single, unrhymed line that recollects, in a detached way, the prospect of death: "Little at Gettysburg we thought." This is not a case of "feeling confessing itself to itself," as in the conventional understanding of modern lyric, but rather of form proscribing deep "feeling."[33] The experience of war, absent from the deictic unrhymed line, remains exterior to the discourses that legitimate war. Thus the stoic recollection of the prospect of death is not recuperated by patriotic song but is formally set apart. Are we to take the unrhymed line's gesture toward free verse (the only such gesture in the volume) as an experiential analogue to the sense of freedom that comes from accepting the inevitability of death? If so, the songlike closing couplet suggests that such moments are both fleeting and incompatible with the commonality of belief or allegiance that constitutes vernacular poetics' relation to its audience. Yet as we have seen, Melville insists on incorporating such moments of recognition or delegitimation into vernacular forms, producing new forms that hail an audience on familiar terms while reflecting critically on those terms.

The late unrhymed line in "The Returned Volunteer" thus emphasizes by way of exception an important pattern in *Battle-Pieces*. Whether in poems of a single stanza such as "Shiloh" or within stanzas of longer poems such as the *abccb* of "The Apparition" or the *abcdbcc* of "The Scout toward Aldie," the pattern is one of increasing density and complexity of rhyme in a movement away from vernacular forms. The resulting echoes and resonances register at the level of form the ideological complexities that Melville addresses at the level of theme. Sometimes the critical alteration of vernacular form is quite subtle, so as to carry the intended reader easily into assent, as in "'Formerly a Slave'"; at other times the alteration is more confrontational, as in "An uninscribed Monument." Throughout the volume, whole poems or stanzas in vernacular forms recur to provide gauges against which the innovative poetics of increasing density can be measured.

The unrhymed line of "The Returned Volunteer" further suggests another possible departure from the vernacular base, free verse, which Melville did not explore. The Victorian-era association of free verse with individual voice made this pattern inappropriate for *Battle-Pieces* as a whole—not merely for commemorative poems whose task by definition is to establish a common memory, but also for the battle poems, which do not attempt to present the individual soldier's subjectivity.[34] Although the model of Whitman was available to him and he was well aware of Emerson's occasional use of unrhymed lines for punctuation, emphasis, or mimetic effect, Melville used unrhymed lines primarily in the openings of poems or stanzas as a means to ground his poetics in familiar forms, such as the unrhymed first and third lines of traditional ballad.[35] Thus he hoped both to hail the audience who had grown up with vernacular poetics and to reconstitute this audience through association as critical citizen-readers. The mechanism for this association was not the subjective self-management that modernist lyric both laments and reproduces, but rather the sense of community produced by and experienced through hymns, ballads, and songs.

Melville regarded vernacular poetics as a vehicle for the rhetorical production of the common "feelings" that, as Christopher Castiglia argues, could move subjects to invest in national identities.[36] In his critical departure from these forms, however, Melville did not accomplish the constitution of a public. The volume was a commercial failure. Reviewers praised some of the more songlike poems, such as "The Temeraire," "Sheridan at Cedar Creek," or "The March to the Sea"—which as we have seen could invoke uncritical collectives—but for the most part they found the forms "uncouth."[37] One reviewer more sympathetic than most seems to have glimpsed the nature of the project when he observed that Melville's "thoughts ... refuse to obey the rigid regimental order of the stanza, but outly [*sic*] its lines, deployed as irregular though brilliant skirmishers."[38] If Melville failed to fulfill the bardic role he evoked in "The Portent," this was because he could not finally speak in a single, nationalizing voice as Whitman claimed to do. Where Whitman presented himself as a microcosm of the United States, his voice standing for each and all, Melville, like Emily Dickinson, "noted" multiple voices, "variable, and at times widely at variance," as the only apt register of the war's memory (3).[39]

In this way, Melville posed the problem of critical citizenship. Recognitions such as the delegitimating force of "Shiloh," or the ambiguity of "law" demonstrated in the pairing of "Dupont's Round Fight" and "A Utilitarian View," or the existential insights of "An uninscribed Monument" or "The Returned Volunteer," could only be accomplished through a departure from the vernacular forms that traditionally produce the emotional satisfactions of national belonging. As we have seen in the paired poems on Sherman's March, the production of such satisfactions could merely reproduce the problem of separate national identities posed by secession. Thus where vernacular poetics traditionally voices patriotism as the nation's cooptation of interiority—Poor Jack is supposed to assent as he sings, "as for my life, 'tis the king's"—Melville explored a patriotism of supplementation, in which interiority remains unspecified and citizens are constituted by means of critical engagements with established forms.

NOTES

I am grateful to Faith Barrett for reading an early draft of this essay.

1. William Spengemann, "Melville the Poet," *American Literary History* 11, no. 4 (1999): 569–609; Hershel Parker, *Melville: The Making of the Poet* (Evanston: Northwestern University Press, 2008); Cody Marrs, "A Wayward Art: *Battle-Pieces* and Melville's Poetic Turn," *American Literature* 82, no. 1 (2010): 91–119; Peter Coviello, "Battle Music: Melville and the Forms of War," in *Melville and Aesthetics*, eds. Samuel Otter and Geoffrey Sanborn (New York: Palgrave Macmillan, 2011), 193–212; Faith Barrett, *To Fight Aloud Is Very Brave: American Poetry and the Civil War* (Amherst: University of Massachusetts Press, 2012), 251–80.

2. Herman Melville, *Published Poems*, ed. Robert C. Ryan, Harrison Hayford, Alma MacDougall Reising, and G. Thomas Tanselle (Evanston: Northwestern University Press; Chicago: Newberry Library, 2009), 2, hereafter documented parenthetically. On elegy's capacity to constitute allegiances among the living, see Max Cavitch, *American Elegy: The Poetry of Mourning from the Puritans to Whitman* (Minneapolis: University of Minnesota Press, 2007).

3. Walt Whitman, *Prose Works 1892*, ed. Floyd Stovall (New York: New York University Press, 1963), 1:115. On Melville's critique of representation, see Timothy Sweet, *Traces of War: Poetry, Photography, and the Crisis of the Union* (Baltimore: Johns Hopkins University Press, 1990), 165–72.

4. John Stuart Mill, "Thoughts on Poetry and Its Varieties," in *Autobiography and Literary Essays*, ed. John M. Robson and Jack Stillinger, vol. 1 of *The Collected Works of John Stuart Mill* (Toronto: University of Toronto Press, 1981), 348. Virginia Jackson argues that William Dean Howells, in a disparaging review familiar to scholars of *Battle-Pieces*, read the volume as attempting, but failing, to develop a modernist lyric voice. "Who Reads Poetry?," *PMLA* 123, no. 2 (2008): 181–87. On the historical development of this sense of lyric during the nineteenth century, see Virginia Jackson, *Dickinson's Misery: A Theory of Lyric Reading* (Princeton: Princeton University Press, 2005). For Howells's review, see Brian Higgins and Hershel Parker, eds., *Herman Melville: The Contemporary Reviews* (Cambridge: Cambridge University Press, 1995), 526–28.

5. Wyston Curnow gives a suggestive psychological account of Melville's bardic ambitions ("'Battles can Heroes and Bards restore': Melville, Whitman, and the Civil War," in *American Studies Down Under*, ed. Norman Harper and Elaine Barry [Victoria: Australian and New Zealand American Studies Association, 1976], 80–98).

6. Rosanna Warren reads Melville as "experimenting with … ways to dramatize the act of knowing" through "elliptical" verse forms ("Dark Knowledge: Melville's Poems of

the Civil War," in Herman Melville, *Battle-Pieces and Aspects of the War* [Amherst, N.Y.: Prometheus, 2001], 280). Helen Vendler argues that Melville "fold[s] the epic matter of history into lyric" by beginning with philosophical generalization and then moving to narration and the expression of "lyric feelings," thus reversing the lyric's typical order of presentation ("Melville and the Lyric of History," in Melville, *Battle-Pieces*, 256). Attempting, like Jackson, to read mid-nineteenth century poetry outside the telos of modernist lyric assumed by Vendler and Warren, I focus here on Melville's relation to the popular poetic ground against which his formal innovations took shape. For pioneering work in this direction, see Jillian Spivey Caddell, "Melville's Epitaphs: On Time, Place, and War," *New England Quarterly* 87, no. 2 (2014): 292–318.

7. "The Soldier's Grave" (New York: Currier and Ives, 1865), color film copy slide, from Library of Congress, http://www.loc.gov/pictures/resource/cph.3b50889/. Caddell notes this lithograph's traditional iconography ("Melville's Epitaphs," 298–300). In the epitaph case, material constraints reinforce the traditional oral form, since three- and four-stress lines require less space than longer lines. In the American Antiquarian Society's Farber Gravestone Collection of images, of the approximately 280 stones dated 1800–1861 bearing poetic inscriptions, only twenty use five-stress lines. Thanks to Harry Brown of DePauw University and his research assistants Jessica Maginity and Ngoc Anh Nguyen for sharing their transcriptions of the AAS Farber Collection photographs; these transcriptions were tagged for poetic form by the author and James Holsinger.

8. Melville also read widely in Francis James Child's *English and Scottish Ballads* beginning in 1859. See Merton M. Sealts, *Melville's Reading: A Check-List of Books Owned and Borrowed* (Madison: University of Wisconsin Press, 1966), 50.

9. Herman Melville, *White-Jacket*, ed. Harrison Hayford, Hershel Parker, and G. Thomas Tanselle (Evanston: Northwestern University Press; Chicago: Newberry Library, 1970), 310–11, 41, hereafter documented parenthetically.

10. Herman Melville, *Moby-Dick or The Whale*, ed. Harrison Hayford, Hershel Parker, and G. Thomas Tanselle (Evanston: Northwestern University Press; Chicago: Newberry Library, 1988), 103, 104, 303, 171, 173. On folksongs in Melville's fiction, see Kevin Hayes, *Melville's Folk Roots* (Kent: Kent State University Press, 1999), 13–24.

11. See Herman Melville, *Typee*, ed. Harrison Hayford, Hershel Parker, and G. Thomas Tanselle (Evanston: Northwestern University Press; Chicago: Newberry Library, 1970), 215; Herman Melville, *Redburn*, ed. Harrison Hayford, Hershel Parker, and G. Thomas Tanselle (Evanston: Northwestern University Press; Chicago: Newberry Library, 1969), 143.

12. Herman Melville, *Billy Budd*, ed. Harrison Hayford and Merton M. Sealts, Jr. (Chicago: University of Chicago Press, 1962), 55.

13. On the question of authenticity in the ballad revival, see Susan Stewart, *Crimes of Writing: Problems in the Containment of Representation* (New York: Oxford University Press, 1991), 86–88, 102–31.

14. Charles Mackay, ed., *The Book of English Songs* (London: Office of the National Illustrated Library, 1851), 157; Sealts, *Melville's Reading*, 77.

15. Compare arguments that *Battle-Pieces* represents Melville's capitulation to the co-

ercive power of the state, for example Michael Paul Rogin, *Subversive Genealogy: The Politics and Art of Herman Melville* (Berkeley: University of California Press, 1986), 257–87.

16. Coviello characterizes Melville's variations on ballad meter here as "strident" ("Battle Music," 198).

17. See Hans Kurath and Raven McDavid, *The Pronunciation of English in the Atlantic States: Based upon the Collections of the Linguistic Atlas of the Eastern United States* (Ann Arbor: University of Michigan Press, 1961), map 32. Samples for this study were taken from speakers born in the 1850s and 1860s. Reviews in New York City and Philadelphia papers objected to Melville's rhyming "law" with "Shenandoah." See Higgins and Parker, *Herman Melville*, 513, 520, 524, 525.

18. Jackson suggests that Melville deliberately cites the folksong "Oh Shenandoah" ("Who Reads Poetry?," 185).

19. Spengemann, "Melville the Poet," 587. Melville may also have been influenced by Emerson's poem about another Welsh bard-prophet, "Merlin," which he read in late 1859 or thereafter. See Parker, *Melville*, 109. On the actual meteor, see Melville, *Poems*, 625.

20. *The Complete Poems of Thomas Gray*, ed. James Reeves (New York: Barnes and Noble, 1973), 79.

21. Ralph Waldo Emerson, "The Poet," in *Complete Works of Ralph Waldo Emerson* (Boston: Houghton, Mifflin, 1903), 1:10.

22. On Melville's use of the *Rebellion Record* here, see Melville, *Poems*, 628–29.

23. Deak Nabers, *Victory of Law: The Fourteenth Amendment, the Civil War, and American Literature, 1852–1867* (Baltimore: John Hopkins University Press, 2006), 39–42.

24. Coviello, "Battle Music," 203–6.

25. For a history of the South Atlantic Blockading Squadron and its action in the Battle of Port Royal (which was less perfectly organized than newspaper accounts made it out to be), see James M. McPherson, *War on the Waters: The Union and Confederate Navies, 1861–1865* (Chapel Hill: University of North Carolina Press, 2012), 31–42.

26. Among the artists represented at the exhibition who used luminist techniques were Albert Bierstadt, Frederick Church, and Jasper Francis Cropsey. Character and genre painters in addition to Vedder included Eastman Johnson and William Sidney Mount. See Stanton Garner, *The Civil War World of Herman Melville* (Lawrence: University Press of Kansas, 1993), 400–401.

27. For details on the battle and Melville's likely source for the imagery, an illustration in *Harper's Weekly* by Alfred Waud, see Melville, *Poems*, 662.

28. Marrs argues that this extra line is a formal register of one of the primary themes of *Battle-Pieces*, Melville's sense of cyclical temporality ("Wayward Art," 115).

29. Michael Warner gives a brilliant account of this line's delegitimating turn in "What Like a Bullet Can Undeceive?," *Public Culture* 15, no. 1 (2003): 41–54.

30. "The Drummer Boy of Shiloh. A Beautiful Ballad by Will S. Hays" (Louisville, D. P. Faulds and Chicago, Root and Cady, 1863), repr. in *The Civil War Songbook*, ed. Richard Crawford (New York: Dover, 1977), 82–86. Barrett speculates on Melville's thematic engagement with this song's appeal to traditional Christian piety (*To Fight Aloud*, 272–73).

31. J. Augustine Signaigo, "On the Heights of Mission Ridge," in *War Poetry of the South*, ed. William Gilmore Simms (New York: Richardson, 1867), 375–76.

32. Barrett, *To Fight Aloud*, 277.

33. Mill, "Thoughts on Poetry," 348.

34. On the Victorian association of free verse with individual voice in the sense of freedom from constraining form, see Susan Stewart, "Rhyme and Freedom," in *The Sound of Poetry, the Poetry of Sound*, ed. Marjorie Perloff and Craig Dworkin (Chicago: University of Chicago Press, 2009), 29–48.

35. It is not clear whether Melville had read Whitman by 1866. See Parker, *Melville*, 97–98.

36. Christopher Castiglia, *Interior States: Institutional Consciousness and the Inner Life of Democracy in the Antebellum United States* (Durham: Duke University Press, 2008), 20.

37. Higgins and Parker, *Herman Melville*, 522.

38. Ibid., 523.

39. Cristanne Miller, for example, finds in Dickinson's Civil War poetry "an amalgam of voices ... taking different emotional and philosophical perspectives" rather than a consistent lyric voice (*Reading in Time: Emily Dickinson in the Nineteenth Century* [Amherst: University of Massachusetts Press, 2012], 148).

"Help'd, Braced, Concentrated"
Transatlantic Tensions and Whitman's National War Poetry

SAMUEL GRABER

This Great Boon

As an era of violent national division, the Civil War years might seem an inhospitable setting for the long-anticipated development of American national literature. Nevertheless, on November 7, 1863, *Harper's Weekly* speculated that such an advent would be one of the war's chief spoils. Tellingly, its front-page editorial avoided the troubled domestic front and directed its readers eastward, to Britain and the aggressively anti-Union tone of its newspapers, led by the *Times* of London. Entitled "One Point Gained," the piece sought to spin the straw of British scorn into the gold of a national culture.

By the time the article appeared, the British government's neutral stance, which was always complex, had been further complicated by two years of combative transatlantic diplomacy and several major crises that threatened to throw the weight of the British Empire behind the southern war effort. The federal navy's seizure of Confederate agents from a British ship in the Trent Affair in 1861 was greeted with popular celebrations in the North, at least until a roused John Bull compelled their release and sent a detachment of British troops to protect Canada against a possible Yankee invasion. For their part, British manufacturers outraged northern sensibilities by illegally outfitting Confederate warships, while British politicians offended them with offers of mediation that would have led to Confederate recognition. Many northerners had trouble understanding why a proudly antislavery empire appeared hostile to their cause, especially once destroying southern slavery became an official war aim. Yet signs of British anti-Unionism were impossible to ignore, for American editors read and often reprinted material from British papers as soon as it crossed the ocean. The attitude of the *Times* proved particularly rankling, for the paper held enormous sway throughout England and beyond. As the editorial in *Harper's* noted, educated northerners often looked to London's greatest daily rather than their own journals when seeking guidance on contemporary affairs—including those touching on literary taste.

Now, however, *Harper's* hoped that the anti-Union record of the British press had eliminated the chief foreign influence on American literature and culture, and settled the long-standing question of literary sovereignty that had previously spawned such cultural movements as Young America. *Harper's* judged the recent transatlantic antagonism "an inestimable benefit. It has enfranchised us from the condition of quasi-colonial dependence—as to public opinion—in which we had previously existed." Despite eighty years of political independence from Britain, "neither the War of Revolution nor the War of 1812 succeeded in emancipating us from the control of the Mother Country in matters of opinion, judgment, and taste." Yet the writer believed the Civil War had achieved what these actual wars with Britain had not: a final cultural break between Americans and their British bellwethers. "We shall hear no more now of what the London *Times* says on this or that subject, or what the British Reviews have decided on this or that book, policy, picture, or play," the article concluded. "We are going to do our own thinking. For this great boon let us be duly thankful."[1]

This essay will argue that the war's transatlantic tensions did play an important and mostly overlooked part in developing a more nationalistic American literature, though not precisely in the way *Harper's Weekly* had suggested. Contrary to its editorialist's hopes, American readers would continue to patronize British literature and criticism in the immediate postwar period. Nevertheless, British anti-Union sentiment clearly left an impression on one of the most important advocates for a distinctively American body of anglophone literature: the war poet, part-time nurse, and full-time observer of the war, Walt Whitman. Whitman's response to the war was deeply affected by perceptions of transatlantic hostility that he, like *Harper's*, regarded as a lever to pry American readers away from dependence on British writers and critics.

Thanks to a growing scholarly and popular consciousness of the Civil War's international aspects and a renaissance of transatlantic scholarship in the humanities, Britain's significance to the American Civil War is now difficult to overlook, especially as a military and diplomatic concern. Yet British influence on the conflict had broader cultural repercussions, for policy orchestrated in back rooms inevitably emerged on front pages, and the exchange of transatlantic news helped shape policy. Leaders, soldiers, and diplomats understood that their convened councils and cabinet meetings had to account for public opinion on both sides of the ocean. Knowing this, partisans did their best to manipulate, spin, and publicize popular responses in newspapers that traveled far and wide. Transatlantic attention to the conflict factored into military strategies and diplomatic stances, and also had ramifications in a literary realm that was similarly organized around transatlantic communication, interest, and influence.[2]

As recent scholarship on anglophone literature has emphasized, a growing tangle of Anglo-American connections in the antebellum era encouraged expressions of both Anglophilia and Anglophobia among American writers, and also allowed sectional and numerous other subnational groups to draw strength from transatlantic associations.[3] Under these circumstances, late antebellum questions of national identity and literature were especially vexed and often contradictory, and the militarization of the sections seemed to confirm the general confusion surrounding questions of where the lines of American national identity and literature should be drawn.

Whether characterized by esteem or antagonism, however, relations with Britain remained an important variable in most Americans' beliefs about their nation and the literature associated with it, and the war brought fresh diplomatic tensions that altered the antebellum calculus for organizing Anglo-American national identity and literature. The literary status of antebellum writing depended partly on British judgments that involved politics as well as aesthetics, and debates over literary merit tended to address the larger question of whether the relatively young United States could yet claim a coherent national culture.[4] Thus, antebellum judgments about American literature were implicitly, and sometimes explicitly, judgments about America's national authenticity. Although dismissive British opinions caused nationalists some anxiety before the war, Britain's uncertain neutrality after 1861 made such opinions appear to be a matter of national survival. For northern readers, the specter of British diplomatic and military intervention—arising in part through British expressions of Confederate sympathy—gave new urgency to the old questions of how to deal with Britain's commanding position within anglophone culture. Publicized British dismissals of nationalist claims, which once might have explained why American books were not worth reading, were now tied to potential intervention and Confederate recognition, giving Unionists a concrete example of the potentially catastrophic effects of transatlantic judgments. *Harper's Weekly* could link Britain's war opinions to its control of American literary taste because both were, at heart, judgments about national legitimacy.

Although Whitman's perspectives on Britain were legion, he was undeniably primed to react similarly to British anti-Unionism; as Kenneth Price has argued, the author of three editions of *Leaves of Grass* stood out among his antebellum peers for the intensity of his refusals of British tradition.[5] Moreover, although the war troubled his antebellum celebrations of American unity, it also gave Whitman's transatlantic resistance a new context and sense of importance. Most significantly, fresh evidence of British hostility to the American republic in the wartime press created an opportunity to deflect attention from the political and literary problem of a divided nation. Indeed, *Drum-Taps* and *Sequel to Drum-Taps* (1865–66) largely ignore the rebellion based a short distance from where the poet spent much of the war; enemies emerge not as southerners but rather as more militant manifestations of the transatlantic oppositions that had inspired much of his previous verse.[6]

In these early postbellum writings, Whitman deployed the war's transatlantic aspects as a counterbalance to the war's legacy of national division in an attempt to recover and expand on his earlier articulations of literary nationalism. Widely publicized European hostility toward the Union allowed Whitman to recast a brutally sectional conflict as a successful transatlantic struggle that would render the American need for independent poetry incontestable. Whitman's antebellum and postbellum volumes of poetry made similar cases for a national literature; nevertheless, the latter could only establish the Civil War as a plausible basis for a common American undertaking because Britain's mainstream press and some of its leaders had predicted and even promoted the American nation's disintegration during the war. This allowed Whitman to reinterpret an internecine struggle poetically as confirmation of his earlier nationalist agenda, though Whitman's wartime experiences contributed new points of emphasis to that project. Most notably, the war poetry would oppose ancient racial bloodlines originating from the Atlantic's eastern shores with the blood of a new western race, blood recently shed in the nation's defense and symbolized by the veterans of the national armies.

In order to explain Whitman's rationale for regarding the war as a transatlantic struggle, I first examine the public challenges to American national legitimacy that had arisen from Britain's tenuous neutrality and from broadly held British assumptions about the sectional conflict. I then demonstrate how such challenges framed Whitman's personal view of the war in ways that would ultimately affect his poetry as well. I conclude with an interpretation of the war collections that treats European war coverage and ensuing northern reactions as significant poetic influences. The poems' multiple references to international hostility support such a reading, and I argue that British war observers in particular spurred Whitman to issue these blunt reminders of transatlantic tensions to assuage the traumatic memory of sectional conflict. At the same time, British imperial fantasies, publicized during the war and predicated on U.S. dissolution and Anglo-Saxon affiliations, helped shape Whitman's poetics in more fundamental ways. The war poetry can be read as a competing national fantasy organized around a new race, veterans of a struggle for independence who the poet insisted were bound to one another, to New World geography, and to a new history of modern war by a shared legacy of spilled blood. In the context of Whitman's vision of the war as a transatlantic contest, such blood displaced the significance of transatlantic bloodlines. Reacting to a recent past in which American nationalities had seemed dependent on transatlantic judgments, Whitman presented his war corpus as a violent defense of an abiding Atlantic divide, obscuring the history of intersectional conflict while promoting a unifying national literature.[7]

Steady Abuse

The apparent precariousness of British neutrality and the ongoing potential for intervention meant that Americans were compelled to track British Civil War news nearly as closely as they did the Confederacy's reportage, and the British press response proved surprisingly antagonistic for northern readers. *Harper's* had reason to single out the *Times* of London as the chief source of this anti-Union animus, for British papers tended to follow its lead. Moreover, the American journal's complaint about "the steady abuse which has been poured upon this country ... since the war began" requires only minor qualification. As Martin Crawford has shown, the *Times* took nearly a year to develop its rabid anti-Unionism.[8] Northern partisans had responded enthusiastically to the *Times*' first special correspondent, the celebrated William Howard Russell. That changed after Russell's scathing account of the federal rout at First Manassas, although the journalist thereafter known to his critics as "Bull Run Russell" remained disdainful of the slave system and sympathetic to the Union's cause, as did a number of prominent Britons. Many Unionist ears were deaf to such nuance, however, and heard only a constantly critical British refrain, especially once the *Times*' relatively unbiased early reporting gave way to echoes of Confederate leaders and the great propagandist for the South, Henry Hotze.[9]

The notable presence of antislavery figures in the British chorus only made their anti-Unionism more troubling, for even liberals often seemed to prefer a slave system to a unified America. A Liberal coalition governed Britain during the war, behind Prime Minister Palmerston and Earl Russell, the foreign minister. Although neither of these venerable British leaders was a friend of slavery, both in different ways appeared to advance the cause of Confederate recognition. Faced with a cotton shortage in 1862, Palmerston determined to revisit British neutrality by year's end, and Americans read news of his cabinet's preliminary discussions late that summer.[10] When Russell's correspondence with Lincoln's secretary of state, William Seward, appeared in northern newspapers in September, *Harper's Weekly* would undiplomatically describe them as "a sneer at our country, our cause, our army, our civilization, and our prospects."[11] At this inopportune time, William Gladstone, chancellor of the exchequer, gave a notorious speech in Newcastle announcing that Jefferson Davis had "made a nation," sending tremors through two continents. Gladstone had been heavily influenced by Hotze, and though he later insisted he had merely disclosed his personal interpretation of the American war, his comments were understood throughout Europe as an indication that official recognition was forthcoming. Although that recognition never came, the uproar over Gladstone's speech arrived at the time that neutrality was being most seriously questioned by Palmerston's ministers, and ensured that arguments against the Union would echo from the height of the British government to the humblest American newsreader.[12]

The following year, a new round of pro-Confederate publicity in the press coincided with the great Confederate victory at Chancellorsville and the surprising British lionization of Stonewall Jackson. That spring the South's parliamentary allies launched a new effort to bring a motion on recognition to the floor, and the motion's sponsor, John Arthur Roebuck, primed the pump with speeches that appeared in major American papers and dismissed America as a failed experiment. Roebuck had once been enthralled by the United States but had now changed his mind. Launching a debate on the American war in the Commons in late April, he described the "shock of opinion" that had accompanied news of its outbreak, and admitted that, "for myself the shock was of a very strong character, for all my early notions were that in America a great experiment was being made in government." Now, however, the war had confirmed democracy's failure. "When the news came, and that great experiment was at an end—*for it is at an end*," Roebuck insisted amid shouts of assent, "I say my heart failed me, for then I was compelled to acknowledge that men, under the most favorable circumstances, proved themselves unworthy of governing themselves."[13]

In place of the dream of democracy, Roebuck had set up a theory of racial supremacy and imperial ambition to which he also appealed in his speech. As "an Anglo-Saxon racist" who "was finishing a gradual transition to Toryism," he habitually disparaged the North's democracy as "mongrelised" and the immigrant population of northern states as "the scum and refuse of Europe."[14] On June 30, in his parliamentary motion for British intervention in the war, he publicly insulted the northern armies as "scum" while praising the southern leaders as "English gentlemen."[15] The North, a militarized racial mélange rather than a nation, stood to wield inordinate power after the war if it prevailed, eclipsing the power the United States had exerted prior to secession. "America while she was one,"

Roebuck reminded his fellow MPs, "ran a race of prosperity unparalleled in the world." The American nation had forced John Bull into galling humiliations. The transatlantic bloodletting was horrific, but southern independence was a godsend, for had the United States continued in its progress, "she would have been the bully of the world." Paraphrasing Shakespeare's *Julius Caesar*, Roebuck imagined a united America that:

> bestrode the narrow world
> Like a Colossus; and we petty men
> Walked under her huge legs and peeped about
> To find ourselves dishonoured graves.

Horrified by the prospect of renewed American power, Roebuck pledged his determination "to do all I can to prevent the reconstruction of the Union" and hoped "the balance of power on the American continent will, in the future, prevent any one state from tyrannizing over the world as the Republic did." If Parliament would rally to this mission, he foresaw a British future in which "we shall be a much greater people, and London will be the Imperial city of the world."[16]

Roebuck was an extreme example of British perspectives on the Union, and his poorly timed and ineptly executed motion would be withdrawn.[17] Nevertheless, abstracts and sometimes full transcripts of his speeches made him infamous among northerners.[18] Moreover, although the government was still unwilling to intervene in a dangerous war, Roebuck's reading of Britain's press and parliament was not entirely mistaken; on the day he proposed his motion, the majority of those who shaped public opinion and policy likely considered the division of America inevitable. While many were opposed to official recognition, the South's secession seemed to confirm that the American nation was little more than an arbitrary confederation of former colonies, an unconvincing nationalist fiction. The *Times* captured the patronizing tone of this widespread British judgment against northern nationalism in the run-up to Roebuck's motion. A May 2 editorial declared: "The United States are not to be the very great, very united, very powerful, very glorious, very free, very wealthy, very unencumbered people that they expected to be. They are to be rather more like the rest of the world." After two years of the Civil War, the British press was ready to join Roebuck in announcing the end of America's national experiment, and the implication was not lost on northern readers.[19] The *Atlantic Monthly* summarized the British refusal to recognize the North's nationalist claims late in the war by quoting Seward: "The United States claim . . . they are a whole sovereign nation, and entitled to the same respect, as such, that they accord to Great Britain. Great Britain does not treat them as such a sovereign."[20]

While Roebuck's racism led him to favor the South and dispute the United States' status as an authentic nation, less antagonistic racial identifications could also diminish British support for the Union once casualties began rising. For example, the idea that bloodlines bridged both the sectional and Atlantic divides caused otherwise supportive Britons, recoiling at the enormous cost in "English" blood required to maintain a dubious national union, to pursue peace even at the expense of the antislavery cause. Because large populations on both sides of the pond shared a language as well as a British heritage, Britons who still regarded most Americans as distant relations could have difficulty understanding why the division between North and South was any less acceptable than the Anglo-American separation of the previous century.[21]

The British blood tie also meant that ending the American cousins' fratricidal war could make London, as Roebuck gleefully predicted, the "imperial city of the world," the metropolitan heart of a global affiliation of Anglo-Saxon states. This imperial fantasy, as much as the prospect of a divided American continent, was anathema to Walt Whitman, especially since Britons like Roebuck appealed to the same Anglo-Saxon bloodline to exclude and slander many of the Union soldiers the poet had come to love while working in army hospitals. While Roebuck and others had publicly insulted these young men as the dregs of Europe, Whitman would craft a competing fantasy that cast them as ideal types of a new American nationality, representatives of a racial identity predicated on a new sort of blood tie and requiring a new kind of war poetry.[22]

"Never Forget"

To read clippings from the ubiquitous *Times* as a northerner in the war's middle years was to encounter one's own nationality weighed and felt wanting by a great transatlantic arbiter. Whenever the Union war effort ebbed, British dismissals of the American nation flowed. At such moments the Civil War appeared in the mainstream British press as a farce as well as a tragedy, in which deluded former colonials violently defended the sham of a nation that had never truly existed— at least in a sense recognizable to the Old World. Britain's characterization of the United States as a pretender nation with only a "thin history" and a culture unworthy of consideration reiterated a major antebellum theme to which Whitman, Emerson, and other advocates for national literature in varying degrees had responded.[23] Contradictions that, as Susan-Mary Grant has argued, had beset northern nationalism since the rise of the Republican party, became more glaring under the British gaze during the war, for the North's claims of national unity were not necessarily more compelling to outside observers than the South's claim to national independence.[24] Thus, even as the Confederacy pursued Britain's official recognition as a military and diplomatic objective, Unionists were forced to grapple with the unofficial but very public British refusal to recognize their own national status.

These fresh judgments and the arc of Whitman's antebellum career gave him an incentive to see the war as a transatlantic struggle against the threat of European domination. Thus, in an intimate letter to a beloved soldier in the spring of 1863, Whitman wrote:

> life would have no charm for me if this country should fail after all, and be reduced to take a third rate position, to be domineered over by England & France & the haughty nations of Europe &c and we unable to help ourselves. But I have no thought that will ever be, this country I hope would spend her last drop of blood, and last dollar, rather than submit to such humiliation.[25]

Somewhat later, he again alluded to transatlantic hostility in the diary that became the basis for *Memoranda During the War*, but now with a stronger sense of that scorn's salubrious effects.

> The happening to our America, abroad as well as at home, these years, is indeed most strange. The Democratic Republic has paid her to-day the terrible and resplendent compliment of the united wish of all the nations of the world that her Union should be broken, her future cut off, and that she should be compell'd to descend to the level of kingdoms and empires ordinarily great![26]

Like *Harper's Weekly*, Whitman saw transatlantic hostility as a "resplendent compliment" that arose from European fears of American power and that would ultimately invigorate American national culture. British animosity had already "help'd, braced, concentrated" the American republic, which otherwise had been "too prone to wander from ourselves, to affect Europe, and watch her frowns and smiles." Wartime tensions seemed bound to alleviate one of Whitman's main literary frustrations: overcoming American subservience to British cultural standards. "We need the hot lesson of general hatred," Whitman reminded himself, "and henceforth must never forget it. Never again will we trust the moral sense nor the abstract friendliness of a single government of the old world."[27] These personal reactions mirrored the northern response to transatlantic tensions that had been publicized during the war to gin up nationalist unity among the populace by the likes of William Seward. Thus Whitman had reason to think, in the aftermath of a national cataclysm, that at least one element of Civil War memory might provide a basis for a renewal of exceptionalist fantasy that could undergird a unified national literature.

The war collections suggest an attempt to validate such a fantasy through direct reminders of "the hot lesson of general hatred." But more broadly, *Drum-Taps* and its sequel can be interpreted as aesthetic constructions designed to carry nationalistically inclined readers through severe fluctuations of national feeling and leave them "help'd, braced, concentrated," and confirmed in their beliefs, partly through imagery that implicitly addressed the threat British observers had posed to northern nationalism. Many Britons had seen secession as historical proof that a democratic experiment within a more general Anglo-Saxon history had failed. Whitman's collections sought to vindicate the poetry of democracy by suggesting a new national history emerging indisputably before the eyes of the world. Britons' anti-Americanism had challenged the North's nationalist notions, but so too had their "abstract friendliness": their interest in the war, judgments about its meaning for American nationalities, and familial attempts to stanch the flow of English blood. Whitman's poetics center American war memory on experiences far removed from any that a transatlantic observer could share. His vision of postbellum America—represented by the racialized figure of the veteran-comrade, rooted in western geography, and energized by intimate associations with war history—invokes an audience immune from transatlantic judgments and therefore primed for a national literature.

At War with the World

In describing *Drum-Taps* to a postbellum collaborator, Whitman had praised an artful arrangement that outshone his previous work: "[*Drum-Taps*] is in my opinion superior to Leaves of Grass—certainly more perfect as a work of art, being adjusted in all its proportions.... I am perhaps mainly satisfied with Drum-Taps because it delivers my ambition of the task that has haunted me, namely, to express in a poem (& in the way I like, which is not at all by directly stating it) the pending action of this *Time & Land* we swim in."[28] Many readers would dispute Whitman's assessment, and perceptive critics have cited *Drum-Taps* for "ineffective organization."[29] Nevertheless, the comment locates a unifying motivation for the war collections in the poet's desire to address national history as a "pending action" and national identity as a fluid construction. As an attempt to express a "time and land" in which one swam rather than walked, Whitman's indirect approach reflected the uncertainties that characterized an unsettled psychological state of an imagined nation with a tenuous claim to shared history.[30]

Yet his relatively direct allusions to transatlantic tensions point toward a recovery project aimed at establishing firmer ground for postbellum nationalism. As reminders of the "general hatred" that had helped destabilize American nationalities during the war, international references reinforced the need among Unionists for independence from such foreign views. Whitman depended on these recalled slights to set the stage for other poems that "braced" and "concentrated" his readers' nationalist desires around a new "race of veterans" determined to resist Old World heritage and transatlantic judgments. Marked by shared intimacy with a purely domestic war history and based in a landscape suffused with their own blood, such a race would demand its own distinctive literature, the poet could hope, because it had demonstrated its national character in the face of insidious British appraisals of its country and its culture.

Several poems in both collections directly recall international challenges to the American nation. The short *Drum-Taps* poem, "World, Take Good Notice," flaunts the national flag before European powers that had advanced territorial claims in North America during the war. Whitman's banner of "coals thirty-six, baleful and burning" does not admit secession's temporary elimination of southern states from the national firmament, but it also cautions against foreign meddlers eager to exploit the republic's distress. Recalling northern worries surrounding British and French schemers who, while pursuing their designs in Mexico, might also have hoped to wrest control of several stars from the American banner, the poem's conclusion promises that a blustery "hands off warning" will "now and henceforth flaunt from these shores" (*DT* 67). "Lo! Victress on the Peaks," one of the last poems of *Sequel to Drum-Taps*, returns to these international conspiracies, as the narrator addresses the sort of feminized colossus that had towered over Roebuck's nightmare of global American power. Whitman's vision raises his Victress Libertad supreme over a continent, but she looks triumphantly east rather than south. "Lo! Victress on the peaks! / Where thou standest, with mighty brow, regarding the world / (The world, O Libertad, that vainly conspired against thee;)" (*SDT* 23). The domestic unity suggested in such visions went hand-in-hand with a threat of transatlantic conflict, for in seeking the Union's enemy abroad Whitman was also avoiding a more obvious enemy at home. Combined with blatant appeals to the sections' shared revolutionary heritage, such as Whitman's long narrative poem, "The Centenarian's Story," these clear reminders of recent transatlantic opposition suggested an American Union compelled to define itself perpetually against a transatlantic foe rather than a southern enemy.[31]

In this fight, as opposed to a war against the South, Whitman could hope to play a role as national bard. Ted Genoways has observed that the poet recognized "it was impossible to construct a national narrative of the war, precisely because it was a *civil* war. For the preservation of the Union to be complete, the prodigal son of the South would have to be welcomed back."[32] Yet precisely this problem helps explain why the transatlantic contest appealed to Whitman as an alternative to a purely domestic struggle, and it had the added benefit of throwing a lifeline to an antebellum project that sectionalism's violence might otherwise have sunk.

Thus, the war's transatlantic aspects enabled Whitman's militarization of his previous declarations of literary independence. When the war collections refer to the poet's writing explicitly, they often rehearse antebellum formulations. In its explicit calls for new literature for a New World, for instance, there seems little to distinguish *Drum-Taps* and *Sequel* from *Leaves of Grass*—or from Emerson's essays for that matter. What is different is the war itself, and Whitman's determination to superimpose war's violence over the previous literary crusade. Yet the conflation of the two struggles would make little sense without a common foe, and this was precisely what the South could not provide. The assumption that the war had liberated the United States from a transatlantic power, supported by a recent history of British antagonism, allowed Whitman to associate his old poetic mission with the historical experience of a war against European dominance. Against a backdrop of transatlantic antagonism, the active physicality of military service could be contrasted to the passivity of traditional verse, and the war's conclusion could be imagined, not as an imperial imposition of North over South, but as a pivot point toward a future freed from antebellum doubts that the poet associated with Old World influences. Thus, the short poem "1861" identifies the war's onset with the ascendency of Whitman's free verse over the pale disciples of a Eurocentric literary tradition, and aligns it with a militaristic history charged with active desire.

> Arm'd year! year of the the struggle!
> No dainty rhymes or sentimental love verses for you, terrible year!
> Not you as some pale poetling, seated at a desk, lisping cadenzas piano.
> But as a strong man, erect, clothed in blue clothes, advancing, carrying a rifle on
>   your shoulder,
> With well-gristled body and sunburnt face and hands—with a knife in the belt
>   at your side. (*DT* 17)

The war's conclusion is similarly recounted as a liberating revolution away from Europe and its slights against the nation in "Turn O Libertad," a *Sequel* poem that implicitly addresses transatlantic tensions and the Old World's outdated models for judging nations and literature. "Turn, O Libertad, no more doubting" the poet advises, "Turn from lands retrospective, recording proofs of the past." Refusing the Old World's retrospective standards and doubt-inducing proofs of the past, the poem echoes an Emersonian vision of national history, and its rejection of staid tradition was perfectly in keeping with Whitman's antebellum work.[33] Yet here again, Whitman could confirm and add to that work by recalling the more recent history of transatlantic animosity. Northern newsreaders, for example, were aware that claims of national unity had been undercut in Britain by analogies drawn from the ancient world. Popularized in bestsellers and newspapers, political theories based on ancient precedents assumed the breakup of the American nation as an inevitable outcome of its continental span.[34] The republic's ability to survive the test intact suggested that ancient standards could not be applied to modern nations, casting doubt on the supposedly reliable "proofs of the past." Similarly, the Union victory brought Whitman renewed hope, after years of lackluster responses to *Leaves of Grass*, that America would turn from outdated literary standards as well and toward a new poetry worthy of their recent and unprecedented experience. This new poetics would attempt to locate a fresh basis for nationalism and national literature in the war's action, energetic spirit, and continental sweep rather than ancient races, European histories, and cultural traditions. "Turn," sings the poet of the present and future, "From the singers that sing the trailing glories of the past, / From the chants of the feudal world—the triumphs of kings, slavery, caste" (*DT* 70).

The chief struggle of Whitman's just-completed war was not to defeat the South nor, more tragically, to free the slave. Rather he sought, as he had before the war, to liberate the American nation from the Old World's influence. As his dedicatory *Drum-Taps* poem, "Shut Not Your Doors to Me Proud Libraries," makes clear, Whitman desperately hoped that a militantly nationalistic "turn" would bring the American public around to a new sort of poetry—a literature just as committed to separating itself from mostly British antecedents as Whitman had imagined his soldier correspondents would be to resisting the threat of European dominance. "A book I have made for your dear sake, O soldiers ... A book separate, not link'd with the rest, nor felt by the intellect. / But you will feel every word, O Libertad! arm'd Libertad!" (*DT* 8). Rather than gazing east for recognition, the poet turned his readers west toward an expansionist and exceptionalist fantasy populated by a new race of veterans whose shed blood, he imagined, could become a renewed nation's bloodline.

Continental Blood

At the conclusion of "Lo! Victress on the Peaks," the poet again presents a globally triumphant Libertad with an offering of poetry, but this time describes it as "a little book, containing night's darkness, and blood-dripping wounds" (*SDT* 70). The macabre image is not hyperbolic; blood is everywhere in the poems. Yet many of Whitman's bloody references do not correspond to how violence was often dealt with in war journalism and literature. The Civil War's brutality had shocked even those who encountered it secondhand through newspapers, illustrations, and photographs. Yet Whitman, who had personally assisted the wounded and dying in the hospitals, sometimes refers to blood in strikingly positive ways. It often appears as a sign of energy or courage: in "Drum-Taps," the poet rejoices in an urban arousal, "the blood of the city up" (*DT* 6); in "Weave in, Weave in My Hardy Life," he promises to "weave in red blood!" (*DT* 69); and in "Song of the Banner at Day-break" he determines to "pour the verse with streams of blood, full of volition, full of joy" (*DT* 9). Of course, blood also appears to mark wounds and even deaths, but does not necessarily indicate the traumatizing or chastening experience that some readers might expect. Rarely are images of spilled blood signs of finality, even when the wounds are mortal; far more often they are precursors to regeneration and movement, historical echoes of spiritual hopes. Thus the blood that spills quite graphically in "The Dresser" makes a lasting mark on the nation that inspires further national life. The wounded soldiers' "priceless blood reddens the grass, the ground" (*DT* 32) inside a hospital tent, as the poem evokes not only the priceless blood of Christian memory but the central symbols of nature's resurrections from *Leaves of Grass*. There, in "Song of Myself," the poetic narrator had answered a child's question about grass by professing that "the smallest sprouts show there is really no death" except death that "led forward life."[35] "The Dresser's" aged narrator conveys a similar indication of a hopeful future "in answer to children" by sharing the image of the blood-stained grass with an imagined distant generation, citizens of the nation such shed blood had secured (*DT* 31). "A March in the Ranks Hard-prest and the Road Unknown," another hospital poem, also emphasizes the memory of blood as an avenue toward movement into the future. Entering a torch-lit church that has become a makeshift hospital, the narrator witnesses a young soldier bleeding to death. Yet within the church, blood and bodies again point to beginnings more than endings: the repeated "odor" of blood and a smile from a dying boy's nearly bloodless lips linger with the narrator as he continues the movement alluded to in the title, out of the church and over "the unknown road still marching" (*DT* 44–45).

If Whitman's book was drenched in blood, so was the nation he imagined. Torn and bloody flags populate the poetry. The country's ground and grass are reddened by it. Moreover, Whitman's poetic narrator never seems utterly revolted by such horrors, and sometimes seems to regard the war's bloodshed as a baptism for the postbellum nation (*DT* 24). As readers we have a right to be disturbed as well as confused by Whitman's apparent readiness to endorse nationalist profiteering from civil conflict's horrendous casualties. In retrospect this certainly seems another tired instance of the nineteenth century's rhetoric of sacrificial suffering, and a refusal to recognize how the mortal results of war's violence, as one critic observes, might also lead to "a less inspiring account of the relationship between death and national community."[36] Nevertheless, the wider global struggle that clearly shaped Whitman's conception of the war suggests another possible interpretation, one that reconciles his two most explicit descriptions of his war collections as books "not link'd to the rest" (*DT* 8) and exhibiting "blood-dripping wounds" (*SDT* 70). If we reimagine the war, as Whitman seems to have done, as a struggle against transatlantic influence, then the spilled blood of soldiers may also reveal an alternative to the authority of a transatlantic bloodline, an alternative that the poet presents as a basis for an independent national culture.

Whitman's tendency to combine images of blood with images of the embattled New World geography supports such a reading. In both collections, American territory is decisively marked by the blood of soldiers on the march. At the same time, Whitman describes the soldiers as an original race; their blood ties them only to one another, in a horizontal lineage not attributable to Europe. Thus they can serve the poet's vision, in the wake of what he casts as a transatlantic struggle, by becoming a sacrament of national unity. Blood spilled over the continent during an internecine conflict creates in Whitman's fantasy a spiritually infused landscape that enforces the Atlantic divide. Union soldiers appear in his poems not as the mongrelized amalgamation of European races that Roebuck perceived.[37] Rather they become, as one of Whitman's shortest war poems describes them succinctly, a "race of veterans" not just on the march over the soil of the New World, but also a race "of" that march and "of" that soil; as Whitman's racial fantasy, they have been produced not by ancient roots, but rather by that history they have also recently made:

> Race of veterans!
> Race of the soil, ready for conflict! race of the conquering march!
> (No more credulity's race, abiding-temper'd race;)
> Race owning no law but the law of itself;
> Race of passion and the storm. (*SDT* 12)

Turned away from their Old World origins, no longer credulously watching for the "frowns and smiles" of Europe, Whitman's imagined veterans are made to carry the passion and storm of the war within their racial makeup, as guardians of a new era of permanent independence.

The absolute division between this new race and the Old World receives its most complete articulation in one of *Drum-Taps*'s better-known poems, but one that some readers have regarded as "unrelated" to the war collections' broader themes of "suffering and heroism."[38] Yet "Pioneers! O Pioneers!," whose central term was used to describe soldiers who traveled in advance of the Union armies, can also be read as a Civil War poem.[39] Bristling with martial imagery of violence and the march, it also suggests transatlantic struggle as a crucial link between the experiences of pioneering and soldiering:

> Come, my tan-faced children,
> Follow well in order, get your weapons ready;
> Have you your pistols? have you your sharp edged axes?
>   Pioneers! O pioneers!
>
> For we cannot tarry here,
> We must march my darlings, we must bear the brunt of danger,
> We, the youthful sinewy races, all the rest on us depend,
>   Pioneers! O pioneers!
>
> O you youths, western youths,
> So impatient, full of action, full of manly pride and friendship,
> Plain I see you, western youths, see you tramping with the foremost,
>   Pioneers! O pioneers!
>
> Have the elder races halted?
> Do they droop and end their lesson, wearied, over there beyond the seas?
> We take up the task eternal, and the burden, and the lesson,
>   Pioneers! O pioneers! (*DT* 25)

In the context of the wider collections, the explicitly racialized imagery of the poem's first stanzas calls to march the western youths who filled the Union ranks and its hospitals in the eastern theaters of war. The depiction of these pioneers as "tan-faced" echoes numerous descriptions of tan, brown, or dusty soldiers from elsewhere in the collections. This resonance complicates the poem's apparently easy compatibility with Anglo-Saxon mythmaking. As a gathering en masse of the historical characters Whitman celebrated in another *Drum-Taps* poem, "O Tan Faced Prairie Boy," the tan-faced pioneers appear as an explicitly racialized rendering of the recruits from America's vast and growing interior who, "detachments steady throwing" into the fray, came east to save the Union from the foreign domination that Whitman believed would follow its defeat (*DT* 57; *DT* 26):

> Colorado men are we,
> From the peaks gigantic, from the great sierras and the high plateaus,
> From the mine and from the gully, from the hunting trail we come,
>   Pioneers! O pioneers!
>
> From Nebraska, from Arkansas,
> Central inland race are we, from Missouri, with the continental blood
>   intervein'd;

> All the hands of comrades clasping, all the Southern, all the Northern,
> Pioneers! O pioneers!⁴⁰ (*DT* 26)

Read in tandem with Whitman's recruitment poems celebrating "an arm'd race ... advancing" (*DT* 7), the first appearance of the pioneers' mastery of frontier lands in these stanzas offers merely a dramatic prelude to how the battlefield will test their youthful manhood under a Union battle flag:

> Raise the mighty mother mistress,
> Waving high the delicate mistress, over all the starry mistress, (bend your
>   heads all,)
> Raise the fang'd and warlike mistress, stern, impassive, weapon'd mistress,
> Pioneers! O pioneers! (*DT* 27)

In this alternative racial fantasy of war, Whitman's fighting men are not reducible to Anglo-Saxons who just happen to stand under a western sky. While British observers like Roebuck may have arranged them in distinct racial categories to be judged based on notions of English purity, the poet's "youthful sinewy races" are a rather proudly "mongrelized" amalgamation of many states, and his fighting men are not white but tan.⁴¹ In identifying the saviors of the nation as an "inland" rather than an Atlantic race—one made superior by their "continental blood intervein'd" and defined by their mustering of diversity rather than common association with any "elder race"—Whitman was contradicting typical British assumptions about the significance of European bloodlines to the war's outcome. The more benign form of these British beliefs merely emphasized the South's supposed racial purity and the North's reliance on German and Irish troops. The more scurrilous generated propagandistic descriptions of the sort Roebuck had spouted, disparaging Union soldiers as a racially degenerate collection of mercenaries drawn from the dregs of Europe. In place of that transatlantic lineage, Whitman's war poetry looks to a new continental bloodline as the sign of an independent nation, revealed in the midst of a bloody war. Yet in order to imagine such a nation, Whitman was compelled to root its racial essence in a West where North and South become one, and to turn its weapons to the East. More problematically, he reoriented the war's discourses of race and emancipation away from African Americans, to whom he seemed increasingly indifferent, and toward Union soldiers who became symbols of racial liberation and empowerment. In these ways he forgot the war even as he remembered it.

Conclusion

In the outcome of Whitman's war fantasy, seen in retrospect from an imagined future, western blood had secured not merely the antebellum republic, but a new nation that no longer had to cater to transatlantic judgments. The national "mother of all" who twice appears to bind South to North in *Drum-Taps*, and who suffuses the soil of the New World with an independent spirit derived from her bleeding and lost children, also promises her sons, "You shall yet laugh to scorn the attacks of all the remainder of the earth. / No danger shall balk Columbia's lovers" (*DT* 49). In the penultimate poem of the first collection, the only mother country the poet is willing to acknowledge, "pensive on her dead gazing," calls to her receiving earth to "absorb them well, taking their dear blood":

> My dead absorb—my young men's beautiful bodies absorb—and their
>   precious, precious, precious blood;
> Which holding in trust for me, faithfully back again give me,
>   many a year hence,
> In unseen essence and odor of surface and grass, centuries hence. (*DT* 71)

Thus, Whitman attempts to mark the postbellum continent with a perpetual bloodline of a new race, a national legacy to be breathed and encountered in nature rather than retrospectively worshiped at a father's tomb. Yet in order for nature and nation to be intermingled in such transformative soil, Whitman had to recall a war that had reestablished the Atlantic border against "the remainder of the earth."

It may be the case that a long-standing tendency to overlook that international "remainder" as a significant component of the Civil War experience has contributed to fairly typical characterizations of both *Drum-Taps* and its sequel as haphazardly organized and thematically inconsistent works. Current interest in international aspects of the war may also help reveal how British constructions and deconstructions of American nationality during the war affected debates over national literature, including those in which Whitman was engaged. If nothing else, an internationalist perspective on war history can contribute to a somewhat more coherent interpretation of *Drum-Taps* and *Sequel to Drum-Taps* as a struggle with national doubt that resolves itself in a national fantasy molded by resistance to transatlantic pressures. If not entirely as artful as its author claimed, the structure of the collections nevertheless demonstrates the poet's determination to salvage from a history of national division, a vision of a land "help'd, braced, [and] concentrated" in its opposition to transatlantic observers.

NOTES

1. *Harper's Weekly*, November 7, 1863, 706.
2. See for example R. J. M. Blackett, *Divided Hearts: Britain and the American Civil War* (Baton Rouge: Louisiana State University Press, 2001); Amanda Foreman, *World on Fire: Britain's Crucial Role in the American Civil War* (New York: Random House, 2010); Brian Jenkins, *Britain and the War for the Union*, 2 vols. (Montreal: McGill-Queen's University Press, 1974–80); Howard Jones, *Blue and Gray Diplomacy: A History of Union and Confederate Foreign Relations* (Chapel Hill: University of North Carolina Press, 2010); Robert E. May, ed., *The Union, the Confederacy, and the Atlantic Rim* (West Lafayette: Purdue University Press, 1995).
3. See for example Elisa Tamarkin, *Anglophilia: Deference, Devotion, and Antebellum America* (Chicago: University of Chicago Press, 2008); Christopher Hanlon, *America's England: Antebellum Literature and Atlantic Sectionalism* (Oxford: Oxford University Press, 2013); and Sam W. Haynes, *Unfinished Revolution: The Early American Republic in a British World* (Charlottesville: University of Virginia Press, 2011).
4. See Robert Weisbuch, *Atlantic Double-Cross: American Literature and British Influence in the Age of Emerson* (Chicago: University of Chicago Press, 1986).
5. Kenneth Price, *Whitman and Tradition: the Poet in His Century* (New Haven: Yale University Press, 1990), 8–34.
6. Walt Whitman, *Drum-Taps* and *Sequel to Drum-Taps* (New York, 1865–66), http://www.whitmanarchive.org. Citations will refer to the page numbers in the combined first edition, hereafter documented parenthetically as *DT* and *SDT*.
7. In addition to repeating antebellum claims, many of the war poems seem to prefigure triumphalist versions of exceptionalism that emerged during the Cold War, and to that extent might be subjected to some of the same criticism that scholars have leveled at these twentieth-century conceptualizations of American distinctiveness. Nevertheless, Cold War–era models of essentialism that treated American nationality as a well-established legacy do not capture the historical contingency of poetry addressed to a very recent political scene in which multiple national and international identities had been explored, contested, and thwarted. Critiques of exceptionalism that stress the role of fantasy in structuring national desires and binding subjects to the state, especially in relation to challenges involving partition and external empires, seem more pertinent to Whitman's immediate postbellum work. For an account of the role of fantasy in later versions of exceptionalism, see Donald E. Pease, *The New American Exceptionalism* (Minneapolis: University of Minnesota Press, 2009), 1–39. See also Donald E. Pease and Robyn Wiegman, eds., *Futures of American Studies* (Durham: Duke University Press, 2002).
8. See Marin Crawford, *Anglo-American Crisis* (Athens: University of Georgia Press, 1987), 128–33; William Howard Russell, *My Diary North and South* (New York: Harper and Row, 1965), 65–68.
9. The same issue of *Harper's Weekly* that excoriated Britain's press identified at least a handful of "English friends." *Harper's Weekly*, November 7, 1863, 706.

10. See Foreman, *World on Fire*, 282–83.

11. "Another Sneer from Earl Russell," *Harper's Weekly*, September 13, 1862, 578.

12. For the most complete study of the 1862 crisis, see Howard Jones, *Union in Peril: The Crisis over British Intervention in the Civil War* (Chapel Hill: University of North Carolina Press, 1992); for Gladstone's response, see Foreman, *World on Fire*, 321.

13. *New York Tribune*, May 7, 1863, 2; for the Sheffield speech and comment, see *New York Tribune*, June 8, 1863, 2, 4.

14. D. P. Crook, *The North, the South, and the Powers: 1861–1865* (New York: John Wiley and Sons, 1974), 311–12. See also J. A. Roebuck, *Life and Letters of John Arthur Roebuck P.C., Q.C., M.P., with Chapters of Autobiography*, ed. Robert Eadon Leader (London: Edward Arnold, 1897), 295.

15. Jones, *Union in Peril*, 272n4. See also, Jenkins, *Britain and the War for the Union*, 2:309–12.

16. Quoted in Frank Lawrence Owsley, *King Cotton Diplomacy: Foreign Relations of the Confederate States of America* (Chicago: University of Chicago Press, 1959), 452. Whitman likely knew of Roebuck's American Colossus, which appeared in the July 13 issues of the *New York Daily Tribune* and the *New York Times*.

17. See Jenkins, *Britain and the War for the Union*, 1:310–12.

18. "What [Roebuck] has recently said and done in reference to this country is too fresh in our memories to require that we should recite or recapitulate it here" ("Who Is Roebuck?," *Atlantic Monthly*, September 1, 1863, 394).

19. *Times*, May 2, 1863, 10.

20. "Our Recent Foreign Relations," *Atlantic Monthly*, August 1, 1864, 251.

21. See "Letter to an English Friend," *Harper's Weekly*, April 4, 1863, 210–11.

22. The relationship of state and national fantasies to imperial alternatives is complicated and varies according to historical context, but may help explain their psychological appeal; Donald Pease describes several ways of theorizing these connections and develops his own model in *New American Exceptionalism*, 1–39.

23. See Haynes, *Unfinished Revolution*, 51–76. See also Weisbuch, *Atlantic Double-Cross*.

24. See Susan-Mary Grant, *North over South: Northern Nationalism and American Identity in the Antebellum Era* (Lawrence: University Press of Kansas, 2000), 130–52.

25. Whitman to Sawyer, April 21, 1863, in *Selected Letters of Walt Whitman*, ed. Edwin H. Miller (Iowa City: University of Iowa Press, 1990), 55–57.

26. Walt Whitman, *Memoranda during the War*, ed. Peter Coviello (New York: Oxford University Press, 2004), 117.

27. Ibid., 118.

28. Whitman to William D. O'Connor, January 6, 1865, in *Selected Letters*, 108.

29. Harold Aspiz, *So Long! Walt Whitman's Poetry of Death* (Tuscaloosa: University of Alabama, 2004), 163. For a defense of the poems that acknowledges such objections, see M. Wynn Thomas, *The Lunar Light of Whitman's Poetry* (Cambridge: Harvard University Press, 1987), 185–93.

30. Luke Mancuso finds that the poetry "bears the incision marks of the immediate

cultural confusion after four years of violence." See "Civil War," in *A Companion to Walt Whitman*, ed. Donald D. Kummings (Oxford: Blackwell Publishing, 2006), 299.

31. The poem's heroes are a brigade of southerners sacrificed to cover Washington's retreat from the Battle of Brooklyn; the poet insists these heroes remain as a ghostly presence within the Union's "Encampments new!" (*SDT* 23–24).

32. Ted Genoways, "Civil War Poems in 'Drum-Taps' and 'Memories of President Lincoln,'" in Kummings, *Companion to Walt Whitman*, 528.

33. See Eduardo Cadava, *Emerson and the Climate of History* (Stanford: Stanford University Press, 1997).

34. James Spence's 1862 bestseller, *The American Union*, helped promote this theory, which underlay many of the mainstream press's pronouncements. See Blackett, *Divided Hearts*, 138.

35. Walt Whitman, *Leaves of Grass* (New York: 1855), 16–17, http://www.whitmanarchive.org.

36. Franny Nudelman, *John Brown's Body: Slavery, Violence, and the Culture of War Singing* (Chapel Hill: University of North Carolina Press, 2004), 4. For a survey of the cultural meanings drawn from the dead, see Drew Gilpin Faust, *This Republic of Suffering: Death and the American Civil War* (New York: Alfred A. Knopf, 2008).

37. Ironically, Whitman had used similar racial logic in his early journalistic work to justify American expansionism in Texas and to dismiss Mexican sovereignty, although as Donald Pease points out, Whitman's emergence as a poet in the 1850s complicated a perspective that had simplistically conflated Anglo-Saxon identity with national legitimacy in the 1840s. See Donald Pease, "Colonial Violence and Poetic Transcendence in Whitman's 'Song of Myself,'" in *The Cambridge Companion to Nineteenth-Century American Poetry*, ed. Kerry Larson (New York: Cambridge University Press, 2011), 227–44.

38. Aspiz, *So Long!*, 163.

39. Timothy Sweet, *Traces of War: Poetry, Photography, and the Crisis of the Union* (Baltimore: Johns Hopkins University Press, 1990), 156.

40. Claimed by the Confederacy, the slave states of Arkansas and Missouri were under at least partial federal control for much of the war and supplied Union troops.

41. For an alternative view of the transatlantic unity of such modified whiteness, see Peter Coviello, *Intimacy in America: Dreams of Affiliation in Antebellum Literature* (Minneapolis: University of Minnesota Press, 2005), 108.

Surplus Patriotism
William Gilmore Simms's War Poetry of the South *and the Afterlife of Confederate Literary Nationalism*

COLEMAN HUTCHISON

In late 1866 the *New York Times* offered a relatively fair and balanced review of a recent collection of Confederate literature, William Gilmore Simms's *War Poetry of the South* (1866).[1] Not yet "the newspaper of record," the *Times* had been a consistently pro-Union, pro-Republican, and pro-Lincoln publication throughout the American Civil War. (Indeed, its offices were a target of the 1863 New York City draft riots.) However, the newspaper often struck a more moderate, reconciliatory tone after the war, when it advocated for the restoration of the Confederate states to the Union.[2]

These print politics might help to explain the newspaper's conflicted, somewhat begrudging assessment of *War Poetry of the South*: "it is, perhaps, well that this phase of the struggle should be represented in our belligerent literature by a volume of this character."[3] Despite such equivocation, the *Times* reviewer was not surprised that the Civil War South had produced such a surfeit of nationalistic poetry: "Ardent, impulsive, and, indeed poetical as the Southern nature is . . . it would have been strange, we say, if the surplus patriotism of non-combatants generally, as well as that of those actually in the field, had not found expression in verse." The reviewer goes on to commend Simms—the southern man of letters par excellence—for choosing not to "suppress those poetic outbursts which even now border closely on the ludicrous, especially when subjected to the test of phlegmatic Northern criticism." Simms had, the review concluded, "apparently done his work thoroughly, and with a sincere desire to make the collection a fair reflex of Southern sentiment as it was in the heat of the great struggle."

For all its ambivalence, this northern review significantly undersells the problems produced by that southern sentiment and heat. In truth, the question of what to do with the South's "surplus patriotism" haunted the *New York Times*, William Gilmore Simms, and Reconstruction-era America in equal measure. How would the newly re-United States manage excess national feeling, especially in the South? What would be the fate and legacy of the South's "poetic outbursts"? Simms's collection of "belligerent literature" provided an uncommon opportunity to ask such questions, not least because public feeling was the volume's sine qua non.

In addition to being one of the largest and most diverse contemporary anthologies of Confederate poetry, *War Poetry of the South* is also, by a significant margin, the most important. Simms drew poetry from all of the Confederate states, as well as several border states; he also included a good deal of his own verse. Not surprisingly, the 205 poems in the collection vary greatly in tone, topic, and literary quality. The result is a generous and more or less representative sampling of Confederate literary culture.

The collection was of great interest to its editor, who took up the ambitious project while his personal and professional life lay in ruins following the dissolution of the Confederate States of America. Simms gave nearly a year of his late life to *War Poetry of the South*, which bears the marks of his editorial care as well as his vast connections to the southern literati. However, since its publication, *War Poetry of the South* has suffered "long years of neglect."[4] Historians and literary critics alike have consistently underestimated this nearly five-hundred-page volume.[5] Like so much of Confederate literature, *War Poetry of the South* is only occasionally cited and rarely discussed. Nevertheless, the collection should be of great interest to twenty-first century readers since it grants us access to a largely evanescent phenomenon: the birth and death of a national literary culture.

In the following pages, I offer a history of this neglected book, one that situates *War Poetry of the South* in relation to other anthologies of Confederate poetry and considers the status of Confederate nationalism after Appomattox. As a result, my readings of Simms's text will be undertaken from some distance: I only offer three "close readings" of poems from this capacious collection—and even those are truncated. This is in keeping with an alternative approach to poetry anthologies, which we rarely read or think about in toto. Yet, as Neil Fraistat reminded us many years ago, we need to attend to the "special qualities of the poetic collection as an organized book: the contextuality provided for each poem by the larger frame within which it is placed, the intertextuality among poems so placed, and the resultant texture of resonance and meanings." Fraistat provocatively dubs these qualities "contexture."[6]

In attending to *War Poetry of the South*'s contexture, I also have in mind the pioneering work of Anne Ferry, who read the poetry anthology as a "public space" or "cultural meeting ground" where "many readers of poetry first and perhaps most of the time meet poems."[7] Indeed, anthologies hold a remarkable indexical power, since they often bring together diverse poetries and then make them available to a broad readership. This is particularly the case with anthologies of Confederate poetry, which began to appear as early as 1862 and continued to be published well into the twentieth century. Because of their relative durability, these books helped to rescue Confederate verse from the dustbin of literary history—to say nothing of the widespread devastation of the Confederate States.

But many wartime anthologists were not content merely to preserve poems; they also aimed to influence how the war would be interpreted *après coup*. William G. Shepperson, for instance, argued that the poems he collected in his 1862 anthology, *War Songs of the South*, "give the lie to the assertion of our enemy that this revolution is the work of politicians and party leaders alone."[8] His pages represent, the anthologist insists, authentic, popular, nationalist feeling. While the majority of such collections argue for the historical and historiographical importance of Confederate poetry, several—including Simms's—also sought to reset the terms of Confederate literary nationalism and to redefine the character of Confederate poetry. Thus, *War Poetry of the South* allows us to see the strange ways of Confederate literary nationalism and to better understand its vexed place in American literary history.

"Present Necessities": Compilation and Production

It is no surprise that William Gilmore Simms deemed an anthology of southern war poetry worthy of both publication and his time. After all, Simms was a lifelong advocate for a distinct and distinctive southern literature. He also thought of himself first and foremost as a poet. The opportunity to collect and help preserve the poetry produced in the Confederacy must have seemed undeniable to the aging literary lion.[9] By late 1865 Simms had taken up the project in earnest. In addition to his far-flung network of correspondents, Simms solicited work from the public. On December 15 the *Daily South Carolinian* (for which Simms served as an associate editor, alongside Henry Timrod) announced and praised Simms's proposed anthology. Simms claimed to want any and all Confederate poems, be they highbrow, lowbrow, or somewhere in between (Guilds 305–6).[10]

At the outset of the American Civil War, Simms was dubious about the prospect of a literary culture springing fully formed from the heads of Confederate nationalists. As late as October 1862, he begged patience from readers and writers alike: "All our thoughts resolve themselves into the war. We are now *living* the first grand epic of our newly-born Confederacy. We are *making* the materials for the drama, and for future songs and fiction; and, engaged in the actual event, we are in no mood for delineating its details, or framing it to proper laws of art, in any province."[11] To Simms's mind, the exigencies of life during wartime—to say nothing of severe shortages of paper, ink, type, skilled labor, and printing presses—meant that a robust Confederate literature might have to wait until after southern independence had been achieved.[12]

And yet, the Confederate States of America was lousy with lyric. Poetry was a ubiquitous and at times tiresome part of cultural life in the Civil War South. As one beleaguered editor of the *Southern Literary Messenger* lamented in July 1863, "We are receiving too much trash in rhyme. What is called 'poetry,' by its authors, is not wanted. Fires are not accessible at this time of year, and it is too much trouble to tear up poetry. If it is thrown out of the window, the vexatious wind always blows it back."[13] *Pace* Simms, Confederates may have been "*living* the first grand epic*" of their new nation, but they were also producing an epic amount of poetry in the process. It was Simms's task to cull from the resulting mass a representative sample.[14]

Simms compiled the anthology during a tumultuous and busy period. Money was an ever-present concern for Simms, who was all but destitute following the burning of his low-country South Carolina plantation home, Woodlands, and the defeat of the Confederacy. An exercised Simms wrote to Evert A. Duyckinck on March 5, 1866, to check on the financial arrangements for *War Poetry of the South* and a proposed collection of Mother Goose stories:

> I need present cash for present necessities, and any arrangement which will give me that, will be welcome. *I have no shelter of my own, in which I can lay my head*, & my children, at present, are living at the plantation in negro houses. A few hundred dollars now would enable me to *restore one wing* of my dwelling there, and give me a tolerable habitation. If I can procure this aid from these two volumes, I should feel comparatively at ease. I should then have an abode where I could live cheaply, write cheaply, & dying, be buried with little cost, among my kindred.[15]

Such "present necessities" forced Simms to settle for a pittance from the New York publisher Charles Benjamin Richardson, to whom he granted the copyright for *War Poetry of the South* rather than "wait upon the lingering returns of sales for one or more seasons" (*Letters* 536). In the end, Simms received only a few hundred dollars for his extensive work on the anthology (*Letters* 581).[16]

This is not to say that *War Poetry of the South* was "hack work" or that Simms's interest in the anthology was merely commercial.[17] From the beginning of the project, Simms was committed to making the anthology a "good book" (*Letters*

536). This may help to explain the remarkable time and energy he lavished on the project. As John C. Guilds notes, "Simms was not content with publishing simply the best random selections sent to him; he recruited poems from the well-known writers, from various regions of the South, attempting to recognize the region's cultural and geographical diversity" (305). Playing on his well-known name, Simms was able to solicit manuscripts and revisions from southern poets both major and minor.[18]

To be clear, publishing the "best random selections sent to him" would have saved Simms a great deal of effort. He was flooded with poems and queries from like-minded collectors. On February 20, 1866, a snippy Simms wrote to Duyckinck: "The book will be quite creditable. There will be a very large mass from which to select.... I find the demand for these things very considerable, North & South; and have received letters from collectors & librarians begging duplicates & annoying me by a fruitless correspondence" (*Letters* 540). One such "fruitless correspondence" with a John A. McAllister (seemingly of Philadelphia, Pennsylvania) reveals a great deal about Simms's editorial labors:

> The war poems of the South are still daily coming in to me, a large proportion of them in M.S. I have not yet attempted classing them, nor do I know what duplicates may be found, nor have I yet decided what selections I shall make from them for publication. It is at present impossible for me to say what I have and what I might wish to have, especially as it is impossible for me to know what things may be scattered over the country to be brought to my knowledge only by accident, or the occasional contributions of persons like yourself making collections. (*Letters* 538)

The tone of this letter suggests just how overwhelmed the editor was by the process of sifting through the "rapidly accumulating" pile of poems. Simms also confessed that, no matter how large this "very large mass" grew, the resulting archive would always be partial and incomplete. Such is the nature of collecting a popular culture. Finally, the fact that Simms was corresponding with someone from Philadelphia bears out his claim that "the demand for these things" was indeed "considerable, North and South" (*Letters* 542).

Undaunted by the challenge, Simms worked on *War Poetry of the South* throughout the spring of 1866. By April he could brag to his old friend Duyckinck, "The Poetry of the South, during the war, will possess (I think) a much higher character, than any thing that has yet been published" (*Letters* 549). Simms traveled to New York in early June, where he was able to personally oversee the volume's composition and proof sheets (*Letters* 590). His work on the anthology was completed by late September, and *War Poetry of the South* appeared in print sometime between November 10 and 23, 1866 (*Letters* 606, 622).

"Emotional Literature": Text and Context

The resulting volume was remarkable for both its size and production values. Printed by George C. Rand and Avery, the duodecimo, 488-page *War Poetry of the South* was a respectable-looking book, with good paper, generally clean type work, plain green boards, and a large gilt stamp of Simms's signature—all for a reasonable $2.50. The publisher, Richardson and Company, hoped that the volume would "prove a family book, to be pored over, with various recollections, and fondly and frequently referred to, as embodying a record precious to the growing generations." As such, the firm also offered a fine edition, with "Morocco Cloth" and gilt edges, for $3.50.[19]

Richardson, who was known for his military titles, seems to have heavily invested in texts sympathetic to the Confederacy and an emergent Lost Cause ideology. During the war he brought out northern editions of John Esten Cooke's hagiographic *The Life of Stonewall Jackson* (1863) and Sally Rochester Ford's best-selling Confederate novel *Raids and Romance of Morgan and His Men* (1864). After the war, Richardson offered a single-volume edition of Edward A. Pollard's *Southern History of the War* (1866) (which was later republished as *The Lost Cause* [1867]) alongside titles like William Parker Snow's *Lee and His Generals* (1867). Indeed, both Pollard's and Snow's books were advertised in the final pages of the second printing of *War Poetry of the South*, suggesting the contours of the literary field Simms's anthology entered.

Even the casual reader—one ignorant of either Richardson's list or Simms's politics—could not mistake *War Poetry of the South*'s sympathies. The anthology's title page includes a melancholy engraving of a broken column, laurel wreath, harp, and discarded sword against the backdrop of a ruined garden. This is followed on the next recto page by a relatively hopeful dedication "To The Women of the South":

> They have lost a cause, but they have made a triumph! They have shown themselves worthy of any manhood; and will leave a record which shall survive all the caprices of time. They have proved themselves worthy of the best womanhood, and, in their posterity, will leave no race which shall be unworthy of the cause which is lost, or of the mothers, sisters and wives, who have taught such noble lessons of virtuous effect, and womanly endurance. (iii)

With its twin evocations of a lost cause and rhetoric of posterity, the dedication seems steadfastly focused on the future.[20] The juxtaposition of the mournful title page with this sanguine dedication captures well the animating tension of the volume—a tension to which Simms gives further voice in his remarkable prose preface.

Dated "Brooklyn, September 8, 1866," Simms's four-page introductory remarks are both deeply rhetorical and deeply conflicted. Simms argues that the "emotional literature" he collects is "essential to the reputation of the Southern people, as illustrating their feelings, sentiments, ideas, and opinions—the motives which influenced their actions, and the objects which they had in contemplation, and which seemed to them to justify the struggle in which they were engaged" (v). Perhaps quietly echoing John Adams ("The Revolution was in the minds and hearts of the people"), Simms plays the disinterested intellectual historian here, urging readers to be sympathetic as they peruse his anthology. Stifling his strongly southern nationalist sentiments, Simms does not offer an apologia for the Confederacy; instead, he hedges a bit. Note the passive construction and use of the past tense here: These motives and objects "*seemed* to *them* to justify" the southern war effort (emphasis added).

The deftness of Simms's rhetoric betrays the delicate political position in which a postwar anthologist of Confederate poetry worked. How could she or he present aggressively nationalistic verse—poems that risk being "too 'fierce' and 'bitter' to suit the taste and temper of the present"—to a newly restored Union?[21] Abram Joseph Ryan, the author of the hugely popular Lost Cause anthem "The Conquered Banner," worried that his incendiary anthology of Confederate verse, *War Lyrics and Songs of the South* (1866), would be censored in the North. As a result, he had the collection printed in London.[22] Thomas Cooper De Leon, a Confederate veteran and older brother of Confederate diplomat Edwin De Leon, instead begged his readers' indulgence and made a familiar appeal to the historical record: "If poems, born of revolution, bore no marks of the bitter need that crushed them from the hearts of their authors, they would have no value whatever, intrinsic or historical."[23]

But it is Simms who makes the most original argument for how to square wartime invective with postwar imperatives to reconciliation. One need only subsume Confederate literary nationalism under a broader American literary nationalism:

> Several considerations have prompted the editor of this volume in the compilation of its pages. It constitutes a contribution to the national literature which is assumed to be not unworthy of it, and which is otherwise valuable as illustrating the degree of mental and art development which has been made, in a large section of the country, under circumstances greatly calculated to stimulate talent and provoke expression, through the higher utterances of passion and imagination. Though sectional in its character, and indicative of a temper and a feeling which were in conflict with nationality, yet, now that the States of the Union have been resolved into one nation, this collection is essentially as much the property of the whole as are the captured cannon which were employed against

it during the progress of the late war. It belongs to the national literature, and will hereafter be regarded as constituting a proper part of it, just as legitimately to be recognized by the nation as are the rival ballads of the cavaliers and roundheads, by the English, in the great civil conflict of their country. (v)

It is as though the American Civil War never happened. Despite having strongly advocated for secession and steadfastly supported the Confederacy, Simms reverts to his antebellum agitations for a national literature. For instance, Simms had argued in a preface to the 1856 version of *The Wigwam and the Cabin* that "to be *national* in literature, one must needs be *sectional*. No one mind can fully or fairly illustrate the characteristics of any great country; and he who shall depict *one section* faithfully, has made his proper and sufficient contribution to the great work of *national* illustration."[24] After a hugely bloody and costly war for independence, the South was once again in the subordinate position, making contributions to a national literature that is not entirely its own.

In fact, Simms argues, northern readers should not think overlong about the sectional character of this verse; instead they should read the collection as indicative of a flourishing regional art. To Simms's mind, *War Poetry of the South* helps to measure the "degree of mental and art development" that the war helped to spur. After all, wars "stimulate talent and provoke expression"; they even give rise to "higher utterances of passion and imagination." Looking to England for a model or precedent, Simms argues that nationalist poetry is, finally, a fungible good. The canon of Confederate poetry is just like the cannon of the Confederate army: a strategic asset that will benefit the newly re-United States (Hutchison 139–42).

Having established a way to read Confederate poetry in a postwar world, Simms then touts the representative nature of his anthology. He boasts that the poems are drawn from "all the States of the late Southern Confederacy, and will be found truthfully to exhibit the sentiment and opinion prevailing more or less generally throughout the whole" (vi). In the same breath he also confesses the partial nature of his archive, noting that he had been unable to "do justice to, and find a place for, many of the pieces which fully deserve to be put on record" (vi). Blaming a shoddy interstate mail system for the exclusion of larger collections from Louisiana, North Carolina, and Texas, the editor goes on to promise a second edition "of like style, character, and dimensions" (vi).[25]

Simms also cannily acknowledges that *War Poetry of the South* was entering a crowded literary field. Indeed, the cessation of Civil War hostilities resulted in a minor publishing boom, as anthologists in the South, North, and England used their collections to commemorate and make sense of the atrocities they had just endured.[26] Simms names in particular anthologies edited by Frank Moore and De Leon, before making a generous concession:

There may be others still forth-coming; for, in so large a field, with a population so greatly scattered as that of the South, it is a physical impossibility adequately to do justice to the whole by any one editor; and each of the sections must make its own contributions, in its own time, and according to its several opportunities. There will be room enough for all; and each, I doubt not, will possess its special claims to recognition and reward. (vii)

Even William Gilmore Simms, the most well-connected and esteemed southern man of letters, could not adequately capture in a single anthology the "genius and culture of the Southern people" (vi). But a series of local anthologies of Confederate poetry might do the trick. Perhaps this is how Louisiana, North Carolina, or Texas could get their poetic due.

Simms closes the preface by briskly defending his editorial rationale and reiterating his belief that these poems are both "highly creditable to the Southern mind" and of great historical interest. The tone of these final three paragraphs is protean, but Simms's rhetoric is skillful throughout. Perhaps the most telling moment is in Simms's discussion of authorship. Speaking in the third person, Simms confesses that "He has been able to ascertain the authorship, in many cases, of these writings; but must regret still that so many others, under a too fastidious delicacy, deny that their names should be made known" (vii). The inclusion of anonymous and pseudonymous poems is an aspect of Simms's editing that has come under particular fire, with critics reading his "regret" as a dereliction of editorial duty. Yet such criticisms misapprehend the function of anonymity and pseudonymity in *War Poetry of the South*.

First, Simms may well have been confessing his own "too fastidious delicacy" here. After all, Simms published poems anonymously and pseudonymously throughout his long career.[27] More to the point, Simms published poems anonymously and pseudonymously in *War Poetry of the South*—a great number of poems, in fact. His name appears next to seven titles in the table of contents. However, James E. Kibler Jr. argues persuasively that the anthology includes another 27 "proved" Simms poems and at least five "probable" Simms poems.[28] Thus, anonymity and pseudonymity worked to Simms's benefit in his anthology, allowing him to quietly publish a significant amount of his own poetry. Second, anonymity and pseudonymity were signal features of Confederate poetry, which often flaunted the rules of polite literature. Indeed, many Confederate poets showed little interest in literary professionalism, and the majority were "amateurs in every sense of the word."[29] Suffice it to say, Simms's decision to include anonymous and pseudonymous poems was in keeping with an important aspect of poetic culture in the Civil War South (Hutchison 99–102).

Simms also betrays his generic biases in the preface. He admits to having excluded a "large proportion of pieces ... of elegiac character"—and with good reason (vii). The extraordinary losses occasioned by the American Civil War meant that elegy was a dominant poetic mode during this period. Given that one in five white southern men of military age did not survive the Civil War, Confederate elegies were particularly common.[30] Thus, Simms includes elegies for only "the most distinguished of the persons falling in battle, or such as are marked by the higher characteristics of poetry—freshness, thought, and imagination" (vii). In turn, he expresses some contempt for those "songs, camp catches, or marching ballads" collected by Moore in his *Rebel Rhymes and Rhapsodies*: "The songs which are most popular are rarely such as may claim poetical rank. They depend upon lively music and certain spirit-stirring catchwords, and are rarely worked up with much regard to art or even propriety" (vii-viii). As a result, Simms only includes a handful of popular song lyrics.[31]

Yet for all this high-literary snobbishness, Simms goes out of his way to say that the pieces he excluded from the *War Poetry of the South* are nonetheless "worthy of preservation"—even those endless elegies and spirit-stirring songs (vii). He closes his discussion of editorial rationale with a concession to literary taste: "Still, many of these should have found a place in this volume, had adequate space been allowed the editor" (viii).

Such is the theory of *War Poetry of the South*; in practice, Simms is surprisingly egalitarian in his selection of poems. The collection opens with perhaps the finest poem produced in the Confederacy, Henry Timrod's Pindaric ode "Ethnogenesis":

> Hath not the morning dawned with added light ?[32]
> And shall not evening call another star
> Out of the infinite regions of the night,
> To mark this day in Heaven ? At last, we are
> A nation among nations ; and the world
> Shall soon behold in many a distant port
> Another flag unfurled ! (7)

But it also includes far less accomplished or ambitious poems, such as Albert Pike's revised lyrics to "Dixie": "Southrons, hear your Country call you! / Up! lest worse than death befall you! / To arms! to arms! to arms! in Dixie" (92). And while *War Poetry of the South* includes many competent sonnets, there are also a number of inept broadside tributes to Stonewall Jackson.

The uneven quality of the poetry seems to have been by design. Again, Simms claims to be preserving these poems for posterity, for the future "philosophical historian." Even bad poetry—perhaps especially bad poetry—will show "with what spirit the popular mind regarded the course of events, whether favorable or adverse; and, in this aspect, it is even of more importance to the writer of history than any mere chronicle of facts" (v). Simms even comes to the defense of those poets who cannot "claim poetical rank"; he argues that "we can also forgive the muse who, in her fervor, is sometimes forgetful of her art" (vi). Apparently the philosophical historian does not require good poetry, merely poetry that "glows or weeps with emotions that gush freely and freshly from the heart" (vi).

We might compare this editorial rationale to that of Thomas Cooper De Leon, who thought that the work of the postbellum anthologist was to protect his or her readers from the "rhymster of low degree," to select out only those rare blooms of poetic beauty: "The garland is to be gathered from a field extensive and teeming with a rank luxuriance of growth, that it must often puzzle the analyst to separate from the really valuable" (v). Calling the popular poetry of the Confederacy "ephemera that have lived out the day for which they were born," De Leon highlights "the quality, and not the quantity, of Southern poetry" (vi). As a result, he includes "few even of the most popular" poems in his *South Songs*, privileging instead "polite" poems by established poets (vi).

Simms's *War Poetry of the South* is by no means a popular poetry anthology. Many of the best known names in southern literature appear in its table of contents: James Barron Hope, James R. Randall, John R. Thompson, Margaret Junkin Preston, Alexander B. Meek, Paul Hamilton Hayne, John Esten Cooke, and James D. McCabe, Jr., to say nothing of Timrod and Simms, among many others. Moreover, the anthology over-represents traditional verse forms. However, unlike De Leon's *South Songs*, Simms's anthology does include some of the Confederacy's poetic "ephemera," if not its "trash in rhyme." Once again, this is in keeping with the dynamics of a nascent Confederate literary culture. The poetry of the Civil War South was overwhelmingly occasional in nature. Whether popular or polite, lowbrow or highbrow, Confederate poems were very much socially contingent productions, nonautonomous works of art largely inseparable from the circumstances in which they were created—especially those of privation, civil war, and emergent nationalism. In turn, a great deal of this poetry was written quickly and rushed to print; needless to say, it bears the marks of such hasty composition (Hutchison 7–8, 99–103). Simms's expansive anthology does well, then, to represent some of the diversity of Confederate literary culture.

One hastens to add, some but not all of the diversity of Confederate literary culture. As the above list suggests, male poets far outnumber female poets in *War Poetry of the South*. Moreover, as Johanna Shields has recently argued, Simms's selections may have been much more provincial and ideological than previous scholars have supposed.[33] Finally, the collection's more or less chronological arrangement—it opens with Timrod's ode to the convening of the Provisional Confederate Congress on February 4, 1861 and closes with a series of poems describing the final furling of the Confederate flag after Appomattox—limits its sense of multiplicity. While chronology may grant the diffuse collection a sense of narrative arc, it also makes the individual poems feel more connected or coherent than they truly are. But such limitations are part and parcel of any literary anthology. As Simms would learn in late 1866 and early 1867, anthologists rarely make everyone happy.

By way of giving a better sense for the collection's "contexture," we might consider three poems that appear on subsequent pages: Mrs. Mary Ware's "Song of Our Glorious Southland" (215–217), Paul Hamilton Hayne's "Sonnet" (217), and the anonymous "Hospital Duties" (218–220). Coming midway through the collection, these poems offer three distinct versions of Confederate literary nationalism; they also vary greatly in terms of topic, form, tone, and address. Yet their close proximity makes a subtle argument about the steadfastness of Confederate nationalist feeling during—and perhaps even after—the Civil War.

Although Mrs. Mary Ware is somewhat lost to history, her "Song" seems to have been well sung during the Civil War era. Simms takes pains to note that her poem was first published in Augusta, Georgia's *Southern Field and Fireside*, a staunchly nationalistic weekly published from 1859 to 1864 that made a particularly ardent case for a distinct and distinctive southern literature.[34] To no one's surprise, Simms was a regular contributor to the *Field and Fireside*. The poem opens with an epic invocation and then quickly settles into a cloying romanticism:

> Oh, sing of our glorious Southland,
>   The pride of the golden sun !
> 'Tis the fairest land of flowers
>   The eye e'er looked upon.
>
> Sing of her orange and myrtle
>   That glitter like gems above ;
> Sing of her dark-eyed maidens
>   As fair as a dream of love.
>
> Sing of her flowing rivers
>   How musical their sound !
> Sing of her dark green forests,
>   The Indian hunting-ground. (215–16)

Fair flowers, dark-eyed ladies, a gendered personification, and a spectral indigenous population: this is a boilerplate celebration of the region's bounty and beauty. As so many nineteenth-century poems argued, the South was an extraordinary physical site, one worthy of poetic encomium after poetic encomium.

And yet Ware's next stanza breaks dramatically from this treacly tradition:

> Sing of the noble nation
> > Fierce struggling to be free ;
> Sing of the brave who barter
> > Their lives for liberty !(216)

The "Southland" is suddenly a "noble nation," and Ware's muse must sing of less natural phenomena, including war, politics, and economic exchange. Put another way, the first three stanzas of the poem render the South as an exceptional space; the fourth suggests that that exceptional space needs to be protected at all costs; and the rest of the poem labors to enumerate said costs. For instance, the poem's second section opens with suppuration not song:

> Weep for the maid and matron
> > Who mourn their loved ones slain ;
> Sigh for the light departed,
> > Never to shine again :
>
> 'Tis the voice of Rachel weeping,
> > That never will comfort know ;
> 'Tis the wail of desolation,
> > The breaking of hearts in woe ! (216)

The apostrophized muse is now asked to emote, to be affected by the "voice of Rachel weeping" and the "breaking of hearts in woe." The once "glorious Southland" is, it seems, beset and besieged, experiencing losses of a biblical proportion. But even that sad state of affairs demands poetic attention.

The final stanzas of "Song of Our Glorious Southland" make clear who is to blame for all this carnage and despair:

> Ah ! the blood of Abel crieth
> > For vengeance from the sod !
> 'Tis a brother's hand that's lifted
> > In the face of an angry God !
>
> Oh ! brother of the Northland,
> > We plead from our father's grave ;
> We strike for our homes and altars,
> > He fought to build and save !
>
> A smouldering fire is burning,
> > The Southern heart is steeled—
> Perhaps 'twill break in dying,
> > But never will it yield. (216–17)

Abandoning the epic invocation of its first two sections, the poem doubles down on its biblical allusions and quietly adopts the ubiquitous "house divided" trope. In Ware's poem, the North is cast as the jealous and angry Cain. The South, in turn, must seek "vengeance" for the murder of Abel, with whom an "angry God" stands. The poem's penultimate stanza shifts this rationale ever-so-slightly, arguing that Confederates are merely protecting the "homes and altars" built by the brothers' father. In any case, the final stanza leaves little doubt about the Southland's steely resolve.

"Song of Our Glorious Southland" encapsulates a number of features of Confederate poetry: romantic representations, biblical allusions, and no small amount of rhetorical swagger. But the version of Confederate literary nationalism it embodies was but one among many, as witnessed by its companion piece, Paul Hamilton Hayne's "Sonnet":

> Rise from your gory ashes stern and pale,
> Ye martyred thousands ! and with dreadful ire,
> A voice of doom, a front of gloomy fire,
> Rebuke those faithless souls, whose querulous wail
> Disturbs your sacred sleep !— "The withering hail
> Of battle, hunger, pestilence, despair,
> Whatever of mortal anguish man may bear,
> We bore unmurmuring ! strengthened by the mail
> Of a most holy purpose !—then we died !
> Vex not our rest by cries of selfish pain,
> But to the noblest measure of your powers
> Endure the appointed trial ! Griefs defied,
> But launch their threatening thunderbolts in vain,
> And angry storms pass by in gentlest showers !" (217)

Hayne's poem appears on the same page as the final two stanzas of Ware's poem. As is so often the case in Simms's anthology, the layout of the poems produces a fascinating apposition. In many ways, Hayne's sonnet seems like a rejoinder to Ware's insistent cries for sympathy. Yet we would do well to note who—or what—answers that call: "Ye martyred thousands." Nearly 150 years before "Vampire Bill Compton" or *The Walking Dead*, here is a southern landscape haunted by the living dead. Bid to rise from their "gory ashes stern and pale" and speak in "A voice of doom, a front of gloomy fire," the Confederate dead are reanimated and rendered as one.

The resulting prosopopoeiac speech expands significantly on Ware's claims of Confederate steadfastness. In both poems, the Civil War provides a limit experience for the "Southern heart." Ware notes that "Perhaps 'twill break in dying, / But never will it yield." Hayne suggests that nothing—not even death, much less "battle, hunger, pestilence, despair, / Whatever of mortal anguish man may bear"—should break the Confederacy's nationalist commitment. And indeed, the poem's undead chorus seems intended to steel southern hearts and minds. After all, these martyr-speakers bore their burden without complaint, "unmurmuring ... strengthened by the mail / Of a most holy purpose !" Still-living Confederates should do the same, "Endure the appointed trial !," and die nobly for their cause.

"Sonnet" offers a characteristically sanguine performance. Paul Hamilton Hayne's wartime poetry is consistently bloody and single-minded. Even his elegies for the Confederate dead show a somewhat callous commitment to cause rather than cost. This is certainly true of his five other poems in *War Poetry of the South*, especially "Our Martyrs" (277–79). Of course, William Gilmore Simms didn't have to go far to find Hayne's red-blooded poetry, since both were denizens of Charleston, South Carolina. The two men were part of the *Russell's Magazine* circle, which met regularly at John Russell's bookstore and at Simms's "Wigwam" house in the immediate lead-up to the war. Hayne, who by 1854 had a national reputation as a poet, served as editor-in-chief of the short-lived magazine (1857–1860). In this capacity, he mentored his young friend Henry Timrod and worked closely with the much older Simms.

Such affinities between Hayne and Simms are relevant because the next poem in *War Poetry of the South* may well be Simms's. "Hospital Duties" is anonymously credited to the "Charleston Courier," but James E. Kibler Jr. cites "reasonable proof of Simms's authorship."[35] The poem saw wide circulation in both the South and the North during the war, and under various titles: "Woman's War Mission," "More Nurses," "A Call to the Hospital," and "Ladies of Richmond," among others. No matter who wrote the eight-stanza verse, it ratifies in complicated ways the nation-building work of Ware's "Song" and Hayne's "Sonnet." Having finished the former and the latter, readers turned the page to find the following lines:

> Fold away all your bright-tinted dresses,
>   Turn the key on your jewels to-day,
> And the wealth of your tendril-like tresses
>   Braid back in a serious way ;
> No more delicate gloves, no more laces,
>   No more trifling in boudoir or bower,
> But come with your souls in your faces
>   To meet the stern wants of the hour. (218)

With its "bright-tinted dresses" and "tendril-like tresses," "Hospital Duties" makes yet another emphatic appeal—this time to the ladies. Employing a deft direct address, the speaker paints an evocative and gory scene:

> Look around. By the torchlight unsteady
>   The dead and the dying seem one
> What ! trembling and paling already,
>   Before your dear mission's begun ?
> These wounds are more precious than ghastly
>   Time presses her lips to each scar,
> While she chants of that glory which vastly
>   Transcends all the horrors of war. (218)

As with the previous two poems, "Hospital Duties" conditions a specific response from its addressee. Here the speaker will not allow the poetic subject to shrink from either the important work before her or those ever-present "horrors of war."

Stanza by stanza, the speaker leads the nameless woman from bedside to bedside, stopping to offer comfort and succor where they can. While many of the wounded are beyond assistance, the speaker urges them on:

> Here's another—a lad—a mere stripling,
>   Picked up in the field almost dead,
> With the blood through his sunny hair rippling
>   From the horrible gash in the head.
> They say he was first in the action :
> Gay-hearted, quick-headed, and witty :
> He fought till he dropped with exhaustion
>   At the gates of our fair southern city.
>
> Fought and fell 'neath the guns of that city,
>   With a spirit transcending his years—
> Lift him up in your large-hearted pity,
>   And wet his pale lips with your tears.
> Touch him gently ; most sacred the duty
>   Of dressing that poor shattered hand !
> God spare him to rise in his beauty,
>   And battle once more for his land ! (219)

After six bewildering stanzas, the "Woman's War Mission" is laid out in stark, forbidding terms:

> They have gathered about you the harvest
>   Of death in its ghastliest view ;
> The nearest as well as the furthest
>   Is there with the traitor and true.

> And crowned with your beautiful patience,
> Made sunny with love at the heart,
> You must balsam the wounds of the nations,
> Nor falter nor shrink from your part. (220)

Although the poem ends with a stanza promising the thanks of a grateful nation and god, it is this penultimate stanza that reveals the poem's sensational designs. Confederate women should eschew common comforts and luxuries and devote themselves wholly to their "Hospital Duties"—which are, finally, hardly less important than men's battlefield duties. Put simply, the work of Confederate nationalism must be undertaken by all.

Per Fraistat, my truncated, contrapuntal readings of these three poems suggest a *contextural* effect. As a heavily organized book, *War Poetry of the South* produces both a contextuality and an intertextuality; the "resultant texture of resonance and meanings" is evident on nearly every page opening. In the case of pages 215–20, that texture suggests a particularly jingoistic nap. "Song of Our Glorious Southland," "Sonnet," and "Hospital Duties" all champion the cause of Confederate nationalism, call for broad personal and collective sacrifices, and capture the intensity of public feeling in the Civil War South. Read together, they also suggest the diversity of Confederate poetry—at least as imagined by the leading advocate for southern literary independence.

"Commendable Industry": Reception and Appraisal

The reception of *War Poetry of the South* was generally warm in both the South and the North—though reviewers on both sides of the Mason-Dixon Line had complaints about Simms's editorial work, in particular his decision to let anonymous and pseudonymous attributions stand. Not surprisingly, the southern response to the volume was at times rapturous. The Georgia-based *Southern Cultivator* saw the publication of *War Poetry of the South* as critically important, since it might occasion a reassessment of southern literature writ large: "by it the literary tastes and talents of the Southern people will be largely measured." Echoing Richardson's puff, the *Cultivator* concluded that it was "a book for every Southern home—a book in which we cannot fail to take a personal and patriotic pride."[36] *The Land We Love* was a bit more equivocal in its two reviews of the anthology. Both praise the "Nestor of Southern Litterateurs" for his "commendable industry" and "zeal and ardor" in the face of the destruction of his homeland.[37] Yet both also complain that Simms excluded several well-known lyrics; misattributed several poems; and did not vigorously pursue questions of authorship.

Indeed, the reviewer for the May 1867 issue seems to prefer the much smaller, more heavily curated De Leon anthology, since "each poem it contains is a gem" (72). Nonetheless, *The Land We Love* concurs with *The Southern Cultivator:* this is "a book which no Southern family can do without" (74).

In the North, the reception was, predictably, quieter. *The Round Table* went further than the *New-York Times* review quoted above, suggesting that Simms's volume compared favorably with northern anthologies edited by Frank Moore and Richard Grant White and showed "the southern poets to have been as much in earnest in celebrating their view of the war as ours were in celebrating ours, and considerably more vehement, not to say vituperative at times."[38] New York's *Old Guard: A Monthly Journal Devoted to the Principles of 1776 and 1787* concurred in a particularly red-blooded, southern nationalistic review: "Whatever might have been said before the War, it can no longer be affirmed that the South has not a literature of its own—a literature which has been born of a struggle that imparted to it the freshest and most endearing elements of immortality."[39]

The only truly negative southern review came from New Orleans's *Crescent Monthly*, which offered some of the harshest criticism—North or South—of Simms's editorial acumen and taste. The anonymous reviewer claimed that Simms's anthology betrayed "too much Palmetto partiality" and "too great a sympathy for mediocrity in verse."[40] Up north, the *New Englander and Yale Review* thought Simms had made "as good a selection as could be made" but rejected outright the claim that such sectional poems would contribute to a national literature: "But we cannot agree with him. They seem to us to be the second-rate effusions of the day, and hereafter they will perish from the knowledge of all but the most curious investigator of the history of these wonderful times."[41]

Following this initial flood of reviews, few writers of the late nineteenth and early twentieth century remarked on Simms's monumental anthology.[42] And as Simms went from being a man "more respected than read" to a man neither respected nor read, his anthology of Civil War poetry was mentioned less and less often. Over the past 150 years, there have been a number of cheap facsimiles but no scholarly edition of *War Poetry of the South*. And, with the notable exceptions of Aiken, Busick, and Shields, few contemporary historians or literary critics have taken up Simms's anthology in earnest.

What, then, is one to do with *War Poetry of the South*? Richardson never commissioned additional volumes from Simms, and there is no conclusive evidence that *War Poetry of the South* went beyond a second printing. Given its "long years of neglect," one might be tempted just to leave the collection amid the welter of Simms's other writings—at least 82 published works—and let it "perish from the knowledge of all." Doing so would be a mistake. *War Poetry of the South* remains the most diverse contemporary anthology of the poetry of the Civil War South. Guilds rightly deems it the "best anthology of its kind" (306). Among other things, it was "creditably" edited by one of the leading lights of nineteenth-century American literature. Moreover, each of its pages embodies the "feelings, sentiments, ideas, and opinions" of Confederates who thought they were in the process of creating a nation and a national literature that would endure. No matter how wrongheaded or offensive those "feelings, sentiments, ideas, and opinions" may seem to twenty-first century readers, they embody the "surplus patriotism" of the South at a moment of extraordinary crisis and creation (v).

It is well past time that *War Poetry of the South* be recognized as a treasure trove of Civil War-era literature and culture. Because poetry anthologies almost always serve a retrospective function—a backward glance over roads traveled, as Walt Whitman might have it—they have the ability to collect, preserve, and make available exuberant and diverse poetic cultures. Anthologies are, as the Australian poet and critic Jennifer Strauss suggests, "essential to the transmission of poetry from the relative ephemerality of periodicals and slim volumes into a more mainstream communication with readers."[43] To read the pages of an anthology like Simms's is to encounter in a single setting poems that likely appeared in a number of other venues and media.[44] Thus, *War Poetry of the South* grants scholars and students intimate access to a short-lived and understudied literary culture. It captures as well as any other single volume the great expectations and stultifying disappointments of Confederate literature.

NOTES

1. *War Poetry of the South* will be republished in 2015 as part of "The Simms Initiatives," an ambitious project to make all of Simms's works available digitally and via print on demand. I am grateful to Todd Hagstette, director of the Simms Initiatives, for allowing me to use material from my critical introduction to that edition here.

2. This movement recapitulated the evolving politics of its cofounder and editor, Henry Jarvis Raymond, who served as a member of the House of Representatives from 1865 to 1867 and chairman of the Republican National Committee from 1864 to 1866. Raymond lost favor with Radical Republicans following his active participation in the 1866 National Union Convention in Philadelphia. See Thomas Wagstaff, "The Arm-in-Arm Convention," *Civil War History* 14, no. 2 (1968): 101–19; also, Meyer Berger, *The Story of the New York Times, 1851–1951* (New York: Simon and Schuster, 1951).

3. *New York Times*, December 12, 1866, 2.

4. John C. Guilds, ed., *Long Years of Neglect: The Work and Reputation of William Gilmore Simms* (Fayetteville: University of Arkansas Press, 1988).

5. No major studies of Simms spend significant time discussing the anthology. For instance, *War Poetry of the South* warrants just two paragraphs in John C. Guilds's stan-

dard literary biography, *Simms: A Literary Life* (Fayetteville: University of Arkansas Press, 1992), hereafter documented parenthetically; garners no mention in J. V. Ridgley's influential introduction, *William Gilmore Simms* (New York: Twayne Publishers, 1962); and appears only in the bibliography of William P. Trent's foundational study, *William Gilmore Simms* (Boston: Houghton Mifflin, 1892). For a persuasive call to action, see Sean Busick, "Simms's *War Poetry of the South*: Notes Toward a Reconsideration," *Simms Review* 17, no. 1–2 (2009): 49–53.

6. Neil Fraistat, ed., *Poems in Their Place: The Intertextuality and Order of Poetic Collections* (Chapel Hill: University of North Carolina Press, 1986), 3.

7. Anne Ferry, *Tradition and the Individual Poem: An Inquiry into Anthologies* (Palo Alto: Stanford University Press, 2001), 128, 1. Ferry goes on to suggest that anthologies are set apart from other kinds of poetry collections because "the anthology is the work of a unique kind of maker, whose presence is felt, inescapably, only in this kind of book" (13). Needless to say, Simms's presence is deeply felt on the pages of *War Poetry of the South*.

8. William G. Shepperson, ed., *War Songs of the South* (Richmond: West and Johnson, 1862), 5.

9. As David Aiken notes, Simms also had an abiding interest in the poetry of war ("Simms's War Poetry: A Battle Cry of Freedom," *Simms Review* 2, no. 2 [1994]: 12).

10. John L. Wakelyn echoes Simms's claim that he had begun collecting the material for his anthology during the war (*The Politics of a Literary Man: William Gilmore Simms* [Westport, Conn.: Greenwood Press, 1973], 258). It is not known whether material from this wartime collection found its way into *War Poetry of the South* or was lost with the plundering and destruction of Simms's library in February 1865.

11. William Gilmore Simms, "Sketches in Greece," *Southern Illustrated News*, October 11, 1862, 2.

12. On the material hardships faced by Confederate litterateurs, see Lawrence F. London, "Confederate Literature and its Publishers," in *Studies in Southern History*, ed. Joseph Sitterson (Chapel Hill: University of North Carolina Press, 1957); Mary Elizabeth Massey, *Ersatz in the Confederacy* (Columbia: University of South Carolina Press, 1952); and Alice Fahs, *The Imagined Civil War: Popular Literature of the North and South, 1861–1865* (Chapel Hill: University of North Carolina Press, 2001), esp. 1–15.

13. "Editor's Table," *Southern Literary Messenger* 37 (July 1863): 447.

14. Coleman Hutchison, *Apples and Ashes: Literature, Nationalism, and the Confederate States of America* (Athens: University of Georgia Press, 2012), 99–142, hereafter documented parenthetically.

15. William Gilmore Simms, *Letters of William Gilmore Simms*, ed. Mary C. Simms Oliphant, Alfred Taylor Odell, and T. C. Duncan Eave, vol. 4: *1858–1866* (Columbia: University of South Carolina Press, 1956), 542–43, hereafter documented parenthetically as *Letters*.

16. On the postwar market for Simms's writings, see James L. W. West III, "William Gilmore Simms and the Postwar Literary Marketplace," *Simms Review* 18, no. 1–2 (2010): 5–14. See also Simms's July 12, 1866, letter to his son (*Letters* 580–82).

17. See Edd Winfield Parks, *William Gilmore Simms as Literary Critic* (Athens: Uni-

versity of Georgia Press, 1961), 9; also, Mary Ann Wimsatt, *The Major Fiction of William Gilmore Simms: Cultural Traditions and Literary Form* (Baton Rouge: Louisiana State University Press, 1989), 218.

18. A March 20, 1867, letter to John R. Thompson suggests Simms's sense of responsibility to his fellow poets: "I regret that the 'Burial of Latané' was imperfectly given in the War Poems. *Mais, mon ami*, what would you have? You were out of the Country, and I had to rely on a newspaper copy. Please send me a revised copy in MS. if you have none in print, and you shall be put *rectus in curia*, through the next edition" (William Gilmore Simms, *Letters of William Gilmore Simms*, ed. Mary C. Simms Oliphant, Alfred Taylor Odell, and T. C. Duncan Eave, vol. 5: *1867–1870* [Columbia: University of South Carolina Press, 1956], 31–32).

19. William Gilmore Simms, ed., *War Poetry of the South* (New York: Richardson, 1866), 483, hereafter documented parenthetically.

20. Aiken, "Simms's War Poetry," 16–17.

21. Emily Mason, ed., *The Southern Poems of the War* (Baltimore: J. Murphy, 1867), 7.

22. Abram Joseph Ryan, ed., *War Lyrics and Songs of the South* (London: Spottiswoode and Co., 1866), iii.

23. T. C. De Leon, ed., *South Songs: From the Lays of Later Days* (New York: Bledock, 1866), vii, hereafter documented parenthetically.

24. William Gilmore Simms, *The Wigwam and the Cabin* (New York: Redfield, 1856), 4. I am not the first scholar to point out that this marks a return to Simms's prewar arguments about the South's contributions to a national literature. See Nicholas G. Meriwether, "Simms's Civil War: History, Healing and the *Sack and Destruction of Columbia, S.C.*," *Studies in the Literary Imagination* 42, no. 1 (2009): esp. 117; and Busick, "Simms's *War Poetry of the South*," esp. 51. David Moltke-Hansen is particularly good on Simms's preface. See his introduction to the edited collection *William Gilmore Simms's Unfinished Civil War: Consequences for a Southern Man of Letters* (Columbia: University of South Carolina Press, 2013), esp. 18. The subject of Simms's movement from "nationalism to secessionism," as Charles S. Watson describes it, has engendered an enormous body of criticism. See especially Watson, *From Nationalism to Secessionism: The Changing Fiction of William Gilmore Simms* (Westport, Conn.: Greenwood Press, 1993); Parks, *William Gilmore Simms*, 89–109; and Wakelyn, *Politics of a Literary Man*, 158–87.

25. This seems to have been more than just poetic sabre rattling. Simms wrote to Duyckinck in August 1866 claiming that the volume "will be quite 450, and yet more than half of the collection will be omitted." See *Letters*, 4:596.

26. Like *War Poetry of the South*, the majority of these anthologies argue for the historical importance of the "emotional literature" of the Confederacy. To read Confederate poetry—in the South, the North, or even England—is to better understand what brought about a conflict with wide-ranging and catastrophic effects. See Shepperson, *War Songs of the South*, 3–5; Frank Moore, ed, *Rebel Rhymes and Rhapsodies* (New York: G. P. Putnam, 1864), v; and *Lays of the South: Verses Relative to the War between the Two Sections of the American States* (Liverpool, 1864), 1. See also Hutchison, *Apples and Ashes*, 139–42.

27. James E. Kibler Jr., *The Pseudonymous Publications of William Gilmore Simms* (Ath-

ens: University of Georgia Press, 1976), 1–8; William Gilmore Simms, *Selected Poems of William Gilmore Simms*, ed. James E. Kibler Jr. (Athens: University of Georgia Press, 1990), xii-xiv.

28. James E. Kibler Jr., *The Poetry of William Gilmore Simms: An Introduction and Bibliography* (Columbia: Southern Studies, 1979), 478.

29. William Moss, *Confederate Broadside Poems: An Annotated Descriptive Bibliography Based on the Collection of the Z. Smith Reynolds Library of Wake Forest University* (Westport: Meckler, 1988), 15.

30. Drew Gilpin Faust, *This Republic of Suffering: Death and the American Civil War* (New York: Alfred A. Knopf, 2008), xi.

31. This is a missed opportunity for Simms, especially in light of recent scholarship that underscores popular song's crucial cultural role in both the United and Confederate States of America. See Christian McWhirter, *Battle Hymns: The Power and Popularity of Music in the Civil War* (Chapel Hill: University of North Carolina Press, 2012); Hutchison, *Apples and Ashes*, 143–72; and Faith Barrett, *To Fight Aloud Is Very Brave: American Poetry and the Civil War* (Amherst: University of Massachusetts Press, 2012), 17–40.

32. Typography in *War Poetry of the South* features an added space before some terminal punctuation. This is retained in my transcriptions.

33. Johanna Shields, "Delusion's Carnival of Death: A Different War Poetry from the South" in *William Gilmore Simms's Unfinished Civil War: Consequences for a Southern Man of Letters*, ed. David Moltke-Hansen (Columbia: University of South Carolina Press, 2013), 112–28. Shields wants us to see the collection "less a reflection of popular opinion than one important part of a larger effort by staunch Confederates to shape public memory in their image" (126). While that may have been Simms's unstated intention, I do not know that the poems bear out this claim. Because of their composite nature, it is often difficult to characterize an anthology in purely ideological terms. As Franny Nudleman notes, anthologies from the postwar period pulled together "a diverse body of poetry that cannot be read through the lens of homogenizing nationalist abstractions." See *John Brown's Body: Slavery, Violence, and the Culture of War* (Chapel Hill: University of North Carolina Press, 2004), 90.

34. Michael T. Bernath, *Confederate Minds: The Struggle for Intellectual Independence in the Civil War South* (Chapel Hill: University of North Carolina Press, 2010), 84–85.

35. Kibler, *The Poetry of William Gilmore Simms*, 433, 435.

36. *Southern Cultivator* 24 (November 1866): 273.

37. *The Land We Love* 3 (May 1867): 71, hereafter documented parenthetically; *The Land We Love* 2 (February 1867): 309.

38. *The Round Table* 4 (November 10, 1866): 244.

39. *Old Guard* 5 (March 1867): 202.

40. *Crescent Monthly* 2 (January 1867): 77–78. The previous April, the *Crescent* had called into question the ethics of Simms's decision to publish his collection while William G. Shepperson was planning to bring out a second edition of his 1862 *War Songs of the South*. See *Crescent Monthly* 1 (April 1866): esp. 168. Southern periodicals were similarly dubious

about the ethics of publishing such a southern book "at the North." See *Scott's Monthly Magazine* 3 (January 1867): 82.

41. *New Englander and Yale Review* 26 (April 1867): 383.

42. Thomas Nelson Page is a notable exception. In an influential 1891 essay, the author of *In Ole Virginia* championed *War Poetry of the South* as an important collection in the history of southern literature. See "Literature in the South Since the War," *Lippincott's Monthly*, December 1891, 741–42.

43. Jennifer Strauss, "Anthologies and Orthodoxies," *Australian Literary Studies* 13, no. 1 (1987): 87.

44. On nineteenth-century poetry anthologies, see Coleman Hutchison and Elizabeth Renker, "Popular Poetry in Circulation" in *U.S. Popular Print Culture 1860–1920*, ed. Christine Bold (New York: Oxford University Press, 2011), 395–413.

PART III

MEDIATIONS OF NATION AND REGION

Traces of the Confederacy

Soldier Newspapers and Wartime Printing in the Occupied South

JAMES BERKEY

Harper's Weekly contains several well-known engravings depicting the prominent role of the press as a mediating institution during the Civil War, including such famous images as Thomas Nast's "The Press on the Field" and Winslow Homer's "News from the War." Lesser known, however, is a single-page illustration from late in the war announcing the arrival of a journalistic newcomer: the *Loyal Georgian*, a soldier newspaper printed and published after the fall of Savannah in December 1864. Inside a printing office, several Union soldiers huddle around a desk, deep in the act of composing a story for the paper. In the background two soldiers stand before a compositor's frame, setting the type for the day's issue. In the center of the image, a young black apprentice, a sheaf of papers curled under his arm, displays a broadsheet heralding the birth of a "New Union Paper, The Loyal Georgian No. 1 Ready at 4 O'Clock."[1] (See figure 2.)

While this scene of printing may be unique in the pages of *Harper's Weekly*, similar situations played themselves out in newspaper and printing offices across the South during the Civil War. Like the *Loyal Georgian*'s printers pictured in *Harper's*, soldier-printers rushed the field of print with their soldier sheets, producing by one estimate close to three hundred papers during the war.[2] The first soldier papers were issued just weeks after the fall of Fort Sumter in 1861, and many papers remained in print as occupation papers well after the Confederate surrender and Lincoln's assassination in April 1865.[3] While some regiments carried the portable Adams "Cottage" Press with them or issued papers from camps in the North, soldier-printers and "typos" in Union regiments more often relied

FIGURE 2. "The Union Army Entered Savannah," *Harper's Weekly*, January 21, 1865. Courtesy of the David M. Rubenstein Rare Book and Manuscript Library, Duke University.

on abandoned civilian newspaper offices and printing presses in the towns they occupied. Edward L. Davenport, a sergeant in the Twenty-Third Massachusetts and soldier-publisher of the *Newbern Progress*, described such a scene after his regiment captured Newbern, North Carolina, in 1862:

> Saturday morning (the day after the battle), in company with other soldiers, the writer left camp on a foraging expedition.... [W]e were in search of a printing-office and soon were on the right track. The door was wide open and we entered but the printers were gone. One or two soldiers were in the room searching for relics. The floor was covered with papers. One press was taken to pieces, ready to move. The balance-wheel had been taken off the small press, a Gordon. There were two pages of matter, set and locked up, which we soon had on the press. On the second impression the press tumbled down. Not to be foiled by this, we covered a planer with a piece of cloth and with that and a mallet we pounded off something like a hundred copies of the paper.[4]

As Davenport's account shows, the material conditions in the abandoned printing offices often created problems for the aspiring soldier-newspapermen. Broken-up presses, damaged type, limited supplies of paper and ink, type already set, papers already partially printed, sudden departures from southern towns, and other difficulties greeted soldiers when they entered through the door of an abandoned southern newspaper office.

The Union soldiers who overcame these material challenges of wartime printing did so because they saw the press not only as a tool for disseminating information, raising morale among the troops, and connecting with the folks back home, but also as an additional weapon in their struggle against the Confederate rebellion in the South. They repeatedly framed their mission as part of the war effort. The editors of the *Cavalier*, originally published by the Fifth Pennsylvania Cavalry in Williamsburg in 1862 before being moved to Yorktown in 1863, identified their paper as part of the Union war "machine": "The great and primary object of the publication shall be to foster and defend loyalty to the Union, and add, though it be but a feeble impulse, to the grand machinery that is crushing the monster 'Treason' from the face of our once happy land."[5] The *Cavalier*'s use of the language of "machinery" not only evokes the industrial economy behind the Union war effort, but also underscores the importance of the very machinery enabling these printing endeavors.

Soldier-printers wielded the editorial scissors as part of that "grand machinery," clipping and reprinting articles, editorials, stories, poetry, and other matter that circulated across the divided nation during the war years. In doing so, they participated in what Meredith McGill has described as a dynamic "culture of reprinting" in the nineteenth century.[6] The *Cavalier*, for example, recirculated fiction by popular authors such as Artemus Ward, Mary Denison, Sylvanus Cobb, T. S. Arthur, and others. Popular poems and songs of national belonging also dotted the pages of the soldier press, bolstering the spirits and resolve of Union forces and buttressing Alice Fahs's contention that "the war was a literary as well as military event."[7] The *Soldiers' Letter of the Ninety-Sixth Illinois Volunteer Infantry*, printed from an abandoned printing press in Harrodsburg, Kentucky, issued a medley of popular nationalistic hymns on its last page, including "Stand Up For Uncle Sam," "The Battle-Cry of Freedom," "Marching On!," and "The Flag of Our Union."[8] In Ironton, Missouri, the printers of the *Normal Picket* inaugurated their paper with "The Picket Guard," commonly known by its refrain, "all quiet along the Potomac tonight," while the *Army Mail Bag* reprinted Joseph Rodman Drake's patriotic "The American Flag."[9]

While these examples of popular literary culture were drawn from the newspaper exchange system and the flourishing literary marketplace of the war years, Union printers often relied, as Davenport's account above suggests, on the abandoned Confederate presses and extraneous materials left behind by absconding Confederate editors.[10] Clipping, reprinting, and, most importantly, reframing materials from their Confederate predecessors on the pages of their newly constituted Union sheets, soldier-printers deployed the tools of the printing trade as editorial weapons, using what Ellen Gruber Garvey calls print's "language of juxtaposition" to challenge Confederate narratives of war and launch new assaults on their southern foes.[11] In doing so, they transformed their papers into a symbolic battleground over which the war's ideological and cultural battles would be fought.

While editorial weapons like scissors enabled soldiers to enact a kind of discursive military cleanup of the Confederate press, the material constraints on printing and soldiers' use of "rebel type" already "set and locked up" had other complex repercussions on the surface of the page.[12] Readers of the *Loyal Georgian* noticed this phenomenon in their reporting on the new paper in Savannah. The *Augusta Chronicle* highlighted what it found to be a particularly "rich feature in the columns of the 'Georgian'": "a quantity of Confederate official advertisement calling upon the citizens to rally to defend Savannah, also other Confederate notices, also prospectuses of several religious Confederate newspapers, and other matter which remind of days gone by." The publisher, according to the *Chronicle*, "shall fill out with these advertisements until his friends furnish him with new ones."[13] Such journalistic traces of daily life in the Confederacy appeared across the South throughout the war. Calls for Confederate victory, rewards for runaway slaves, anti-Lincoln diatribes, and notices for Confederate literary monthlies, among other things, occupied the pages of the soldier press alongside Union proclamations of victory and other articles extolling the virtue of Lincoln and the North.

This essay follows these traces of the Confederacy across the pages of Union soldier newspapers, attending to what Katy Chiles has brilliantly described as the periodical form's "production of intratextuality." Describing the juxtaposition of texts and meanings in the *Weekly Anglo-African*'s serialization of Martin Delaney's *Blake*, Chiles explains, "Written at different times by assorted authors, these various texts come together to form the text of each periodical, but not as seamlessly as we might believe. The friction, overlay, and conversations among these 'texts within a text' can be best explored as the production of intratextuality."[14] While such an intratextual reading method can help us to interpret the striking juxtapositions that result from northern soldiers' practice of occupation printing, Chiles's allusion to the lack of "seamlessness" indicates her critical distance from Benedict Anderson's "imagined community" thesis. It has become a commonplace to think of newspapers as coterminous with national boundaries and, as Chiles points out, to consider their "texts within a text" as analogous to the citizens of a nation, each brought together through the "extraordinary mass ceremony" of the "simultaneous consumption ('imagining')" of the newspaper.[15] Just as Chiles's reading of the serialization of Delaney's *Blake* complicates Anderson's "imagined linkages," other scholars, most notably Trish Loughran, have challenged the "seamless," incorporative power of Andersonian "simultaneity."[16] For Loughran the integration of the material infrastructure of the United States in the antebellum period failed to produce ideological cohesion and national solidarity, instead generating increased sectional discord and national disintegration. My focus on the often messy and chaotic material conditions out of which soldier newspapers were forged similarly reveals a deeply fractured nation, struggling to integrate its disparate and openly hostile parts into an indivisible Union. "Simultaneity," in the practices of Union soldier-printers, results in division and fragmentation, a collision of divergent worldviews and social practices brought together by the unstable vicissitudes of wartime printing.

Although these traces of the Confederacy could shatter the "imagined community" of the soldier paper, this essay will conclude by examining how Union printers tried to frame and contain their "disintegrative potential" (Loughran 24). Indeed, given the ideological incongruity and potentially treasonous hostility of Confederate advertisements appearing in a Union paper, it seems surprising that soldier-printers would let such material stand at all in their papers. Certainly, the appearance of Confederate "dead matter," as one soldier paper called it, may be attributed to the material conditions of textual production under which Union "typos" labored.[17] While some Confederate material appeared unscathed in inaugural issues of soldier papers, however, Union printers quickly effaced and reinterpreted that material. Refashioning Confederate narratives of the war within a framework of Union victory, soldier papers enacted an occupation on the pages of what had been the Confederate press that was analogous to their military and political occupation of the southern landscape.

Print Battlefields: Reprinting as an Editorial Weapon of the Soldier-Printer

Soldier papers throughout the war saw their enterprise not only as a means of spreading Union sentiment, but also as a strategic endeavor that complemented the "work of the sword" on the field of battle. As we saw with the *Cavalier* above, soldier-editors often cast their work as part of the larger war strategy. In resuming the publication of the *Newbern Progress*, Edward L. Davenport and George Mills Joy, also a member of the Twenty-Third Massachusetts Regiment, review the *Progress*'s earlier advocacy of the Confederacy:

> The Progress has been heretofore one of the most virulent and bitter opposers to the government, in the South.... That government so foully and wickedly wronged, has taken possession of this office, and henceforth all publication ema-

nating from it will aim to disabuse the southern mind of that prejudice and error which has been encouraged by previous publications.... [W]e war rather with those demagogues who have so inflamed the public mind and caused an appeal to arms necessary to vindicate the majesty of law and good government.[18]

For Davenport, Joy, and other soldier-editors, the battle for the "southern mind" was a vital part of the war effort, and the occupation of newspaper offices enabled a discursive war with Confederate "demagogues" that complemented and supplemented the maneuvers of soldiers on the field.

In addition to stating their general opposition to Confederate principles and Confederate editors, soldier papers used the tools of print culture to turn their papers into print battlefields in their own right. The "Yankee Printers" of the *Newbern Progress* reprinted an article from their Confederate predecessor in order to signal the shift in perspective of the paper and resignify such key terms as "enemy." Appearing a few columns away from their inaugural salutatory where they declare war on southern demagogues, "The Enemy in Sight" describes the preparations being made in Newbern at the "approach of the enemy," here meaning the Union forces. Originally published in the Confederate *Progress* on March 13, the article reported that "a battle is certainly expected today, and the day will probably decide the fate of Newbern." On the very next line, the Union printers add: "Saturday, March 15. Friday did it. We have taken Newbern. The enemy endeavored to burn the town, but were unsuccessful, the inhabitants using the fire engines and other means in their power to extinguish the flames. YANKEE PRINTER."[19] On the one hand, this "triumphant comment," as Davenport later described it, shows the Union soldiers having some fun with their newfound press.[20] More importantly, though, the *Progress*'s new proprietors not only re-determine the meaning of "enemy," but also expose the Confederate forces as hostile to the material and security interests of Newbern citizens, relating the civilians' efforts to save the town from a fiery destruction by the departing rebels. Such a "triumphant comment" positions the Yankee printers as sympathetic to their new readership while undermining the rebel campaign's promises to protect southern citizens from Yankee invaders.

The *Progress*'s reprinting of "The Enemy in Sight" and its ensuing critical commentary brings to mind Ellen Gruber Garvey's "language of juxtaposition," a practice of recontextualization made possible by the conditions of wartime printing.[21] The *Progress* was hardly unique in this practice. Printers from the First Minnesota Regiment, who took over the offices of the *Berryville Conservator* in Virginia in early March 1862, littered their paper with short snippets and reprints from earlier *Conservator*s, exemplifying what another soldier paper deemed the "frank and fearless use of tongue and pen" in their critical reframing of the *Con-*

servator's Confederate point of view.²² Upon taking over the *Conservator*'s offices, the First Minnesota's printers discovered that H. K. Gregg, the previous editor, and his staff had already printed three of the four pages of the *Conservator*'s March 12 edition. The Union printers quickly set their type and on the remaining blank page printed the *First Minnesota*, dated March 11, 1862.²³ What would have been Gregg's front page contained an account of Confederate General Joseph Johnston's official report of the Battle of Manassas on October 14, 1861, which continued on the inside second page. Like the *Newbern Progress*'s "triumphant comment" on "The Enemy in Sight," the Minnesota printers added three lines after Johnston's report, their only emendation to the original *Conservator*: "The above is all that was in type of the report, and the copy could not be found—more's the pity—Eds. FIRST MINNESOTA." The remaining page and a half lists various Confederate Congressional Committees and prints local advertisements. The soldier-printers took this situation in stride, however, making light of "being caught ... in bad company" in their opening salutation: "Our only apology for making our appearance in 'secesh' company is, that the employees of Mr. Gregg hearing, doubtless, that we Vandal Yankees had crossed the Potomac and were on their way to the pleasant little village of Berryville, were kind enough to 'set up' and 'work off' the first side of the paper."²⁴

Despite lamenting their "appearance in 'secesh' company," the *First Minnesota*'s "typos" hardly seemed to mind as they assembled their type. Scattered across their single page were the print remains of the *Conservator*'s earlier Confederate issues. Informing their readers on several occasions that "the above was in type before we took charge of the office" or "the above extract is from the previous issue of the 'Conservator,'" the *First Minnesota* reprinted and re-"justified," to use the language of printing, the "dead matter of the Conservator" in order to lampoon its Confederate perspective.²⁵ In so doing, they took aim with their "shooting-sticks" at Confederate ideology, misinformation, and moxie, composing their own type to counter the discursive attacks marshaled by their opponents in the pages of the very paper they now controlled. The *First Minnesota* poked fun at the *Conservator*'s previous editor on several occasions and reprinted almost a dozen short one-to-two-sentence lines from earlier *Conservators*. Some pieces, like "Run Away Editor," were humorous shots at Gregg for his "sudden absquatulation" from Berryville.²⁶ Reviling Gregg for his role as editor of the *Conservator*, they declared that he "sent forth column after column in vile abuse of the best government the world has ever known—the government that towered above all others, and on whose banners might be written 'PEERLESS.' This Gregg was 'lost' to all true principles of manhood, has 'strayed' from the tuition of his youth, has 'stolen' what?—the true impulses of many, perhaps nearly all of his readers."²⁷ Such moments paint Gregg not only as a traitor to their "peerless" government, but also as derelict in his duties to the public as an editor and newspaperman.

Elsewhere the *First Minnesota*'s editors made more aggressive advances against southern representations of the war, reprinting selections from the *Conservator*'s pages to correct and reinterpret the meaning of the Confederacy. They skewer Confederate type in an article titled "Confed. Notes" that explains how to recognize authentic Confederate currency. The quoted *Conservator* reads, "The genuine Confederate Notes are all numbered with RED ink. As there are some counterfeits in Richmond (numbered with BLACK ink), it would be well to observe this particularity." The symbolism of this southern ink is too much for the Union printers. They respond with a reinterpretive volley of their own: "Genuine in red ink—what more symbolical of the red-handed outrages of Jeff. and his advisers. Red—with what? The blood of Virginians."[28] Reprinting these lines and then reinterpreting their meaning allows these soldier-printers to undermine the Confederacy in at least two ways. On the one hand, the presence of counterfeit money in Richmond suggests the weak foundation of the Confederacy, its capital rife with hucksters and frauds intent on swindling the people, a common refrain in Union-leaning papers throughout the war. On the other hand, and building off the notion of Confederate duplicity, the semiotics of red ink enables the printers to cast Jefferson Davis and the CSA as the war's true villains, villains who are ultimately responsible for the bloodshed suffered by their own people, the very same Virginians that the First Minnesota had so recently been fighting. Such a rendering of the red ink as the "blood of Virginians" also allows the Union soldiers to position themselves as the genuine protectors of Berryville, Virginia, a brilliant tactical maneuver that asserts the benevolent power of the Union and its soldiers.

While the *First Minnesota*'s editors reinterpreted snippets of news from the *Conservator*'s pages, other soldier printers launched poetic volleys to attack southern literary culture and its nationalistic myths. Having chased Stonewall Jackson's brigade from Winchester, Virginia, in March 1862, the soldier-printers of the *Connecticut Fifth* lampooned Jackson by reprinting and then parodying a poem they discovered in the pages of their southern predecessor, the *Winchester Virginian*. Written as a "Tribute to Jackson's Command," the reprinted "Jackson's Stone Wall Brigade" begins with a historical allusion to Confederate general Barnard Bee's famous christening of Jackson at the Battle of Bull Run:

> "Look, men," cried General Bee—
> "At yonder ranks—and see
> Jackson's brigade standing firm
> Looking resolute and stern
> As a Stone Wall."[29]

The remainder of the Confederate poem emphasizes the steadfast bravery and impending fame of Jackson and his men, who "fight with heart and hand; / And they ne'er retreat, but stand / 'Like a Stone Wall.'" Immediately beneath this southern homage, however, the *Connecticut Fifth* prints its own "Jackson's Stone Wall Brigade," this one a "Tribute to Jackson's Command, by the very Old Boy in Winchester, Virginia." Borrowing the title, but not the sentiment, this parody rewrites Jackson and his men as cowards:

> Look, men, look sharp, and see
> Their coat tails as they flee,
> And Jackson drawing a bee-
>   Line for a *safe stone wall*.
>
> That Brigade must have a name
> To live in future fame—
> And suppose we call the same
>   "The Stone Wall Brigade."[30]

Echoing the opening lines of the reprinted original, the *Fifth*'s parody offers an alternative meaning of the famous moniker before asserting the strength of Union fighters in its final stanza. The *Fifth*'s poet concludes,

> Or if they ever make a stand,
> They will find a Yankee hand
> Will crush into the sand
>   The Stone Wall Brigade.

Just as the *First Minnesota* undermined the meaning and strength of the Confederacy by reprinting articles like "Confed. Notes," the *Fifth* reworks the materials it finds at hand in the offices of the *Winchester Virginian* to challenge a storied figure in the Confederate pantheon.

Whereas some soldier papers reprinted material from the presses they were occupying in their battle for the southern mind, other soldier-printers reached into the broader culture of song and symbol that circulated throughout the North and South, appropriating and reworking such songs as "The Bonnie Blue Flag" and "Dixie" in their pages. In doing so, they participated in what Coleman Hutchison has called the war's "broader culture of lyrical revisionism."[31] Printing from the abandoned offices of the *Athens Post* in Tennessee in September 1863, members of the Eighth Michigan Cavalry rechristened the paper the *Athens Union Post*, an addition that "very materially changes its *complexion*," and printed an original composition titled "No 'Bonnie Blue Flag' For Me," penned in Athens on September 12, 1863.[32] Alluding to the popular Confederate song that trumpets the defense of southern rights and cheers on the order of secession, the

Union Post's lyric upends southern claims to liberty and rights. Although "some people sing of the 'Bonnie Blue Flag,' / And call it the flag of the free," the anonymous soldier-poet intones the fabled history of the "stripes and stars":

> On Bunker and Yorktown the stripes and stars
>   Floated proud o'er the conquerors head,
> And still they will float o'er the stars and bars
>   That dishonors those honored dead.
> So rally, and fight for the lands,
>   Your forefathers fought to make free;
> There the stars and stripes we'll plant with firm hands
>   No "Bonnie Blue Flag" for me.[33]

While the Confederate anthem establishes a genealogy of secession for the fledgling Confederate nation, this Union poem asserts the temporal priority of the Union flag at "Bunker and Yorktown," repudiating the South's declaration of freedom and independence. The South, the poem claims, is already a part of the Union; it is land that "your forefathers fought to make free."

Soldiers in the Thirty-Third Illinois Volunteers rewrote "Dixie," one of the most popular and hotly contested cultural objects of the wartime period, in the pages of their soldier sheet, the *Normal Picket*, in Ironton, Missouri, in the winter of 1861–62. Written "for the Picket," "Our Dixie" appropriates the lyrics and melody of the popular tune, but the titular *our* "materially changes its complexion," to borrow a phrase from the *Athens Union Post*, disputing their "Southern brethren's" proprietary claim to the imagined space of "Dixie." Like other "local appropriations and rewritings," the *Picket*'s "Our Dixie" reimagines the tune from a northern perspective and redraws the boundaries of national allegiance:[34]

> And so we'll go to Dixie.
>   Huray! Huray!
> For Uncle Sam we'll take our stand
> And drive secesh from Dixie's land
>   Away! away! away down South in Dixie![35]

This Union variant even attacks King Cotton, challenging cotton's status as the South's national commodity:

> Then away! away! away! away!
> We'll make a break for Dixie
>   Huray! Huray!
> We'll teach the traitor rebel band,
> That Cotton won't grow in Dixie's land
>   That corn! that corn! that corn is king in Dixie!

Given the song's "extraordinary ideological flexibility," it is hardly surprising that Union troops stationed in a border state at the beginning of the war would find in "Dixie" a lyrical weapon of war.[36] As part of the larger arsenal of reprinting and rewriting explored here, the poems and songs found among soldier papers such as the *Connecticut Fifth*, the *Athens Union Post*, and the *Normal Picket* demonstrate the ingenuity of the Union and its printers in the face of challenging material conditions in occupied newspaper offices. Taking up the tools of print and literary culture, they transformed their papers into print battlegrounds and waged war over the meaning of the Confederacy.

Traces of the Confederacy: Southern Advertising on the Pages of Soldier Newspapers

Occupying southern newspaper offices enabled Union printers to launch media critiques of Confederate narratives of the war through the very medium and machinery of the Confederate printing trade. However, such conditions also brought with them various constraints on the production of soldier newspapers, including scarcity of paper and ink, ransacked printing offices and broken-up presses, and little time to prepare a paper. While the vicissitudes of wartime printing enabled the critiques of the Confederacy that we have seen in the *First Minnesota*, for example, these material constraints also meant that the pages of Union-held papers in the occupied South became sites of contested meaning in other, more complicated ways. Alongside the humorous editorializing of Union printers, readers also discovered other journalistic traces of daily life in the Confederacy: advertisements for slave sales, rewards for runaway slaves, anti-Lincoln diatribes and bounties, Confederate recruiting advertisements, and notices for nationalistic Confederate literary monthlies, among other things. By existing on the space of the same page, this collision of divergent worldviews and social practices showed the breakdown of Anderson's "imagined linkages," as competing material, social, and ideological traces jostled for control and authority over the space of the page.

Such traces of the Confederacy appear in soldier newspapers at all stages of the war. Because Union printers were working with the extraneous materials they found in occupied printing offices and were trying to issue their papers quickly, it was a common practice to reuse old advertisements, even entire pages of advertisements that were most likely already set, thus enabling the quicker printing of the paper and by extension the Union's claim to the town and its public sphere. Nevertheless, soldier newspapers often apologized or at least sheepishly commented on the practice. In addition to asking their readers

of my late partners, BARTON & WILLIAMS.
T. T. FAUNTLEROY, JR.,
October 30, 1861—tf   *Receiver C. S. A.*

$100 REWARD.

Ran away from the subscriber, in the months of August and October last, TWO SLAVES; one a GIRL, about 18 years old, bright mulatto, tall and slender, hair quite straight, teeth little decayed in front, no mark remembered save a mole quite conspicuous near the right eye. She calls herself MARY RANDOLPH. She ran away the 2d of August, taking with her a quantity of clothing, among it several fancy dresses. The other, a BOY of 15 years, bright mulatto, about 5¼ feet high, with low forehead, hair growing closely around it, not very intelligent, and stammers slightly in talking. He is a brother of the girl, calls himself FREDERICK RANDOLPH, and ran off in October, wearing a coarse leghorn hat, brown pants with stripes down the sides, and a dark sack coat.

I will give $50 apiece if they are taken in Clarke, $60 apiece in Frederick, and what the law allows if taken in any of the border Counties, or out of the State.   A. L. P. LARUE.
December 18, 1861—6m

TULEYRIES FOR RENT.

I wish to rent this elegant MANSION HOUSE and GARDEN to a gentleman who has a family, until I can sell the whole estate. The Tuleyries is the healthiest and most beautiful residence in the Southern Confederacy.

Early application is desired, and will not be rented to any one unless binding themselves to take good care of the House, &c. One room will be reserved for myself, as it is necessary for me to be on the farm several times during the year.
JOS. T. MITCHELL,
Agent and Attorney in fact for the heirs of
July 26, 1861—tf   *Col. Jos. Tuley, dec'd.*

$100 REWARD.—The above reward will

be given for the apprehension of NEGRO MAN, JAMES JOHNSON, belonging to the estate of Jacob Isler, dec'd. Said Negro is about 5 feet 4 inches high, of copper color, and about 20 years old. Fifty Dollars reward will be given if taken out of the County of Clarke, in this State, and $100 if taken in Maryland or any of the Free States. Said Negro to be delivered in the jail of Clarke or Jefferson.   WM. A. CASTLEMAN,
August 8, 1861—tf   *Adm'r of Jacob Isler, dec'd.*

WILLIAM R. DENNY,
(SUCCESSOR TO J. H. CRUM & CO.,)
Dealer in Books and Stationery, Dry Goods and Notions,

Will continue the sale of the same style of Goods heretofore sold at the old stand, ☞ one door South of Taylor Hotel, ☜ and will continue to sell Goods at the small profits for which this Store has been famous.   [Winchester, September 25, 1861

FROM WINCHESTER TO LEESBURG.

LLOYD & BYRD are now running a *Tri-Weekly Line of Stages* between Winchester and Leesburg. Leaves Winchester every Tuesday, Thursday and Saturday morning. Leaves Leesburg every Monday, Wednesday and Friday morning.   [July 12, 1861

will be prepared to give general satisfaction.
His material being *all cash*, he will be thankful to his friends to keep him so respect. *Country Trade* will be received in exchange for work at fair market prices.
April 16, 1861   JOHN AVIS.

NEW SHOE ESTABLISHMENT.

I have again commenced the Shoemaking business on my own account at Wickliffe, and have procured the best workmen in the State of Virginia, and the best selection of materials that could be had. I would return my sincere thanks for the patronage I received when in business before, and hope for a liberal share for the future. I ask you to come and look at my work, ask my prices, and you will surely deal. I will keep constantly on hand a good assortment of *ready-made Boots and Shoes*, to which I would invite the attention of the public.

I will also repair all kinds of *HARNESS*, and will pay the highest market price for *HIDES*.
January 15, 1861   M. L. SINCLAIR.

HO! FOR THE TOBACCO AND CIGAR STORE!

Another wagon-load of Tobacco, Cigars, Snuff, &c., &c., just received, and purchased for the cash. Returning my thanks to my customers and the public generally for the liberal patronage extended to me, I would inform them that I can sell Tobacco and Cigars at *greatly reduced prices*, having bought another large and well-selected stock at surprisingly low prices. *Tobacco worth 37½ and 50 cents, selling at 20 and 25 cents per pound!* My stock embraces the finest and best brands of Tobacco and Cigars manufactured, which I am selling at nearly *one-half* of regular prices. Don't forget the sign of "Pompey," opposite the Post-Office.
Berryville, April 9, 1861   Z. GRAY.

NOTICE.—All persons indebted to JOHN

H. CRUM & Co., will as speedily as possible settle their accounts, at the old stand, to myself or FRANK G. WALTER. This is necessary because of the death of Mr. CRUM, whose business his Administrator desires to settle speedily. All persons having claims against JOHN H. CRUM & CO., will please at once present them for payment.
WILLIAM R. DENNY,
Winchester, Sept. 25, 1861   Surviving Partner.

MORE GOODS!

I have this day (September 26th) bought the entire STOCK OF GOODS of the house of J. P. HEIRONIMUS & Co., for cash, amounting to about $10,000, and will be sold at low figures for *cash*.
Winchester, Oct. 2, 1861   C. B. ROUSS.

WILLIAM R. DENNY,
ONE DOOR SOUTH OF TAYLOR HOTEL,
Has on hand a lot of good quality of *Ladies' Home-Made Morocco Shoes*, which will be sold at the *old* prices.   [Winchester, September 25, 1861

NAILS.—250 kegs best Wheeling Nails,
for sale by   BAKER & BRO.
Winchester Depot, January 8, 1861

OILS, PAINTS AND GLASS—In large
quantities and great variety, for sale by
Winchester, April 17   BAKER & BROS.

FIGURE 3. Advertising page, including two runaway slave ads, *First Minnesota*, March 11, 1862. Courtesy of the David M. Rubenstein Rare Book and Manuscript Library, Duke University.

to "be lenient with us" because the "sheet was gotten up in a few hours," the *First Minnesota*'s printers also apologetically explained that "a few advertisements appear on our last page. We were in a hurry and had to do it."[37] Such explanations and apologies suggest some uneasiness on the part of the Union printers, and I would venture, based on tracing the fate of this advertising material in subsequent issues of the papers, that this discomfort was due at least in part to the content of the advertisements themselves.

Much of the advertising material that appeared in soldier-newspapers was innocuous. The *First Minnesota* contained one and a half pages of advertisements, which covered all aspects of daily life in Berryville and nearby Winchester, Virginia: hardware stores, cabinet makers, pump makers, and pipe borers; hay, straw, and fodder cutters; boot and shoe establishments; saddle and harness makers; tobacco and cigars; watches, jewelry, silver, and plated ware; etc. Other ads were for drug stores and general goods stores. While some, such as W. C. Cooper's "Saddles! Saddles!" notice, included prefatory nationalistic admonitions such as "Encourage Home Enterprise!," most offered simple, nonpartisan descriptions of their products and services. The *Opelousas Courier*, taken over by Union troops on April 25, 1863, and printed on wallpaper, included several announcements of public sales of land, houses, personal belongings, and livestock; estray notices for mules and other livestock; and various advertisements for a surgeon-dentist, a doctor, and a parish surveyor as well as hotel and ferry services.[38]

Not all of the Confederate advertising material that appeared in soldier newspapers, however, was politically innocent in the eyes of northern soldiers; some advertising material underscored the stark differences between the North and the South. Readers would also discover advertisements for runaway slaves, notices for slave sales, or requests to purchase slaves. On the inside-left page of the *First Minnesota*'s morning edition, for example, there are two advertisements for runaway slaves, both offering a hundred dollar reward.[39] (See figure 3.) While jarring to our contemporary eye, these advertisements appear on the page as just an advertisement for any other product or service. While one sees images of boots or saddles adorning advertisements for saddle makers and shoe establishments elsewhere on the page, the runaway slave ads are embellished with the print iconography of the runaway slave—a male slave in full stride carrying a stick and sack over his shoulder, a female slave holding her sack in her hand.[40] The text itself remains descriptive and matter-of-fact:

> Ran away from the subscriber, in the months of August and October last, TWO SLAVES; one a GIRL, about 18 years old, bright mulatto, tall and slender, hair quite straight, teeth little decayed in front, no mark remembered save a mole quite conspicuous near the right eye. She calls herself MARY RANDOLOPH.

She ran away the 2d of August, taking with her a quantity of clothing, among it several fancy dresses.[41]

Such descriptions echo the lists of prices and descriptions of materials found in other advertisements on the same page, one way in which southern discourse reinforced slaves' status as commodities. Advertisements like these appeared in other soldier papers as well, some as late as April 1865. In one of those intratextual ironies that is only possible in the soldier papers that bring the divergent worlds of the Union and Confederacy together on the same page, the *Sixth Corps*, issued from the press of the *Danville Register* on April 27, 1865, printed a $150 reward notice for the "recovery" of "a mulatto boy William, between 17 and 18 years of age" only three columns away from the announcement that Danville had been "captured" by Union forces.[42] Unremarked upon by the Union printers of the *Sixth Corps*, the juxtaposition of these starkly different moments of *capture* is indicative of the nineteenth century's "ongoing processes of cultural integration" and "the simultaneous experiences of *dis*integration and national fragmentation" that Trish Loughran attributes to the remarkable, axiomatic "time-space compressions" of print culture and that are here produced by material conditions of occupation printing in the South (3).

While the presence of runaway slave ads and other traces of the South's "peculiar institution" are particularly jarring for contemporary readers, other competing discourses of the Confederacy appeared in the advertising pages of soldier newspapers. The *Newbern Progress*, *Opelousas Courier*, and *First Minnesota* all included Confederate recruiting advertisements for cavalry brigades and heavy artillery companies. The *Sixth Corps* provides an interesting glimpse of the last days of the Confederacy in one of the notices in its first issue, printed from Danville, Virginia, the last capital of the CSA. In the ad, titled "Danville Defences" and dated April 16, R. E. Withers, Colonel Commanding Post, calls on citizens to "send voluntary labor to erect Defences around Danville" as "recent events make the safety of this place a matter of grave importance to every loyal and patriotic citizen."[43] It is unclear if the Union printers who issued the *Sixth Corps* purposely included this notice in their paper, but, like the reward for the "recovery" of the runaway slave William, such a Confederate call for Danville's defense is ironically undercut by the presence of a competing article titled "To the Citizens of Danville" on the far left, Union side of the page. Here, Union printers promise readers that they have "always ensured protection to peaceably disposed and loyal citizens. . . . [I]t is the intention of the General commanding the Corps to make the presence of his troops in this place, a time long to be remembered and talked over as the period when safety to life and property was restored, and the sun of prosperity again dawned, after being obscured for four years behind the dark clouds of secession."[44] Although the war was over and Union forces clearly controlled Danville, for a moment on the pages of the *Sixth Corps*, in the haste to produce a Union paper, the Confederacy seems to make one final posthumous stand against those same Union forces.

Occupying, Effacing, and Reframing the Confederacy

Runaway slave ads, recruiting announcements, and notices like "Danville Defences" underscored the sharp divisions between the North and South, making the space of the soldier newspaper a terrain fraught with semantic and ideological peril. It is hard to know if the juxtaposition of narratives—different meanings of "capture," Union and Confederate calls for protecting citizens—on the pages of the *Sixth Corps*, for example, was purposeful, but we can discern something of soldier-printers' intentions by tracing the fate of these advertisements in subsequent editions. Indeed, Union printers engaged in a variety of tactical print maneuvers to forestall print's disintegrative potential and create a space for national reconstruction and consolidation. Many of the innocuous advertisements mentioned above reappeared in later issues of soldier papers. Other advertisements, like the runaway slave ads and Confederate recruiting announcements, simply disappeared from their pages, as soldier-newspapermen effaced these traces of the Confederacy and left them on the floor of the printing office. In the advertising pages of the *Newbern Progress*, for instance, we see an interesting progression between the first and fifth numbers of the Union-issued *Progress*. Of the six columns on the page, the two left-side columns are gradually populated with new stores and services, many of which are Union-based. P. C. Cummings, the sutler of the Eleventh Regiment, Connecticut Volunteers, announces the opening of his store, while the Adams Army Express offers its reasonable rates and G. & D. Cook of New Haven, Connecticut, advertises bulletproof vests. Such ads replaced those by local southern general goods stores, a process of occupying the page akin to the geographical occupation of southern space that brought Union printers into the *Progress*'s office in the first place. The page's other four columns remain almost identical, the only difference being the disappearance of a recruiting notice for Confederate cavalry that appeared in the first number of the Union *Progress*. Originally appearing between ads for a new manufacturing co-partnership Miller & Co. and the High Point Female Seminary, Cooper Huggins's call for "forming a Cavalry Company for two years, or the war" is silently erased, a simple line now separating High Point's female seminarians from Miller & Co.'s manufacturing venture. (See figure 4.)

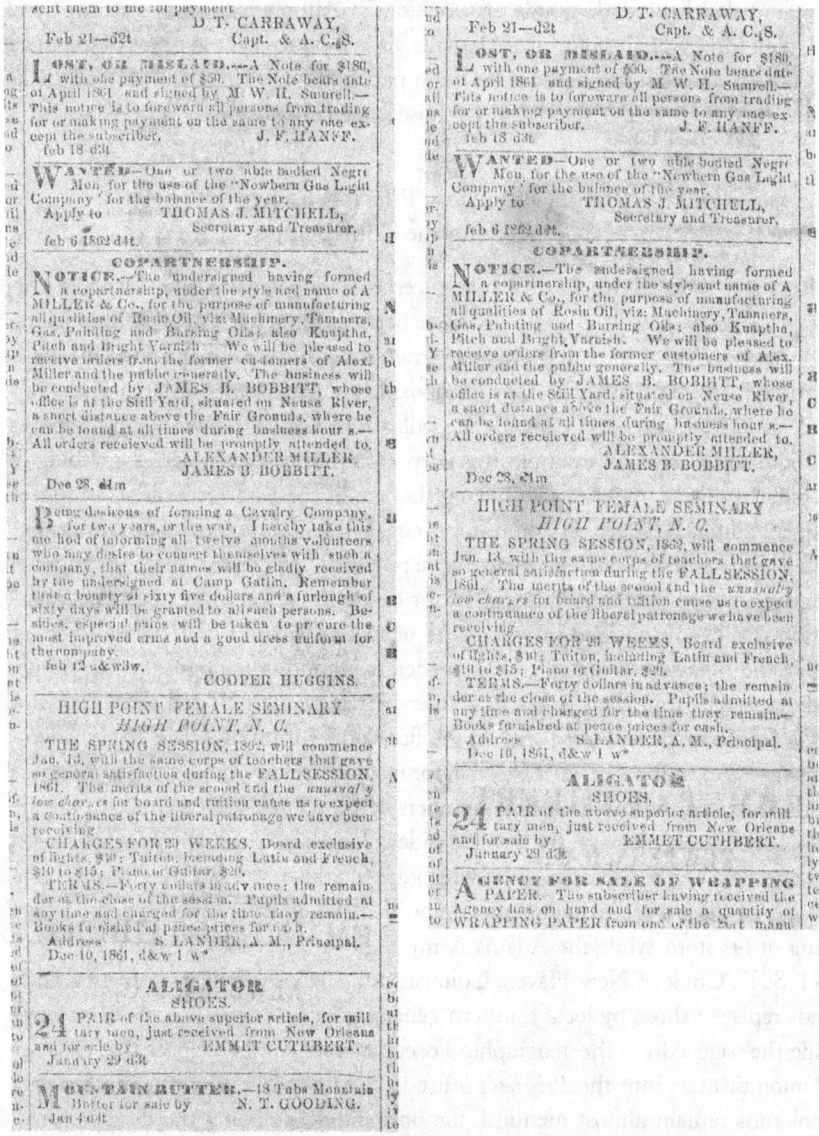

FIGURE 4. Cooper Huggins's recruitment ad appears in the advertising page of the *Newbern Progress*, March 22, 1862 (left). It has been effaced from the page by the April 5 issue (right). Courtesy of the David M. Rubenstein Rare Book and Manuscript Library, Duke University.

In addition to this strategy of silent erasure and colonization by Union-leaning ads, Union printers also self-consciously reframed and reinterpreted the traces of the Confederacy they encountered in their first issues. The *Opelousas Courier*, printed on wallpaper on April 25, 1863, by soldiers in the Forty-First Regiment, Massachusetts Volunteers, includes a similar request as the "Danville Defences" notice in the *Sixth Corps*, but the editors of the *Courier* strategically frame this ad to emphasize the Union's control over the geographical and imagined space of its southern readers. Directly beneath a short piece announcing the Union's capture of Butte-a-la-Rose by General Nathaniel Banks, the *Courier* ran "To the Patriotic Citizens of St. Landry." (See figure 5.) The original ad calls on the citizens of St. Landry to help erect fortifications at Butte-a-la-Rose "with all the available negroes they can spare," ending their ad with this appeal: "Let every man come to the rescue before it be too late!" The Union printers of the *Courier* then inform the public that "the public spirited firm of N. P. Banks & Co., have decided to complete the work of rendering Butte-a-la-Rose impregnable," casting aspersions on the "absconding . . . former overseer (a person named Taylor)," noting the "subsequent strike of [Taylor's] hands," and explaining that the "well known character of the gentlemen who have now undertaken the work" ensures the success of the effort.[45] The soldier-printers of the Massachusetts Forty-First are clearly poking fun at their Confederate opponents at this moment, but their reframing maneuver also demonstrates how they slotted their capture of Butte-a-la-Rose into larger narratives of the war. It is hardly a coincidence that General Banks and the Union army are referred to as a "public spirited firm" and C.S.A. Major General Richard Taylor is cast as an "overseer" whose laborers "strike" as soon as he departs. Underscoring the differences between the North's industrial economy and the South's plantation economy through such allusions, the Union printers undermine Confederate belief in the supremacy of the southern way of life, suggesting the duplicity of its leaders and the discontent of its laborers (i.e., slaves). Furthermore, their ability to complete the job started by Taylor demonstrates their own strength, fortitude, and benevolence as occupiers of the South and future architects of a newly constituted nation.

Whereas the Union printers of the *Opelousas Courier* reinterpreted a Confederate advertisement from an earlier *Courier*, the *First Minnesota*'s staff self-reflexively aimed their shooting stick at their own paper, tactically reframing the Confederate advertisements they had let stand in their first issue when they reissued their paper in a second edition later that same evening. Their first edition—the four-page *First Minnesota/Berryville Conservator* combination—sold out rapidly, and they issued a second, two-sided evening edition on the same day, effacing almost all of the earlier Confederate material as if removing casualties from the field of battle.[46] We have already seen how they critically re-

FIGURE 5. Reframing a Confederate advertisement. "To the Patriotic Citizens of St. Landry," *Opelousas Courier*, April 25, 1863. Courtesy of the David M. Rubenstein Rare Book and Manuscript Library, Duke University.

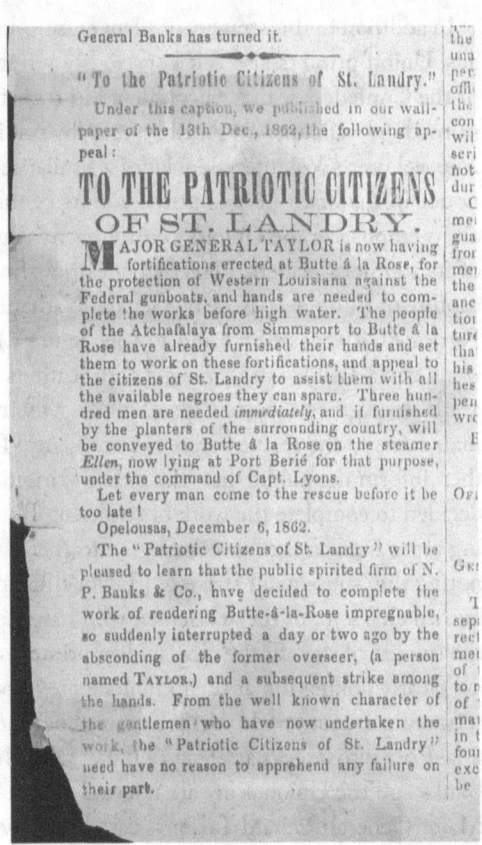

interpret articles like "Confed. Notes" from earlier *Conservator*s, but their engagement with Confederate advertisements reveals a deeper awareness of the strange collision of worlds that occurred in their morning edition. Calling them "specimens of the modern style of advertising in the South," they reprinted only three advertisements from the morning edition.[47] The soldier-printers, for example, strategically reframe and repurpose "To the Brave Soldiers of the South," an advertisement for C. B. Rouss's store in Winchester. Far from advertising the "goods" of his store, Rouss maligns Lincoln, comparing him unfavorably to Arnold and Judas, who "were white men compared to this scoundrel": "He has done more harm than any other man since the creation. He has, with a fiendish malignity, unsurpassed by the savage or barbarian, brought a calamity upon a happy country and a mighty people, amounting to universal destruction." Rouss concludes by offering a bounty of "$20,000 for the head of Lincoln." Then as an afterthought, he reminds readers that he is "selling GOODS very cheap." Not to be intimidated or to relinquish control over the framing of the war, the *First Minnesota*'s printers preface Rouss's advertisement with their own threat: "Read it, and remember he lives in Winchester, where we are going. We venture the prediction that Mr. Rouss will be strong Union before another moon—he is too brave to run." By reproducing Rouss's advertisements, these soldier-printers not only poke fun at his "brave" posturing and Confederate moxie, a strategy meant to rally their own side, but also reveal their complete mastery of the military and political field. Rather than simply eradicating these Confederate sentiments from the evening edition, the Union printers reincorporate them into a second edition printed fresh on blank sheets unlike the morning edition, allowing them to exist in the same space as their own articles and perspectives. They make a place for an inhospitable, seditious political perspective within the territory they now control, actively engaging and debating its positions. By doing so, they reinforce the very democratic ideals of the Union they are fighting to preserve, demonstrating for their soldier and civilian readership the potential for and desire of the Union to reincorporate "Secessia" at even its most vitriolic and slanderous.[48]

NOTES

I wish to thank Jon Blandford, Josh Davis, Lynn Badia, and Zack Vernon for their valuable feedback on earlier drafts. I also want to thank Elizabeth Dunn and Jessica Janecki for their intrepid efforts in tracking down soldier newspapers at the David M. Rubenstein Rare Book and Manuscript Library at Duke University. The images reproduced in this article are from holdings in the Rubenstein Library. Finally, the staffs at the Boston Athenaeum, the Western Reserve Historical Society in Cleveland, and the North Carolina Collection at the University of North Carolina were very helpful during my research for this project.

1. "The Union Army Entered Savannah," *Harper's Weekly*, January 21, 1865, 36.

2. Earle Lutz estimates close to three hundred papers, although he acknowledges that many no longer exist. See "The *Stars and Stripes* of Illinois Boys in Blue," *Journal of the Illinois State Historical Society* 46, no. 2 (1953): 132. For more information on Civil War soldier newspapers, see Bell Wiley, "Camp Newspapers of the Confederacy," *North Carolina Historical Review* 20, no. 4 (1943): 327–35; Bell Wiley, "Soldier Newspapers of the Civil War," *Civil War Times Illustrated* 16, no. 4 (1977): 20–29; Lester Cappon, "The Yankee Press in Virginia, 1861–1865," *William and Mary Quarterly* 15, no. 1 (1935): 81–88; and Chandra Miller, "'A Perfect Institution Belonging to the Regiment': The *Soldier's Letter* and American Identity Among Civil War Soldiers in Kansas," *Kansas History* 22, no. 4 (1999/2000): 284–97.

3. The difficulty of categorizing soldier papers makes the process of identifying the first or last Civil War soldier newspaper problematic. Earle Lutz identifies the *U.S. American Volunteer*, published in De Soto, Missouri, on May 21, 1861, as the first camp newspaper. In

my research, I have found one earlier paper, the *Camp Register*, published in Camp Defiance, Cairo, Illinois, on May 6, 1861, by the Illinois Volunteer Militia. For more on the challenges of categorizing soldier papers, see Earle Lutz, "Soldier Newspapers of the Civil War," *Bibliographical Society of America Papers* 46 (1952): 373–80.

4. Davenport's account is reprinted in James Emmerton's regimental history, *A Record of the Twenty-Third Regiment Mass. Vol. Infantry in the War of Rebellion, 1861–1865* (Boston: William Ware & Co., 1886), 79–80.

5. "Salutatory," *Cavalier*, June 25, 1862.

6. Meredith McGill, *American Literature and the Culture of Reprinting, 1834–1853* (Philadelphia: University of Pennsylvania Press, 2003).

7. Alice Fahs, *The Imagined Civil War: Popular Literature of the North and South, 1861–1865* (Chapel Hill: University of North Carolina Press, 2001), 60.

8. See "The Songs We Sing," *Soldiers' Letter of the Ninety-Sixth Illinois Volunteer Infantry*, November 28, 1862.

9. See "The Picket Guard," *Normal Picket*, December 24, 1861; and "Drake's Ode to the American Flag," *Army Mail Bag*, June 13, 1864.

10. For a general overview of the printing industry in the South during the Civil War, see Ellen Gay Detlefsen, "Printing in the Confederacy, 1861–1865: A Southern Industry in Wartime" (PhD diss., Columbia University, 1975), ProQuest (AAT 7804357).

11. Ellen Gruber Garvey, *Writing with Scissors: American Scrapbooks from the Civil War to the Harlem Renaissance* (New York: Oxford University Press, 2013), 131.

12. The phrase "rebel type" comes from "Union Paper in Petersburg," *Grant's Petersburg Progress*, April 10, 1865.

13. "From Savannah," *Augusta Chronicle*, January 5, 1865.

14. Katy Chiles, "Within and without Raced Nations: Intratextuality, Martin Delaney, and *Blake; or the Huts of America*," *American Literature* 80, no. 2 (2008): 325. The relationality of Chiles's intratextual reading practice has many intellectual bedfellows in print culture and periodical studies. For one particularly compelling theory, see Ann Ardis's discussion of "internal dialogics" in "Staging the Public Sphere: Magazine Dialogism and the Prosthetics of Authorship at the Turn of the Twentieth Century," in *Transatlantic Print Cultures, 1880–1945: Emerging Media, Emerging Modernisms*, ed. Ann Ardis and Patrick Collier (New York: Palgrave Macmillan, 2008), 38.

15. See Benedict Anderson, *Imagined Communities: Reflections on the Origin and Spread of Nationalism*, rev. ed. (New York: Verso, 1991), 35.

16. Trish Loughran, *The Republic in Print: Print Culture in the Age of U.S. Nation Building, 1770–1870* (New York: Columbia University Press, 2007), 7, 12, hereafter documented parenthetically.

17. "At Home," *First Minnesota*, March 11, 1862.

18. "Salutatory," *Newbern Progress*, March 22, 1862. Despite the paper's continuance under the same title as the previously pro-Confederate *Newbern Progress*, we can unequivocally categorize it as a soldier paper as the first issue indicates that the "gallant twenty-third Mass., has the honor of furnishing the entire editorial and typographical force."

19. "The Enemy in Sight," *Newbern Progress*, March 22, 1862.
20. Emmerton, *Record of the Twenty-Third Regiment*, 80–83.
21. Garvey, *Writing with Scissors*, 28–36.
22. "'Loyal Georgian' Hail," *Savannah Daily Loyal Georgian*, December 28, 1864.
23. Rapidly selling out of their first edition, they issued a second, evening edition that was shorter and substantially altered. While the morning edition was printed on a single sheet, 16-by-22-inches, printed on both sides and folded to produce four pages, the evening edition was produced on a single 11-by-16-inch sheet printed on both sides.
24. "To Our Friends," *First Minnesota*, March 11, 1862.
25. For printers, justification is the art of spacing the words in a line of type, and matter is a term for composed type. Like other soldier-printers, the First Minnesota's "typos" often played with the language of printing in their columns, occasionally noting the semantic potential of the printer's "shooting stick" on both the field of battle and the field of print. See "At Home," *First Minnesota*, March 11, 1862.
26. "Sudden absquatulation" comes from "An Apology," *First Minnesota*, March 11, 1862.
27. "Run Away Editor," *First Minnesota*, March 11, 1862.
28. "Confed. Notes," *First Minnesota*, March 11, 1862.
29. "Jackson's Stone Wall Brigade. A Tribute to Jackson's Command, by a very young lady, of Selma, Virginia," *Connecticut Fifth*, March 18, 1862.
30. "Jackson's Stone Wall Brigade. A Tribute to Jackson's Command, by the very Old Boy in Winchester, Virginia," *Connecticut Fifth*, March 18, 1862.
31. Coleman Hutchison, "Secret in Altered Lines: The Civil War Song in Manuscript, Print, and Performance Publics," in *Cultural Narratives: Textuality and Performance in American Culture before 1900*, ed. Sandra M. Gustafson and Caroline F. Sloat (Notre Dame: University of Notre Dame Press, 2010), 263.
32. "Our Paper," *Athens Union Post*, September 17, 1863.
33. "No 'Bonnie Blue Flag' For Me," *Athens Union Post*, September 17, 1863.
34. For a discussion of the "complex revisionary history" of "Dixie," see Coleman Hutchison, "Whistling 'Dixie' for the Union (Nation, Anthem, Revision)," *American Literary History* 19, no. 3 (2007): 604.
35. "Our Dixie," *Normal Picket*, February 12, 1862.
36. Faith Barrett, *To Fight Aloud Is Very Brave: American Poetry and the Civil War* (Amherst: University of Massachusetts Press), 18.
37. Untitled, *First Minnesota*, March 11, 1862.
38. On wallpaper newspapers, see Hugh Awtrey, "Wall Paper News of the Sixties," *Regional Review* 3, no. 6 (1939): 14–20; and Clarence S. Brigham, "Wall-Paper Newspapers of the Civil War," *Bibliographical Essays: A Tribute to Wilberforce Eames* (Cambridge: Harvard University Press, 1924), 203–09.
39. In the four-page *First Minnesota/Berryville Conservator* paper, this would have been the second (inside left) page of a front-paged *First Minnesota* edition or the back page of the front-paged *Berryville Conservator* issue.

40. For a discussion of the semiotics of slave advertisements, see Marcus Wood, *Blind Memory: Visual Representations of Slavery in England and America, 1780–1865* (New York: Routledge, 2000), 78–142.

41. "$100 Reward," *First Minnesota*, March 11, 1862.

42. "General Order No. 1" and "$150 Reward," *Sixth Corps*, April 27, 1865. The *Sixth Corps* included another runaway slave ad, a $250 reward notice for the capture of "my boy Ned," placed in the *Danville Register* by James M. Walker in February.

43. "Danville Defences," *Sixth Corps*, April 27, 1865.

44. "To the Citizens of Danville," *Sixth Corps*, April 27, 1865.

45. "To the Patriotic Citizens of St. Landry," *Opelousas Courier*, April 25, 1863.

46. Royal Tholl details the *First Minnesota*'s printing career in "The Typographical Fraternity of the First Minnesota Volunteers," *Minnesota History* 62, no. 7 (2011): 258–67.

47. "To the Brave Soldiers of the South" appears under the heading "Louder," *First Minnesota*, March 11, 1862, 2nd ed.

48. Another new feature of the evening edition was titled "Latest New from Secessia," a compilation of humorous news flashes from the southern press. See *First Minnesota*, March 11, 1862, 2nd ed.

The Turn against Sentiment
Kate Cumming and Confederate Realism

―――――♦―――――

JANE E. SCHULTZ

An "altar of sacrifice" is scarcely visible in Kate Cumming's 1866 *Journal of Hospital Life in the Confederate Army of Tennessee* unless it is figured through the bodies of Confederate warriors. As a metaphoric shorthand commemorating southern womanhood's willing concessions to the Confederate cause, the altar was as useless to Cumming as a shelter tent in a downpour.[1] Cumming's unvarnished, three-year account of medical work with surgeon Samuel Stout's "flying hospital" corps resounds with a Confederate nationalism that turns away from the sentimental voice and idiom of midcentury southern writers such as Augusta Evans or Constance Cary.[2] Trapped in a kind of half-life between the registers of sentiment and romance on one hand and verisimilitude and graphic depiction on the other, *A Journal of Hospital Life* presents wartime realism as a mode of representation based on the inescapable facts of the Confederacy's medical crisis. Although critics have traditionally considered realism to be a *postwar* phenomenon consequent to the war's spectacular reckoning with death and driven by northern sensibilities, Cumming's chronicle of the dying and dead suggests that realism's traces had also seeded southern sensibilities by the 1860s.[3] Despite the *Journal*'s ideological alignment with the aims of the slaveholding South, it was part of a literary culture that valued experiential reportage, a characteristic that transcended the sectional construct and was a near cousin to the clinical modes of narration that flourished with medicine's professional emergence in the mid-nineteenth century. Given the evolution of medical genres, specifically the case study, which "sought authenticity in unprecedented quantities of minute observation," it is neither surprising to find realistic depiction in nursing narratives like Cumming's nor to discover the scrutinizing clinical lens trained on nonmedical subjects.[4]

Chris Hager and Cody Marrs have recently challenged the periodization of realism and its generic embedding in fiction. Earlier in the nineteenth century, realist sensibilities were visible in "epic poems, travelogues, autobiographies, lyrics, essays, and other genres alien to scholarly narratives that present the history of postwar literature as a history of narrative fiction."[5] Such a corrective, that the threads of realism are woven into a denser fabric of genres than heretofore acknowledged, invites us to examine the realist tendencies in life writing. In the midcentury, American life writing was more multigeneric than narrowly autobiographical, reflecting flexibility in generic definitions and boundaries. Life writers made use of novelistic, dramatic, and lyrical forms, even as they presented nonfictional accounts of their lives. Cumming described her journal as a "literary" endeavor and sprinkled it with poetry, letters, and excerpts from newspapers rather than restricting it to medical reportage. An 1870 study of "Southland writers" placed her alongside novelists Evans and Sallie Rochester Ford, indicating the extent to which Dixie's cultural commentators ranked life writers among the literati.[6] Sarah Gardner also observed this mix of genres and conventions in her 2004 study. Evans saw nothing romantic about the horrors of battle, though she could wax triumphal about Confederate valor.[7] For Cumming, too, the romantic and realistic were permeable rather than taxonomically distinct.

In its representation of Confederate hospital culture, Cumming's *Journal* strays from more polemical examples of southern life writing. The first southerner to publish an account of medical relief work and the first of those to publish an unreconstructed diary, Cumming had no thought to blaze a new narrative trail. Few Confederate hospital accounts were published before the twentieth century, most as memoirs.[8] Hoping to generate income in the months after the armistice, Cumming published her eyewitness account to give readers a window into the medical malfeasance resulting from inadequate hospital support. The original text, which Cumming could scarcely get into the marketplace, features what Coleman Hutchison has labeled the proleptic qualities of Confederate literature, "a national literary culture in aspiration": the sense that the Confederate nation could be conceived through literary products that promised victory as a foregone conclusion.[9] Cumming's aspirations for southern nationhood are visible throughout the *Journal*, even late in the war when medical supplies have all but vanished and hospitalized soldiers eat with their hands. Under such a regime, it is not surprising that Cumming voiced frustration and fatigue. But low morale neither silenced her pen nor occluded her faith in ultimate Confederate success. Paeans to the nation-that-might-be sit uneasily beside depictions of bodily trauma and moral failure, a reasoned narrative through-line missing in the diarist's attempt to capture the material confusion of her surroundings.

The intersection of the registers of Confederate nationalism and embodied realism, of sectional optimism and medical malaise, produces an array of perspectives that the *Journal* does not entirely succeed in resolving. Cumming's disgust at Yankee barbarity—an experiential reality she cannot ignore—initially feeds her nationalism. A monolithic Union is held to account for mounting casualties, galvanizing Cumming's political partisanship. But as the war progresses, her patriotic declarations and medical denunciations become relationally dissociated. Whereas body counts at first prompt connections to Confederate ideology, incessant and inescapable evidence of deteriorating relief efforts drives a wedge between nationalism and realism. As the war wears interminably on, a third relationship between nationalism and realism emerges—one in which the increasing bleed-through of bodily horrors undermines political confidence. Keeping up the pretense of certain victory requires a human energy that is no longer supportable, and all that is left is a forced march of survival. Instead of the earlier disentangling of the two registers, we see the real seeping into Cumming's Confederate aspirations. Thus, Cumming moves relationally in three distinctive ways between the two registers, moving toward a destination that strikes down Unionism with Confederate moral superiority.

As a strategy of representation temporally conceived, Cumming's realistic depiction of medical trauma breaks down over time. It is not so much her inability to chronicle what she sees as it is the sense that language no longer has the power to represent the witness-able. Timothy Sweet's analysis of Whitman's conviction that the "real war" was unrepresentable proves instructive here. The textual production of memory must necessarily "interdict certain aspects of 'reality' [and] 'experience.'" Physical residue of war-torn bodies can only be hinted at; it can never be placed into memory through fully embodied acts of representation. As Sweet reminds us, "the lived experience of war will always exceed the representation capacity of any medium." Cumming's increasing awareness of the futility of clinical observation does not, however, dampen her faith that readers will comprehend the enormity of the trials faced by relief workers—a suggestion that "shifts the burden of representational responsibility" onto them.[10] That faith in the reader's power to discern fuels Cumming's continued attachment to the goals of Confederate nationalism.

The *Journal* depends on what I have termed "Confederate realism," a methodology that brings war's medical spectacle into personal focus but also leaves room to acknowledge Confederate valor and righteousness. Simply put, Cumming's witness of war's ghastly toll on human beings is sublimated into political transcendence. Soldiers' bodies are not the sacrifice for which national sovereignty is exchanged; rather they *become* building blocks of the new nation, cementing honor to manhood as a foundational mythology. Cumming's diary chronicles *what* happens to the sick and wounded but offers no explanation of *why* such misery prevails. Catalogs of the numberless fallen hide in plain sight, where the refrain of Confederate triumph is logically disconnected from the visible data. While a process of selection governs what the diarist chronicles, she does not produce a contextual narrative—an intention central to authors who used wartime diaries to create memoirs.[11] Diarists like Cumming did not merely reflect the visual world around them like "passive mirrors" but instead negotiated what David Shi has called "a coherent and accessible world of objective facts capable of being known through observation, understood with the use of reason, and accurately represented in thought, literature, and the arts."[12] This definition rests on the proposition that a "truth" can be ascertained in the presentation of visible facts, an idea that might have been difficult for wartime nurses to process, given their emotional freight. Yet Cumming finds language to chronicle her hospital work without pausing to interpret the moribund signs or ascribe dire political meanings to them. Cushioning that chronicle is a religious devotion invoked on almost every page of the diary, a devotion that buttresses faith in Confederate success.

Like scores of narratives written by those who cared for the sick and wounded, the shocking materiality of Cumming's rendering of the medical war opens the way for clinical observation. From her disgust at countrywomen who refrained from helping fallen soldiers to her anger at unreasonable surgeons, Cumming charts the specific injuries, illnesses, and prospects of hospitalized Confederates and the "cheerless places" they took quarter. Her voice is sharp and uncensored—nothing belle-like about it. Diary entries reflect an archival impulse, a desire to inaugurate nation through historical legacy. Functioning initially as a clerical exercise, Cumming's lists of soldiers also serve a literary purpose: to record the present moment before it has passed into the realm of memory, or worse, into oblivion.[13] Her account of Chickamauga's casualties conveys both the clerical and nation-building imperatives:

> On entering [the ward], the first man to the right is Mr. Robbins, about fifty years of age. The doctors say he is one of the worst wounded.... There is very little hope of his recovery. Near him is Mr. McVay, an Irishman, much emaciated. One of his legs has been amputated above the knee and the bone is protruding about an inch.... To the left is Mr. Groover, wounded in both knees. While marching, a cannon-ball took off the cap of one, and the under part of the other, and his back is one solid bed-sore.... The very sight of his face is distressing.... The effluvia from his wounds is sickening. Further on are a dozen or

so badly wounded: one without a leg; another without an arm, and some with wounds which are awful to look at.... At the head of this group is Mr. Conda, an Irishman, with his leg in a sling. His wound ... is very painful.... There is no need of asking him how he is. Opposite him is Mr. Horton, another great sufferer. Just beyond is a man who has about two inches of his shin-bone cut out, and it is growing up. Alongside of him is Mr. Sparks [whose leg wound makes him] groan day and night.... A little ways from him is Mr. Robinson, a lad about seventeen. The calf of his leg is a solid sore. He wails most dolefully, and we find it impossible to assuage his pain.[14] (166)

Though not technically a clinical summary, Cumming's description of the afflictions besetting her patients might be compared structurally to Whitman's poetic catalogs: both attempt linguistically to seize the material textures of what is passing beyond reckoning. The list becomes the vessel for representing, but also apprehending, the awful consequences of military strife—literally, a gauge by which to measure the passing away of human lives. Physical immersion in this underworld blots out everything but the material inescapability of death—a journey of Dantean rather than Odyssean proportions. Whether or not prompted by therapeutic intent, Cumming's *recitative* reflects a desire to bring order out of chaotic surroundings.[15]

Initial exposure to war at Shiloh occasions Cumming's use of locutions and conjugations concerning the real. It is language that signals transport to a new consciousness, one that apprehends war's terrors but does not shrink from meeting them. "We began to feel that we were in the *service in reality*" (13), she proclaims, as she approaches the field by wagon.[16] While still at a distance, Cumming imagines the proximity of the wounded: "We could *realize* the condition of an army immediately after battle" by picturing men "wading" through the "slop and mud" (14, italics added). Here realization amounts to a projection in which Cumming anticipates a future state of understanding. But such psychological preparation has little utility, despite a coworker's graphic account of what she will soon encounter. Nine days after her departure from home, Cumming has not yet changed her clothes, has slept soundly on boxes, and knelt in blood to attend soldiers. "Nothing that I had ever heard or read," she attests, "had given me the faintest idea of the horrors witnessed here. I do not think that words are in our vocabulary expressive enough to present to the mind the *realities* of that sad scene. Certainly none of the glories of the war were presented here" (14–15, italics added). Expecting something more romantic, Cumming is disappointed. Only now can she "realize" (16) how sleep and food deprivation create hungers previously unimaginable; how social decorum about one's dining companions and their gracelessness pales in comparison to meeting basic needs. In effect, she has traveled from a world of familiar routines and social protocols to one where it is not uncommon to see a soldier's "brains... oozing out" (25)—a realism that so fundamentally alters her sense of the past that the past can no longer be represented in familiar terms. Disturbing sights initially feed her indignation and energize her partisan views.

Cumming's intimacy with death is not figured en masse but in the relentless step-by-step details of individual passings. As the death toll rises, she increasingly displaces emotional turmoil by resisting its absorption, an act that signals the intermediate phase of the relationship between Confederate nationalism and realism. More accurately a scribe of death than a witness, she shields herself from experiencing pain, despite a willingness to inform, assure, and sympathize with her charges. She is skeptical about the military initiatives that result in the heavy losses but does not flinch when citing the particulars. Ian Finseth has noted that the anonymity and spectacle of death epistemologically challenged witnesses' attempts to find meaning in the war's bloodbath: "The nameless Civil War dead, especially when visibly and horribly unburied, represented an extravagant corporeality that made it more difficult to dispose of their complexities symbolically."[17] Cumming's labor obliged her to weigh the physical evidence of shattered bodies, but she resisted self-pity. As diarists removed from scenes of war carnage mused about gallantry and southern character, Cumming came to terms with a grittier phenomenological reality.

Her growing awareness of and ability to articulate the normalization of death's horrors facilitates the turn from sentiment to realism. Confronting war's medical mayhem is transformational, destabilizing Cumming's sense of the past and requiring alignment with a "new normal," a materially recalibrated daily regimen. Many of the war's middle-class relief workers experienced this jarring change from relative domestic tranquility to a blood-spattered war zone, where they marveled at their capacity to objectify others' suffering.[18] Cumming's shock in realizing that she had washed the face of a corpse at Shiloh is only surpassed by her recognition that death's "terrible things" go unremarked. "No one seems to mind them" (20), and, like amputation, it is "so common that it is scarcely noticed" (27).[19] The pull of medical necessity against the emotional push of sympathy creates psychological tension in Cumming's changing perceptions of reality, where caregivers undergo trauma comparable to combatants'; but these dynamics do not lead her to question the war's efficacy.

Fearing desensitization, Cumming avoids acts of interpretation, which can only exacerbate the tension, and performs her duties with a perfunctory obedience: "We... act as if [death] was something that might happen to others, but never to ourselves" (21), she notes. To be useful to sufferers is to consciously distance oneself from their pain. "Many a time through the night we hear the men cough and groan, but we can not [*sic*] even allow our minds to dwell on these things, as it would unfit us for our duties" (91). By mid-1863, as Confederate military prospects dimmed, avoiding emotional engagement becomes mechanical, like flipping a switch to move into higher gear. In a field hospital near Newnan, Georgia, Cumming refuses eye contact with the wounded: "I tried to look neither to the right or left, for I knew that there were many pairs of eyes looking sadly at us from the sheds and tents." She rationalizes, "I could do nothing for them, and when that is the case, I try to steel my heart against their sorrows." Even a surgeon's appeal is fruitless: when asked to remain in the ward, she "told him no; I had seen enough" (153–54). In order to perform effectively, she has to reject any stimulus that will prick her composure, even if it means leaving the needy behind.

Cumming's avoidance of emotional interaction with individual soldiers does not completely insulate her from the dark implications of the body count, however. Even as she recounts the laurels won by Confederate warriors at Malvern Hill in the summer of 1862, she cannot help but think of the concomitant casualties: "The brave dead and wounded—alas! how the thought of them comes up, like a specter, to mar our triumphs" (54). Realistic reminders of war's waste function like hemorrhages constantly seeping through Cumming's consciousness, a tendency increasingly visible in later diary entries.[20] Aesthetic pleasures only veneer a baseness that cannot be tamped down. A cavalry review "appeared splendid" to Cumming until "the ambulances passed in review," which "cast a blight over the whole" (31). A pristine snowy landscape should produce visual enjoyment "but for the knowledge of what our men were suffering . . . half-clad" (74). A Confederate victory at Murfreesboro in January 1863 yields "four thousand prisoners and spoils of all kinds; but I can scarcely rejoice, for our wounded are coming in by the hundreds" (84). A visit to a well-run Chattanooga hospital warrants praise, "but I cannot look on those things with the same pleasure which I have heretofore, as it is impossible to feel that any thing connected with our army is permanent" (124). The psychology of apprehension cut short by correlation to medical damages goes beyond pessimism. Like the imagery that summons post-traumatic stress in war veterans, Cumming's thought pattern short-circuits from neutral description to trauma and instability. All roads lead to pain.

Although many hospital attendants labored in dismal circumstances, Cumming's clinical perspective is rare among Confederate testimonials. From Chattanooga in 1863 she provides a panoramic narration, describing the hospitals in her division, enumerating the staff and bed capacity, explaining the funding, and assessing her foraging opportunities (95–96). "We get up in the morning about 4 o'clock, and breakfast by candle-light, which meal consists of real coffee without milk, but sugar, hash, and bread; we eat it in our room.... I see that the delicacies for the sick are properly prepared. After the duties of the day are over, we then write letters for the men, telling their relations they are here, or informing them of their decease; other times mending some little articles for them" (94). From here she describes the convalescents who serve as cooks and their culinary impediments. The delineation is pictorial, leaving little to the imagination. Ada Bacot, a widowed planter from Darlington, South Carolina, devotes herself to dramas of manners and marital controversy in Charlottesville hospitals, in contrast to the phenomenological summaries that Cumming's eye records.[21] So too with Susan "Grandma" Smith's 1867 account of four years in the hospital service, published as a reminiscence and subject by her own admission to the vagaries of poor recall. Smith's object was not so much an appraisal of medical work as an evangelical and patriotic defense of southern sensibilities.[22] Even Phoebe Yates Pember's *A Southern Woman's Story* (1879), which recounts her civil war with tippling surgeons and uncouth patients at Richmond's Chimborazo Hospital, emphasizes the social aspects of her service. Several northern nursing accounts are comparable to Cumming's in their depiction of graphic medical detail and their thorough directory of hospital inmates. But Cumming's diary may be the most comprehensive, unreconstructed record of day-to-day practices over an extended period, given her conscientious accounting of the hospitals' frequent movements and her architectural descriptions of their configuration and operations.[23]

As Cumming adjusts to the relentless suffering, she questions whether she can endure the protracted emotional suppression needed for hospital work. The routine of watching men die moves her from an initially unshakeable faith in the Confederate cause to a more epistemologically skeptical place, where she defaults to material depiction in lieu of more sentient reactions. The extreme nursing that she is called on to perform exposes her to a pathology of complexity, where she must negotiate the transient rigors of medical work, even as she absorbs a bombardment of social stimuli that she must distill into appropriate military conduct. After months of retreat and hospital removals following the spring and summer campaigns of 1863, for example, Cumming sees the pragmatic wisdom of focusing on healing instead of healers: "No movement astonishes me now, and like a true soldier, I obey orders and *try* to *ask* no questions" (122). In effect, her low status in the military-medical infrastructure of the Confederacy allows her to accept her subordination as a survival tool. The learning curve is steep, but it approaches a calculus of diminishing returns when one has learned too much. Once again the detachment of painful realities from patriotic commitment is visible.

Recognizing an essential contradiction between her charge to nurse sufferers, which demands agency and endurance, and a southern code of femininity built on performances of submission and guilelessness, Cumming quickly abandons cheerfulness and her desire to please. She is careful in the first months to provide the name and regiment of each man she nurses and to identify his hometown, along with any disposition of his property and body if he dies. But by the second year of service, she has scaled back her effort. Men die nameless in amputation wards, men she never sees, men brought in at night who are dead by morning and whose "bearers have not the least idea of the inmate's name" (91–92). She can no longer account for patients attended by other workers, nor of soldiers whose friends are on site to look after them (97, 234). And yet it is only the scale of the narrated spectacle that she abbreviates, not the specifics of the medical encounters in her charge. These particulars are apparent in her account of the death of James Scott: "After lying on his back for four months, he was able to walk about; he was then taken with pneumonia; recovered from that; was taken with diphtheria; from that he also recovered; and died from the effects of erysipelas. Poor child! What a happy release from woe and suffering!" (97). Limiting the scope of death but not its etiology helps Cumming cope with the comprehensible components of mortality.

Realistic assessment of female peers is out of place in the realm of southern manners, which dictated benign forms of address. Yet Cumming loses patience with countrywomen who decline hospital service and become verbally combative. When acquaintances elliptically suggest to her that any woman who willingly serves will compromise her respectability, Cumming snaps, "Not respectable! And who has made it so? If the Christian, high-toned, and educated women of our land shirk their duty, why, others have to do it for them.... Have we not thousands who, at this moment, do not know what to do to pass the time that is hanging heavily on their hands?" (65–66). Taking no prisoners, Cumming's direct address is unsparing. More than a year later, she is still on the defensive. When a coworker receives a letter "entreating" her to abandon her post, Cumming fires off a lengthy rebuttal:

> A lady who feels that her modesty would be compromised by going into a hospital and ministering to the wants of her suffering countrymen, who have braved all in her defense, could not rightly lay claim to a very large share of that excellent virtue—modesty—which the wise tell us is ever the companion of sense.... I am thoroughly disgusted with this kind of talk.... There is scarcely a day passes that I do not hear some derogatory remarks about the ladies who are in the hospitals, until I think if there is any credit due them at all, it is for the moral courage they have in braving public opinion.... It seems strange

that [Sisters of Charity] can do with honor what is wrong for other Christian women to do. Well, I cannot but pity those people who have such false notions of propriety.... As for no "refined or modest" lady staying in them, from my own experience, and that of every surgeon whom I have heard speak on the subject, I have come to the conclusion that, in truth, none but the "refined and modest" have any business in hospitals. (178–79)

The beauty of a diary is that a tirade of this order can be consigned to privacy, but it may also be useful to understand this assault as an act of transference whereby patriarchal contempt of women stands in for contempt of Confederate decision-makers. In manuscript form, Cumming rehearses frustrations that are best left unspoken, but her decision to publish laid her open to public condemnation. She attempted to placate readers in the 1866 introduction: "I know that the women of the South will think that I have said too much against them; but let them remember that I, too, am a woman, and that every slur cast on them falls on me also" (4). Calling women out for their false delicacy, Cumming could scarcely expect to curry favor as she acknowledged her guilt by association. Her confrontational style surely abetted the realistic register; neither censoring it nor euphemizing it would suffice.

She is no more charitable to the southern men she nurses. Throughout the diary, she alludes to Confederate heroism, but the iron of her pronouncements is punctured by criticism of individuals. Happy to applaud honorable warriors setting a courageous example, like those invoked in Henry Timrod's verses, she sees but few.[24] While Confederate poets were busy crafting classical models of chivalrous conduct, Cumming paints a duller portrait of sufferers who steal hospital property and reveal cowardice. Debilitated warriors in her wards do not recover as quickly as Yankees (24–25, 28), and she concedes that she cannot harden her heart against the latter: "Seeing an enemy wounded and helpless is a different thing from seeing him in health and in power. The first time I saw one in this condition every feeling of enmity vanished at once" (18).[25] Cumming can more easily countenance care for the hospitalized foe than tolerate gratuitous Rebel misdeeds. She is horrified when she learns of a captain who, upon taking a Union soldier prisoner, shoots him in cold blood (216). Even the admired General Braxton Bragg comes under scrutiny when he has a soldier executed for killing a pig and "a negro" ("I can not [sic] think it is right to take the life of a fellow-mortal, unless it is for a flagrant crime" [48]). Apparently, Cumming sees the soldier but not the slave as a "fellow-mortal." She is equally scandalized by surgeons who rationalize overdosing patients with morphine (33) and by the "Pharaoh" of the Kingston hospital, Dr. Avent, who takes pleasure in refusing every supply request and then blames Cumming for her charges' inadequate nourishment (123).

The terrible swift sword of Cumming's witness wrings from her a realistic candor that few southerners were inclined to enunciate, yet these denunciations do not alter her confidence in Confederate victory.

By midwar Cumming regards human woe as ransom for the Confederate state: "Amid all this suffering, the star of hope for our cause shines brighter and brighter," she gushes. "Our armies are improving every way" (82). She even quotes "A Call to the Hospital," an eighty-eight-line ballad in the *Charleston Courier* that celebrated the courage of the sick and wounded:

> Pause here by the bedside; how mellow
> > The light showers down on that brow!
> Such a brave, brawny visage! Poor fellow!
> > Some homestead is missing him now.[26] (ll.17–20)

The idealized soldier "lies faint, but unfearing / With the enemy's ball in his breast" (ll.23–24). A second is "picked up on the field almost dead" with "a horrible gash in the head" (ll.26, 28); his suffering severe, but his military bearing already the stuff of legends:

> They say he was first in the action;
> > Gay-hearted, quick-handed, and witty;
> He fought till he dropped with exhaustion
> > In the front of our fair southern city.
> Fought and fell 'neath the guns of that city,
> > With a spirit transcending his years. (ll.29–34)

The "call" of the ballad's title was calculated to enlist the labors of reluctant women. The speaker confronts women with a list of imperatives that require sacrifice on their part:

> Fold away all your bright-tinted dresses,
> > Turn the key on your jewels to-day,
> And the wealth of your tendril-like tresses
> > Braid back in a serious way.
> No more delicate gloves, no more laces,
> > No more trifling in boudoir or bower;
> But come with your souls in your faces,
> > To meet the stern wants of the hour! (ll.1–8)

Echoing the pronouncements of the Union's nursing superintendent, Dorothea Dix, the speaker asks women to shed the material appurtenances of femininity but not to turn from sentiment itself. The womanly ideal of this "call" wipes sweat from the soldier's brow and "balsams the wounds of a nation . . . to comfort, to counsel, to cure" (ll.71, 76). The speaker concedes the difficulty, but insists that these Joans of Arc rise to the occasion, despite the peril:

> I grant you the task's superhuman,
>   But strength will be given to you
> To do for these dear ones what woman
>   Alone in her pity can do. (ll.77–80)

The altar of sacrifice is never far off in this rendering of hospital life, which concludes with an exhortation and benediction:

> But e'en if you drop down unheeded,
>   What matter? God's ways are the best;
> You have poured out your life where 't was needed,
>   And He will take care of the rest. (ll.81–88)

Even if you die anonymously amid the chaos, the poem implies, you will have given that "last full measure" and will have the satisfaction of eternal blessing. "A Call to the Hospital" both reprises conventional gender roles (male = brave, stoic warrior; female = angelic, sacrificial nurse) and suggests the possibility that such roles cannot be fully contained in medical spaces. The paradox is figured in Cumming's struggle to reconcile the brilliance of Confederate prospects with the daily slough of details that, in their realism, compromised those prospects; the constant seepage of the real pollutes the romance of nationalism.

Inasmuch as she sought to depict the Confederacy as a stately bulwark against northern aggression, Cumming's nationalistic enthusiasm begins to ebb by late 1863, after the debacles at Gettysburg and Vicksburg. Worn-out surgeons are frequently "intoxicated" (148), a field hospital presents nauseating sights (151–52), and gangrene wreaks havoc in the wards ("A wound which a few days ago was not the size of a silver dime is now eight or ten inches in diameter" [169]). Quartermasters who fatten through graft lead her to disparage the "moral leprosy which is eating at the very vitals of the Confederacy" (181). The Confederacy is a diseased soldier to whom prosaic surgeons deal "bitter medicines" (179). The following year opens with no better prospects. Cumming survives hospital fires at Newnan and Americus, and months of withering fighting around Dalton. She reports from Atlanta on May 17, 1864,

> that morning was one of the gloomiest I ever passed. It was damp and cheerless.... Hundreds of wounded men, dirty, bloody, and weary, were all around us. And when I thought of the many more which were expected, I was filled with despair.... In the afternoon, [we] went to the cars on their arrival from the front; and O, what a sight we there beheld! No less than three long trains

filled, outside and in, with wounded. Nearly all seemed to be wounded in the head, face, and hands.... I commenced to dress one man's hand which was badly wounded.... These men were called by the surgeons slightly wounded. One poor fellow from Alabama had both hands disabled. From one he had lost all the fingers excepting the fourth and thumb; and on the other he was shot through the wrist. This man was perfectly helpless. There were many just such *slight* wounds. One or two had lost an eye. (197–98, italics in original)

If Cumming has any rhetorical objective in this passage aside from the erosion of hope, it is her default to a clinical scan of the setting. Like an automaton, she records with near-photographic precision what her eye takes in, emphasizing the medical particulars of the ordeal instead of assigning blame or responsibility to any individual. Jason Puskar has posited the tendency of realists to collapse causation into a more ambiguous form, and Cumming's observations of mangled men resemble this way of seeing. The "radical instability at the heart of modern life," Puskar notes, is produced "in narratives of causeless and blameless catastrophe"—a feature characterizing Cumming's late-war entries in contrast to early missiles hurled at Union malefactors.[27] Though she doggedly associates Yankee soldiers with scenes of carnage, the connection breaks down as the war closes and her ability to interpret specific causes languishes.

Not only was causation under siege in the medical amphitheater, which incidentally had not yet glimpsed the invincibility of microbes, but the diary itself faltered. At the end of 1864 Cumming goes for six weeks without drafting a single entry. In the last dismal months of the war, she writes only sporadically, abandoning narrative for a practice more closely resembling medical charting. When a soldier of the Third Florida Infantry dies unexpectedly, she notes that "he is one of five brothers who have died in the service. What a record and a tale is [*sic*] in these few words!" (207). Cumming alludes via metonymic shorthand to the emotional fallout that must surely beset the soldier's family and friends upon learning of the loss. Even though she is still able to recite the graphic litany of woe that surrounds her—piles of bloody rags, bullet wounds to the head requiring trephination, soldiers who cut off their fingers with axes to avoid further combat, a man with pierced lungs whose slightest movement "causes the blood to run in streams from his wound" (213)—she is unable to unpack ontologically why such horrors exist. At this juncture the use of satire and caricature is more succinct and satisfying. She calls General Sherman a "despoiler" who "has marched through Georgia with his *invincible* army, and ... encountered *perils* of all kinds in defenseless old age, women, and children. But that kind of warfare seems to suit these *chivalrous knights*" (258, italics in original). Instead of celebrating the armistice, which she does not hear about until April 22, 1865, she wonders sarcastically whether "the enemy will *honor* us [with its presence] to-day" (273, italics in original). And when a Federal officer elicits their hospital report, she notes derisively that Confederate surgeons "*reciprocated*" when the Yankee "passed the compliments of the day" (74, italics in original). As she heads home, she "sicken[s]" at the sight of battered Newnan, beside herself that there appears to be no immediate redemption for the Confederacy. Such gut checks are in accordance with the last phase of Cumming's nationalism: Rather than acquiesce to a tyrannical foe, she belittles Union valor and bravado but cannot help from retching at the prospect of impending defeat—a case of embodied matter over mind.

On May 4, 1865, Cumming commences the ten-day, 445-mile journey home by wagon, by rowboat, and on foot to Mobile. Upon arrival, she discovers her brother at the kitchen sink washing dishes; no sign of the family "servants." Though never prosperous, the Cummings claimed elite friends, like Mary Custis Lee, and were proud of their social standing as Scottish immigrants.[28] Having settled in Mobile in the 1840s with their ten children, they embraced the Confederacy. As the eldest child "at home" (brother Jamie served in an Alabama artillery regiment), Kate aspired to be the good daughter, determined to contribute to family income, as Louisa May Alcott had done with *Hospital Sketches* and *Little Women*. But it was no small matter in 1865 to find a publisher for a Confederate diary ("the Methodist House in Nashville is not in working order").[29] After many rejections, John Morton of Louisville agreed to publish, but only if Cumming fronted him printing costs. She borrowed four hundred dollars from a family friend, hoping that royalties would allow her to reimburse the debt and make a modest living.

A Journal of Hospital Life in the Confederate Army appeared in June between two six-by-nine-inch rust-colored covers, each page ruled with two columns in nine-point type, a concession to the continuing scarcity of paper. Cumming dedicated the two-dollar volume "to the members of the Confederate Army of the Tennessee, whether living or dead, to whose suffering and heroism I bear witness" and concluded with tables that recorded the inflationary prices of provisions like molasses, corn meal, and chickens—an appendix that did not appear in Richard Harwell's 1959 edition. In the spring of 1866 Cumming deputized friends to sell subscriptions, but complained in May, when books had still not arrived, "I am afraid I shall lose the sale of a number of copies as so many of my friends are leaving for Europe."[30] Whether or not she was sincere about potential customers' departure, it is clear that she was anxious about the income.

Cumming's belief that former Confederates would welcome a realistic chronicle of the medical war proved unfounded, and her opening salvo—that her decision to publish was prompted by "a great thirst for revenge" (3)—did little to encourage northern readers, while southerners could ill afford to buy the book. In July 1866 Cumming "pray[ed] that [she would] be able to make some money from [her] book"; by August, so few copies had sold that she begged Philadelphia's J. B. Lippincott to take them off her hands—"they meet with favor every place in which they are for sale," she fibbed. Lippincott declined.[31] By winter, distributors were mailing back unopened boxes. One of Cumming's friends lamented from Fredericksburg, "I fear, Miss Kate, that the chances for the sale of the book are very poor in this community.... Our people *have not the means* to gratify their literary tastes."[32] Two years after publication, Cumming still had not earned enough money to discharge her debt: "When I think about the money that I owe on my book," she wrote, "I feel as if I would go crazy..... I never had anything distress me like this."[33] Though the diary was published fourteen months after Lincoln's assassination, Cumming had not mollified her critique of the martyred president. With statements like "Human lives are nothing to him" (81), it is no wonder that Harper and Brothers replied that they "would not care to place their imprint on a book containing some of the sentiments herein expressed."[34] Neither northerners nor southerners were ready to absorb the graphic realism of miseries so recently documented.

Cumming would more easily publish a sanitized version of the diary thirty years later as *Gleanings from Southland* (1895), at a time when conciliatory figures saturated war discourse. *Gleanings* included much of the original diary but expunged its more fiercely partisan commentary. A far cry from Confederate implosion, *Gleanings*' introduction celebrated technological, educational, and commercial advances in "the new South." In his 1959 edition of the diary, Richard Harwell called *Gleanings* "a poor shadow of the original" (xviii), alluding to its reconstructed, temperate voice.[35] The later work sacrificed the edge and immediacy of the 1866 text to please a broader audience that included northerners, an irony that could not have been lost on Cumming. In it Cumming emphasized brotherly love and family ties (its white supremacist comments notwithstanding), two elements in short supply in the original.

Cumming embraced the Confederate cause like a religious convert and voiced a distinctly unsentimental nationalism that never collapsed under the weight of medical negligence. Confederates could not have tolerated a scolding and were not ready for medical realism in 1866; looking back through a gentler lens at most of the same events was more appealing to them in 1895. Though the literary world was experimenting with naturalism at the same time, Confederate reconstructions of the war remained far from that orbit. In a literary culture whose articulators called into being a sublime new state and then enshrined it in amber, the Confederate nurse, a purveyor of embodied realities so graphic and unapologetic that they moved, wave-like, over the familiar skin of sentimentality, was an outlier. Cumming's diary marked a turn from sentiment that was evident in wartime Confederate letters but not recognized for the realism it represented. Attaching temporal boundaries to literary modes has kept us from fully appreciating how permeable those modes have been; specifically from seeing how realistic formulations were both an ingredient of earlier nineteenth-century life writing and of a broadly national trend not exclusive to northern publications. Just as the border states represented an intermingling of political views that could not be consolidated by the Mason-Dixon Line, Kate Cumming's *Journal* shows us how one southerner negotiated forms of nationalism and realism that defied points of origin and termination.

NOTES

1. With reference to Drew Gilpin Faust's article, "Altars of Sacrifice: Confederate Women and the Narratives of War," *Journal of American History* 76, no. 4 (1990): 1200–1228.

2. Evans's war-era novels, *Beulah* (1859), *Macaria* (1864), and *St. Elmo* (1866), are all written as romances. See, for example, Coleman Hutchison's discussion of *Macaria* in *Apples and Ashes: Literature, Nationalism, and the Confederate States of America* (Athens: University of Georgia Press, 2012), 74–98. Cary's novel, *Flower de Hundred* (1890), sits squarely within the romantic tradition. Her war memoir, *Recollections Grave and Gay* (1912), is chiefly sentimental.

3. See, for example, Edmund Wilson, *Patriotic Gore: Studies in the Literature of the American Civil War* (New York: Oxford University Press, 1962); and Daniel Aaron, *The Unwritten War: American Writers and the Civil War* (New York: Knopf, 1973).

4. Lisa Herschbach, "True Clinical Fictions: Medical and Literary Narratives from the Civil War Hospital," *Culture, Medicine, and Psychiatry* 19, no. 2 (1995): 185. In this article, Herschbach draws the connection between the advent of literary realism and clinical medicine's representations of physical embodiment.

5. Christopher Hager and Cody Marrs, "Against 1865: Reperiodizing the Nineteenth Century," *J19: The Journal of Nineteenth-Century Americanists* 1, no. 2 (2013): 271.

6. Ida Raymond, *Southland Writers*, vols. 1 and 2 (Philadelphia: Claxton, Remsen, and Haffelfinger, 1870). Ford (1828–1910) is best known for her novel *Raids and Romance of Morgan and His Men* (Mobile, 1864). Neither Cumming's "The Bostonians" nor "Isabella" was ever published. See manuscripts in Kate Cumming Collection, folder 15, Alabama Department of Archives and History, Montgomery, hereafter referred to as CC-ADAH.

7. See Sarah Gardner, *Blood and Irony: Southern White Women's Narratives of the Civil War, 1861–1937* (Chapel Hill: University of North Carolina Press, 2004), 28–29.

8. Susan Smith published *The Soldier's Friend*, her account of thrilling adventures that Richard Harwell believes was ghostwritten, in 1867. Phoebe Pember, Fannie Beers, and Julia Morgan produced reminiscences in 1879, 1888, and 1892, respectively, but no Confederate surgeon published an account until 1899, when Ferdinand Daniel's *Recollections of a Rebel Surgeon* appeared.

9. Hutchison, *Apples and Ashes*, 20.

10. Timothy Sweet, *Traces of War: Poetry, Photography, and the Crisis of the Union* (Baltimore: Johns Hopkins University Press, 1990), 48, 55.

11. Compare Amanda Stearns's diary fragment, Manuscripts, National Library of Medicine, Bethesda, Md., to her memoir, *The Lady Nurse of Ward E* (New York: Baker and Taylor, 1909). See also Phoebe Pember, *A Southern Woman's Story: Life in Confederate Richmond* (New York: G. W. Carleton, 1879); and Fannie Beers, *Memories: A Record of Personal Experience and Adventure during Four Years of War* (Philadelphia: J. B. Lippincott, 1888).

12. David Shi, *Facing Facts: Realism in American Thought and Culture, 1850–1920* (New York: Oxford University Press, 1995), 6, 4–5.

13. See, for example, the diary entries of May 10, 18, and 24, 1863, and those of June 7, 19, and 27, 1863, in *Kate: The Journal of a Confederate Nurse*, ed. Richard Barksdale Harwell (Baton Rouge: Louisiana State University Press, 1959), 103–4, 106, 108–11, hereafter documented parenthetically from the 1987 reprint.

14. *A Journal of Hospital Life* is filled with such catalogues. See, for example, 212–13.

15. Gardner categorizes the female-authored southern diary as an instrument calibrated to seek certainty in uncertain times. See *Blood and Irony*, 19.

16. In this passage Cumming italicizes "service," while I emphasize "in reality."

17. Ian Finseth, "The Civil War Dead: Realism and the Problem of Anonymity," *American Literary History* 25, no. 3 (2013): 536.

18. Frances Clarke notes that working-class Americans were better acquainted with scenes of physical pain than elites, in a cultural climate where suffering was the visible expression of individual worth. See *War Stories: Suffering and Sacrifice in the Civil War North* (Chicago: University of Chicago Press, 2011), 9–10.

19. See my *Women at the Front: Hospital Workers in Civil War America* (Chapel Hill: University of North Carolina Press, 2004). For example, Nurse Harriet Eaton wrote, "Another man died this morning, and one last Monday. I closed his eyes, bound up his face, cut off a lock of his hair, and wondered at my indifference as I passed back and forth by his body all day." See Harriet Eaton, *This Birth Place of Souls: The Civil War Nursing Diary of Harriet Eaton*, ed. Jane E. Schultz (New York: Oxford University Press, 2011), 97.

20. An emerging scholarship on "war's waste" provides a rich context for this discussion. See Beth Linker, *War's Waste: Rehabilitation in World War I America* (Chicago: University of Chicago Press, 2011); Drew Gilpin Faust, *This Republic of Suffering: Death and the American Civil War* (New York: Knopf, 2008); and Mark Schantz, *Awaiting the Heavenly Country: The Civil War and America's Culture of Death* (Ithaca: Cornell University Press, 2008).

21. See *A Confederate Nurse: The Diary of Ada W. Bacot, 1860–1863*, ed. Jean Berlin (Columbia: University of South Carolina Press, 1994).

22. Susan E. D. Smith, *The Soldier's Friend; Being a Thrilling Narrative of Grandma Smith's Four Years' Experience and Observation, as Matron, in the Hospitals of the South, during the Late Disastrous Conflict in America* (Memphis: Bulletin Publishing, 1867), 33.

23. Cumming's diary compares favorably with the more peripatetic accounts of Hannah Ropes of Massachusetts and Harriet Eaton of Maine. See Hannah Ropes, *Civil War*

Nurse: The Diaries and Letters of Hannah Ropes, ed. John R. Brumgardt (Knoxville: University of Tennessee Press, 1980); and Eaton, *This Birth Place of Souls*. Libra Hilde affirms the comprehensiveness of Cumming's diary in *Worth a Dozen Men: Women and Nursing in the Civil War South* (Charlottesville: University Press of Virginia, 2012), 191–92.

24. See Hutchison's discussion of Confederate poetry in *Apples and Ashes*, 99–142.

25. Clarke notes that northerners accused Rebels of weakness in bearing their suffering—a slight to their honor. See *War Stories*, 60.

26. The poem was reprinted in William Gilmore Simms's *War Poetry of the South* (New York: Richardson, 1867), 218–20. With thanks to Coleman Hutchison, who says that the poem also appeared under different titles in other southern venues, including broadsides, but without attribution. Cumming notes in a diary entry of November 10, 1898, that she recited this poem at a United Daughters of the Confederacy meeting. See CC-ADAH.

27. Puskar calls this phenomenon of "spontaneous and blameless violence," also present in modernist texts, "chance collectivity," a kind of panacea for "lingering regional antagonisms after the Civil War." See his *Accident Society: Fiction, Collectivity, and the Production of Chance* (Stanford: Stanford University Press, 2012), 2–3.

28. Lee wrote to Cumming four times to praise her book. See especially the letters of November 30, 1868, and May 18, 1869, CC-ADAH.

29. Cumming to "My Dear Friend," February 27, 1866, CC-ADAH.

30. Cumming to John Morton, May 21, 1866, CC-ADAH.

31. Cumming to "My Dear Brother," July 2, 1866; and to J. B. Lippincott, August 24, 1866. J. B. Lippincott to Cumming, July 29, 1867, CC-ADAH.

32. F. P. Wellford to Cumming, February 11, 1867, CC-ADAH, underlining in original.

33. Cumming diary, February 13, 1867, CC-ADAH.

34. Harper and Brothers letter to Cumming, August 26, 1867, CC-ADAH.

35. Gardner places similar emphasis on New York publisher Appleton's edition of Mary Chesnut's diary, which "northernized" it for a more lucrative reception in the populous East. See *Blood and Irony*, 170.

Mourning and Substitution in *The Gates Ajar*

SHIRLEY SAMUELS

"I will make her so much at home in my house that she shall not remember that it is not her own."

The Gates Ajar

Border Wars

Published after the last battles of the Civil War and the tragedy of Lincoln's assassination, the best-selling first novel by Elizabeth Stuart Phelps, *The Gates Ajar*, tells a tale remarkable for its stillness. At the beginning of the novel, the narrator, Mary, spends her time as a chronicler of grief. Her brother, Roy, has been killed on the battlefield, and the consolations offered by the community members of her small New England town appear to her muted and inadequate. Not until the appearance of her dead mother's sister Winifred, herself a widow, does she find comfort. In her arms, both literally and figuratively, Mary can imagine heaven.

That consolation is at once thwarted and confirmed at the novel's close when Winifred also dies, leaving the narrator as a substitute mother for Winifred's orphaned child, not very subtly named Faith. The story that the novel tells, insofar as it is a story rather than simply a meditation on grief and faith, consists mainly of conversations between the two women who are the last remaining adults of their family. The popularity of a tale of finding faith in the face of a violently diminished family might stem directly from the similar situation of its audience. In the wake of the war, nearly every family in the newly reconstituted United States had been diminished by violence. It seems not at all surprising that readers sought consolation.

The novel's popularity was such that any novel published by Phelps containing the word "gates" was sure to sell. She subsequently wrote, among others, *Beyond the Gates* (1883), *The Gates Between* (1887), and *Within the Gates* (1901). Her most admired novel today is *The Story of Avis*, a tale loosely based on her mother's marriage.[1] Her mother, named Elizabeth Stuart Phelps, also a writer, had named her Mary. She was a child when her mother died and renamed herself in her mother's honor, subsequently publishing under that name. Such cross-identifications with the name of the author's deceased mother and the name her mother gave her reappear in *The Gates Ajar*, where the narrator's name is Mary, and in her life, where her father's second marriage was to her mother's sister, also named Mary.[2]

This essay proposes that the novel's strong thesis that life after death provides a literal home—a thesis that emerges through scenes showing women's affection for each other—connects with the under-recognized role of Kansas as a place for the tragic loss of homes. Far from placing the geographical location of Kansas at the center of the novel's emotional territory, however, the essay asserts that the violence associated with Kansas was a central enough fact for nineteenth-century progressive readers that Phelps has no need to elaborate on its significance. Although the novel's action occurs in an unnamed domestic location, mostly confined to the space of one house in a small New England town, the place of Kansas in its events locates the memory of loss in the West rather than on any battlefield in the southern United States.

Directly or indirectly because of losses suffered in the American Civil War, women in this best-selling postbellum sentimental novel confront the boundary between heaven and earth as they cling to each other.[3] Mourning lost loved ones, they live in an emotional border territory. This emotional territory alludes to and sometimes metaphorically resembles border territories between Missouri and Kansas, the site of violent skirmishes and deadly betrayals as the newly forming states fought about slavery. As Winifred and her daughter, Faith, cross this physical boundary to return to the novel's eastern location, they substitute the violence in Kansas for the violence of slavery even as the narrator and Winifred, and later Faith, substitute each other's bodies for the bodies they have lost in the Civil War.[4]

In this essay, the argument follows two chains of substitution. With the first substitution, the novel invokes forms of violence in Kansas connected with the westward expansion of national boundaries to stand in for the violence of slavery, that is, both the violence involved in the practice of slavery and the violence associated with the westward expansion into Kansas. Such violence in the West involved the failed desire for an unbroken antebellum nation. In the second substitution, the narrator's aunt Winifred stands in, via forms of intimacy that also seem to allude to incestuous sister–brother desire, for the narrator's never-to-arrive husband. Winifred, having lived through the historical tragedy of Quantrill's raid on Lawrence, Kansas, forms the link between the two chains. Winifred subsumes the narrator's grief as she comes to stand in for any woman who's been affected by the violence of the war. Insofar as her presence in the novel with her daughter, Faith, performs an allegory, in addition to her religious teachings, Winifred brings peace to the narrator. The narrator's grief over her death suggests a national lesson: Winifred's death from cancer alludes to the cancer of slavery that killed the antebellum body politic, but her child Faith lives.

The question remains: does that put heteronormativity and the structure of slavery in the antebellum nation in the same position? For the novel's characters, the war seems to have abolished both, though the specter of each remains. The new nation, after one more substitution (Faith for Winifred), is structured by a maternal bond and by the absence of men. To orient this emotional energy along the east–west axis rather than the north–south axis is to recognize that even as westward expansion might be seen as the cause of the war, the extension of slavery westward was the logic of its own undoing. So the novel performs, in a register interwoven with its attention to a vision of the afterlife as a natural mirror of rural happiness, a national mourning connected to westward expansion.

Because it is precipitated by an arrival from Kansas, the novel's primary relationship, the courtship of two women, invokes the violent extension of the nation's boundaries. Implicitly, the extension of national boundaries also becomes a crisis about what forms of the family can exist anywhere in the reconstituted nation. The allusions to the violence in Lawrence, Kansas, that precipitated the move back east for Winifred involve a violence at the nation's boundary and a proposed extension of that boundary directly related to the novel's core emotional relationship.[5] The arrival in the home of this widow and her daughter escaping the violence in Kansas silently invokes the lingering doubts cast by debates over the Kansas-Nebraska Act.

Violence in Kansas

The Kansas-Nebraska Act has received a great deal of attention from historians as the catalyst of the unraveling of the balance between free and slave states articulated in the earlier Missouri Compromise of 1820, an unraveling that led more or less directly to the Civil War, but it may be considered to be more invisible for literary critics because there exist few performances of its implications in literary terms. The best language associated with the crisis occasioned by admitting both Kansas and Nebraska as states may appear in the debates between Abraham Lincoln and Stephen Douglas as they competed for a seat in the United States Senate. For all that Lincoln has been considered as a politician whose resistance to slavery evolved fairly slowly, his statements about the extension of slavery into Kansas resonate today.[6] The outrage that Lincoln expressed concerned the question of a broken promise about the boundary between slave and free states that was first proposed by the admission of the state of Maine into the union, a legal compromise that sought a balance between free and slave states resulting in the agreement known as the Missouri Compromise. The broken promise also concerned an artificial symmetry between slaveholding and non-slaveholding states, and resulted in visible bloodshed, to the extent that a senator emerged with a bloody head from the floor of the senate.[7]

The damaging effects of the Kansas-Nebraska Act, an act proposed by Lincoln's rival Stephen Douglas, included gang violence in reaction to how it marred the concept of a national balance, termed a compromise from the start, and especially to how it legislated boundary expansion and the extension of the practice of slavery into new territories. In the earlier Missouri Compromise, slavery in the new territory "shall be, and is hereby, forever prohibited." All the words in that declaration became suspect after the Kansas-Nebraska act. The linguistic move from "shall be" to "is" holds in suspension a process of becoming free that the language of "forever prohibited" seems to contradict.[8] For Stephen Douglas, the principle of "popular sovereignty" represented an apparently democratic appeal to states rights that made the issue of determining the extension of slavery a simple matter of arithmetic. Understanding that numbers mattered, settlers stampeded Kansas to stake out claims that supported either abolition or slavery. Controversial abolitionists like John Brown traveled to Kansas armed to fight precisely because of the appeal of exerting the rights of a citizen to oppose slavery. The principles were sound; the practices were bloody.

The violence in Kansas between 1854 and 1861 led to its being termed "bleeding Kansas."[9] The literal shedding of blood presaged the bloodshed that would prevail across the eastern half of the United States from 1861 to 1865. Little considered in terms of cultural memory is how much the border warfare in Kansas became sanctioned by the federal government. Not only were the "border ruffians" later commissioned as loosely designated official soldiers by both the Confederate army and the Union army, the acts of retaliation that spilled across the Mississippi were rarely addressed as criminal acts.[10] The criminal acts that took place continued after the war and led to the formation of notorious groups such as that headed by the outlaw Jesse James. Some of these same outlaws, including the James brothers, were present at the massacre to which *The Gates Ajar* alludes at Lawrence, Kansas, in 1863.

The guerilla warfare on the western frontier does not usually appear in discussions of Civil War battles, a place usually occupied by Gettysburg, Chancellorsville, or the Wilderness. Nor do we consider, when we consider a nineteenth-century town, the drama of a group of 450 ruffians riding into town, lining up the men and boys, shooting them, and then burning down their houses, outside of the dusty drama of a spaghetti western. But it was very much the war experience in Kansas and Missouri, and it formed a different kind of challenge to what it meant to have a home, one that I am considering here in juxtaposition to the domestic drama of *The Gates Ajar* for the very obvious reason that it compels the widow and her child to move into the narrator's eastern home, doubling the impact of emotional displacement caused by battlefields to the South and the West.[11] As a newspaper headline of the time stated: "The Lawrence Massacre by a Band of Missouri Ruffians under Quantrell; August 21, 1863; 150 Men Killed Eighty Women Made Widows and 250 Children Made Orphans." The emphasis on widows and orphans leads me back to *The Gates Ajar*. I want to raise here the question of how the concept of substitution may also invoke how the violence, including the sexual violence, of Quantrill's raid, invokes or makes possible both the queer desire and the quasi-incestuous longings that the novel expresses.

Within *The Gates Ajar*, the events that have brought Mary's aunt Winifred to her doorstep begin with her presence in Kansas. She has lived through "Quantrell's raid."[12] It is possible to think of Winifred's husband, John, who had been a Christian missionary to Kansas and then died of an unspecified disease, as a victim of Civil War violence on the western frontier. Not only was his health affected by the raid on Kansas, but also his death by disease invokes the detail that many casualties of the Civil War died of disease. The death toll from the battlefield includes the movements of populations that introduced disease along with violence. Like the death of young Willie Lincoln of typhoid because of the waters of the Potomac River, many so-called civilians died from tainted waters because they lived near battlefields and massive encampments.

The story of Quantrill's Raiders changes according to the teller since their exploits were considered simultaneously as heroic for the South and villainous for the North. The attack on families in Lawrence, Kansas, appears as an intimately disturbing aspect of Civil War violence. Even more significantly, the hidden story of what happened to the women in that town remains under-specified.[13] The Confederate Congress passed a law in 1862, known as the Partisan Ranger Law, that authorized what had been outlaw activities, including murder. Quantrill was a well enough known bandit that he was not authorized to act under it, but he claimed license nonetheless. When engaged with Federal troops, Quantrill's Raiders were reported to castrate and later even to scalp their male victims. Left untold is the story of their treatment of female victims, but the implications are present in contemporary political cartoons that show women struggling in the arms of bandits.[14]

Mourning and Substitution

The Gates Ajar does not reference the history of the entire political struggle that led to the violence in Lawrence, Kansas, but it does specifically reference that violence, and the main character's loving companion, her aunt Winifred, has gone to Kansas as if to a foreign country to help in a missionary assignment. Her appearance in the household of the mourning narrator, Mary, brings together two women who mourn the loss of men, but it might also be seen to presage a shift in emotional attachment from men to women. The proliferation of death that forms the backstory for the novel has taken place away from home, on an unseen battlefield, leaving mourners to remain at home. To mourn is to live on the border between life and death. To see life in the world beyond death, within the world of the novel, relies on a Christian vision of both life and death. But what I also want to suggest here is that the disrupting violence in Kansas that has precipitated many of the novel's key events permeates the vision of Christian hope with a hidden agenda about the westward expansion of the nation's boundaries as well as an act of occlusion or displacement about the matter of slavery.

Mary spends the first part of the novel in mourning for the loss of her dead soldier brother, Royal, the only remaining member of her immediate family, as well as declaring her certainty that her future will contain no children. In the closing off of futures, nonfunctional heterosexuality fuses with the loss of future reproductive possibility to make women bond with other women—and with orphans. Remanufactured families obsess the narrator, whose parents died long before her brother was killed in the Civil War. The disruption of her expectations that occurs with Winifred's arrival involves both a renaming of her emotional connections and a remapping of familial norms.

The effects of haunting, violence, and redemption in this novel have a precursor in the religious invocations of Susan B. Warner's very popular *The Wide, Wide World* (1850), in which Ellen Montgomery loses her mother and must find new attachments. Like *The Gates Ajar*, that novel opens with women waiting in a room and with domestic scenes of cooking. Attention to lessons from the Bible appear at first significant in the way that conscience works at the edge of consciousness. Ellen Montgomery, the daughter who loses her mother and mourns, must learn lessons from an attractive older woman who seems possessed of an enormous library in terms of citation and reference. Many of these lessons are about patience and about mourning lost objects. Ellen first feels as though her grief will "rend soul and body in twain." As she lies dying, her mother, torn between conscience and her own conscious grief, insists that "though we may sorrow, we must not rebel."[15] The lessons, drawn from the Bible and from Milton, seem designed to produce more patient women, but also more learned women. As Mary says of Winifred in *The Gates Ajar*, she is a "woman who knows something about fate [and] free-will, ... who is not ignorant of politics, and talks intelligently of Agassiz's latest fossil, who can understand a German quotation, and has heard of Strauss" (108).

In *The Gates Ajar*, the novel's attention to a consciousness that cannot bear its object—specifically the work of mourning—literally describes what lies at the edge of the Civil War. This physical and metaphysical challenge also becomes the challenge of how to inhabit simultaneously a place in a heterosexual normative order and the "new normal" of a world of women. The matter of reproduction in heavenly terms is the matter of another life beyond the body. After forming a new domestic unit with her mother's younger sister, who has survived the terrible violence of the raid on Lawrence, Kansas, only to succumb to illness, the narrator is left to perform the role of a mother to her cousin Faith, named by a dying father to bring hope to a now deceased mother. The novel links the reforming, or public, identities that Christianity provided in accounts of slavery with the private domestic lives that mourning women could live, producing a postwar combination of mourning and a life lived doubly on heaven and on earth.[16]

The substitution that the novel enacts has the dead mother's sister take the place of the dead brother who has previously substituted for dead parents and proleptically taken the place of a never-to-be found husband.[17] The dead mother's sister's child has been named Faith to emphasize her redemptive positioning when her father dies, leaving her mother adrift in the wake of the border warfare in Kansas. Faith becomes the crossing point of biological ties and erotic connections, substituting her small body for the lost body of her own mother, who has been substituting for the body of Mary's lost brother.

To consider the forms of erasure in fiction set in a historical place that draws on a tragedy only seen out of the corner of the eye is not therefore to claim that the search for historical origins is the most important trace, but rather that the search for erasure can lead to gestures of substitution that are themselves significant. Critical commentary on concepts and theories of substitution has relied on Joseph Roach, who talks about substitution in ideas about performance. Roach cites Homi Bhabha on mimicry as "at once resemblance and menace"; performances "raise the possibility of the replacement of the authors of the representations by those whom they imagined into existence as their definitive opposites."[18] The convolution of prepositional phrases here at once masks and reveals the kind of substitution that intrigues Roach. What agent and what action might be called onto the playing field becomes obscured—and yet the obscurantist action of performing substitution also becomes the point. As Roach asserts, "'That is why the surrogated double so often appears as alien to the culture that reproduces it and that it reproduces. That is why the relentless search for the purity of origins is a voyage not of discovery but of erasure."[19] To state the concept more plainly, in terms relevant to the novel's rewriting of domestic happiness, the narrator mourns the loss of her brother, who has substituted both for the past loss of their parents and for her unexplained resistance to having a future family. Her desire for him suggests incestuous longing, but both the presence and the loss of a loved family member are reenacted by the substitutions carried out by her aunt's body.

In thinking about how substitution can work, I also draw on Rebecca Schneider's work in *Performing Remains: Art and War in Times of Theatrical Reenactment*.[20] Schneider cites Elizabeth Freeman on the compulsions of repetition and queer identification and asserts that "mimesis, theatricality, imitation, simulation, the copy, the double, and the fake cross and confuse each other."[21] That is, in thinking about substitutions, I acknowledge the difficult ways in which both religion and war stand in for gestures of desire in this fiction, as in others. And in performing a sort of pilgrim's progress, in novels from *The Wide, Wide World* through Louisa May Alcott's *Little Women* and *The Gates Ajar*, women's fiction often takes advantage of the teleology of religion to move women toward one another. In unpacking the possibilities that the question of performance might bring onto the stage of this novel, what I propose is a kind of queer and possibly incestuous doubling that accompanies religious instruction.[22]

Within the world of *The Gates Ajar*, for example, Mary sits on the lap of her mother's sister and puts her arms around her neck when she asks her to move into the house. Placing herself in the position of both a child and a lover, she performs a substitution where her body at once takes the place of the daughter Faith and enacts a substitution for the beloved. The discipline that encourages an intimate relation to religion in all three of the novels that focus on grieving and loss in the mid-nineteenth-century United States (*The Wide, Wide World*, *Little Women*, and *The Gates Ajar*) involves a relationship with a strong spiritual woman who is deeply loved and then lost. The intimacy of the relation is at once nicely enhanced and deflected through death. What has been erased in order to make this double substitution occur are the bodies of the male brother and husband who might otherwise be positioned in such physical intimacy. What has also been erased in *The Gates Ajar* are allusions to the struggle over slavery long associated with the violence in Kansas.

Scenes of Writing

The opening pages of *The Gates Ajar* appear written as a journal in a house where a woman feels confined; these pages present scenes of a woman writing. The narrator is preoccupied with the question raised in Charlotte Perkins Gilman's iconic short story "The Yellow Wallpaper": where can she find the paper to write on? As the work of women performed in a domestic space, the act of writing is interrupted by a reminder of housekeeping, even as the novel reminds us that she is not doing the housekeeping because her class position enables her to have help. The place of the domestic servant who enters to scold her away from her writing and encourage her to come to dinner recurs in *The Gates Ajar* as it does in other fiction, such as Fanny Fern's earlier novel about a woman who begins to write, *Ruth Hall* (1850). In *The Gates Ajar*, the narrator is told: "Put away them papers and come right along!" (5). Her first visitor suggests that she will want to come and sew. The intersection of public and private writing appears in the dating of entries as though she were simply writing a journal.[23]

The novel's first section does not have a date at the top. Instead, the narrator indicates that, as of the twenty-first of February, "the house feels like a prison. I walk up and down and wonder that I ever called it home" (2). Attention to how to name a location gives way to the visceral effects of language: "Those two words—'Shot dead'—shut me up and walled me in, as I think people must feel shut up and walled in, in Hell" (4). As the narrator describes the confusion between a confinement at home and the more insubstantial rendering of being sent to hell, the auditory effects suggest a different meaning for confinement. The first pages of the novel describe the sensation of life in a home in a village where children laugh in the streets. The intrusion of this laughter produces pain, but may also proleptically suggest the intrusion of children.

The narrator recalls a winter day when she returns from a walk to the post office and describes the joy that she feels in reading a letter she found there from her brother, Roy, who has been away fighting as a soldier for so long that "they" tell me that she should have expected the news that has just come by telegram. The news brought by the telegram cancels the joy of the letter; the telegraphed words have paralyzed her. She speaks of the paralysis even as she opens with the scene of writing, finding a notebook in a drawer that she now fills with words. Writing her own words serves to rewrite the words that have confined her.

The narrator writes to recover from a blow. As she puts it, "A solid blow has in itself the elements of its rebound; it arouses the antagonisms of the life on which it falls; its relief is the relief of a combat." The writing that she does has a resistance and pressure: "Perhaps I write excitedly and hardly. I feel excited and hard" (6). The hardness and excitation that she feels in this parallel, yet chiasmic structuring of emotion and writing, makes writing into a container for emotion. Named Mary Cabot, the narrator calls her brother Roy, short for Royal. As she describes the life that has led to this encounter with her brother's death, there's an oddity, she recognizes, in being so close to her brother that she doesn't think about possibly wanting a husband in the future. Without explaining, she says, "That was settled so long ago.... Roy was all there was" (8). She quotes from Elizabeth Barrett Browning: "God keeps a niche / In Heaven to hold our idols"

(21). This quotation reinforces the sense that the bond with her brother is that of lovers and that the appearance of her mother's sister will substitute in more than one way.

Winifred Forceythe, her (dead) mother's youngest sister, writes to her from Kansas a letter dated the same day that she begins writing. The strange coincidence encourages the reader to look for parallels in their acts of reading and writing. When they are first living together, the narrator and her aunt read Charles Lamb's "Elia" (33) and the essay "Dream Children," with its "pathos and symmetry" (35).[24] Charles Lamb and his sister lived together; their closeness persisted in the wake of the tragedy that she had stabbed their mother to death. This detail is not explained in *The Gates Ajar* and it is quite possible that Phelps expected her well-educated readers to know the allusion not only to the work but also to the biography and to understand that behind the scenes is an account of another brother and sister who lived together after the death of parents. If I am to consider the semi-outrageous implication that death makes incest possible, then I would also look at the symmetry where Mary has lost her brother and Winifred has lost her husband, losses that make it possible for them to cling to each other's bodies.

When her aunt arrives, Mary finds that she has a young girl named "Faith" with her (40). Contemplating the change in her household, she says, "Take her altogether, I like to look at her" (42). Faith is three years old, a "round, rolling, rollicking little piece of mischief" (42). They talk about "the surrenders and the assassination" (43). With the arrival of this sympathetic auditor, Mary can cry for the first time since her brother's death. The reference to "the surrenders and the assassination," not elaborated on, place the arrival in the summer of 1865, after Appomattox and the Ford Theatre killing of Abraham Lincoln. Lincoln is not named here, at once because the assassination has happened so recently that readers of the novel will not need reminding, and possibly as though the naming of the president who was killed on Good Friday is still too close to a sacred invocation. Mary's tears enable her to reflect; she says to her aunt, "It is just as if a great black gate had swung to and barred out the future" (50). The related implication in the title is how to have a gate "ajar," or how to open a gate to the future. To write the gate into existence becomes an act of researching spiritual beliefs as well as physically inhabiting a metaphor.

The Sensuous Afterlife

When Mary asks her aunt to come and live with her, she sits in her lap first, and she recalls, "I put my arms about her neck" (100). What it will mean to form this new union remains unclear, since the terms must evolve from the situation: "*I* am not 'a family,'" protests Mary (101, emphasis in original). Even as she explores "this new promise of home," Mary asserts an odd combination of belonging and amnesia: "I will make her so much at home in my house that she shall not remember that it is not her own" (105). The containing unit of the "house" becomes the boundary for an act of will ("I will make her") that is also designed to erase a past home ("she shall not remember that it is not her own"). The inaugural act of sitting in her aunt's lap at once suggests a persistence of maternal attachment from mother to aunt and an erotic performance of desired intimacy.[25]

The further container or boundary for this new intimacy of "home" is the small town in which Mary has her house. The inadequacy of the town and of the town's concept of emotional attachments and religious beliefs emerges repeatedly. After her brother's death, Mary notes that she cannot be comforted and explains that various members of the town come to tell her how to feel. The appropriately named Deacon Quirk, for example, asks why she hasn't been to church and then looks at her as if at a "Mormon or a Hottentot" (16). The very odd pairing, emphasizing an alien identity, prevails in the question of substitutions and pairings extending to the analogies used between humans and animals. The strangeness applied to domestic objects, or domestic objects made strange, appears in the sermon Mary attends, with its "speculation as to whether Maltese kittens were mulattoes" (68). The racism here at once extends across human and animal lines and indicates confusion about what country is invoked. She is "bewildered and disheartened" by the sermon because it makes heaven out to be an abstract place where one meditates on the goodness of God (70). According to such a creed, members of the town should "subdue" earthly affections to God (71).

Such a subjugation of earthly desires and attachments, for the narrator, is not at all what she wants: "Going hungry, hopeless, blinded, I came back empty, uncomforted, groping" (73). Responding to the groping that Mary presents, Winifred supplies an intimacy in terms at once physical and spiritual, a private form of affiliation for a narrator who needs to feel that the idea of relationship is valued. For Winifred, "wherever the Bible touches the subject, it premises our individuality" (80). That individuality provides specific attachment that is physical as well as spiritual.

The narrator says, "I never supposed before that God would let anyone laugh in heaven" but this supposition is followed immediately, and perhaps oddly, with an allusion to the recent death of someone who was widely known as a practical joker, the president of the United States. "I wonder if Roy has seen the President" (83). Her aunt tells her that Roy is *"only out of sight"* and that in the unseen place he inhabits, he must still love her (87, emphasis in original). Winifred proposes not only an emotional but also a physical life after death: "To love must mean to think of, to care for, to hope for, to pray for, not less out of a body than in it" (55). Her assurances lead to a long discussion on whether life beyond the grave is embodied or disembodied. "Disembodied?" asks Mary. "I do not think so," replies her aunt. Invoking the Resurrection of Christ, she continues, "All the *tendency* of Revelation is to show that an embodied state is superior to a disembodied one" (113, emphasis in original). Her preaching becomes increasingly mystical—and mystifying—until it really becomes almost a challenge to established Christian doctrine. Certainly within the world of the novel, Winifred's sermons present a challenge to the preaching of the town minister, Mr. Bland. Speaking of life after death, she asserts, "I suspect that we have some sort of body immediately after passing out of this, but that there is to come a mysterious change, equivalent, perhaps, to a re-embodiment, when our capacities for action will be greatly improved" (114). As she draws further away from the minister's sermon, Winifred's lessons begin to sound like the defiance of Anne Hutchinson.[26] At the same time, the concept of action that will be "greatly improved" suggests an ambiguous re-embodiment.

Winifred does not think bodies will be the same on heaven as on earth, for reasons "too tedious to specify" (114). Her first example is anything but tedious. Drawing on an exoticism that reminds us that the New England they inhabit is full of missionaries who have returned with tales of other beliefs, she laughs at the option of a "Hottentot" cannibal resurrected within the body of another "Hottentot" who has consumed it. She turns to the concept of the Mohamedan "little bone" that is imperishable (116).[27] In spite of all these strange speculations about the immateriality of the body, there persists a celebration of touch in Aunt Winifred's assertions. "What would be the use of having a body that you can't see and touch? A body is a *body*, not a spirit" (117, emphasis in original). Roy is thus "*only out of sight*" (87, emphasis in original). And that means that Mary will again be able to kiss and hold her brother, to "feel his kiss on your happy lips" (117). The celebration leaves open the potential for a re-embodiment that will be "greatly improved" in its capacity to have physically intimate encounters.

The novel presents the challenge of learning how to inhabit simultaneously a place on earth and a place in heaven, learning to substitute the actual tastes of life on earth with the anticipated tastes of heaven, even to the particular flavor of gingerbread. The speculation continues into appearance. Shall we look the same after death? Why not? replies her aunt in an extended (and footnoted) catechism.[28] According to her, the "human form has been borne and dignified forever by Christ" (120). Nonetheless, after death, the "spiritual body is real, is tangible, is visible, is human," but also is ambiguously "changed" (122). Our "future bodies" will be "vastly convenient," she continues, entering what seems almost a science fiction realm after reminding her auditor that, after death, Christ could appear and disappear at will (124). The "powers of which there is no dreaming" will, for example, mean that she can time travel to Kansas (124). As she puts it, "I, for instance, sitting here by you and thinking that I should like to be in Kansas, will be there" (124).

Winifred's vision of heaven includes "mountains and trees" (137) because she continually proposes a relation to the world that includes the pain of human interaction as well as the joy. Oddly, perhaps, she imagines that we need to remember sorrowful memories of humans, but at the same time she wants the "*ideal* of mountains which we catch in rare glimpses—as we catch the ideal of everything" (137, emphasis in original). Winifred also wants a "home of my own" in heaven, with flowers outside the window. Since the narrator seems shocked, she quotes back at her, "in the Father's house are many mansions." As Winifred mentions that her husband, John, will be waiting for her, the narrator says, "I believe that gave me some thoughts that I ought not to have, and so I made no reply" (139). The potential for jealousy persists in this imagined heaven.

Wanting a "local habitation and a name" (140) in heaven is also wanting a location in heaven that will have names. Winifred proposes "living under the conditions of organized society. Organized society involves homes, not unlike the homes of this world" (140). Many questions emerge from this assertion. What happens with the home of someone who is poor or who has been living under the conditions of slavery in someone else's home? The aspirational quality of this heavenly ideal erases race and involves a middle-class home that can be recreated in heaven. Winifred goes on to say, "I conjecture nothing that the Bible contradicts" (141). The odd placement of subject–verb–object here might implicate the antinomian assertions of Anne Hutchinson. She continues: "I do not believe as truth indisputable anything that the Bible does not give me. But I reason from analogy about this, as we all do about other matters" (141–42).[29] In her sensuous lists, Winfred continues, "I hope for heavenly types of nature and of art" (144). She has the idea that the material world of pleasure in heaven will be like synonyms: "their pianos and machinery may not be made of literal rosewood and steel" (186). Yet when Winifred thinks of building a home in heaven, she thinks of Kansas (225). The oddity that she transplants the violent location of Kansas into heaven almost echoes the statement in *Uncle Tom's Cabin* that heaven is "better than Kintuck" (a statement uttered by the dying Uncle Tom).[30]

The world of *Uncle Tom's Cabin* might be appropriately referenced here both because it is the "other" best seller of nineteenth century United States and because its religious lessons are so explicitly bound up with the physical facts of slavery that *The Gates Ajar* seems to elide. In calling this elision apparent rather than actual, I am arguing that the significance of Kansas for the novel is also about how it relocates the Civil War from the South to the West, and makes its location as a site of violence tied up with the resistance to slavery that the novel never names. The substitutions that the novel enacts, in other words, include the substitution of the violence of Kansas for the violence of slavery.

The tragedy at the novel's close is that moments that might indicate sensual connections become encounters with the physical precursors of death. Apparently Winifred has breast cancer. She "opened the bosom of her dress....." and the ellipses are part of the original (231). The last pages of the novel are immersed in mourning the impending death of Winifred. Her death stands in for and invokes both the loss of Mary's brother and symbolic losses. When she thinks of going to heaven, Winifred thinks of "President Lincoln, or Mrs. Browning" as though they were hanging out there together (238). Her sense of a pantheon has the promise of intimacy with her heroes. Her dying holds other promises of intimacy.

As Winifred lies in bed dying, her physical body becomes less able to use language. The deathbed intimacy between Mary and Winifred includes a scene that would otherwise have been sensual: "I crept up on the bed beside her, for she seemed to wish it.... After that I kissed her." The scene of intimacy suggests a possible union in the afterlife, but they are interrupted by Winifred's vision of John, who has preceded her there: "'John!'—she said,—'why, John!'" (246). The turn from the living woman to the dead husband, a husband buried in Kansas, interrupts the novel's suggestion of a dying romantic kiss, even as it suggests that John has appeared in order to interrupt the kiss.

Finally, in the intense world of Elizabeth Stuart Phelps's *The Gates Ajar*, the matter of reproduction in heavenly terms is the matter of another life beyond the body. The novel links the "other" identities that Christianity provided in accounts of slavery with the lives women could live in the postwar combination of mourning and a life lived doubly in heaven and on earth. The double life of mourning and mobility includes the discipline that encourages an intimate relation to religion arrived at through a relationship with a strong spiritual woman who is loved and lost. The intimacy of such a relation is at once enhanced and deflected through death. That the deaths of the novel invoke the absent boundary of Kansas makes the invocation of Kansas into a metonymic instantiation of the national mourning that cannot speak its name, a mourning at once for lost women and for the loss of a nation forever divided by slavery.

NOTES

1. The title page for the initial publication of *The Story of Avis* (Boston: James Osgood, 1877) calls attention to Phelps as "Author of 'The Gates Ajar,'" but it tells a story very far removed from it. In *The Story of Avis*, the woman's desire to be a writer is thwarted by her conventional marriage and no religious consolation appears.

2. The novel's expansion of a consolation available through religion drew on a learned family background. Her mother's father, Moses Stuart, had been the president of the Andover Theological Seminary. Her own father, Austin Phelps, was a minister who became president of the Andover Theological Seminary the same year that *The Gates Ajar* was published. There is no current biography of Phelps. Details on her life can be found in her autobiographical writing as well as in the multi-authored nineteenth-century illustrated tome *Our Famous Women*. The typically ornate subtitle is *An Authorized Record of the Lives and Deeds of Distinguished American Women of Our Times* (Hartford, Conn.: A. D. Worthington, 1884).

3. Published in the United States without securing international copyright protection, the novel in various editions sold more than a hundred thousand copies on both sides of the Atlantic in the decades after its publication, making it one of the top novels of the nineteenth century. See Stephanie Palmer, "Reframing *The Gates Ajar*: British Responses to Elizabeth Stuart Phelps' Novel" (paper presentation, Italy, 2013). See also Desiree Henderson, *Grief and Genre in American Literature, 1790–1870* (Burlington, Vt.: Ashgate, 2001), 139–45.

4. For helpful readings of the novel, see Justine Murison, *The Politics of Anxiety in Nineteenth-Century American Literature* (Cambridge: Cambridge University Press, 2011); and Elizabeth Duquette, *Loyal Subjects: Bonds of Nation, Race, and Allegiance in Nineteenth-Century America* (New Brunswick: Rutgers University Press, 2010), 94. See also Elizabeth Young, *Disarming the Nation: Women's Writing and the American Civil War* (Chicago: University of Chicago Press, 1999). Duquette pairs *The Gates Ajar* with John De Forest's *Miss Ravenel's Conversion from Secession to Loyalty* (1867). She reads both as examples of the "reunion romance," where political struggles are solved through a form of remarriage (85). See also Lisa Long, "'The Corporeity of Heaven': Rehabilitating the Civil War Body in *The Gates Ajar*," *American Literature* 69, no. 4 (1997), 781–811, and Cindy Weinstein, "Heaven's Tense: Narration in *The Gates Ajar*," *Novel* 45, no. 1 (2012): 56–70.

5. See "Reynolds's Political Map of the United States" (New York: Wm. C. Reynolds and J. C. Jones, 1856), Geography and Map Division, Library of Congress, http://www.loc.gov/item/2003627003. This map was produced to show the importance of Kansas, a territory presented as a blank white space in the midst of a series of states and territories marked by color as free or slave.

6. In particular, the speech that Lincoln gave in Peoria, Illinois, on October 16, 1854, has been understood as a turning point in his announced views on slavery and an origin moment for his work toward the presidency. See *The Collected Works of Abraham Lincoln*, ed. Roy P. Basler (New Brunswick: Rutgers University Press, 1953), 2:275.

7. Senator Charles Sumner, well known as an abolitionist politician, was beaten over the head with a cane by Preston Brooks, a southern senator, on the floor of the Senate in 1856 and nearly killed. In retaliation, John Brown, who had arrived to carry out abolitionist agitation in Kansas in 1855, conducted several violent raids, dragging men suspected of proslavery sentiments from their homes and killing them with swords. See Nicole Etcheson, *Bleeding Kansas: Contested Liberty in the Civil War Era* (Lawrence: University of Kansas Press, 2004). See also "Report of the Special Committee Appointed to Investigate the Troubles in Kansas" (1856; repr., Ann Arbor: University of Michigan Library,

2005), http://name.umdl.umich.edu/AFK4445.0001.001. This report notes that territories inhabited by Indians have previously been barriers to settlers and anticipates that the troubles in Kansas have "endangered" the continued existence of the United States (2).

8. The language of compromise operates in conjunction with the language of "forever"—a language reiterated in the Emancipation Proclamation's words, "forever free." It also might suggest the way that the Declaration of Independence, as read by Derrida, establishes a moment of "becoming" built into the declarations of nation and state alike. See Jacques Derrida, "Declarations of Independence," in *Negotiations: Interventions and Interviews, 1971–2001* (Stanford: Stanford University Press, 2002), 46–54. See also Bonnie Honig, "Declarations of Independence: Arendt and Derrida on the Problem of Founding a Republic," *American Political Science Review* 85, no. 1 (1991): 97–113; and Jacques de Ville, "Sovereignty without Sovereignty: Derrida's Declarations of Independence," *Law and Critique* 19, no. 2 (2008): 87–114. That sense of both land and body as a process of becoming in relation to belonging emerges in several legal decisions of the antebellum period.

9. Horace Greeley of the *New York Tribune* has been credited with the phrase.

10. Such well-known religious leaders as Henry Ward Beecher, father of Harriet Beecher Stowe, became involved in raising funds to purchase arms for the so-called "free soilers" in Kansas during the 1850s. These guns were referred to as "Beecher's Bibles," further confusing the relation between violence and religion that the novel never directly confronts. The violence in Kansas has also been associated with John Brown because he and his sons carried out violent retaliations for the slaughter that took place in Lawrence. See David Reynolds, *John Brown, Abolitionist: The Man Who Killed Slavery, Sparked the Civil War, and Seeded Civil Rights* (New York: Harper, 2005). See also Stephen B. Oates, *To Purge This Land with Blood: A Biography of John Brown* (New York: Harper and Row, 1970), http://xroads.virginia.edu/~hyper/hns/kansas/jbrown.html.

11. See also Donald R. Hale, *We Rode with Quantrill: Quantrill and the Guerrilla War as Told by the Men and Women Who Were with Him, with a True Sketch of Quantrill's Life* (Kansas City, Mo.: D. R. Hale, 1992); and Michael Fellman, *Inside War: The Guerilla Conflict in Missouri* (New York: Oxford University Press, 1989). A contemporary book by John Edwards, *Noted Guerillas* (1867), appeared the year before *The Gates Ajar*; the full title is *Noted Guerrillas, or The Warfare of the Border. Being a History of the Lives and Adventures of Quantrell, Bill Anderson, George Todd, Dave Poole, Fletcher Taylor, Peyton Long, Oil Shepherd, Arch Clements, John Maupin, Tuck and Woot Hill, Wm. Gregg, Thomas Maupin, the James brothers, the Younger brothers, Arthur McCoy, and Numerous Other Well Known Guerillas of the West* (Chicago: Thompson and Wakefield, 1877). See also Jay Monaghan, *Civil War on the Western Border, 1854–1865* (Boston: Little, Brown, 1955) and Thomas Goodrich, *Bloody Dawn: The Story of the Lawrence Massacre* (Kent: Kent State University Press, 1992).

12. The date of the raid also makes it possible to conjecture other dates in the novel and to understand that her daughter, Faith, was born close enough to the events of this raid as to leave some doubt about her paternity. See *The Gates Ajar* (Boston: Fields, Osgood and Co., 1869), 61, http://www.letrs.indiana.edu/cgi/t/text/pageviewer-idx?sid=d8952b729b48 foe8f1cob35836512498;c=wright2;cc=wright2;seq=0001;idno=Wright2-2628; hereafter documented parenthetically. This novel is out of print and only available on line.

13. See the "as told to" story by one of the raiders, John McCorkle and O. S Barton. *Three Years with Quantrell: A True Story* (Armstrong, Mo.: Armstrong Herald Print, 1914). See also Duane Schultz, *Quantrill's War: The Life and Times of William Clarke Quantrill, 1837–1865* (New York: St. Martin's Press, 1996).

14. There are several pictorial examples of the violence directed at women. A symbolic version appears in reaction to the violence of the 1850s as "Liberty, the Fair Maid of Kansas in the Hands of the 'Border Ruffians'" (Philadelphia, 1856), Alfred Whittal Stern Collection, Library of Congress, http://memory.loc.gov/cgi-bin/ampage?collId=lprbscsm &fileName=scsm0331/lprbscsmscsm0331.db&recNum=0&itemLink=D?scsmbib:4: ./temp/~ammem_ukQN. In this suggestive cartoon, as Liberty begs for mercy, a "ruffian" laughs.

15. "Elizabeth Wetherell" [pseud. for Susan B. Warner], *The Wide, Wide World* (New York: George P. Putnam, 1851), 12, 13. As Jane Tompkins notes in her important attention to that novel, the subsequent making of tea in the scene of parting between mother and daughter performs a very significant ritual in *The Wide, Wide World*; see *Sensational Designs: The Cultural Work of American Fiction, 1790–1860* (New York: Oxford University Press, 1986). The first thing Mary does for Winifred is make tea.

16. For a comparison of *Uncle Tom's Cabin* and *The Gates Ajar*, see Ashley Barnes, "The Word Made Exhibition: Protestant Reading Meets Catholic Worship in *Uncle Tom's Cabin* and *The Gates Ajar*," *Legacy* 29, no. 2 (2012): 179–200.

17. Another articulation of incest in a novel of the 1850s appears in the resemblance between the erotic attraction of Pierre for his mother and "sister" Isabel in Herman Melville's *Pierre, or The Ambiguities*, and that possibly provides a way to think about the connection between Mary and Roy in *The Gates Ajar*.

18. Joseph Roach, *Cities of the Dead: Circum-Atlantic Performance* (New York: Columbia University Press, 1996), 6.

19. Ibid.

20. Rebecca Schneider, *Performing Remains: Art and War in Times of Theatrical Reenactment* (New York: Routledge, 2011).

21. Ibid., 14, 18. See also Elizabeth Freeman, *Time Binds: Queer Temporalities, Perverse Histories* (Durham: Duke University Press, 2010); and Dana Luciano, *Arranging Grief: Sacred Time and the Body in Nineteenth-Century America* (New York: New York University Press, 2008).

22. Such doubling resembles that described by John Irwin's attention to William Faulkner's novels in his critical work *Doubling and Incest, Repetition and Revenge: A Speculative Reading of Faulkner* (Baltimore: Johns Hopkins University Press, 1996). See also Tavia Nyongo, *The Amalgamation Waltz: Race, Performance, and the Ruses of Memory* (Minneapolis: University of Minnesota Press, 2009).

23. On the first page of the novel, a week has passed since she found out about her brother's death, but she has not yet opened the "yellow" packets, packets that never reappear in *The Gates Ajar*—are these packets with his "effects"? As she searches her desk for paper, the narrator finds a "poor little book" where she has previously kept "memoranda of the weather, and my lovers" (1).

24. *Essays of Elia*, first published in 1823, was quite popular in the United States.

25. It also suggests a form of what has been described as the nonreproductive futurity aroused by unions that are not presumed to result in the birth of children. My terms allude to the work of several critics, including Lee Edelman, *No Future: Queer Theory and the Death Drive* (Durham: Duke University Press, 2004); and Sarah Ensor, "Spinster Ecology: Rachel Carson, Sarah Orne Jewett, and Nonreproductive Futurity," *American Literature* 84, no. 2 (2012): 409–35.

26. Sources for the words of Anne Hutchinson are to be found in the words of the judges at her trial, and for that reason bear something beyond the difficulty of oral history. The judges, according to John Winthrop's account, have their own agenda, but they also record a spirited defense. I have in mind here Hutchinson's insistence on the idea of "union with the person of the Holy Ghost . . . so as to amount to a personal union" (John Winthrop, journal entry, October 25, 1636). See David Hall, ed., *The Antinomian Controversy, 1636–1638: A Documentary History* (Durham: Duke University Press, 1990), 43. See also Amy Schrager Lang, *Prophetic Woman: Anne Hutchinson and the Problem of Dissent in the Literature of New England* (Berkeley: University of California Press, 1987). Thank you to Tim Sweet for a discussion of this matter.

27. For those in the dark about the "little bone," the concept is that the tip of the coccyx is imperishable. It is most likely that Phelps found out about it from a translation of the Koran that was much discussed in the mid-nineteenth century: George Sale, trans., *The Koran: Commonly Called the Alcoran of Mohammed* (Philadelphia: J. W. Moore, 1856). The commentary by Sale explains the coccyx as a "seed" for reincarnation: "as it was the first formed in the human body, it will also remain uncorrupted until the last day, as a seed from whence the whole is to be renewed" (54).

28. These are not literal footnotes, but rather embedded citations. For example, Aunt Winifred cites "Dr. Chalmers" on "spiritual materialism." He has given a sermon on "New Heavens and Earth" and Winifred interrupts herself to say "which, by the way, you should read" (77). On spiritualism and its relation to the Scottish "divine" Thomas Chalmers, see Murison, *The Politics of Anxiety*, 140. Chalmers proposed that a body could be both spiritual and material.

29. As part of her lesson, Winifred quotes from Isaac Taylor, *Physical Theory of Another Life* (conveniently to hand on the book shelf) in order to connect "argument from analogy" to "abstract reasoning" (89).

30. Harriet Beecher Stowe, *Uncle Tom's Cabin* (New York: Penguin, 1986), 590.

"Near Andersonville"

Place and Race in Early American Regionalism

JILLIAN SPIVEY CADDELL

What does it mean to be an African American woman near Andersonville, the most notorious southern death camp, during the American Civil War? Winslow Homer posed this question when he named a painting created in the war's immediate aftermath *Near Andersonville*. (See figure 6.) The preposition *near* and the proper place-name locate the viewer and the woman the painting depicts not in some abstract place of the war, but proximate to a location heavy with meaning. The soldiers in the upper left-hand corner are not just any Union soldiers; they are soldiers who are being led, perhaps to their deaths, to the infamous Confederate prison at Andersonville, Georgia. While atrocities occurred in prisons both North and South, no other prison became as charged with anger and political significance as Andersonville. As early as the spring of 1864, reports of the prison's horrible conditions seeped into the northern press, and as the war came to an end, photographs of survivors shocked the North. If the nation was to reunite, Andersonville would have to be forgotten or, at least, the memory of it scrubbed and altered. But the painting does not depict the horrors of Andersonville that polarized the country but the experience of being *near* it, and it does so through an enslaved or formerly enslaved woman while giving no indication of her feelings toward the soldiers: her face gives nothing away.[1]

The centrality of the woman in Homer's painting contrasts with the marginal role that African Americans are supposed to have played in art and literature about the Civil War. Daniel Aaron summarizes this belief in his founda-

FIGURE 6. Winslow Homer, *Near Andersonville*, 1865–66. Oil on canvas, 23" x 18". Newark Museum, gift of Mrs. Hannah Corbin Carter; Horace K. Corbin; Robert S. Corbin; William D. Corbin; and Mrs. Clementine Corbin Day in memory of their parents, Hannah Stockton Corbin and Horace Kellogg Corbin 1966.

tional work *The Unwritten War*: "Without the Negro, there would have been no Civil War, yet he figured only peripherally in the War literature. Often presented sympathetically (which ordinarily meant sentimentally and patronizingly), he remained even in the midst of his literary well-wishers an object of contempt or dread."[2] For Aaron, race is the reason the war remains unwritten, a source of "emotional resistance" that "blur[s] literary insight."[3] In a recent essay that appeared during the sesquicentennial of the war, the African American writer Ta-Nehisi Coates echoed Aaron, describing the black experience of the Civil War in this way: "For my community, the message has long been clear: the Civil War is a story for white people—acted out by white people, on white people's terms—in which blacks feature strictly as stock characters and props."[4] While it is undoubtedly true that in postwar literature by white writers, African American characters often serve placating and racialized roles, this essay will survey works like *Near Andersonville* in which the creative impasse that Aaron finds when African Americans appear "peripherally" in Civil War literature becomes a site where the war's meaning is productively analyzed. Aaron points us toward this productive space when he describes African Americans as appearing "peripherally" in war literature, since the descriptor links the experience of war with place and distance. I will argue that certain places touched by war lend writers during and after the war's duration specific settings for exploring race and structures of power that are imaginatively untethered from the political and ideological dictates of the nation.

Aaron's adverb "peripherally" also may remind us of Toni Morrison's formative claim in *Playing in the Dark* that an Africanist presence, however often silenced, constitutes American literature: "The contemplation of this black presence is central to any understanding of our national literature," she writes, "and should not be permitted to hover at the margins of the literary imagination."[5] This discourse of marginalization mirrors, in ways both illuminating and obfuscating, discussions of the place of the region in pre-recovery literary studies of regionalism. "Grounded in a specific geography and a local history," write Thomas Constantinesco and Cécile Roudeau, "the region has indeed been commodified as the nation's picturesque other, a gendered entity that stands in consistent counterpoint to the universal as pleasantly quaint or dangerously peculiar."[6] With these words in mind, we might return to Homer's woman in the doorway, who serves as the "picturesque other" to the Union soldiers representing the nation. In this essay, I will consider the relationship between marginalization (of black subjects like the woman in *Near Andersonville*) and regionalization (of local perspectives and places) suggested by this shared critical language. While I do not wish to suggest that these two processes are commensurate in effect, they are far more intimately bound in postwar regionalist literature than has been previously explored, as black experience is co-opted by white artists to understand othered places within the nation.

In recent years, scholars of the postwar genre of regionalism have gone beyond the initial feminist recovery efforts that reappraised regionalism—once considered minor, feminized, and nostalgic—to show how the genre is fully implicated in the construction of the nation, even as it questions the nation's governing structures. In the words of Stephanie Foote, regionalism "must be approached as a genre that participates in and responds to the late nineteenth-century social discourses from which it initially seems to be turning its delicate face."[7] Several studies, most importantly Judith Fetterley and Marjorie Pryse's *Writing Out of Place*, have done so by focusing on the genre's participation in *regionalization*—which we might define, following from Fetterley and Pryse, as the process by which nations control smaller regions politically, economically, and ideologically—in order to focus less on the region as a geographical place and more on the region as a discursive site where regionalization can be charted and, at times, contested. With this approach, Fetterley and Pryse can go so far as to say that regionalism "is not a feature of geography" and that the genre "is therefore a discourse ... rather than a place."[8] Taking geography to be a concretization of the nation's space that obscures, quoting Frank Davey, "the politically oppositional aspects of regionalism," Fetterley and Pryse effectively do away with the region in regionalism as it invokes a specific geographical space (6). Considering the region as a discursive rather than a geographic site suggests new ways of assessing the political investments of canonized regionalists, like Sarah Orne Jewett and Kate Chopin. It also potentially opens the genre's boundaries to include new texts and authors outside the established regionalist canon who depict the operations of regionalization, including the writers I will study here, Rebecca Harding Davis and Constance Fenimore Woolson.[9] I will suggest that in order to understand the process of regionalization that occurs in regionalist texts, we must pay more attention to a crisis that fundamentally concerned questions about the relation of the region to the nation: the American Civil War.[10] When we attend to the war's presence in these works, we see that they negotiate regionalization through race in ways that rewrite the values of regionalism and how it participates in projects of national critique and consolidation at the same time.

This essay considers three texts, a painting and two stories, that take the Civil War and black experience as their subject—Homer's *Near Andersonville* (ca. 1866), Rebecca Harding Davis's "John Lamar" (1862), and Constance Fenimore Woolson's "Rodman the Keeper" (1877)—asking how these works seek to understand regionalization through depictions of black subjects in particular places of war, like Andersonville. These places contain an inherent instability that allows them to challenge dominant social structures, like race, and therefore critique national hegemony. To perform this critique, these texts move African Americans from the margins of histories about both the Civil War and the postwar genre of regionalism, depicting black characters as subject to the processes of regionalization. Recognizing the way these texts portray black characters opens up new readings of the racial construction of the United States imagined by, and sometimes precluded by, regionalism, as well as new insight into the role the Civil War played in a genre thought to be unconcerned with it. While several canonical regionalist writers, most notably Jewett, wrote stories that took the Civil War as their subject, these stories have never appeared in major anthologies of regionalist works. This may be because they do not fit our prescribed idea of the subjects and plots of regionalist stories, or because these stories often feature racist depictions of black subjects. I read such stories, and their sometimes uncomfortable representations of African Americans, not as unsuccessful anomalies but as another way that regionalist writers sought to understand the relationship between the regionalized subject and the nation. Thus, to understand how the war influenced regionalism, we must first address how the war affected the American spatial imaginary, how it "restored a familiar map but also opened new territory for expansion," as Amy Kaplan has written, and how it also generated places that could not be subsumed into that national map or shaped to fit traditional narratives of national reunion.[11]

Contested Places and the Civil War

The Civil War was fought over and through questions of place. The war's military context was grounded in geographic questions and problems, including the conquering and garrisoning of territory to physically reclaim place for the Union (or, for the Confederacy, to maintain a real, independent geography), and the impact that geography (especially topography and hydrography) had on the overall conduct of the war, the direction of campaigns, and the outcome of battles. The Civil War taught Americans that questions of geography were not benign facts from schoolbooks but issues of national importance that cost lives. Further, after the war ended, place provided Americans with a source of pride and a means of visualizing nationalism. As Ralph Waldo Emerson wrote, "in every house & shop, an American map has been unrolled, & daily studied,—& now that peace has come, every citizen finds himself a skilled student of the condition, means, & future, of this continent."[12] A knowledge of American place, learned by heart through the hard years of war, became a prerequisite of postwar citizenship.

With map in hand and borders settled, America went forward from its moment of crisis into its imperial heyday—or so tidy narratives of American history might have us believe. Although the country's borders would shift with territorial annexation, its size would not be reduced, and its existence would not be threatened, at least not by rebellions from within. Anne Baker summarizes this view when she states that the Civil War "established the Union on a new, firmer footing" such that "national boundaries came to seem more solid and more real."[13] While postwar nationalist rhetoric may have trumpeted this sense of settled space, within these borders contested places remained: sites where questions of national affiliation had acquired heightened importance through being contested during the war. Even after Lee's surrender restored the American map, places associated with the war—including explicitly related localities like battlefields, cemeteries, and former prison sites, as well as places that appeared less directly related, like the new state of West Virginia—retained a residue of contingency that allowed them to serve as sites where the nation's existential moment was preserved and the effects of regionalization could be countered.

In their capacity to reflect on and reorient real places within the nation, offering alternate possibilities for structuring society, contested places resemble what Foucault termed heterotopias. Heterotopias, according to Foucault's foundational formulation, are "real places—places that do exist and that are formed in the very founding of society—that are something like countersites, a kind of effectively enacted utopia in which the real sites, all the other real sites that can be found within the culture, are simultaneously represented, contested, and inverted."[14] Heterotopias are a "simultaneously mythic and real contestation of the space in which we live" that expose the oftentimes invisible ways that place orders culture (24). John Funchion has shown how Foucault's relatively brief explication of these countersites can be used to understand regionalization. For Funchion the local is a "protean phenomenon" rather than a fixed place, one always subject to greater forces; heterotopias, therefore, offer "a compelling way of examining localities as being as perpetually iterative as the networks that connect them."[15] Take, for instance, Andersonville. The prison was unlike others created on either side of the Civil War in several important ways that underwrite its heterotopic nature. The largest Confederate prisons before Andersonville were located in cities like Richmond, while Andersonville was, according to one prisoner, "merely a hole cut in the wilderness. It was as remote a point from our armies, as they then lay, as the Southern Confederacy could give."[16] After the war, Andersonville was preserved as a national cemetery and national park, each a type of heterotopia that reflects on what the nation purportedly values and the image it conceives of itself. Although Andersonville's meaning has been co-opted for American nationalist purposes—it even serves today as the site of the National Prisoner of War Museum—it retains vestiges of a past in which the future of the United States remained an open question. The tiny town for which the camp was unofficially named, for instance, boasts the Henry Wirz Monument, dedicated in 1909 to the controversial Confederate commander held responsible for and ultimately executed for causing much of the suffering at Andersonville. The Wirz monument reminds any visitor that however national Andersonville may now be, the vitriol of the Civil War lives on from a time when the nation's survival was not guaranteed. This retained contingency makes Andersonville a contested place, a particular type of war heterotopia that retains an unsettled essence even after war ends.

Not all contested places were distinct sites like Andersonville, however. For Rebecca Harding Davis, whose publishing career in the *Atlantic* began concurrently with the Civil War, the contested place of foremost concern was the one where she grew up, the mountains of what was then western Virginia. At the same time that Davis was describing the paralyzing effect of industrialization on her home state in "Life in the Iron-Mills" (1861), a convention was held in Wheeling to prevent Virginia from seceding from the Union; later, in 1863, West Virginia voted to secede from Virginia, though support remained divided between Union and Confederacy within the new state.[17] Nearly fifty years after the war had ended, Davis described the divisions of loyalty within West Virginia in this way: "In every village opinions clashed. The elders of the family, as a rule, sided with the government; the young folks with the South."[18] Regional scales are diminished here while local differences matter most: not only do opinions differ from town to town, but even within individual families. It was not simply West Virginia's vexed location between slave and free states that led to its divided affiliations: the geographical terrain of the state, mountainous and densely forested, allowed small-scale guerilla warfare to flourish. Davis noted broadly that the side one supported during the war came down ultimately to a question of location: "[Women's] loyalty, like their husbands," she wrote, "depended almost wholly on their geographical point of view."[19] In both politics and topography, West Virginia was highly localized in a way that transformed and reversed the war's vast national scope into a matter of differences between families from one valley to the next. The texts to which I will now turn consider contested places as heterotopias in order to escape thinking about them through binaries like center/periphery that are sometimes reified in discussions of regionalization. Rather than serving as sites of pure subordination or pure resistance, these are "places where uneven hegemonic forces collided," and the struggle for power between North and South played out across scales ranging from the nation to the community to the individual, generating a multiplicity of possibilities for what the United States would become.[20]

"That vague country":
The Divided Loyalties of "John Lamar"

"John Lamar," published in the *Atlantic Monthly* in April 1862, details the experiences of a Confederate soldier who is being held prisoner by Union forces camped out on a farm owned by his family in West Virginia. The farm's owner, Captain Dorr, has enlisted with the Union and is now head of the regiment camped on his farm, but his cousin, Lamar, is a Georgia "Secesh" sympathizer being held prisoner there along with his slave, Ben. While the story begins as an explication of Lamar's confused loyalties between his family in West Virginia and his family in Georgia, the narration eventually transitions to describe Ben's struggle between protecting his master and striking out for freedom, a shift in perception that Fetterley and Pryse identify as a hallmark of regionalism.[21] When Ben chooses not just to run away but to kill his master first, however, "John Lamar" closes off its empathetic relation of black experience, marking the limits of regionalist sympathy. The story's complicated questions concerning loyalty, family, and emancipation are staged in a setting that reproduces the system of slavery, using the contested place of West Virginia to show that regions are not apart from the nation but constitutive of it (and its evils) in miniature.

The farm where "John Lamar" takes place has become a camp for Federal troops, providing "a sort of wedge in the Rebel Cheat counties of Western Virginia."[22] A Union stronghold in a Rebel county, ancestral home to those who support both the Union and Confederate sides, the farm serves as synecdoche to the divided state of West Virginia. Reflecting the future state's conflicted loyalties, the farm also replicates its topography in miniature:

> Around there were hills like uncouth monsters, swathed in ice, holding up the soggy sky; shivering pine-forests; unmeaning, dreary flats; and the Cheat, coiled about the frozen sinews of the hills, limp and cold, like a cord tying a dead man's jaws. Whatever outlook of joy or worship this region had borne on its face in time gone, it turned to [Lamar] to-day nothing but stagnation, a great death. He wondered idly, looking at it, (for the old Huguenot brain of the man was full of morbid fancies,) if it were winter alone that had deadened color and pulse out of these full-blooded hills, or if they could know the colder horror crossing their threshold, and forgot to praise God as it came. (3–4)

This description of setting, which occurs early in the story, reveals Lamar's worldview. Lamar ascribes a sentience to the land that allows it to reflect the dire circumstances of the nation at war: it has a face and pulse and, perhaps, a knowledge of "colder horror." Importantly, Lamar is able to read the land and humanize it more so than he can his own slave Ben, who is "talked of ... like a clod" by Lamar and Dorr even while Ben is in the room (13). Slavery is a system of subjugation, Davis insists through the character of Lamar, one that confuses land/property for people and people for land/property. The connection between Lamar's spatial imaginary and slavery is further emphasized in this passage by the mention of the "full-blooded hills," which calls to mind the deep rhetorical and legal connections between race and blood in America. The coiling river, which wraps around the hills "like a cord tying a dead man's jaws," could be a specter of the chains of the enslaved and the system that Lamar fights to protect. In this passage, then, West Virginia is portrayed as a heterotopia reflecting in miniature the South's monstrous relationship to slavery, a system that permeates the sensory perceptions of the slaveholder Lamar.

Existing on the border between North and South, the story's setting not only depicts the evils of southern slavery but the complicity of the rest of the nation in perpetuating such a dehumanizing system for so long. Although Captain Dorr fights for the Union, for instance, he argues that the slave question should be kept out of the war, and he regards Ben with the same lack of humanity that Lamar does. Meanwhile, to bring into relief the corrupting effects of slavery, Davis's story reverses the racial hierarchies perpetuated by the system of enslavement. The prison that occupies the space at the geographical and theoretical center of "John Lamar" reverses the logic of slavery, holding the white owner captive and leaving his slave free to roam and, ultimately, to decide his own and his master's fate. Ironically, the jail where Lamar is held is actually a shed built by Lamar and Dorr the year before, a detail that illustrates how the system of slavery morally incarcerates those who participate in it.

Lamar hatches a plan for his slave Ben to spring him from prison in the night; as this plan progresses, the story, which is initially focalized through the southerner Lamar, shifts to catalog Ben's dawning awareness of his subjugation and ability to resist. The contested place of West Virginia makes Ben's self-emancipation possible because of its proximity to the North, a region that he has dreamed of since his father escaped there and his lover was freed and moved there. The narrator describes Ben's longing for the North in this way: "So it came, that the slow tide of discontent ebbing in everybody's heart towards some unreached sea set in his ignorant brooding towards that vague country which the only two who cared for him had found" (11). The "vagueness" of the country compels Ben to discover the imaginative power within himself that would bring about his emancipation. Likewise, it is only in the undetermined topography of West Virginia, as opposed to the languid space of the South, that Ben is able to run away:

The world had grown new, strange; was he Ben, picking cotton in the swamp-edge?—plunging his fingers with a shudder in the icy drifts. Down in the glowing torpor of the Santilla flats, where the Lamar plantations lay, Ben had slept off as maddening hunger for life and freedom as this of to-day; but here, with the winter air stinging every nerve to life, with the perpetual mystery of the mountains terrifying his bestial nature down, the strength of the man stood up. (16–17)

While indulging in the folk belief that warmer climates slow the blood, the narrator draws on stereotypically racist notions of the bestiality of the black man in ways that foreshadow the story's ultimately ambiguous feelings about emancipation. Yet even as the narrator uses racialized stereotypes to depict Ben's coarseness, Davis employs a familiar regionalist trope typically reserved for white characters that associates a relationship to place with the "discovery of self."[23] Ben's vision of the North and his growing awareness of his own agency enabled by the overturned hierarchies in place in West Virginia are central to his burgeoning desire for freedom.

Davis marks this developing desire through her narration, which increasingly invokes a hypothetical reader to gain sympathy for the enslaved man's dilemma. After hearing an abolitionist preacher speak, calling him "a man and a brother," and learning from a sentry that the northern soldiers "had come to set the slaves free," Ben slowly comes to realize his own agency to free himself while his master is in prison. Davis signals this shift in awareness by engaging the reader in Ben's plight through direct address. After relating how Ben's father escaped to the North, for example, the narration seeks to describe the boy's "comical" longing for his absent parent: "very different his, from the feeling with which you left your mother's grave,—though as yet we have not invented names for the emotions of those people" (10). Davis initially sets the reader's emotions against those of the slave, suggesting that the difference in feeling is so disparate between the slave and the presumed *Atlantic* reader that there are no words to express the former. (Note, too, that it is the presumed *Atlantic* reader, as well as the narrator, who own and "invent" the language of the day, another assertion of white dominance.)

Gradually, however, words *are* assigned to Ben's consciousness. As he looks north, imagining his freedom, "his nerves grew cold and rigid, as yours do when something wrings your heart sharply: for there are nerves in these black carcasses, thicker, more quickly stung to madness than yours" (11). The narrator continues to relate the reader's emotions with those of the slave, eventually implicating the reader in a system that objectifies black people (a point viciously made in the word "carcasses") in order to rule it. As Dorr and Lamar discuss the philosophical underpinnings of the war, forgetting about Ben's presence, the narrator simultaneously lets them off the hook while damning them and her readers with the simple phrase, "we all do the same, you know" (13). The narrator's ironic stance initially seems to valorize white superiority in intellect and emotion but develops to demonstrate that it is not difference in intellect that separates whites from blacks but difference in experience: whites can never understand the black experience because they have never been enslaved. Thus, we learn that when Ben decides to kill Lamar, his "thick blood throbbed and surged with passions of which you and I know nothing: he had a lost life to avenge" (21).

Davis's narration moves Ben from the literal and figurative margins of the story into a figure through which the slave's place in the postslavery nation can be imagined, yet this vision is shut down when Ben is armed and chooses not to fight with the North but to kill his master. Even as Ben's agency, however placated, awakens in the cold mountain air, he feels the placelessness of the contested place, which as a heterotopia is, in Foucault's words, "outside of all places" (24). "It's a big world," Ben says, "but der's no room in it fur poor Ben" (17). The violence that he enacts in killing his master perpetuates the violence of the slave system, shutting off his vision of the North and rendering him a slave again, a person without a place or home. He is, to echo the title of the famous Civil War story, a man without a country, "a man, wifeless, homeless, nationless, hawked, flung from trader to trader for a handful of dirty shinplasters" (18). In a setting that reproduces and reverses the ruling structures of slavery, Ben becomes as savage as the system in which he was trapped: "It was his turn to be master now!" insists the narrator as Ben escapes after killing Lamar (21). Ben turns away from the imagined land of the North that had previously fueled his desire for freedom, as instead he is "[drawn] back" by "his native air, torrid, heavy with latent impurity": "He panted, thinking of the saffron hues of the Santilla flats, of the white, stately dwellings, the men that went in and out from them, quiet, dominant,—feeling the edge of his knife" (21). The violence that Ben enacts ties him to the southern space he so desperately wishes to escape. The story gives Ben no resolution; we leave him feeling the terrible thrill of his newfound power as the narrative returns to the dying Lamar. In his last moments, Lamar realizes Ben's action, and "in that dying flash of comprehension, it may be, the wrongs of the white man and the black stood clearer to his eyes than ours: the two lives trampled down" (22).

In the story's closing scene, a sentry looks down at the dead body of Lamar and feels that "the war, which had become a daily business, stood suddenly before him in all its terrible meaning" (23). The war's meaning as Davis wrote, just one year into the conflict, was of violence perpetuating violence in a border region that both offered possibilities for black emancipation and ultimately foreclosed those possibilities, abandoning Ben in the mountains. Ben's inability to escape the terrible system in which he has always toiled is evidence that resistance is not rendered any easier in heterotopic contested regions. Reading "John Lamar" alongside recent attempts to delineate the generic values of regionalism shows how particular sites could encapsulate, on a local scale, the ways that race inexorably structured both North and South. Getting outside this regionalizing structure is, in "John Lamar," impossible. These inescapable contested sites, Davis indicates, were the real places where the war, in all its scales of struggle, took place, and where questions about black emancipation would continue to be based. Although three years later the war would end, reuniting the warring sides and settling borders, unsettled places of war remained, continuing to challenge the nation's authority.

"His island marked out": Crossing Internal Borders in "Rodman the Keeper"

If "John Lamar" depicts how American places reflected a multitude of forces struggling over the fate of the nation, Woolson's "Rodman the Keeper" portrays the afterlives of those places as the reunited nation sought to control their meaning. "Rodman the Keeper," first published like "John Lamar" in the *Atlantic*, in March 1877, reverses the circumstances of the earlier story. Rather than cataloging the experiences of a Confederate sympathizer imprisoned by Union forces, it describes a former Union soldier, John Rodman, who is virtually imprisoned at the site of a former prisoner camp and current national cemetery in the South. Rodman serves as keeper of the cemetery, which renders him the embodiment of the recent northern enemy to the townsfolk who live nearby, "and upon him, therefore, the bitterness fell, not in words, but in averted looks, in sudden silences when he approached, in withdrawals and avoidance, until he lived and moved in a vacuum."[24] The story tracks Rodman's tentative friendship with a dying ex-Confederate soldier, Ward De Rosset, and the friction he encounters from De Rosset's fiery southern-sympathizing niece, Bettina. Rodman's growing bond of sympathy with De Rosset and Bettina suggests that the story will act as a parable of reconciliation.[25] Yet "Rodman the Keeper" maintains that contested places, even those that intend to heal the nation, instead perpetuate acrimony, despite the ability of some to traverse their borders.

Woolson's tale about a national cemetery built on the remains of a notorious prison is based on the real site of Andersonville, and like Homer's *Near Andersonville* it seeks to understand the prison's lasting impression in American memory. During the war, prisons created unnatural boundaries in which islands of opposing soldiers were surrounded by enemy territory; when the war ended, these unnatural places persisted through their cemeteries, which stranded northern soldiers in southern climes and vice versa. While Foucault described all cemeteries as heterotopias, American national cemeteries, Woolson's story makes clear, are another memorial genre altogether, one that seeks to create identical spaces of mourning throughout the nation, binding otherwise disparate locales. Only the cemeteries for northern soldiers, however, were called "national"; the bodies of Confederate soldiers were not allowed in these government cemeteries. The acrimony generated by the creation of national cemeteries and their exclusion of southern soldiers poisoned the promised reunion of the nation and fomented racial tension that would come into full force during the post-Reconstruction era of Jim Crow laws.[26]

"Rodman the Keeper" focuses on the boundaries of the national cemetery and the question of who will or will not enter its grounds, reminding us of Foucault's description of how heterotopias "presuppose a system of opening and closing that both isolates them and makes them penetrable" (26). At the story's outset, Rodman functions solely within the cemetery's boundaries; we are told that after being rejected by the townspeople, Rodman "withdrew himself, and came and went among them no more ... and began the life of a solitary, his island marked out by the massive granite wall with which the United States Government has carefully surrounded those sad Southern cemeteries of hers" (126). Others, like Ward De Rosset and Bettina, resist entering the cemetery. The only characters who are willing to cross the boundaries of the cemetery, Woolson suggests, are the local black townspeople. Thus, though "Rodman" largely sidesteps racial unrest, it does consider the relationship between former slaves, memorialization, and education in its errand to envision the South's future.

The story features a marginal character named Pomp, a former slave of the De Rossets who remains with them after emancipation and cares for his former master. Pomp's type is familiar in tales about the Reconstruction South: he resembles Aaron's sympathetically yet patronizingly portrayed black presence, whose speech is rendered in dialect and who is loyal to his "family" although he is no longer owned by them (132). Pomp, however, is not simply a stock character: he is also the only named character who is willing to pay reverence to the dead of the prison, to remember and commemorate, and to traverse boundaries between the "national" cemetery and the hostile territory that surrounds it. Pomp's role in "Rodman the Keeper" gestures toward the historical connection between Andersonville and the slavery question over which the war was fought. Massive prisons like Andersonville only came into existence midway through the war, after the Confederacy vowed to return African American soldiers fighting for the Union to southern states for punishment and the Union ended its prisoner exchange cartel.[27] It could be said, then, that prisons, and the cemeteries they generated, emerged in direct relation to African American participation in the war. The Union's refusal to continue prisoner exchanges with the Confederacy was bound up in a recognition of personhood and can be seen as a version of why the war itself was being fought: the North wanted the South to recognize that black and white soldiers were interchangeable, and the South refused.

In the story, Rodman the northerner takes in De Rosset, the Confederate, and Pomp when it is clear that they cannot care for each other. Pomp, though "bent and shriveled," is told he must learn to read by Rodman, who feels that "after all these years of theory, he, as a New Englander, could not stand by and see precious knowledge shut from the black man" (132, 137). Rodman uses as primer a government placard hanging on the wall of his caretakers' house. It reads, "In this cemetery repose the remains of Fourteen Thousand Three Hundred and Twenty-One United States Soldiers," and is followed by two stanzas from Longfellow's "A Psalm of Life" (139). "The only known instance of the Government's condescending to poetry," Rodman thinks as he teaches the ex-slave to read. Woolson's narration then describes the placard as follows: "It was placed there for instruction and edification of visitors; but, no visitors coming, [Rodman] took the liberty of using it as a primer for Pomp. The large letters served the purpose admirably, and Pomp learned the entire quotation; what he thought of it has not transpired" (140). Since there are no actual visitors to the cemetery, Pomp must serve as interpreter—but, as a former slave, interpretation is closed off to Pomp by the text. Undoubtedly this is a moment like those in "John Lamar" in which the racialized other is depicted as unknowable because of his difference; the narrator, after all, has access to other (white) characters' thoughts. Yet we can also locate within this scene of monumental pedagogy a sense that this ex-slave will have a far better understanding of the words of the memorial than any other character in the story, all of whom have incomplete or biased access to memory of the war: Rodman is a former Union soldier who feels contempt for the southerners who surround him; De Rosset is a Confederate dying of war wounds in much the same way that Confederate sympathies must die if the country is to prosper; and Bettina is too full of vitriol on behalf of her southern countrymen to desire reconciliation.

Further, this scene suggests that with education combined with commemoration, African Americans will have a role to play in the future of the nation. This theme is continued later in the story when black Americans are the only characters to remember Memorial Day.[28] None of the white townsfolk come to the cemetery on that day, and even Rodman has forgotten the holiday until a stream of African Americans, old and young, bring flowers to the Union dead in a ceremony that unites them with citizens across the nation. Although the narrator portrays the black memorializers patronizingly, noting that "they know dimly that the men who lay beneath those mounds had done something wonderful for them and for their children," the importance of the ceremony to the future of black participation in the nation is clear (141). That evening, Rodman spies Pomp taking flowers to the cemetery mounds; "he had performed his part," says the narrator (141). In this moment of memorialization, Pomp and the other ex-slaves of Woolson's scarred town are able to cross boundaries—hostile town and "national" cemetery—that others in the story cannot or refuse to traverse.

The story suggests that it is only those who possess this ability to move across boundaries who will prosper in the unified country and enjoy the benefits of citizenship and belonging. For example, the story ends with Rodman visiting the old De Rosset home and encountering the new owner, "one of those sandy-haired, energetic Maine men, who ... were often found through the South, making new homes for themselves in the pleasant land" (145). While many of Woolson's characters are defined in relation to the cemetery's borders, the Maine man cannot see them at all; he "already knew everybody within a circle of five miles" (146). The story's exploration of internal boundaries uncovers where the nation's power does and does not extend. The national cemetery represents a physical space embodying U.S. control in an unruly region that would like as little to do with it as possible; as Bettina states, "the South *is* our country, and not your North" (145). Woolson analyzes the fissures still apparent in the reunited nation that were increasingly effaced as the U.S. government effectively colonized the Reconstructed South.[29] Within the story, nostalgia is always for a prewar version of the South, and it is clear through her portrayal of the desolated land and the dying De Rossets that Woolson has some sympathy for these nostalgic southerners. We might read "Rodman the Keeper" as a critique of American imperial aggression within its own borders, though by refusing to marry Bettina to Rodman and exiling her and her brand of Lost Cause memory to another part of the South at the story's end, Woolson's tale seems reluctant to blame either the restored Union or the embittered former Confederacy for the borders erected by both sides.

Though "Rodman the Keeper" portrays some characters who are able to cross boundaries, like Pomp and the Maine man at the story's close, its ending reasserts the hegemony of those boundaries: Rodman will return to the cemetery; De Rosset is dead, and Bettina and Pomp have retreated to Tennessee. A scene in which Pomp learns to read from the memorial may suggest that education and commemoration together will allow blacks full participation in the country's future. The first version of the story, published in the *Atlantic*, affirms this point in a conversation between Rodman and Bettina. As Bettina pays her last and only visit to the cemetery, their talk turns to what Bettina calls "the state of our servants." Rodman says that they are in "transition" and that education will be the savior of southern blacks and whites alike (147–48). This conversation was later excised from the version collected in *Rodman the Keeper: Southern Sketches* (1880). Woolson's (or her publisher's) decision to remove these key lines betrays the tale's ultimate doubt in the ability of monumental pedagogy to dissolve the internal boundaries of the purportedly reconstructed nation and heal the scars of war made visible by national cemeteries. This skepticism about the possibilities of racial uplift in the orderless occupied South, particularly with regard to black education, is also evident in Woolson's story "King David." The white South will continue to reject national rule, both stories insist, rendering the attempts of black southerners to enter the nation's citizenry futile. "Rodman the Keeper" thus portrays the postwar regionalization of the South as both an occupation (of the land that white southerners claim as their own) and an opportunity (for black southerners to realize the promises made to them by the nation), ending in stalemate and the persistence of borders that keep out and keep in.

Reframing the Margins of Regionalism

The contested places that emerged during and after the Civil War were settings in which multiple forces contended for power, particularly over the fate of African Americans. Davis's vision of war-torn America shows how slavery destroys black and white men alike, while Woolson's postbellum rendering of southern and northern war memory attempts to but ultimately cannot reconcile African Americans into a nation still divided by place *and* race. Both Davis and Woolson emphasize that the war's real impact took place at the local level, in grievances between families and within relationships modeled on families, like those between masters and slaves, in specific places that bore traces of the war's impact. These stories remind us that while the genre of regionalism indeed serves as a site where the evidence of regionalization can be catalogued and resisted, we cannot get rid of the place in regionalism. Indeed, certain characteristics of the places where these stories are set—the borderland of West Virginia and the internal island of the "national" cemetery—lend these tales a logic through which the nation can be critiqued from within.

To close, I will return to *Near Andersonville* by way of an 1874 letter by Woolson titled "In the South" and published in the *Cleveland Daily Herald*.[30] At the end of a folksy epistle brimming with observances about southern character, Woolson tells the story of her trip to a national cemetery built on the location of a Confederate prison in North Carolina. With a few spare hours between trains, Woolson visits the cemetery and meets its keeper, a man much like Rodman, who laments the few visitors to the hallowed ground, even on decoration day: "The colored people come in crowds, bringing their best flowers," he tells Woolson, "but not a white face."[31] Woolson returns to her traveling companions and one of them, a white southern woman, asks how she spent her time in Salisbury:

> "Can you not imagine," I said, "where I would naturally go?" No; she evidently had no idea. A colored maid stood in the corner of the room, Southern fashion, in case I should need something; I beckoned to her to come forward.
> "I am a Northerner, as you probably know," I said; "now where do you think I went in the hour I had here before dark?"
> "To the soldiers' cemetery, m'am," she answered, instantly, dropping a little courtesy as she spoke.
> "You see *she* knows," I said.[32]

Woolson's peripheral maid, who seems to have directly inspired the story of Pomp's remembrance in "Rodman the Keeper," leads us back to the woman in Homer's *Near Andersonville*. By placing an African American woman at the center of his Civil War painting, Homer prioritizes her experience of war in a way that these stories initially license but eventually shut down. Depicted on a threshold—is she coming or going?—the woman's fate remains uncertain, unlike the fates of Ben and Pomp. What will be her place in the nation that remained after the Civil War? Homer reframes the margins of the war to focus on the periphery as an end unto itself, shifting perspective in order to demonstrate that race is central to making meaning out of the war. Regionalism, in its desire to make sense of national space, to sort through the complex structures of power governing the region in relation to the nation and the individual citizen in relation to the land, attempts to perform a similar sort of reframing. As we continue to explicate how regionalism intervenes in processes of national power and local resistance, we must also remain attentive to the ways it perpetuates certain societal hierarchies even as it disputes others.

NOTES

1. For a thorough study of the painting's history and meanings, see Peter H. Wood, *Near Andersonville: Winslow Homer's Civil War* (Cambridge: Harvard University Press, 2010).

2. Daniel Aaron, *The Unwritten War: American Writers and the Civil War* (Tuscaloosa: University of Alabama Press, 1973), xxii.

3. Ibid.

4. Ta-Nehisi Coates, "Why Do So Few Blacks Study the Civil War?," *The Atlantic*, November 30, 2011, http://www.theatlantic.com/magazine/archive/2012/02/why-do-so-few-blacks-study-the-civil-war/308831/.

5. Toni Morrison, *Playing in the Dark: Whiteness and the Literary Imagination* (Cambridge: Harvard University Press, 1992), 5.

6. Thomas Constantinesco and Cécile Roudeau, "Limning New Regions of Thought: Emerson's Abstract Regionalism," *ESQ: A Journal of the American Renaissance* 60, no. 2 (2014): 285.

7. Stephanie Foote, "'I Feared to Find Myself a Foreigner': Revisiting Regionalism in Sarah Orne Jewett's *Country of the Pointed Firs*," *Arizona Quarterly* 52, no. 2, (1996): 37.

8. Judith Fetterley and Marjorie Pryse, *Writing Out of Place: Regionalism, Women, and American Literary Culture* (Urbana: University of Illinois Press, 2003), 7, hereafter documented parenthetically.

9. The dividing lines between the genres of realism, local color, and regionalism are notoriously difficult to draw. I categorize Davis and Woolson as early regionalists because of their engagement with locations outside the nation's cosmopolitan centers and with issues of regionalization. Davis and Woolson have rarely been anthologized as regionalist writers, though *The Portable American Realism Reader* (New York: Penguin, 1997) includes "Rodman the Keeper" under the category "Regionalism and Local Color" (while leaving out Davis altogether). For more on anthologies and generic descriptors, see Fetterley and Pryse, *Writing Out*, 8–9.

10. Although a great deal of important critical work has considered regionalism's complicity with American colonialism and structural racism, not as much attention has been paid to the genre's relation to the great national crisis of the Civil War. For one example of a reading of a key regionalist text in light of its rewriting of the Civil War, see Edward Gillin, "Joshua Lawrence Chamberlain and the Old Soldier of *The Country of the Pointed Firs*," *War, Literature, and the Arts: An International Journal of the Humanities* 16, nos. 1/2 (2004): 86–103.

11. Amy Kaplan, "Nation, Region, and Empire," in *The Columbia History of the American Novel*, ed. Emory Elliott, Cathy N. Davidson, Patrick O'Donnell, Valerie Smith, and Christopher P. Wilson (New York: Columbia University Press, 1991), 242.

12. Ralph Waldo Emerson, *The Journals and Miscellaneous Notebooks of Ralph Waldo Emerson*, ed. Linda Allardt, David W. Hill, assoc. ed. Ruth H. Bennett, vol. 15, *1860–1866* (Cambridge: Harvard University Press, 1982), 64.

13. Anne Baker, *Heartless Immensity: Literature, Culture, and Geography in Antebellum America* (Ann Arbor: University of Michigan Press, 2006), 9.

14. Michel Foucault, "Of Other Spaces," trans. Jay Miskowiec, *Diacritics* 16, no. 1 (1986): 24, hereafter documented parenthetically.

15. John Funchion, "Reading Less Littorally: Kentucky and the Translocal Imagination in the Atlantic World," *Early American Literature* 48, no. 1 (2013): 63.

16. John McElroy, *Andersonville: A Story of Rebel Military Prisons* (Toledo: D. R. Locke, 1879), 127.

17. Western (West) Virginia sent nearly thirty-five thousand soldiers to fight for the Union, but another ten thousand enlisted with the Confederacy. See Sharon M. Harris and Robin L. Cadwallader, introduction to *Rebecca Harding Davis: Stories of the Civil War Era* (Athens: University of Georgia Press, 2010), xxxiv.

18. Rebecca Harding Davis, *Bits of Gossip* (Boston: Houghton, Mifflin, 1904), 109.

19. Ibid., 111–12.

20. Funchion, "Reading Less Littorally," 65.

21. Judith Fetterley and Marjorie Pryse, *American Women Regionalists 1850–1910* (New York: W. W. Norton, 1992), xvii–xviii.

22. Rebecca Harding Davis, "John Lamar," in *Rebecca Harding Davis: Stories of the Civil War Era*, ed. Sharon M. Harris and Robin L. Cadwallader (Athens: University of Georgia Press, 2010), 1, hereafter documented parenthetically.

23. In their introduction to *American Women Regionalists*, Fetterley and Pryse assert that this relationship between place and self-discovery is one of the defining themes of regionalism (xvi).

24. Constance Fenimore Woolson, "Rodman the Keeper," in *Constance Fenimore Woolson: Selected Stories and Travel Narratives*, ed. Victoria Brehm and Sharon L. Dean (Knoxville: University of Tennessee Press, 2004), 126, hereafter cited parenthetically.

25. For more on stories of postwar reconciliation, see Nina Silber, *The Romance of Reunion: Northerners and the South, 1865–1900* (Chapel Hill: University of North Carolina Press, 1997).

26. For more on the role of the national cemetery in Woolson's story, see Martin T. Buinicki, "Imagining Sites of Memory in the Post–Civil War South: The National Cemetery in Woolson's 'Rodman the Keeper,'" in *Witness to Reconstruction: Constance Fenimore Woolson and the Postbellum South, 1873–1894*, ed. Kathleen Diffley (Jackson: University Press of Mississippi, 2011), 162–76.

27. Benjamin G. Cloyd, *Haunted by Atrocity: Civil War Prisons in American Memory* (Baton Rouge: Louisiana State University Press, 2010), 9.

28. For more on the origins of Memorial Day, see David W. Blight, *Race and Reunion: The Civil War in American Memory* (Cambridge: Belknap Press, 2001), esp. chap. 3, "Decoration Days."

29. For a summarization of studies that have argued for considering the postwar South as an occupied U.S. colony, and for more on Woolson's ambivalent relation to the Reconstructed South, see Anne E. Boyd (Rioux), "Tourism, Imperialism, and Hybridity in the Reconstruction South: Woolson's 'Rodman the Keeper: Southern Sketches,'" in *Witness to Reconstruction: Constance Fenimore Woolson and the Postbellum South, 1873–1894*, ed. Kathleen Diffley (Jackson: University Press of Mississippi, 2011), 56–72.

30. My thanks to Anne Boyd Rioux for bringing this letter to the attention of the Woolson Listserv.

31. Constance Fenimore Woolson, "In the South," *Cleveland Daily Herald*, October 7, 1874, 2.

32. Ibid.

Emancipation and Grizzly Reckoning
The Advent of Photography,
California's Overland Monthly,
and the Model of Parallax

——————◆◆◆——————

KATHLEEN DIFFLEY

The principle of parallax is older than the nineteenth century, older than Copernicus, older than Ptolemy. Even Aristotle, who believed the earth stood still, knew that a stellar body seemed to move when observed from different vantage points. That apparent shift does not have to be Greek to anybody: just hold a finger out at arm's length, cover one eye, then cover the other. Any pair of eyes provides two slightly different points of view, which help to place what is observed and also secure a depth of field as the stereo camera once did in the nineteenth century. (See figure 7.) On a larger scale, the parallax of heavenly bodies can be determined from at least two different sites more than a few miles apart, or from the same site more than a few weeks apart and therefore at different stages of the earth's yearlong revolution around the sun. Adept at such measurements, Asaph Hall at the U.S. Naval Observatory determined, between August and October 1877, that the planet Mars had two undiscovered moons, which he named Phobos and Deimos or "Panic" and "Terror," after the *Iliad*'s two minions of the god of war.

In a similar fashion, the United States, which only slowly began taking a singular verb after the principle of a looser confederacy was defeated, coalesced during the nineteenth century. Out of differing points of view and then the invocation of war, a powerful General Government emerged in 1865 together with a newly paramount national citizenship, as the jurisdiction of postwar states receded. At this tense moment of political consolidation and cultural opportunity, what quite a few Americans had in hand as they tried to define a reconstructing

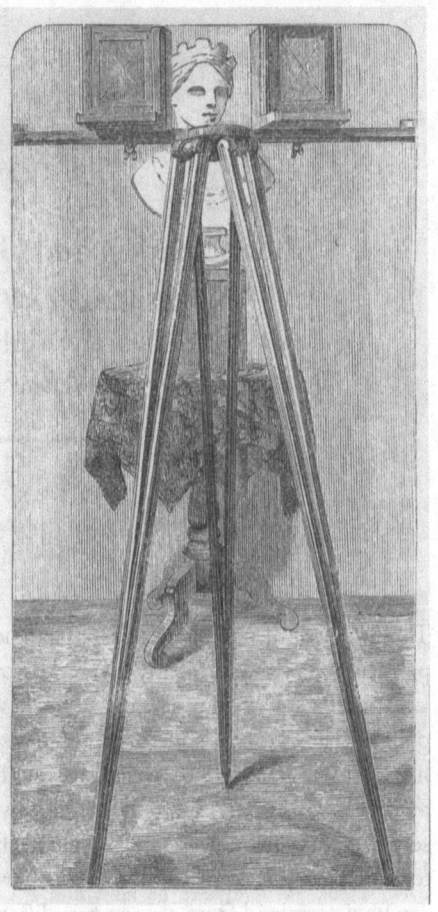

FIGURE 7. "Taking Stereoscopic Picture of Near Objects," from Austin Abbott, "The Eye and Camera." *Harper's Monthly*, September 1869, 480. Wood engraving. Courtesy of the University of Iowa Libraries.

union were battlefield pictures, most provocatively, the first stereo views of Antietam soldiers where they fell in September 1862. Indeed, what the *New York Times* called "dripping bodies" with "a terrible distinctness" were made both more familiar and more unnerving by the fact that Mathew Brady had been marketing these Maryland pictures to northern parlors, while operator Alexander Gardner had anticipated Brady's gallery business by taking most of his Antietam photographs as stereo views.[1]

From photography's wartime advances as well as Asaph Hall's heavenly spectacle, three instructive points follow for understanding how many Americans first made the Civil War coherent. These points are grounded, like binocular vision, in the principle of parallax. First, the irregular double image of the stereo view, which is constructed of two photographs taken roughly two-and-a-half inches apart like a pair of eyes, may serve as a model for the irregular double vision of the Civil War that would emerge after Antietam's horrific casualties. In late 1862 disquieting photographs were suddenly compared in record numbers to the artistic drawings made for new illustrated magazines, which often celebrated the regiments with which special artists traveled. Also made on the spot, such drawings contrasted sharply with the "dripping bodies" that Gardner discovered and Brady displayed. Even more insistently, these new visual technologies clashed at the very moment that Abraham Lincoln announced the Preliminary Emancipation Proclamation. The stereo model of "fraternally twinned images," in Miles Orvell's apt phrase, thus offered an available cultural logic across representational mediums that were at odds and across civil rupture to the emancipated postwar nation, not at all the Union as it was.[2]

Second, the stereo model can also be extended to Civil War stories as decidedly different exercises in commemoration from decidedly different sites like Boston and San Francisco. In fact, postwar California and Bret Harte's new literary magazine, the *Overland Monthly*, took advantage of an unusual distance from the East and its parochial perspective to cast San Francisco as exotically polyglot, truly Olympian Boston's fraternal twin and the country's demographic future. In issue after issue, the magazine's booster agenda favored a keen sense of otherness that proved receptive to the claims of new black citizens. In its backward glance to the war years, the *Overland Monthly* also published a clutch of stories so idiosyncratic that they can be explained, in part, by the earlier crowding of the Forty-Niners and the continuing pull of San Francisco for so many from so many other places, even years after gold was first discovered. Repeatedly, the Civil War narratives circulated by the *Overland Monthly* directly challenged eastern priorities through their unusual witness, which intensified the competition of visual logics with a further dissonance in perspective that readers were left to resolve.

Finally, the emerging habit of seeing stereoscopically, like the more recent hankering for instant replay, created a significant postwar opportunity for imagining how new African American citizens might augment the body politic. Again, the stereo view is instructive since its illusory depth bespoke the necessary ascendancy of the viewer, who alone could contrive a merging of images and a "virtual reality" whose three-dimensional field was nowhere visible on the pasteboard card. By analogy, it was up to magazine readers to envision a parallactic postwar nation, one whose imagined dimension and reconstructive audacity might spring in part from perusing regional magazines. In the culture wars that actually intensified after 1865, when the Thirteenth Amendment unlocked slavery's chains without defining emancipation's freedoms, magazines like the *Overland Monthly* published unpredictable Civil War stories whose promise and invitation have remained largely unexplored. Similar to other regional contenders during the 1860s and 1870s, which were all cultural moons of a sort with any new satellite's unexamined trajectory, Bret Harte's magazine was both captured by and separate from the eastern periodical behemoths that students of Reconstruction have been slow to set aside.

Such developments had yet to crest the national horizon as negotiations surrounding the Emancipation Proclamation took shape during the summer of 1862, when Lincoln willingly tied the extension of civil liberties to elusive battlefield success. The Union victory in September at the battle of Antietam allowed Lincoln to move forward and ultimately tied the rights of black citizens to the force that new social relations would require. "Thenceforward and forever," as Stephen Sears has written, "the United States would be a very different nation."[3] As James M. McPherson has added, "the symbolic power of the Proclamation changed the war from one to restore the Union into one to destroy the old Union and build a new one purged of human bondage."[4] Unfortunately for the president and the "new birth of freedom" he would underline at Gettysburg, what the Army of the Potomac found along Antietam Creek in the midst of a warm Indian summer was a bloodbath, as Mathew Brady's photographic exhibition would shortly reveal.[5] More than 150 years later, September 17, 1862, remains the single bloodiest day in American military history, a day on which more than 23,000 men were reported dead, wounded, captured, or missing in action.

Yet the threat of military disaster little more than sixty miles from Washington produced a further opportunity, even before the Preliminary Emancipation Proclamation was issued on September 22, less than a week later. Fortuitously, Antietam Creek and the town of Sharpsburg lay close enough to Brady's Washington gallery for Alexander Gardner and his assistant James Gibson to make their way into Maryland with armloads of photographic supplies right after the smoke cleared.[6] The Army of Northern Virginia actually refused to retire following the long afternoon's losses, and the battle of Antietam remained a standoff for another hot September day, while intermittent truces were declared so the wounded could be moved. On the field that General Lee and his army finally left behind, Brady's operators discovered burial parties just setting out and bloated bodies beginning to decompose, like those photographed along the right wing's sunken mill road soon to be known as Bloody Lane. (See figure 8.)

The raw force of such stereo views can best be understood by way of the visual norms these images defied. In the immediate wake of battle, anxious readers generally looked to the new illustrated weeklies, whose wood engravings quickly augmented battlefield dispatches and casualty reports. By the fall of 1862 special artists like Edwin Forbes, who had been traveling with the Army of the Poto-

FIGURE 8. Alexander Gardner, "The 'Sunken Road' at Antietam." Stereo view. Courtesy of the Library of Congress, LC-DIG-ppmsca-07751.

mac for months, were "on the spot" for what he called "the most picturesque battle of the war," by which he meant that specials at Antietam could see the battle unfold across open fields from the comparative safety of reserve batteries.[7] What Forbes witnessed and then drew that September afternoon was printed in *Frank Leslie's Illustrated Weekly* as "Brilliant and Decisive Bayonet Charge of Hawkins's Zouaves," a double-page engraving of the moment when the 9th New York Volunteers poured across fields and meadows, then up over a stone wall and into the roar of Confederate artillery, the flash of rebel muskets. (See figure 9.) Their charge was to cost the larger brigade of 940 some 455 men, but the cheering New Yorkers would see rebels running through the streets of Sharpsburg.[8]

In the illustration that *Leslie's* engraved, some of the New York volunteers have already fallen, but Forbes's composition takes its visual excitement from those still standing: from the distinctive uniforms of the Zouaves, as well as the muzzles they load and the bayonets they hoist to give the illustration its title. Significantly, the flag that the soldiers raise in the left foreground has not yet been struck down, as it would be repeatedly when Confederate guns opened fire. Instead, those Confederate batteries are consigned to the engraving's sketchy background, an arrangement that translates the shallow field of the medium into the sketchy inadequacy of the Confederate cause. Special artists like Forbes, who traveled at the pleasure of Union generals and the expense of the army they accompanied, had every reason to align their political loyalties with their professional interests as they drew for the wood block, especially since the newsmagazines they supplied were serving largely northern audiences by 1862.

As a result, the "picturesque" moments that readers discovered usually gave

FIGURE 9. Edwin Forbes, "Brilliant and Decisive Bayonet Charge of Hawkins's Zouaves." *Frank Leslie's Illustrated Weekly*, October 11, 1862, 40–41. Wood engraving. Courtesy of the University of Iowa Libraries.

FIGURE 10. Edwin Forbes, "The battle of Antietam—Charge of Burnside's 9th Corps, on the right flank of the Confederate army, 3:30 p.m., Sept. 17th, 1862." Sketch in pencil and Chinese white. Courtesy of the Library of Congress, LC-DIG-ppmsca-22526.

greater dimension and weight to the Union regiments they celebrated, which were often filled from the ranks of weekly readers.[9] In northern parlors as well as Union camps, it was thus reassuring to peruse New York's *Leslie's Illustrated*, which had been founded in 1852 and generally relied for its war coverage on artistic drawings made hastily from the field. No matter what special artists chose to portray, they began with a blank sheet that invited quick lines, like those Forbes made in his pencil sketch of the Zouave charge. (See figure 10.) In the scribbled notes he added to guide the New York art department, Forbes even numbered the points of interest he had decided to include, like "2—The old Lutheran church" and "5—Rebel line of battle." From blank sheet to sketch and from notes to engraving, specials thereby articulated a logic of constructed space.

No wonder, then, that Brady's October exhibition of Antietam photographs brought New York gallery visitors up short, while stirring local journals to consider an unpicturesque war stripped of apparent design. Noting the difference between the morning casualty lists and the startling images Brady displayed, like a view of Antietam's vicious early fighting, the *New York Times* spoke of their "dull, dead, remorseless weight" on breaking hearts and of "the horrible significance that dwells amid the jumble of type."[10] (See figure 11.) Where the dead in Forbes's drawing amounted to battlefield obstacles and visual litter, Alexander Gardner's views for Brady took such obstacles as central, and the litter of battlefield concussion became Gardner's recurring visual theme. Routinely, photographic operators were confronted with a scene that was always already there, always already what Peter Galassi has called "the intractably three-dimensional stuff of the world."[11] Particularly along the fence line of the Hagerstown Pike, Gardner's photographs from Maryland suggested a logic of irrelevant detail: among the rotting bodies of the Confederate dead, it scarcely mattered which arm was raised or which rail was down. Instead of Forbes's converging lines of battle, Gardner's stereo view of Antietam's "contest" favored endless detritus; William Frassanito speculates, in fact, that Gardner could identify General Starke's Louisiana brigade by the insignia on one soldier's knapsack, which gallery visitors could inspect with a magnifying glass.[12] But when growing numbers of viewers recalled what they had seen in illustrated weeklies, the divergences of the new mediums were difficult to reconcile.

In negotiating the clash between Forbes's boundless glory and Gardner's boundless litter, the very task of seeing stereoscopically, baffled Americans were likeliest to get help from other pages of the illustrated weeklies and from other magazines that carried stories of the Civil War. Particularly in the aftermath of Antietam's losses, the stories circulated in literary magazines revealed a similar dissonance when they began fluctuating between the familiar and the unconventional in their narrative design. Sentences in Antietam stories started to fall apart with the "whir" of chance bullets, the broken mutterings of rough soldiers,

FIGURE 11. Alexander Gardner, "Antietam, Maryland. Bodies of dead, Louisiana Regiment." Stereo view, right half. Courtesy of the Library of Congress, LC-DIG-cwpb-01105.

and the abrupt emergence of dialect. In addition, customary past-tense narration sometimes faltered when present-tense interruptions became more acute. More broadly, the formal tension between narrators in their summaries and characters in their scenes accelerated as authoritative narrators lost verbal ground to a vernacular litter. In these Antietam stories for a host of magazines across the country, the rounded perspective that narrative omniscience shared with artistic drawing was increasingly challenged by the rude details, irrelevant and obtrusive, that surfaced in dialogue and photograph alike as the insurgency of characters with things to say challenged the directing hand of a narrator and the assurances of a stable order. In place of photographic sprawl, however, the stories of Antietam repeatedly favored the ascendancy of a minor character, one able to read a divided *dramatis personae* and therefore likely to teach magazine readers how to discover depth by bringing disparities into focus.

The quiet mediation of these nameless narrators suggests not only the synthetic task of the midwar reader but also the growing importance of the midcentury "observer," Jonathan Crary's term for marking the nineteenth-century shift away from the status of things seen and toward the dynamics of seeing. For Crary, the stereoscope serves as the representative medium of that shift, while the camera obscura embodies the certainties of perspective that were fast dissolving. As he points out, the stereoscope imitated human vision by achieving depth through reconciling disparities, specifically through the observer's "apprehension of differences" when images were inexact.[13] But reconciling disparities could be a dangerous undertaking during and after the Civil War, as George Ward Nichols revealed in "The General's Story" (*Harper's Monthly*, June 1867), where narrative complications provide a revealing example. Years after the shock of casualty lists, it was not the friction of glory and litter that torqued his account but the frightening possibility of becoming stereoscopic, of playing different parts long enough that identity itself became malleable across an ever deepening field.

In "The General's Story," doubling is so rampant (the double identity of the narrator as spy, the double spy he meets in prison, the double narrative generated by the frame story) that observation repeatedly invites "metamorphosis," until the Antietam captain retreats into himself while the postwar general he becomes drops the narrative reins for the safety of the frame story's fireside. Returning home to Washington, the general declares: "With the name of Peters I shook off that terrible nightmare of suspense. I awoke, as it were, from a horrible dream where I had been playing a part, where I had been a helpless actor to my own personality. A restful, thankful, happy consciousness was it, when I was free, when I came to know myself again." The "horrible significance" of the general's "dream" is that personal freedom for a spy depended on acting the helpless twin, the hapless citizen of Baltimore instead of the resourceful Pennsylvania captain, the "careless flaneur" of Richmond instead of Secretary Seward's spy.[14] It was an unsettling lesson in binocular vision, what W. E. B. Du Bois would later call "double consciousness," that the country's slaves and freedpeople already knew. Even before *The Souls of Black Folk* appeared in 1903, Du Bois wrote in "Strivings of the Negro People" for the *Atlantic Monthly* (August 1897) about how "being a problem" felt. "It is a peculiar sensation," he observed, "this double consciousness, this sense of always looking at one's self through the eyes of others."[15] As "The General's Story" reveals, something akin to double consciousness was a wartime lesson that many white Americans were only beginning to learn.

By January 1863, when the Emancipation Proclamation went into effect, the habit of seeing stereoscopically was spreading almost as quickly as the handheld stereoscope, which was invented by Oliver Wendell Holmes in 1861 and became an immediate mainstay on parlor tables. Holmes himself wrote of the eye's uneasy balance in "The Professor's Story," which was serialized in the *Atlantic Monthly* beginning in December 1859 and would be retitled *Elsie Venner*, Holmes's first novel. Taking up the real and the ideal that the infatuated lover "blended," Holmes in one installment (October 1860) observed: "The heart's vision cannot unite them stereoscopically into a single image, if the divergence passes certain limits."[16] Still, the *Atlantic Monthly* kept the possibility alive some years later in a review of Thomas Wentworth Higginson's *Oldport Days* (January 1874), which cast the poet as seeing the "literal" and the ideal "in one stereoscopic view," just as Asa Gray's earlier review of Darwin's *Origin of Species* (August 1860) played the radical claims of Darwin against those of the temperate Lyell "like the two counterpart pictures for the stereoscope" that together made "one apparently solid whole."[17] Such a reasoned venture, the making of "one apparently solid whole," eluded the domestic Holmes when he looked at Brady's views of Antietam. In "Doings of the Sunbeam" (July 1863), he admitted that he shoved the photographs of "fragments and tatters" into the far corners of his cabinet where "mutilated remains" belonged.[18] Like so many other viewers who recalled illustrated periodicals, Holmes and the *Atlantic Monthly* were left with what Keith Davis calls "the brutal inertness of death" and a troubling tension between litter and glory.[19]

It is therefore significant that the *Overland Monthly* (1868–75) was founded in a decidedly plural San Francisco as an alternative register, a fundamental challenge, a fraternal twin. The magazine's very name was coined, in fact, to defy the cultural hegemony of the Northeast. Writing his first "ETC." column for the magazine's debut in July 1868, editor Bret Harte began his two-and-a-half-year tenure by declaring: "'Pacific Monthly' is hackneyed, mild in suggestion, and at best but a feeble echo of the Boston 'Atlantic.'"[20] Harte further dismissed possibilities like the "Wide West" as "threadbare," the "Occidental" as "cheap pedantry," and the "Sunset" as "cheaper sentiment." Instead, it was the railroad, "the highway of our thought" as he put it, that would deliver western "breadth and liberality" in one direction and eastern "refinement" in the other, a transaction that was important enough to put the railroad track on the magazine's title page. (See figure 12.) Astutely, Harte sketched the track's twin lines beneath California's grizzly bear and its "primitive" defiance, a sign that the *Overland Monthly* would not take backwater status kindly when the "development of the country" was uppermost.[21]

By way of contrast, consider what the *Atlantic Monthly* held dear, embodied

FIGURE 12. First issue title page. *Overland Monthly*, July 1868. Wood engraving. Courtesy of the University of Iowa Libraries.

on another title page. (See figure 13.) From its founding in 1857, the Boston magazine had opposed slavery with the kind of zeal that added a postwar liberty cap to its iconic stars and stripes. The New England pledge to individual freedom was thereby celebrated in a national commitment to "Yankee humanism," as Ellery Sedgwick has described the *Atlantic*'s mission in his study of its nineteenth-century enterprise. But the extension of civil rights to African Americans did not abbreviate the magazine's certainty that the common good, figured in the nation's flag, required New England's leadership and the priorities of its educated elite. As Sedgwick observes, "This resistance to the democratic principle of majority rule in intellectual, aesthetic, and ethical issues and the attempt to reconcile social democracy with an authoritative hierarchy of cultural values were reflected in the *Atlantic* throughout the 19th century and beyond."[22] An

FIGURE 13. Wartime title page image. *Atlantic Monthly*, January 1865. Wood engraving. Courtesy of the University of Iowa Libraries.

antebellum allegiance to Old Glory, in other words, was an allegiance to Yankee oversight and to the literary mastery that gave the *Atlantic Monthly* unparalleled cultural capital.

Naturally Boston's smug prestige inflected narrative priorities in stories about the war, most noticeably through the verbal grip of contributors like western Virginia's Rebecca Harding Davis. In "John Lamar" (April 1862), Davis casts the conflict between soon warring sections as a competition between rivals in love, two western Virginia boys whose continuing friendship and toast to "Liberty!" epitomize antebellum ideals, North and South, that were already diverging. Committed to their sectional differences, Davis's protagonists nonetheless share a thoughtless disregard for two unexpected characters: an evangelical Union volunteer from Illinois and the "gladiator" slave he inflames to murder.[23] These two arresting portraits—sharp-edged, colloquial, malignant—make mincemeat of ongoing sectional debate and John Lamar's southern solution to slavery's injustice, a gradual education in work and ambition that miscalculates his slave's gathering revenge.

Thanks in part to Davis's deft hand, the *Atlantic Monthly* sustained its early lien on canonical authority. But emancipation complicated the stories that less elitist magazines would tell, especially from a polyglot western metropole where social relations were already unsettled. In *The Public City: The Political Construction of Urban Life in San Francisco*, Philip Ethington points to what he calls "the climate of the social revolution unleashed by the Emancipation Proclamation," which made race rather than republican virtue a determining priority and thereby upset an antebellum sense of the common good.²⁴ Beginning in 1863, Ethington argues, the country's prevailing political model would derive instead from social groups and their competing interests. In the ten eccentric Civil War stories that the *Overland Monthly* circulated, and particularly in the four that reckoned with race, a fundamental shift from individual initiative to group dynamics, from personal liberty to public service, and from established consensus to social contention defied Boston's high-toned example and reoriented the play of postwar storytelling.

San Francisco's rough iconoclasm and the *Overland*'s journeyman challenge produced a Davis "twin" in the lesser known, un-famous Freeman S. Bowley. As Keith Wilson has documented, Freeman Sparks Bowley was a seventeen-year-old from Maine when he enlisted as a white officer in the Thirtieth United States Colored Infantry (USCT) during the war's final year, before he emigrated to San Francisco in 1868 for work as a fireman on the Southern Pacific Railroad and began publishing stories drawn from his wartime experience.²⁵ Bowley's "A Dark Night on Picket" (July 1870) in the *Overland* depicts black military service with none of Davis's verbal audacity, none of her narrative recalculations, none of her slave Ben's vengeful muscle. Bowley's recollection of colored troops near Richmond foregrounds the "groan of superstition" and faceless voices in the dark, especially when contrasted with his well-spoken Division Officer of the Day. What Bowley describes as the "maniac laugh" of a great horned owl is actually more memorable than his colored men in the ranks ("a Sergeant," "my reserve," "the vidette") who come and go in a less accomplished narrative economy without names, without features, pretty much without character. Against Davis's sharp portraits, they are a blur.

Yet they can handle musket barrels and bayonets, and they capture rebel prisoners despite their carbines while fending off their "large, ferocious, yellow dogs."²⁶ Narratively inexact, they nonetheless register the African American claim to the perquisites of citizenship via military service. Bowley's black soldiers on picket do not talk much and when they do it is in the predictable dialect of "good Lordy hab mussy!"²⁷ But where Davis casts the fight for freedom as an exercise in bold initiative, personal and insurgent, Bowley's narrative fumbles treat the black lien on civil liberties en masse, not only as an undifferentiated group effort but as an effort by the only group—the USCT—that historically counted. Davis could not have served Boston's *Atlantic* better than in her slave master's parting tribute: "When we stand where New England does, Ben's son will be ready for his freedom."²⁸ Even in its irony, her delineation of black power amounts to single-handed combat, personal gumption, and a commitment to the founding ideals that rippled on the magazine's title page. But Bowley's submergence of character in crowd, of fetching talk in silent obedience, of Ben's "glittering knife" in the musket barrels of disciplined troops, is a reminder that slave revolts were ultimately less numerous than black enlistments, which the *Overland Monthly* was almost the only postwar magazine to portray.

Two decades after the discovery of gold and the California dream of instant wealth, readers who encountered Bowley's story were accustomed to the western habit of self-promotion and what David Wyatt has called "the peculiarly overdeveloped ability of Californians to frame experience as spectacle."[29] Almost without exception, the Civil War stories that appeared in the *Overland Monthly* run like Bowley's on a kind of theatricality, similar to the tableaux vivants of nineteenth-century theater. Arguably, all stories are portals to another place and an imagined sequence of events. But the *Overland Monthly*'s stories of the war are repeatedly and consciously staged, with a surreptitious wink to readers as spectators. Sometimes that means street scenes as theater sets; in G. T. Shipley's "Saint Saviour of the Bay" (October 1868), a Federal naval officer entering Bahia notes "doors opening into nowhere; columns carrying nothing; windows giving light to nobody; stairways ending in vacancy; red walls, green walls, blue walls, yellow walls, all jumbled together."[30] Elsewhere, that means phantasmagoric vision; in Henry King's "The Cabin at Pharaoh's Ford" (December 1874), an abolitionist parson's addled daughter is chained to her Kansas bed when he departs for his midnight errands, and it is her "fevered dream" that includes a "monster harp of gold" and a "chorus of many voices" in a scene of orchestrated glory.[31] More generally, there's a tendency toward roles, masks, spies, and disguises, often conspicuously described by minor characters who narrate. The magazine's most conventional story about race, written by later kindergarten activist Sarah B. Cooper and titled "Old Uncle Hampshire" (November 1872), easily recalls the best-selling Uncle Tom in an aging slave's convenient loyalty to a white plantation home. But in the *Overland Monthly*, he fends off local bushwhackers through the "outward meekness that served as an opportune disguise for a burning indignation."[32] In the drama Uncle Hampshire stages on Cooper's "spacious verandah," even a stereotype gets to direct because he understands both implicit theatricality and how to ad lib.[33]

Far from Boston's "Yankee humanism," these narratives seem born of deft staging and ready script, no doubt for good reason. As Douglas Henry Daniels has observed in *Urban Pioneers*, his social and cultural history of black success in California's premier city, "life in San Francisco was itself a charade, for appearances counted as much as origins."[34] Scratch an *Overland Monthly* story of the war, and it is worth noticing who sees, since even minor characters can play major roles when bringing Ethington's "interest groups" into focus. As Crary puts it when describing his paradigmatic stereoscope, its cards, and their viewers, "the illusion of relief or depth was thus a subjective event, and the observer coupled with the apparatus was the agent of synthesis or fusion."³⁵ The quiet vehicles for synthesis, Crary's observers can become the unacknowledged center of their mediated narratives, the kinds of stories that Wendy Bellion describes as "artifacts of spectatorship as well as place."³⁶ So it is worth looking more closely at a final and more intricate story, "An Episode of 'Fort Desolation'" (March 1871), probably the *Overland Monthly*'s most peculiar venture in charting emancipation.

Written by Josephine Clifford, who eventually escaped her abusive husband and a frontier fort by heading west to family in San Francisco, this "episode" concerns the military shift after Appomattox from a sectional civil war to a western assault on the Indians, specifically after "colored" regiments were redeployed. In 1866, as the Union's armies were disbanding and their men mustering out, the 125th USCT was posted instead to the New Mexico Territory. Having volunteered in Kentucky during 1865 and thus the war's final spring, the newly enlisted black recruits were not on their way home, because they were obligated for three years rather than the duration of the war. Like them, Clifford and her lieutenant husband were sent with the Third U.S. Cavalry to one of New Mexico's frontier forts, where she sets her account of simmering violence. Because her marriage grew rocky, it is no surprise that her story focuses on the murderous expense of adultery in a distant outpost, though it is the bewitching wife who strays and her "true-hearted" captain who grows vulnerable. Unlike tales of homecoming in the East, the *Overland Monthly* here stages Reconstruction's desolation as stereo view, with surrender in Virginia offset by uprisings along the frontier, liberty's ripples pitched against the magazine's grizzly snarl.

Clifford actually structures her story around three startling developments that recall both the play of theatricality in the *Overland Monthly*'s Civil War and the "horrible significance" of Antietam. The first is the erring wife's fondness for display, not only of imported luxuries in the Captain's quarters but also through her own unexpected poses in "Indian country."³⁷ At one point, Mrs. Arnold grabs a couple of hidden derringers as though scripted, Clifford writes, "like a heroine in velvet trowsers on the stage" (210). Just as she plays at posing, she also toys with her husband's dog and her own plunging horse to "see him dance." She laughs "like an imp" at the horse's groom and takes her amusement from the "stage-play" of a houseboy's small losses, usually thefts she engineers (209). If she is the "better half" of the western union the Arnolds suggest, the "Mrs. Captain" of a reconstructing national household, it is at least troubling that she stages disaster, in her home with the steady Captain and in a marriage about to be smashed along with her imported china.

Even more unexpectedly, both the boy she torments and the groom she teases are black, and so is the Captain's cook, Constantia, who is more constant in her service than her mistress in her marriage. The black boy shares the household work, despite whimpering over his disappearing cake and stolen cap. The groom is a mulatto sergeant, a reminder of wartime emancipation, black enlistments, the creation of the USCT, and the army's insistence on white officers. As Elizabeth Leonard has pointed out, though approximately 180,000 black volunteers became soldiers, they generally rose no higher than sergeant;[38] as Thomas Mays has added, even USCT sergeants were sometimes white since their duties required the ability to read.[39] The groom's rank and his "flashing black eyes" (209) therefore suggest his unusual skill and self-possession, which will survive both his mistress's mistreatment and his own criminal conduct when he frees two "White Men" who kill the Captain (211). Yet Clifford's sergeant lends a grizzly stature to the story's semblance of a black family, while the cook brings constancy and the boy an innocent devotion. Theirs is a second and parallactic story of the Civil War's "desolation," a Reconstructive story of black service and white theft.

The third development comes as early as Clifford's first sentence. The story is narrated by a version of Josephine Clifford in 1866, when she was a dutiful lieutenant's wife recently arrived with the Regular Army. In this twilight "episode," the narrator sees what she might become, once military barracks have been completed, domestic luxuries have been imported, and a wartime marriage has run aground. She is more than a captain's wife in the making; she actually looks like *this* captain's wife, as one character after another exclaims. The story's opening line is an outburst that becomes a refrain: "'How much you resemble Mrs. Arnold!'" (207). It is as though the seer melds with the scene, the viewer becomes part of the view. As the narrator puts it when she first meets the Captain's wife, "I could see that she looked like—a sister" (208). A gendered reminder of Orvell's "fraternally twinned images," she is also the reader's representative, the viewer embodied, a minor character writ large. The depth of field she contrives in uncharted postwar territory ends in a trail "farther and farther from the road" where ambush and the "flashing black eyes" of the sergeant lurk. If theirs is to be a continuing story, which Clifford's "episode" implies, it is the story of elusive liberties and predator appetites, even in the unpicturesque solitudes of the West.

Metaphorically, the belittled sergeant, the constant cook, the whimpering boy, the bewitching wife, and even the off-stage Apaches are all moons of a sort, all revolving around the "true-hearted" Captain as an imploding sun and a vanishing common good. He is their walking U.S. flag, the fort commandant whose domestic dependents are in revolt. As a result, "An Episode of 'Fort Desolation'" becomes a story of conflicting emancipations—for those Lincoln proclaimed free, for those the army obligated, for those constrained by marriage, and for those sent to the guardhouse. If their center holds in the *Overland Monthly*, it is thanks to the new frontier wife with binocular vision, the minor character who sees from fort to fort, from barracks to plains, and from black sergeant to white mistress, in whom she sees herself. In Clifford's story, the unusual physical resemblance between one post mistress and another gnaws at the distance between spectacle and spectator, between view and viewer, with disconcerting implications for magazine readers and the nation's comfortable armchairs.

After discovering the moons of Mars in 1877, Asaph Hall thoughtfully observed that, in order to get a fix on distant bodies, he had to find a new perspective. "All that was needed was the right way of looking," he later wrote, "and that was to get rid of the dazzling light of the planet."[40] If the "dazzling" marketplace success of eastern "quality journals" like the *Atlantic Monthly* is displaced as insistently as Clifford's Captain Arnold, the "panic" and "terror" that the Civil War engendered recover some of their regional urgency and parallactic promise, especially after emancipation and African American service were imaginatively acknowledged. Long neglected satellites of another sort, journals like the *Overland Monthly* are always double visioned, always attending to the gravity of eastern norms and their own tangential velocity. They can offer, therefore, a startling integration of national order and local detail, of national opportunity and local expense, for growing numbers of readers just discovering grizzly bear claws. Even in postwar San Francisco, however, the stereoscopic shimmer of true national reconstruction, like New Mexico's gilded china and Antietam's Zouave glory, was a distant spectacle, at once beckoning and precarious.

NOTES

1. "Brady's Photographs: Pictures of the Dead at Antietam," *New York Times*, October 20, 1862, 5. Of the seventy photographs that Brady's operators brought back from Maryland, only eight were large 8" x 10" plates; sixty-two were stereo views, including fifty-five taken by Alexander Gardner and another seven by his assistant. Robert Taft has noted that wartime operators almost always carried a stereoscopic camera, which was small, easy to use, and likely to produce the popular sales that would underwrite future fieldwork; see *Photography and the American Scene: A Social History, 1839–1889* (1938; repr., New York: Dover, 1964), 234. That was demonstrably the case with the stereo views of Antietam. As Alan Trachtenberg has observed, "Whether translated into wood engravings and lithographs in the daily press and in periodicals or offered for sale as freshly made prints, mainly in stereo-cards or carte-de-visite format, the photographs were destined for home consumption ... with domestic audiences in mind"; see *Reading American Photographs: Images as History, Mathew Brady to Walker Evans* (New York: Hill and Wang, 1989), 88. More than simply a New York event during the weeks that followed the battle, Brady's exhibition was a marketing venture and a far-flung financial success.

2. Miles Orvell, *The Real Thing: Imitation and Authenticity in American Culture, 1880–1940* (Chapel Hill: University of North Carolina Press, 1989), 78.

3. Stephen W. Sears, *Landscape Turned Red: The Battle of Antietam* (1983; repr., New York: Mariner Books–Houghton Mifflin Harcourt, 2003), 45.

4. James M. McPherson, *Crossroads of Freedom: Antietam, the Battle That Changed the Course of the Civil War* (New York: Oxford University Press, 2002), 139.

5. Abraham Lincoln, "The Gettysburg Address," in "The Dead Heroes," *Harper's Weekly*, May 28, 1864, 338.

6. As a self-described "Photographer to the Army of the Potomac," Gardner had been photographing maps and charts for the Secret Service under Allan Pinkerton since early 1862. He had also enjoyed unlimited access to troops in the field and early information about their movements, information that brought him to Antietam before Robert E. Lee's army slipped away during the night of September 18. Particularly useful in documenting Gardner's ties to McClellan's staff and the secret activities of the U.S. Topographical Engineers are Francis Trevelyan Miller, ed., *The Photographic History of the Civil War* (1911; repr., New York: Thomas Yoseloff, 1957), 8:14–15, 23; Josephine Cobb, "Alexander Gardner," *Image* 7, no. 6 (1958): 124–36; Mark D. Katz, *Witness to an Era: The Life and Photographs of Alexander Gardner* (New York: Viking, 1991), 22–103; William F. Stapp, "'To . . . Arouse the Conscience, and Affect the Heart,'" in *An Enduring Interest: The Photographs of Alexander Gardner*, ed. Brooks Johnson (Norfolk, Va.: Chrysler Museum, 1991), 23; and, above all, William A. Frassanito, *Antietam: The Photographic Legacy of America's Bloodiest Day* (New York: Scribner's, 1978). Earlier accounts that mistakenly place Mathew Brady at Antietam, despite his failing eyesight, should be used with caution.

7. Edwin Forbes, "Watching a Battle," in *Thirty Years After: An Artist's Memoir of the Civil War* (1890; repr., Baton Rouge: Louisiana State University Press, 1993), 258.

8. For a fuller description of the 9th New York's extraordinary charge and the brigade's heavy casualties, see Sears, *Landscape Turned Red*, 281–84. For the impact of that charge and its expense, see also McPherson, *Crossroads of Freedom*, 125–28.

9. In the description printed alongside his drawing, Forbes failed to mention the late arrival of A. P. Hill's division from Harper's Ferry, Confederate troops that appeared just in time to flank the Union advance and force the New Yorkers to fall back. See "The Last Bayonet Charge of Hawkins's Zouaves at Antietam," *Frank Leslie's Illustrated Weekly*, October 11, 1862, 45–46. For a brief allusion to the final "repulse," plus Forbes's later recollections of Antietam ("The battle was a dramatic and most magnificent series of pictures"), see Forbes, "Watching a Battle," 258. Further discussion of how special artists functioned at the front may be found in Theodore R. Davis, "How a Battle Is Sketched," *St. Nicholas* (July 1889): 661–68; William P. Campbell, *The Civil War: A Centennial Exhibition of Eyewitness Drawings* (Washington, D.C.: National Gallery of Art, 1961); Pat Hodgson, *The War Illustrators* (New York: Macmillan, 1977); Kathleen Diffley, "Musquitos, Rattlesnakes, and Perspiration," *Books at Iowa* 63 (November 1995): 3–13; W. Fletcher Thompson Jr., *The Image of War: The Pictorial Reporting of the American Civil War* (Baton Rouge: Louisiana State University Press, 1994); Robert Knox Sneden, *Eye of the Storm: A Civil War Odyssey*, ed. Charles F. Bryan Jr. and Nelson D. Lankford (New York: Free Press, 2000); and Joshua Brown, "Illustrating the News," in *Beyond the Lines: Pictorial Reporting, Everyday Life, and the Crisis of the Gilded Age* (Berkeley: University of California Press, 2002), 32–59. For an-

other thoughtful contrast between competing "image makers" at Antietam, see Anthony W. Lee, "The Image of War," in *On Alexander Gardner's "Photographic Sketch Book" of the Civil War*, ed. Anthony W. Lee (Berkeley: University of California Press, 2007), 16–43.

10. "Brady's Photographs," 5.

11. Peter Galassi, *Before Photography: Painting and the Invention of Photography* (New York: Museum of Modern Art, 1981), 17.

12. Frassanito, *Antietam*, 131.

13. Jonathan Crary, *Techniques of the Observer: On Vision and Modernity in the 19th Century* (Cambridge: Massachusetts Institute of Technology Press, 1992), 120.

14. George Ward Nichols, "The General's Story," *Harper's Monthly*, June 1867, 73.

15. W. E. B. Du Bois, "Strivings of the Negro People," *Atlantic Monthly*, August 1897, 194.

16. Oliver Wendell Holmes, "The Professor's Story," *Atlantic Monthly*, October 1860, 491.

17. "Recent Literature: Higginson's *Oldport Days*," *Atlantic Monthly*, January 1874, 108; Asa Gray, "Darwin on the Origin of Species," *Atlantic Monthly*, August 1860, 231.

18. Oliver Wendell Holmes, "Doings of the Sunbeam," *Atlantic Monthly*, July 1863, 12.

19. Keith F. Davis, "'A Terrible Distinctness': Photography of the Civil War Era," in *Photography in Nineteenth-Century America*, ed. Martha Sandweiss (Fort Worth: Amon Carter Museum, 1991), 152.

20. "ETC.," *Overland Monthly*, July 1868, 99.

21. For Harte's quick hand with a pencil, as well as his tenure as the *Overland Monthly*'s first editor, see Axel Nissen, *Bret Harte: Prince and Pauper* (Jackson: University Press of Mississippi, 2000), 87–112; Ernest R. May, "Bret Harte and the *Overland Monthly*," *American Literature* 22, no. 3 (1950): 260–71; Madeleine B. Stern, "Anton Roman: Argonaut of Books," *California Historical Society Quarterly* 28, no. 1 (1949): 1–18; Noah Brooks, "Bret Harte in California," *Century*, July 1899, 447–51; Noah Brooks, "Early Days of 'The Overland,'" *Overland Monthly*, July 1898, 3–11; and W. C. Bartlett, "Overland Reminiscences," *Overland Monthly*, July 1898, 41–46.

22. Ellery Sedgwick, *The "Atlantic Monthly," 1857–1909: Yankee Humanism at High Tide and Ebb* (Amherst: University of Massachusetts Press, 1994), 6.

23. Rebecca Harding Davis, "John Lamar," *Atlantic Monthly*, April 1862, 411–23.

24. Philip J. Ethington, *The Public City: The Political Construction of Urban Life in San Francisco, 1850–1900* (Berkeley: University of California Press, 1994), 241.

25. Keith Wilson, introduction to *Honor in Command: Lt. Freeman S. Bowley's Civil War Service in the 30th United States Colored Infantry* (Gainesville: University Press of Florida, 2006), 3.

26. Freeman S. Bowley, "A Dark Night on Picket," *Overland Monthly*, July 1870, 36.

27. Ibid., 35.

28. Davis, "John Lamar," 417.

29. David Wyatt, *Five Fires: Race, Catastrophe, and the Shaping of California* (Reading, Mass.: Addison-Wesley, 1997), 7.

30. G. T. Shipley, "Saint Saviour of the Bay," *Overland Monthly*, October 1868, 347.

31. Henry King, "The Cabin at Pharaoh's Ford," *Overland Monthly*, December 1874, 513.
32. Sarah B. Cooper, "Old Uncle Hampshire," *Overland Monthly*, November 1872, 437.
33. Ibid., 431.
34. Douglas Henry Daniels, *Urban Pioneers: A Social and Cultural History of Black San Francisco* (Berkeley: University of California Press, 1990), 127.
35. Crary, *Techniques of the Observer*, 129.
36. Wendy Bellion, "Vision and Visuality," *American Art* 24, no. 3 (2010): 22.
37. Josephine Clifford, "An Episode of 'Fort Desolation,'" *Overland Monthly*, March 1871, 207, hereafter documented parenthetically.
38. Elizabeth D. Leonard, *Men of Color to Arms! Black Soldiers, Indian Wars, and the Quest for Equality* (New York: W. W. Norton, 2010), 258n29.
39. Thomas D. Mays, "The Battle of Saltville," in *Black Soldiers in Blue: African American Troops in the Civil War Era*, ed. John David Smith (Chapel Hill: University of North Carolina Press, 2002), 205.
40. Quoted in William Sheehan, *The Planet Mars: A History of Observation and Discovery* (Tucson: University of Arizona Press, 1996), 63.

CONTRIBUTORS

FAITH BARRETT is Associate Professor of English at Duquesne University. She is the author of *To Fight Aloud Is Very Brave: American Poetry and the Civil War* (University of Massachusetts Press, 2012) and coeditor of *"Words for the Hour": A New Anthology of American Civil War Poetry* (University of Massachusetts Press, 2005). Her essays have appeared in *Emily Dickinson Journal* and *Arizona Quarterly*.

JAMES BERKEY is Assistant Professor of English at Penn State Brandywine. He has published articles on soldier newspapers from the Spanish-American War in *The Journal of Transnational American Studies* and *The Journal of Modern Periodical Studies*.

JILLIAN SPIVEY CADDELL is lecturer in English at American University. She is at work on a book that explores the intersections of geography and war. Her essay on Melville's epitaphs appeared in *The New England Quarterly*.

KATHLEEN DIFFLEY is Associate Professor of English at the University of Iowa. She is the author of *Where My Heart Is Turning Ever: Civil War Stories and Constitutional Reform, 1861–1876* (University of Georgia Press, 1992) and editor of *To Live and Die: Collected Stories of the Civil War, 1861–1876* (Duke University Press, 2002) and *Witness to Reconstruction: Constance Fenimore Woolson and the Postbellum South, 1873–1894* (University Press of Mississippi, 2011).

JOHN ERNEST is Professor and Chair of English at the University of Delaware. He is the author of *Liberation Historiography: African American Writers and the Challenge of History, 1794–1861* (University of North Carolina Press, 2004), *Chaotic Justice: Rethinking African American Literary History* (University of North Carolina Press, 2009), and *A Nation Within a Nation: Organizing African American Communities before the Civil War* (Ivan R. Dee, 2011); and he is editor of *Narrative of the Life of Henry Box Brown, Written by Himself* and William Wells Brown's *My Southern Home; Or, The South and Its People*.

SAMUEL GRABER is Assistant Professor of the Humanities and Literature at Christ College, the honors college of Valparaiso University. He has published essays in *Walt Whitman Quarterly Review* and *American Nineteenth Century History* and is preparing his dissertation, "Twice Divided Nation: The Civil War and National Memory in the Transatlantic World," for publication.

CHRISTOPHER HAGER is Associate Professor of English at Trinity College. He is the author of *Word By Word: Emancipation and the Act of Writing* (Harvard University Press, 2013), which won the 2014 Frederick Douglass Book Prize. Two of his essays have appeared in *American Literature* and another in *J19*.

COLEMAN HUTCHISON is Associate Professor of English at the University of Texas. He is the author of *Apples and Ashes: Literature, Nationalism, and the Confederate States of America* (University of Georgia Press, 2012), co-author of *Writing about American Literature* (Norton, 2014), and editor of *A History of American Civil War Literature* (Cambridge University Press, 2015). Hutchison has two books in progress: "The Ditch is Nearer: Race, Place, and American Poetry, 1863–2009" and a popular biography of "Dixie."

SHIRLEY SAMUELS is Professor of English and American Studies at Cornell University. She is the author of *Romances of the Republic: Women, the Family, and Violence in the Literature of the Early American Nation* (Oxford University Press, 1996), *Facing America: Iconography and the Civil War* (Oxford University Press, 2004), and *Reading the American Novel 1780–1865* (Blackwell, 2012); and she is editor of *The Culture of Sentiment: Race, Gender, and Sentimentality in 19th Century America* (Oxford University Press, 1992), *Companion to American Fiction, 1780–1865* (Blackwell, 2004), and *The Cambridge Companion to Abraham Lincoln* (Cambridge University Press, 2012).

JANE E. SCHULTZ is Professor of English at Indiana University–Purdue University–Indianapolis. She is the author of *Women at the Front: Hospital Workers in Civil War America* (University of North Carolina Press, 2004) and editor of *This Birth Place of Souls: The Civil War Nursing Diary of Harriet Eaton* (Oxford University Press, 2010). Her essays have appeared in *Signs*, *Literature and Medicine*, *Civil War History*, and numerous other journals and collections.

TIMOTHY SWEET is Eberly Family Distinguished Professor of American Literature at West Virginia University. He is author of *Traces of War: Poetry, Photography, and the Crisis of the Union* (Johns Hopkins University Press, 1990) and *American Georgics: Economy and Environment in Early American Literature* (University of Pennsylvania Press, 2002).

JEREMY WELLS is Assistant Professor of English at Indiana University Southeast. He is author of *Romances of the White Man's Burden: Race, Empire, and the Plantation in American Literature, 1880–1936* (Vanderbilt University Press, 2011).

INDEX

Aaron, Daniel, 5–7, 10, 14, 25, 225–27, 237
abolitionists, abolitionism. *See* antislavery
Adams, Henry, 5–6, 59–60, 74, 147
adventure fiction, 9, 13
Agassiz, Louis, 212
Aiken, David, 158
Alcott, Louisa May, 8, 11, 12, 202, 214
Anderson, Benedict, 11, 13, 170–71, 177
Anderson, Henry, 86–90
Antietam, Battle of, 247–54, 259, 261
antislavery, 24, 31, 41, 58, 66, 70–73, 78, 85, 93, 103, 119, 123, 126, 210, 220, 234
Army Mail Bag, 169
Arthur, T. S. 169
Athens Union Post, 175–77
Atlantic Monthly, 16, 55, 68, 232, 253–57, 261
Augusta Chronicle, 170
Avent, Dr. ("Pharoah" of Kingston hospital), 198

Bacot, Ada, 196
Baker, Anne, 230
ballad, 9, 15, 46–47, 82, 100–113, 148, 199
Bancroft, George, 59–60, 64, 70, 74
Banks, Nathaniel, 183
Banks, William, 80, 92–93
Barrett, Faith, 10, 12–15
Bee, Barnard, 174–75
Bellion, Wendy, 259
Bernath, Michael, 11
Berryville Conservator, 172–74, 183
Bhabha, Homi, 213
Bierce, Ambrose, 5 6, 9, 10
Binnington, Ian, 11

Bleeding Kansas, 41
Blight, David, 14–15, 65, 69
Bloody Lane, 248–49
"The Bonnie Blue Flag," 175–76
Boston Transcript, 68
Bowley, Freeman S., 269–70
Brady, Mathew, 246–51, 254
Bragg, Braxton, 198
Branham, Robert James, 45
Brown, John, 8, 14, 41, 102–3, 210
Brown, Sterling, 54
Brown, William Wells, 13, 57–74
Browning, Elizabeth Barrett, 215, 220
Bryant, William Cullen, 112
Bull, John, 119, 125
Bull Run, First Battle of (Battle of Manassas), 123, 173–74
Burns, Robert, 80
Busick, Sean, 158
Butler, Benjamin, 33–34, 80–81
Butte a la Rose, Capture of, 183
Byers, S. H. M., 86
Byron, Lord, 80

Cable, George Washington, 4, 6
Calhoun, John C., 72–73
"A Call to the Hospital," 152, 155–57, 199–200
Camp Saxton 44–45
Cary, Constance, 189
Castiglia, Christopher, 113
Catton, Bruce, 3
Cavalier, 169, 171
Cavitch, Max 81

Chancellorsville, Battle of, 124
Charleston Courier, 199
Chesnut, Mary, 3, 6, 10–12
Chesnutt, Charles, 11, 57
Chickamauga, Battle of, 192
Chiles, Katy, 170
Chopin, Kate, 4, 228
Christian Recorder, 32
citizenship, 2, 7–16, 25–29, 42–45, 54, 60–61, 72, 99, 113–14, 132, 170–172, 180–84, 210, 229, 238, 240–41, 245, 247–48, 257
civil rights movement, 3, 6–7, 17
Civil War centennial, 2–7, 12–17, 36
Civil War sesquicentennial, 2, 14–17, 227
Clark, Edward H. G., 69
Cleveland Daily Herald, 240
Clifford, Josephine, 259–61
Coates, Ta-Nehisi, 227
Cobb, Sylvanus, 169
Cohen, Michael, 46
Cold War, 3–7, 17
Colored National Convention, 66–67
Confederate States of America (CSA), 142, 144, 174, 180
Connecticut Fifth (soldier newspaper), 174–77
Conwell, Russell, 43
Cooke, John Esten, 146, 151
Cooper, Anna Julia, 67
Cooper, James Fenimore, 4
Cooper, Sarah B., 258
Crane, Stephen, 1, 5, 7
Crary, Jonathan, 253, 258–59
Crawford, Martin, 123
Crescent Monthly, 158
Cruz, Jon, 47, 50
Cumming, Kate, 16, 189–204
Cummings, P. C., 181
currency, Confederate, 174–75, 184
Currier and Ives, 100

Daily South Carolinian, 143
Daniels, Douglas Henry, 258
Danville Register, 180
Darwin, Charles, 254
Davenport, Edward L., 168–72
Davey, Frank, 228
Davis, Jefferson, 8, 124, 174

Davis, Keith, 254
Davis, Rebecca Harding, 13; "How the Widow Crossed the Lines," 9; "John Lamar," 16, 228, 231–36, 240, 256–57; "Life in the Iron-Mills," 231
Dawes, James, 8
De Forest, John W., 5–6, 9, 10–11
Delaney, Martin, 170–71
De Leon, Edwin, 147
De Leon, Thomas Cooper, 147, 148, 151, 158
Denison, Mary, 169
Dibdin, Charles, 101, 111, 114
Dickinson, Emily, 7, 10, 11, 13, 14, 55
Diffley, Kathleen, 9, 13, 16
Dingledine, Don, 41
Dix, Dorothea, 199
"Dixie," 12, 150, 175–77
Dixon, Thomas, Jr., 56
Douglas, Stephen, 209–10
Douglass, Frederick, 6, 25, 27, 43
Drake, Joseph Rodman, 169
"The Drummer Boy of Shiloh" (Will S. Hayes), 108
Dryden, John, 102
Du Bois, W. E. B., 3, 13, 65; *Black Reconstruction*, 65–66; *The Souls of Black Folk*, 40, 54–55, 253; "Strivings of the Negro People," 253
Dunbar, Paul Laurence, 13, 35
Duquette, Elizabeth, 10–11
Duyckinck, Evert A., 145

elegy, 82–83, 150
Eleventh Connecticut Infantry Regiment, 181
emancipation, 2, 9, 15–16, 24, 27, 28, 32, 35, 44, 73, 83, 85, 107, 232–33, 235–37, 256, 259–61
Emancipation Proclamation, 44, 247–48, 253–54, 256
Emerson, Ralph Waldo, 78, 126, 229
"The Enemy in Sight," 172–75
epic, 5–6, 9–10, 14, 100, 144, 152–54, 190
epitaph, 15, 100–101, 110
Ethington, Philip, 256–58
Evans, Augusta Jane, 11–12, 190

Fahs, Alice, 11, 13, 65–66, 169
Farrison, William Edward, 58
Faulkner, William, 7, 49

INDEX

Faust, Drew Gilpin, 9, 11
Fay, Miss, 86
Fern, Fanny, 215
Ferry, Anne, 143
Fetterley, Judith, 228, 232
Fifteenth Amendment, 7, 9
Fifth Connecticut Infantry Regiment, 174–75, 177
Fifth Pennsylvania Cavalry, 169
Fifty-Fourth Massachusetts Infantry Regiment, 41
Finseth, Ian, 13, 194
First Minnesota (soldier newspaper), 172–75, 177–80, 183, 185
First South Carolina Volunteers, 26, 41–46, 55
"The Flag of Our Union," 169
Foote, Stephanie, 228
Forbes, Edwin, 248–53
Ford, Sally Rochester, 146, 190
Fort Beauregard, 104
Fort Sumter, Battle of, 167
Fort Wagner, Battle of, 27, 69
Fort Walker, 104
Forty-first Massachusetts Infantry Regiment, 183
Foucault, Michel, 230, 235, 237
Fourteenth Amendment, 7, 9
Fraistat, Neil, 142, 157
Frank Leslie's Illustrated Weekly, 249–50
Frassanito, William, 251
Freedmen's Bureau, 31
Freedom's Journal, 66
Freeman, Elizabeth, 214
Fugitive Slave Act, 5, 59
Fuller, Randall, 11
Funchion, John, 230

Galassi, Peter, 251
Gardner, Alexander, 8, 246–52
Gardner, Sarah, 190
Garvey, Ellen Gruber, 170, 172
Gates, Henry Louis, 81
Gazette (Chapel Hill), 79
Genoways, Ted, 129
Gettysburg Address, 1, 4, 248
Gettysburg, Battle of, 111–12, 200, 210
Gibson, James, 248

Gilman, Charlotte Perkins, 214
Gladstone, William, 124
Grant, Susan-Mary, 126
Grant, Ulysses S., 5, 8, 69
Gray, Asa, 254
Gray, Thomas, 103
Gregg, H. K., 173–74
Griffin, Martin, 10–11
Grimke, Charlotte Forten, 12
Guilds, John C., 143, 145, 159

Hager, Christopher, 14, 81, 190
Hale, Edward Everett, 13
Hall, Asaph, 245, 261
Harper and Brothers, 203
Harper, Francis E. W., 10, 12–13, 69
Harper's Monthly, 246, 253
Harper's Weekly, 27, 119–21, 124, 127, 167–68
Harris, Joel Chandler, 67
Harte, Bret, 16, 254
Harwell, Richard, 202–3
Hawthorne, Nathaniel, 6, 11
Hayne, Paul Hamilton, 13, 151, 152, 154, 155
Hays, Will S., 108
Helper, Hinton, 70
Higginson, Thomas Wentworth, 11, 14; *Army Life in a Black Regiment*, 23–28, 32, 35, 39–55; *Oldport Days*, 254
Holmes, Oliver Wendell, Jr., 3, 5–6
Holmes, Oliver Wendell, Sr., 254
Homer, 80, 102
Homer, Winslow, 16, 167, 225–28, 236, 241
Honey Hill, Battle of, 69
Hope, James Barron, 151
Hoppin, W. J., 86
Horton, George Moses 10, 13, 15, 77–94, 193
"Hospital Duties" (also "A Call to the Hospital"), 152, 155–57; 199–200
Hotze, Henry, 123–24
Howells, William Dean, 6, 35
Huggins, Cooper, 181–82
Hunt, Leigh, 68,
Hutchison, Coleman, 12, 15, 149, 151, 175, 190
hymn, 15, 23, 52, 78, 82, 86, 100, 101, 104–06, 113, 169

The Index (London) 12

Jackson, Andrew, 70
Jackson, Stonewall, 69, 124, 150, 174–75
"Jackson's Stone Wall Brigade," 174–75
James, Henry, 5, 6, 10, 11
James, Jennifer, 12
James, Jesse, 210
James, William, 3, 5
Jefferson, Thomas, 81
Jewett, Sarah Orne, 228–29
Johnson, Andrew, 69
Johnson, George, 30, 33–35
Johnston, Joseph, 173
Joy, George Mills, 171–72, 215

Kansas-Nebraska Act, 16, 209–10
Kazin, Alfred, 3–8
Keckley, Elizabeth, 8–9, 12
Kete, Mary Louise, 81
Kibler, James E., Jr., 149, 155
King, Henry, 258
King, Martin Luther, Jr., 36

Lamb, Charles, 216
The Land We Love, 157–58
Lee, Mary Custis, 202
Lee, Robert E., 69, 102, 248
Lenin, Vladimir, 4
Leonard, Elizabeth, 260,
The Liberator, 69
Lincoln, Abraham, 3–6, 8, 9, 31, 68, 81, 82, 124, 141, 170, 177, 184, 209–11, 220; assassination of, 86, 167, 203, 207, 216; 1861 Address to the New Jersey Senate, 73–74; Emancipation Proclamation, 247–48, 260; Gettysburg Address, 1
Lincoln, Mary Todd, 8
Lippincott, J. B., 203
Long, Lisa, 8
Longstreet, James, 69
Looby, Christopher, 42, 47, 49
Loughran, Trish, 171, 180
Louisville Journal, 68
Lowell, James Russell, 10, 112
Loyal Georgian, 167, 170
Lyell, Charles, 254
lyric poetry, 10, 50, 82, 100, 108, 110, 112–13, 175

Malvern Hill, Battle of, 195
Manassas, First Battle of, 123, 173–74
"Marching On!," 169
Marrs, Cody, 190
Marx, Karl, 3
Mays, Thomas, 260
McAllister, John A., 145
McCabe, James D., 151
McGill, Meredith, 169
McPherson, James M., 248
Mead, John, 42
Meek, Alexander B., 151
Melville, Herman, 6–11, 85; "The Apparition (A Retrospect)," 107, 112; *Battle-Pieces*, 3–4, 9–10, 15, 99–114; "Benito Cereno," 8; *Billy Budd*, 101; *The Confidence-Man*, 99, "Dupont's Round Flight," 103–6, 113; "Formerly a Slave," 106–7, 112; "The Frenzy in the Wake," 101, 106; "The House-top," 101–02; "Lee in the Capitol," 102–03; "The March into Virginia," 109–10; "The March to the Sea," 86, 106, 113; *Moby-Dick*, 100; "On the Slain Collegians," 110–11; *Pierre*, 99; "The Portent," 8, 102–03, 113; "The Returned Volunteer to his Rifle," 111–13; "The Scout toward Aldie," 112; "Sheridan at Cedar Creek," 113; "Shiloh," 108–10, 112; "Stonewall Jackson (Ascribed to a Virginian)," 101; "Stonewall Jackson. Mortally Wounded at Chancellorsville," 101–02; "The Temeraire," 106, 113; "A Utilitarian View of the Monitor's Fight," 103–05, 11; "An Uninscribed Monument," 110–11, 113; *White-Jacket*, 100–101
Mercherson, Abram, 30
Mill, John Stuart, 100
Milliken's Bend, Battle of, 69
Milton, John, 80, 212
Minstrel, 12, 47, 52
Missouri Compromise, 103, 209–11
Mitchell, Douglas L., 69
Mitchell, Margaret, 12
Mitchell, Silas Weir, 8, 13
Moore, Frank, 148–49, 150, 158
Morrison, Toni, 227

INDEX

Morton, John, 202
Moses, Wilson Jeremiah, 73
Motley, John Lothrop, 59–60
Murfreesboro, Second Battle of, 195
"My Country 'Tis of Thee," 44–45

Nabers, Deak, 9, 104
Nast, Thomas, 167
National Prisoner of War Museum, 230
Nell, William C., 58, 63
Newbern, Battle of, 168, 172
Newbern Progress, 168, 171–73, 180–82
New Englander and Yale Review, 158
Nichols, George Ward, 253
Ninth Michigan Cavalry, 10, 15, 77, 79–80, 82–83, 86, 90, 92
Ninth New York Volunteers, 249–50
"No 'Bonnie Blue Flag' For Me," 175–76
Normal Picket, 169, 176–77
Nudelman, Franny, 8

Old Guard: A Monthly Journal Devoted to the Principles of 1776 and 1787, 158
Olustee, Battle of, 69
125th United States Colored Infantry, 259
"One Point Gained," 119
Opelousas Courier, 179–80, 183–84
Orvell, Miles, 247, 260
"Our Dixie," 176
Overland Monthly, 16, 247–48, 254–61
Owen, Wilfred, 108

Pacific Monthly, 254
Page, Thomas Nelson, 4, 10
Palmerston, Viscount, 123–24
Parkman, Francis, 59–60
pastoral, 107–111
Pattee, Fred Lewis, 1–2, 6
"Peace: National Hymn in the Form of a March," 86
Pember, Phoebe Yates, 196
Petersburg, Battle of, 107
Phelps, Elizabeth Stuart, 8–9, 11, 16, 205–20
Piatt, Sarah, 10, 13
Picker, John M. 40, 47, 50, 53
Pike, Albert, 150

Poe, Edgar Allen, 4, 39
Pollard, Edward A., 146
Pope, Alexander, 102
Port Hudson, Battle of, 69
Port Royal, Battle of, 104–5
pragmatism, 3–7, 11
Prescott, William H., 59–60
Preston, Margret Junkin, 151
Price, Kenneth, 121
print culture, 2, 11, 13–15, 51–52, 66, 44–45, 167–85
Pryse, Marjorie, 228, 232
Puskar, Jason, 201

Quantrill's Raid on Lawrence, 208, 211

Radano, Ronald, 40, 53
Randall, James R., 151
realism, 1, 4–5, 15–16, 189–91, 194, 200, 203–4
Rebellion Record, 104
Reconstruction, 13, 66, 73, 104, 142, 237, 259
regionalism, 2, 4, 228–29, 236, 240–41
Register (Raleigh), 79
The Reporter, 3
Republican Party, 126, 141
Revolutionary War, 60, 70, 120, 147
Richards, Eliza, 81
Richardson, Charles Benjamin, 144, 146, 157, 158
Roach, Joseph, 213
Roebuck, John Arthur, 124–26, 129, 135
romance fiction, 9–11, 13
The Round Table, 158
Rowan, Carl, 3
Royce, Josiah, 11
"Run Away Editor," 173
Russell, Earl, 123
Russell, John, 155
Russell, William Howard ("Bull Run Russell"), 123–24
Russell's Magazine, 155
Ryan, Abram Joseph, 147

Samuels, Shirley, 8, 16
Savannah, fall of, 167–68, 170
Scarry, Elaine, 7–8
Schneider, Rebecca, 214
Scott, Sir Walter, 46–47

Sears, Stephen, 248
secession, 114, 124–25, 128–29, 148, 175–76, 181
Sedgwick, Ellery, 255
segregation, 24
sensationalism, 13, 157
sentimentalism, 16, 31, 35, 45, 86, 111–12, 189, 194, 199–200, 203–4
Seward, William, 124–25, 127, 253
Shakespeare, William, 80, 125
Shepperson, William, 143
"Sherman's March to the Sea," 86, 106, 113
Sherman, William Tecumseh, 8, 29, 69, 83, 201
Shi, David, 192
Shields, Johanna, 151, 158
Shiloh, Battle of, 193–94
Shipley, G. T., 258
Signaigo, J. Augustine, 108–09
Silber, Nina, 9–10
Simms, William Gilmore: *War Poetry of the South*, 11–12, 15, 109, 141–59; *The Wigwam and the Cabin*, 148, 155
Sixth Corps (soldier newspaper), 180–81, 183
Sixth United States Infantry Regiment, 64
Sizer, Lyde Cullen, 12
slavery, 3, 5, 6, 10, 11, 12, 24, 31, 45, 60, 61, 68–69, 70–71, 78, 79, 178, 179–81, 208–10, 212, 220, 225, 232, 233, 256. *See also* antislavery; emancipation
Smith, John David, 62–63, 73
Smith, Mark M., 61, 66
Smith, Susan "Grandma," 196
Snow, William Parker, 146
Soldiers' Letter of the Ninety-Sixth Illinois Volunteer Infantry, 169
song, 10, 12, 13, 14, 39–41, 44–55, 62, 80–83, 85–86, 100–102, 105–06, 108, 113, 150, 152–55, 169, 175–77. *See also* ballad
sonnet, 10, 111, 150, 152, 154–55, 157
South Atlantic Blockading Squadron, 105
Southern Cultivator, 157–58
Southern Field and Fireside, 152
Southern Literary Messenger, 12, 79, 144
Southern Pacific Railroad, 257
spiritual, 40, 46–47, 50–55
"Stand Up For Uncle Sam," 169
Stanton, Edwin, 31–33, 35

Starke, William Edwin, 251
Stereograph, 16
Stereoscope, 253–54, 258
Stern, Julia, 10, 11
Sternhell, Yael, 27
Stout, Samuel, 189
Stowe, Harriet Beecher, 4, 9, 12, 45, 219, 258
Strauss, Jennifer, 159
Strother, David Hunter (pseud. Porte Crayon), 6
suffrage, 30, 69
Swedenborg, Emanuel, 9
Sweet, Timothy, 7, 191

Taylor, Richard, 183
Taylor, Susie King, 28
temperance movement, 58, 82
Third Florida Infantry, 201
Third United States Cavalry, 259
Thirteenth Amendment, 247
Thirtieth United States Colored Infantry, 257
Thirty-Fifth United States Colored Troops, 29
Thirty-Third Illinois Volunteers, 176
Thompson, John R., 151
Thoreau, Henry David, 8, 9
Times (London), 120, 123
Times (New York), 62, 68, 141–42, 158, 246
Timrod, Henry, 6, 11–13, 143, 150–51, 155, 198
"To the Citizens of Danville," 180–83
"To the Patriotic Citizens of St. Landry," 183–84
Tourgée, Albion, 4
Transcendentalism, 40
Trent Affair, 119
"Tribute to Jackson's Command" (also "Jackson's Stone Wall Brigade"), 174–75
Turner, Nat, 8, 70
Twain, Mark, 6, 9, 13
Twenty-third Massachusetts Volunteer Infantry, 168, 171

United States Colored Troops (USCT), 62, 257, 259–60
U.S. Constitution, 7, 9, 31, 60, 247

Vedder, Elihu, 106
Velazquez, Loreta Janeta, 12

INDEX

Vesey, Denmark, 70
Vicksburg, Battle of, 200
Virgil, 80, 102

War of 1812, 70, 120
Ward, Artemus, 169
Ward, Thomas J., 58, 61–62, 71
Ware, Mary, 152–55
Warner, Susan B., 212, 214
Warren, Kenneth, 24, 35
Warren, Robert Penn, 3–6, 9, 11, 14
Wars of the Roses, 103
Washington, Booker T., 65
Washington, George, 8
Washington, Madison, 70
Watts, Isaac, 78, 100
Webster, Daniel, 5
Weekly Anglo-African, 32, 170
Weems, Parson, 74
White, Richard Grant, 158
Whitman, Walt 2, 4, 6, 7, 10, 11, 13, 85, 99, 113, 120–23, 159, 191, 193; "The Centenarian's Story," 129; "The Dresser," 132; *Drum-Taps*, 1, 3, 8, 9, 15, 122, 128–34, 136; "1861," 130; *Leaves of Grass*, 122, 128, 130–32; "Lo! Victress on the Peaks," 129, 131; "A March in the Ranks Hard-prest and the Road Unknown," 132; *Memoranda During the War*, 127; "O Tan Faced Boy," 134–35; "Pioneers! O Pioneers," 133–35; *Sequel to Drum-Taps*, 122, 129–30, 133, 136; "Shut Not Your Doors to Me Proud Libraries," 131; "Song of Myself," 132; "Song of the Banner at Day-break," 132; *Specimen Days*, 3, 7–8; "Turn O Libertad," 130–31; "Weave in, Weave in My Hardy Life," 132
Williams, George Washington, 58, 60–61, 64
Wilson, Edmund, 4–7, 10, 11, 12, 14, 25
Wilson, Ivy, 81
Wilson, Keith, 257
Winchester Virginian, 174–75
Wirz, Henry, monument, 231
Withers, R. E., 180
Wolosky, Shira, 7
Woolson, Constance Fenimore, 9, 16, 228, 236–41
Wyatt, David, 258

Young, Elizabeth, 8, 12

www.ingramcontent.com/pod-product-compliance
Lightning Source LLC
Chambersburg PA
CBHW011755220426
43672CB00018B/2968